Quality Assurance
for Individuals with
Developmental Disabilities

Quality Assurance for Individuals with Developmental Disabilities

It's Everybody's Business

edited by

Valerie J. Bradley, M.A.
President
Human Services Research Institute
Cambridge, Massachusetts

and

Hank A. Bersani, Jr., Ph.D.
Community Integration Associates
Manlius, New York

·P·A·U·L·H·
BROOKES
PUBLISHING C°

Baltimore • London • Toronto • Sydney

Paul H. Brookes Publishing Co.
P.O. Box 10624
Baltimore, Maryland 21285-0624

Typeset by The Composing Room of Michigan, Inc., Grand Rapids, Michigan.
Manufactured in the United States of America by
The Maple Press Company, York, Pennsylvania.

Cover image courtesy of Peter Garrison.

Library of Congress Cataloging-in-Publication Data

Quality assurance for individuals with developmental disabilities :
  it's everybody's business / edited by Valerie J. Bradley, Hank A.
  Bersani, Jr.
          p.   cm.
     Includes bibliographical references (p.   )
     ISBN 1–55766–038-7
     1. Developmentally disabled—Services for—Standards—
United States.   I. Bradley, Valerie J.   II. Bersani, Hank A.
HV1570.5.U65Q35   1990
362.1'968—dc20   89-25447
                                                        CIP

contents

section I   Conceptual Overview

section II   Consumers' Point of View

section III   Families' Point of View

section IV   Governmental Issues

section V   Management Issues

contributors

John W. Ashbaugh, M.B.A.
Vice President
Human Services Research Institute
2336 Massachusetts Avenue
Cambridge, MA 02140

Hank A. Bersani, Jr., Ph.D.
Community Integration Associates
4508 Watervale Drive
Manlius, NY 13104

David Braddock, Ph.D.
Associate Professor, Community Health
  Sciences
and
Director, Illinois University Affiliated
  Program in Developmental
  Disabilities
The University of Illinois at Chicago
1640 West Roosevelt Road
Chicago, IL 60608

Valerie J. Bradley, M.A.
President
Human Services Research Institute
2336 Massachusetts Avenue
Cambridge, MA 02140

Senator John H. Chafee, L.L.B.
U.S. Senate
Washington, D.C. 20510

James W. Conroy, M.A.
Temple University Developmental
  Disabilities Center
9th Floor Ritter Annex
Philadelphia, PA 19122

Derrick F. Dufresne, M.B.P.A.
President
Community Resource Associates
736 Crab Thicket Lane
Des Peres, MO 63131

Celia S. Feinstein, M.A.
Temple University Developmental
  Disabilities Center
9th Floor Ritter Annex
Philadelphia, PA 19122

Sue A. Gant, Ph.D.
Division of Quality Assurance
Department of Mental Retardation
90 Pitkin Street
East Hartford, CT 06108

James F. Gardner, Ph.D.
Chief Executive Officer
Accreditation Council on Services for
  People with Developmental
  Disabilities
8100 Professional Place
Suite 204
Landover, MD 20785

Robert M. Gettings, M.P.A.
Executive Director
National Association of State Mental
  Retardation Program Directors, Inc.
113 Oronoco Street
Alexandria, VA 22314

Richard Hemp, M.A.
Coordinator
Information Center on Financing
  Services
Illinois University Affiliated Program in
  Developmental Disabilities
The University of Illinois at Chicago
1640 West Roosevelt Road
Chicago, IL 60608

Michael J. Kennedy
Center on Human Policy
Syracuse University
200 Huntington Hall
Syracuse, NY 13244-2340

Madeleine H. Kimmich, D.S.W.
Human Services Research Institute
112 Grove Avenue
Post Office Box 327
Washington Grove, MD 20880

James A. Knoll, Ph.D.
Human Services Research Institute
2336 Massachusetts Avenue
Cambridge, MA 02140

Robert Lehr, Ph.D.
Box 188
R.R. # 3
Tully, NY 13159

Susan Lehr, M.A.
Box 188
R.R. # 3
Tully, NY 13159

Michael S. Lottman, L.L.B., L.L.M.
Executive Director
Mansfield Class Panel of Monitors
991 Main Street
East Hartford, CT 06108

John O'Brien
Responsive Systems Associates
58 Willowick Drive
Lithania, GA 30038

Catherine E. Parsons, M.S.
Director of Surveys
Accreditation Council on Services for
  People with Developmental
  Disabilities
8100 Professional Place
Suite 204
Landover, MD 20785

C. Kaye Pearce, M.A.
Associate Director
Commission on Accreditation of
  Rehabilitation Facilities
101 North Wilmot Road, Suite 500
Tucson, AZ 85711

Gerald Provencal, M.S.W.
Director
Joseph M. Synder Macomb-
  Oakland Regional Center
16200 Nineteen Mile Road
Mt. Clemens, MI 48044

Nancy K. Ray, Ed.D.
Policy Director and Special Assistant to
  the Chairman
New York Commission on Quality of
  Care
99 Washington Avenue, Suite 1002
Albany, NY 12210

Gary A. Smith, B.A.
Director of Special Projects
National Association of State Mental
  Retardation Program Directors, Inc.
113 Oronoco Street
Alexandria, VA 22314

**Members of Speaking For Ourselves
  as told to Karl Williams**
Suite 625
One Plymouth Meeting
Plymouth Meeting, PA 19462

Lyle D. Wray, Ph.D.
County Administrator
Dakota County
1560 Highway 55 West
Hastings, MN 55033

foreword

Meterologists have a metaphor, the notion that "a butterfly stirring the air today in Peking can transform storm systems next month in New York" (Gleick, 1987). The "butterfly effect" has come to stand for the sensitivity of large, complex systems (such as world weather) to miniscule perturbations. It's time for another paradigm shift in services for people with developmental disabilities, and this book may just be the butterfly that sets it in motion.

Small perturbations may create what appear to be chaotic conditions, or put a system out of control. Scientists have been grappling for most of this century with a sense that uncertainty is the only certainty. But now the phrase "making order out of chaos" is taking on a new meaning as mathematicians create new unifying paradigms for the management of the unpredictable. Since the mid-1970s a new cross disciplinary science has emerged that deals with "complex (nonlinear) dynamical systems," *chaos* for short. Its insights have been of interest to specialists in fields as dissimilar as astronomy and zoology, and have generated new questions about what we know, what we can know, and how we know it. This new way of thinking may also provide insights into the complexities evident in the interactions among human services systems and the people who populate them.

This chaos theory goes well beyond classical statistics familiar to many of us as a tool for managing large numbers of idiosyncratic events or objects, such as births, molecules, or experimental data; it deals more with systems that evolve according to certain rules but tend to develop spontaneous irregularities that are not predictable in practice, especially when the rate of change in the system accelerates markedly. Examples abound in the natural world and include (in addition to weather) the occurrence of earthquakes, the patterns of turbulence in the wake following a ship, the growth of dendrites in the human brain, and the evolution of species. The behavior of the stock market provides another example.

The new geometry of "fractals" (as a branch of chaos) is capturing popular imagination, partly because fractals can be visualized and embraced esthetically by people who do not think of themselves as scientists. Like many mathematical constructs, a particular fractal may be used to represent any one of a number of physical phenomena, for example the branching of a tree and the erosion patterns of rivulets on an unsodded hillside. A fractal in graph form can also be used to represent an idea, a concept, a set of social relationships. Although generated by a computer with no such representation in mind, the fractal reproduced on the cover of this book can be interpreted to represent the sinuous interactive relationships among the forces at work within human services. Without being too literal about it, one can also see it as symbolizing the intermingling of macro- and microforces, the latter at the finest discernible level representing unique individuals in small social clusters.

Thus far, as a scientific approach, "chaos" has been embraced primarily by the more adventurous among people in the physical and biological sciences. Economists have expressed an interest, with results described by Pool in *Science* (Pool, 1989). At the Santa Fe Institute a dozen men with sophisticated backgrounds in theory and representing equally the fields of physical science and economics have been applying their respective problem-solving methods to commonly defined problems. They have had to overcome culture shock, to develop a common language, to dispel their mutual preconceptions, to find a common ethic. But when they did so, new solutions became possible. It will take a similar willingness to work through to a higher level of communication and mutual learning if the burgeoning ideas about quality and quality assurance that abound in this book are to come into synergistic apposition.

Many apparent differences between the disciplines represented in Santa Fe turned out to be cosmetic, but some real ones have had to be contended with. "A fundamental difference between the physical sciences and economics is that in economics the agents are conscious. People and corporations, unlike protons and proteins, determine their actions according to what they expect to happen in the future" (Pool, 1989, p. 702). We all know something about what can happen when too many decisions on buying or selling securities are programmed to be automatic. To move beyond this simplistic approach, the Sante Fe teams are developing a mathematical model to represent "bounded rationality," using "genetic algorithms" to simulate personal decision-making in which the decisionmaker learns by experience, but no individual can ever reach perfection. There are clear precedents here for us in the field of developmental disabilities, both as to the incorporation of individual prerogatives and as to the melding of the predictable and unpredictable to produce optimum outcomes.

That the field of developmental disabilities is chaotic is reflected well in this book in two principal ways. First, the subject of the book necessarily superimposes one chaotic system on another. Second, the editors have done a commendable job of providing a forum for authors (appropriately including themselves) with varying perceptions of what constitutes quality or of how to assure it.

On the first count, the chaos in the field of quality assurance in human services generally is superimposed on the chaos in conceptualization and organization of the services themselves. It is as if the Bureau of the Census were to try to carry out its mission without being certain who is a person to be counted (is Fido a member of the family?) or where one would need to look for people. For census takers it is not enough to visit only households, as does the National Center for Health Statistics in conducting its influential sampling surveys. As with census studies, the structure of any quality assurance system must reflect not merely contemporary values but also the underlying social system, in this case the structures that determine the character of the service delivery systems. These are, of course, very much in flux at this time.

Somewhat coincidentally and for different reasons both systems (quality assurance and service delivery) are now undergoing a certain disaggregation and internal diversification. In quality assurance, as reflected in this book, this takes the form of proliferation of stakeholders, each laying claim to a piece of the action. Suddenly quality assurance is everyone's business: people using or needing services, families, hands-on providers, public administrators, legal advocates, policy analysts, self-appointed monitors, official monitors, voluntary accrediting bodies, politicians, researchers, clinicians, and interested spectators. Although it is not possible to reflect through one or two authors the range of views and diversity of needs to be found in each of these sectors, plenty of conflict and contrast is laid before us. Amidst the chaos we can discern a potential for constructive complementarity.

Whether readers take full advantage of these juxtapositions is, of course, up to each of them. It is well-known that most of us can report more accurately to others on ideas with which we agree than on ideas with which we disagree. This may be because we spend more time with the ideas and the authors who reinforce rather than challenge our own views. Most readers of this book will recognize some authors' names in the table of contents and will be unfamiliar with others. Those readers who resist the temptation to limit their reading to the chapters written by their own ideological allies may get a useful earful of the loud dissonance among the competing contemporary paradigms in both the service systems and the quality assurance systems.

In the summer of 1989, the dissonance rose to a shrill crescendo in the halls of Congress. The eye of the storm no longer focused on the size of residential facilities but rather on the appropriate structure and choice of architect and custodian for the proposed mandatory system(s) of quality assurance. At issue was a question as to whether the traditional structure and strong federal presence affirmed by Congress for nursing homes can or should be translated to encompass the decentralized, multi-provider patterns of service delivery that now characterize the community service systems for people with developmental disabilities, and whether the federal or state bureaucracy should have the leading role.

Political outcomes are among the most chaotic, so often dependent on some distant and seemingly irrelevant butterfly; this one may well be resolved by an accident having nothing to do with quality per se. But political confrontations may also be resolved purposefully and creatively, if each side (and in this case there are many sides) is prepared to participate in finding new paradigms. Critical outcomes hang in the balance as this highly relevant book comes on the scene.

Michael Kennedy, a young man with a developmental disability, is among the present authors who has had a voice in the political debate of 1989. The last major communication from the Consortium for Citizens with Disabilities that went to the House Committee of jurisdiction before it acted on Medicaid Community and Facility Habilitation Amendments of 1989 contained Kennedy's plea that quality assurance activities not impair quality by invasion of the privacy of the individuals on whose behalf they are conducted.

Kennedy is a highly visible member of an especially large 10-year birth cohort that peaked in the early 1960s. He is visible because, as a former resident of a large public institution, he has been known to the system for a long time, and because he is articulate and uses a wheel chair. He has become a prototypical example of successful deinstitutionalization. We like to think that there are another 94,000 like him who have been emancipated in the last quarter century. He embodies our ideals of independence, integration, and productivity. But, successful as he now is, he is not entirely typical of his generation, so many of whose members are crowding state waiting lists at this time.

A waiting list for service, whether it is for a living arrangement, supported employment service, a personal attendant, or some other support service, is an antithesis of quality assurance, an outcome that requires zero sophistication to measure.

Most states now have waiting lists for various services, especially for "alternative living arrangements," and they are growing. In contrast to the situation a quarter century ago, most people on waiting lists are adults, adults who have grown up as children in their own or foster families. We do not need an elaborate system of monitoring to know that remedies are urgently needed, and we are not without visions of what they might look like.

Statistics do not, however, tell the whole story of the shortcomings in quality of living experienced by many of today's young adults, Michael Kennedy's contemporaries. Two particularly revealing books have been published about two young people who have grown up in the era launched by President Kennedy. Nicole Kaufman and Adam Dorris have the good fortune not to be on any waiting list at the moment. Their life histories, one with mild mental retardation, the other with fetal alcohol syndrome, are told insightfully by their mother and father respectively (Kaufman, 1988; Dorris, 1989). Unlike Michael Kennedy, Nicole Kaufman and Adam Dorris had many of the right opportunities; they grew up in their family homes with parents of exceptional patience, competence, and commitment to their progress toward independence. They lived in university towns with more than the average in community supports. They attended their local schools. Since leaving, they have held—and lost—jobs; they have moved away from their families. Their impairments are clearly in the area of self-direction. Their stories, well written by perceptive and loving parents, are poignant and true. But there is no escaping the fact that their lives are precarious. They are and will continue to be at risk. Failing parents, there is not now in place or in prospect any way to assure the quality, or even the existence, of any continuing support network for either of them.

We need some new paradigms.

Advances in applying chaos have depended heavily on sophisticated computer technology. We, who are in the behavioral and social sciences, have not yet entered this arena. Of course we have late model personal computers and plenty of software, but for the most part it is used to keep fiscal records or simple demographic data, to punch out objectives to be included in individual habilitation plans, and to expedite analysis of experimental data using traditional statistical methods. Our tests of significance still refer to a formula, not to a question of substance. To remain on the cutting edge will indeed require another major paradigm shift. In short:

- We need to figure out how to evaluate whole life outcomes for individuals, not just how to collect and measure random bits.

- We need to recognize that strategic planning and implementation is a prerequisite for quality in the future; no one should spend 10 weeks, let alone 10 years on a waiting list.

- We need to recognize that every author represented in this book, and many more, is a protagonist for some unique technique or perspective that can contribute right now to the enhancement of quality for at least some people with developmental disabilities, but that not one of these programs or systems can do a complete job by itself for even one person with a severe disability.

- We need to conceptualize our systems as complex, dynamic, nonlinear, and not entirely predictable, and to apply the best tools available to their analysis, their understanding, and ultimately to their management.

By putting together a compendium of the state of opinion in 1990, Bradley and Bersani are helping us to focus on these tasks and to navigate in a sea of fractals.

Elizabeth Monroe Boggs, Ph.D.

REFERENCES

Dorris, M. (1989). *The broken cord.* New York: Harper and Row.
Gleick, J. (1987). *Chaos: Making a new science.* New York: Viking.
Kaufman, S.Z. (1988). *Retarded ISN'T stupid, Mom!* Baltimore: Paul H. Brookes Publishing Co.
Pool, R. (1989). Strange bedfellows. *Science, 245,* 700–702.

preface _____

More public resources are being spent on community services than ever before. However, we are concerned that as the service system has grown in size and complexity, there has not been a commensurate increase in the sophistication of our efforts to safeguard the interests of the people served in these settings, much less to assure true quality for people who depend on our human services.

This book is an amalgam of insights and experiences derived from people who have been directly involved as consumers as well as professionals in the evolution of community services to persons with developmental disabilities and mental retardation. Though each author comes from a different perspective and position in the system, they all share a long tenure in the movement to create more humane and responsive homes and workplaces for people with disabilities. Their ideas about what constitutes quality and the ways in which it can be assessed are not merely theoretical but are derived from the gritty experience of making service systems work through advocacy, service development, or program oversight.

Each author in this volume has taken a particular perspective—a point of view toward quality assurance. The fact that we have all presented a particular perspective should not imply that each author supports only that perspective. Rather, as editors, we have asked each author to describe a different piece of the puzzle. We believe that each of the perspectives represented here is necessary in a complete quality assurance system, but no one of these approaches is sufficient. In quality assurance, as in the rest of life, the whole is greater than the sum of the parts.

The collaborators in this book are colleagues and friends and are all individuals who at one time or another played an important role in the editors' professional development and understanding of quality assurance. Through our acquaintance with these individuals, we have developed a growing admiration for people who choose to make systems work against the very real constraints of inadequate resources and bureaucratic inertia. Being a successful advocate, monitor, state quality assurance official, or legislator requires both a strong sense of values and purpose as well as a mastery of the "art of the possible." We think that all of the contributors in this book embody these qualities, and their combined wisdom should provide important and practical lessons for the reader.

The concept for this book grew out of our mutual experiences in the field of developmental disabilities and with the specific forces at work in a number of states around the country in which we have worked as consultants, researchers, presenters, providers of technical assistance, and advocates. Given this wide exposure to multiple systems and approaches, we know that there is no one quality assurance technique that will provide an adequate picture of a diverse programmatic landscape. However, we do think that the concepts and examples outlined in the ensuing pages will spark ideas and assist the reader to think more broadly about quality assurance and to see the goal of developing quality assurance structures as not only within reach but also imperative to the well-being of people with disabilities.

There are many volumes that deal with specific issues of program evaluation and various issues in service monitoring. However, we are aware of no single volume that approaches, in a systematic way, the building of a comprehensive system to promote quality assurance in services to people with developmental disabilities. Furthermore, we know of no other volume that affords equal footing for consumer self-advocates, parents, working professionals, and policymakers.

Given the fluidity of the field, the mechanisms and ideas advanced in this book will continue to evolve and change well after our publication date. It is our hope that these chapters will stimulate people working at the federal, state, local, and service delivery level to build on these concepts using their own creativity and tempering them within their own unique constraints and opportunities. The abiding idea, which we are confident will not change over time, is the necessity to involve people with disabilities as well as those who are their friends and family in the conduct of quality assurance. Without their participation and input, quality assurance becomes a sterile exercise that reinforces the paternalistic practices that traditionally characterized services to vulnerable people.

In this book, we have attempted to move past the current state of practice of quality assurance and describe the state of the art. We focus on approaches that are being applied today, but have not been uniformly accepted into common practice. Our goal is to provide direction for the future that is grounded in the best that is being offered now. Together with our colleagues, we trust that this volume will provide the information needed to bring quality assurance into the 1990s.

In conclusion, we would like to take this opportunity to thank Paul Nurczynski from Human Services Research Institute for all of his help in preparing the manuscript, translating foreign word processing programs, and generally maintaining a sense of humor throughout. We want to especially recognize Elizabeth Boggs for her thoughtful advice and generosity—both intellectual and personal. We would also like to thank Gunnar Dybwad, Professor Emeritus, Brandeis University, for reading some of the early versions of the manuscript and providing thoughtful reactions and suggestions. Finally, we would like to thank Melissa Behm and Sarah Cheney for their patience and unfailing good cheer.

Quality Assurance for Individuals with Developmental Disabilities

CONCEPTUAL OVERVIEW

chapter 1 ———————

Conceptual Issues
in Quality Assurance

————————— *Valerie J. Bradley* —————————

The field of developmental disabilities and mental retardation has been characterized since the early 1970s by a furious and intense effort to construct a network of community living and working environments for persons with disabilities that could serve as alternatives to large institutions. This frantic activity has involved people at all levels of the service delivery system in the difficult and gritty work of building the community foundation.

During the course of this evolution, planners and policymakers have also been drawn into relentless debates about such issues as the virtues of institutional versus community programs, the merits of the medical versus developmental versus functional model of service delivery, the efficacy and moral acceptability of aversive interventions, and the definition of "least restrictive environment." These arguments have enlivened the field but have left many without time to step back and view the emerging delivery system with all of its virtues and flaws.

Furthermore, many have spent endless hours seeking support for developing services in the increasingly complex game of funding stream manipulation. Even when funding was identified, there was considerable work involved to stretch the eligibility requirements to fit the specific service needing support. The quest for funding has become even more manic as federal and state budgets have begun to tighten. Once funding had been corralled and allocated, program managers became obsessed with the need to ensure that the funding was spent in ways that conformed with contracts and auditing regulations.

In the early 1980s, the attention of system builders turned to the development of an "infrastructure" to manage the service delivery system, including the creation of case management, contracting and auditing systems, rate-setting formulas, and management information systems. Personnel management has also absorbed a substantial amount of time and has included the development of a range of certification and competency-based training regulations and strategies to recruit staff to fill key direct care jobs that turn over with dismal regularity.

Throughout this development, a major issue has been overlooked—assuring that the quality of those services so laboriously constructed is maintained. Without a solid series of mechanisms for quality assurance at all levels of the system, the considerable investment of time and precious resources will be compromised. The chapters that follow provide the reader with a comprehensive overview of the issues surrounding quality assurance, the dilemmas and tensions that inevitably arise in designing a quality assurance system, and the multiple constituencies and levels of the system that of necessity must be involved in the quality assurance enterprise. This book also elucidates the emerging state of the art in quality assurance, and it is hoped that it will instill in the reader an appreciation for its complex and multifaceted character.

IMPORTANCE OF QUALITY ASSURANCE

There are significant and compelling reasons why quality assurance is a crucial element of the system of services and supports for persons with developmental disabilities. First, the community system is serving more individuals with severe disabilities. Responsive quality assurance mechanisms are necessary to ensure that the promises that have been made to these sometimes vulnerable individuals and their families are kept and that community placement does not leave them stranded in potentially exploitative and abusive situations (see Provencal, Chapter 21, this volume).

Second, quality assurance systems are an important means of communicating high expectations for the service delivery system. Thoughtfully conceived, quality assurance standards should embody the state of the art as well as society's values about service delivery. These standards should reflect expectations about the shape and content of services and should exhort providers of service to greater levels of performance.

Another major reason for concern with quality assurance is the importance of giving feedback to providers of services in order to assist them to improve and enhance their programs. Service providers around the country have been asked to make modifications in their programs and to adapt to ever-changing conceptions of how services should be designed and implemented.

Responsive quality assurance systems make it possible to assist providers to accommodate evolving program expectations by giving them periodic feedback about their performance (see Dufresne, Chapter 11, this volume).

Federal concern regarding program quality also provides a substantial impetus for an intensified focus on quality assurance issues. Such concern is coming from two branches of government—the Health Care Financing Administration (HCFA) in the executive branch, and the Congress. With respect to HCFA, attention to the adequacy of so-called active treatment has grown as evidenced by increased federal monitoring of intermediate care facilities for persons with mental retardation (ICFs/MR) by HCFA "look-behind" teams. The heightened interest of HCFA reviewers was manifest in the following speech:

> . . . policymakers will receive increasing pressure to further account for costs incurred within dispersed systems. We as a system must accept the challenge to refine predictors of optimum client growth and change; to identify how well resources that may become scarcer and scarcer can best be coalesced to enhance dignity and worth and increase client independence; to find "best indicators" or "powerful markers" that measure performance and tie effectiveness of services provided for the dollars spent. Increasingly we will need to be able to identify just what it is we're spending billions of dollars on! (Spaar, 1987)

In addition to HCFA, the other jaw of this federal pincer movement is Congress. Beginning with Senator Lowell Weicker's hearings on the quality of care in the nation's ICFs/MR (U.S. Senate Subcommittee on the Handicapped, 1985), Congressional interest has been evident in several pieces of legislation, including Senator Chafee's Medicaid Home and Community Quality Services Act of 1989 and other Medicaid reform legislation introduced by Congressmen Henry Waxman and James Florio. Debates about how best to structure the federal role continue, but one thing is clear: unless states and others concerned about services to people with developmental disabilities begin to mount a concerted effort to fashion comprehensive federal quality assurance systems, the federal government will, in one form or another, move into the vacuum (see Smith and Gettings, Chapter 8, this volume).

Furthermore, as resources become scarce, the need to justify the relatively generous funding that services to people with developmental disabilities have enjoyed since the late 1970s will become more immediate. Quality assurance provides program administrators and advocates with the information necessary to impress upon policymakers the very real value, in terms of improved lives, that they are receiving for their money (see Conroy and Feinstein, Chapter 18, this volume).

Finally, quality assurance mechanisms are necessary to ensure that the gains that have been made in service delivery are maintained. Service systems, not unlike automobiles, need periodic tune-ups. One certainly wouldn't buy a $20,000 car and then go 5 years without following the recommended maintenance schedule. Likewise, by not adopting comprehensive quality assurance systems, the services that have been created will steadily deteriorate.

In the remainder to this chapter, some terminology and conceptual issues are introduced in order to provide a framework for the book. Specifically addressed are the issues surrounding the definition of quality, the purposes and objectives of a comprehensive quality assurance system, the dimensions of service quality, the components of any quality assurance system, the methods for collecting quality assurance information, and the key constituencies of the quality assurance effort.

WHAT IS QUALITY?

The term "quality" is increasingly used not only in the field of disabilities but also in business. Advertisements for automobiles in particular stress the virtues of their products in statements such as, "Quality is Job 1," and others claim, "the quality goes in before the name goes on." These concerns, like those in the field of disabilities, are the result of a desire for standards that yield a product that performs reliably and predictably (Bersani, 1989). Clearly, these criteria should form the expectations for services to persons with developmental disabilities. The added dimension in human services is the desire to find out if the service that is delivered has the intended effect. In other words, quality is the promise that is made to the client and quality assurance is necessary to ensure that the promise is kept.

To ensure that the promise of a full life in the community mainstream is kept, quality assurance systems must be available that both monitor the fulfillment of this overarching goal and assist in facilitating the implementation of these concepts. Values like community integration are not self-implementing; they need to be nurtured and supported.

The concepts of quality and quality assurance are somewhat hazy. One cannot hope to create a coherent picture of the phenomenon without first understanding the multifaceted character of this versatile notion. To some extent, ideas about quality in the field of disabilities read like Roshamon—the story that describes a dramatic event using the recollections of each of the three participants, all of whom recall the event through their own self-interest and self-conception. Like the conclusion to the story, quality or truth is really found at the illusive intersection of multiple perspectives. Keeping this admonition in mind, there are four elements of the definition of quality and quality assurance.

Characteristic

The word "quality" can mean a characteristic or an aspect of some phenomenon. Thus, quality assurance must be concerned with the essence of particular service modalities. For instance, are residences in fact homes or homelike? Do the programs display those characteristics that are associated with community integration (see Bersani, Chapter 6, this volume)?

Aspiration

Quality is an aspirational term and refers to a high level of achievement and expectation. Quality assurance, therefore, should assess the extent to which services are being delivered in ways that coincide with the most current knowledge of the state of the art (see Knoll, Chapter 17, this volume).

Subjective Notion

Quality is a subjective notion. Just as reasonable people disagree about the "quality" of a movie or a meal, people in the field of disabilities disagree about what constitutes a "quality" program. Though some of these debates revolve around disputes over the efficacy of particular service modalities, most grow out of the clash of perspectives inherent in a field made up of multiple constituencies including consumers, their families, professionals, legislators, federal regulators, administrators, advocates, the public, and researchers. Quality assurance systems, if they are to be reflective of this diverse set of players, must embody all points of view. This book, therefore, reflects the perspectives of consumers (Kennedy, Chapter 3, and Speaking for Ourselves, Chapter 4), families (Lehr and Lehr, Chapter 5), policymakers (Chafee, Chapter 7), public agencies (Wray, Chapter 10), service providers (Dufresne, Chapter 11), advocates (Lottman, Chapter 12, and Ray, Chapter 13), and state program officials (Gant, Chapter 20).

Value

Quality is commensurate with value. Therefore, quality assurance systems must be aimed at the value or the outcome of services (see O'Brien, Chapter 2, and Conroy and Feinstein, Chapter 18, this volume). Value or benefit comes from increased integration, choice, functionality, and productivity. Without a focus on outcomes, it is impossible to assess whether any benefit has in fact been passed on to the client.

WHAT IS A QUALITY ASSURANCE SYSTEM?

As noted in *Assessing and Enhancing the Quality of Services: A Guide for the Human Services Field* (Bradley et al., 1984), the conduct of quality assurance around the country has been hampered by a variety of problems. In part, these problems reflect a failure to understand the overall aim of quality assurance, which is to enhance services as well as to regulate them. Specifically, quality assurance systems are almost always aimed at past abuses and not on future capacity. They are punitive and rarely generate the needed training or resources necessary to rectify the problems uncovered. Furthermore, many quality assurance standards codified in state regulations are aimed at the lowest common denominator and do not provide benchmarks or incentives that can inspire providers to attain higher levels of accomplishment. They, therefore, do not provide any psychic or other rewards for outstanding performance.

Finally, as the ability of states to monitor services in an increasingly decentralized system has shrunk, regulators have been forced to rely on paper documentation as a proxy for quality. This burden of documentation has been visited on providers already stretched and depleted by a shrinking resource base. Paperwork requirements have also been coupled with increasing audit and cost reporting requirements. Though such oversight is important, monitoring priorities appear to be moving away from the essence of service delivery—the well-being of the client. This message is not lost on providers who feel alienated from a system of regulation that seemingly does not respect that they are in business to supply services to enrich the lives of people with disabilities (see Dufresne, Chapter 11, this volume).

These problems can be avoided if designers of quality assurance systems remember the importance of a balance between regulation and enhancement (e.g., training and technical assistance) as well as the following realistic objectives (adapted from Bradley et al., 1984):

To assure that providers of human services have the capability to provide an acceptable level of service

To assure that client services are provided consistent with accepted beliefs about what constitutes good practice

To assure that a commitment of resources produces a reasonable level of service from the point of view of the consumer as well as the one supplying the funds

To assure that the services that are provided have the intended effect

To assure that the limited supply of services is provided to clients most in need

To assure that the legal and human rights of people with disabilities are protected

The capacity and practice aspects of quality assurance are described by a range of authors in this book. For instance, Michael Lottman (Chapter 12, this volume) provides the reader with a discussion of the strategies used by the court to stimulate the achievement of the range of quality assurance objectives. James Gardner and Catherine Parsons (Chapter 15, this volume) and Kaye Pearce (Chapter 16, this volume) discuss related concerns in their descriptions of two national accreditation bodies. James Knoll (Chapter 17, this volume) grapples with the evolution of assumptions about best practices over time, and Sue Gant (Chapter 20, this volume) addresses the ways in which these issues have been built into the Connecticut quality assurance system.

Issues surrounding the ability of service delivery systems to ensure an adequate return on the public dollar are discussed by John Ashbaugh (Chapter 9, this volume) in his overview of performance contracting. The ability of quality assurance systems to ascribe outcomes is covered in depth by James Conroy and Celia Feinstein (Chapter 18, this volume). Finally, the issue of rights protection is clearly articulated by both Lottman (Chapter 12, this volume) and Ray (Chapter 13, this volume).

DIMENSIONS OF SERVICE QUALITY

Another way of understanding quality assurance is by concentrating on those aspects of service delivery that are the targets of quality assurance systems. Specifically, there are four:

- *Inputs* Inputs or "structural" measurements of the service system are the "raw material" or capacity that the provider brings to bear on the delivery of services. They include the physical facility, the nature of the clients being served, the number and competency of the staff, and the regulatory framework in which the service is delivered. Program inputs are relatively straightforward and are reasonably easy to identify and measure. Concern about inputs characterized many early quality assurance schemes that were premised primarily on staffing ratios and staffing standards (Scheerenberger, 1983).

- *Process* The process of the service enterprise reflects the interaction between the client and the organization providing the service and has to do with "practice." As noted earlier, many providers complain that paperwork compliance has come to dominate quality assurance monitoring. Many of these documentation requirements are directed at process functions such as planning, charting, developing manuals, reporting incidents, and so forth. Given staff shortages, direct and regular observation of the service transaction is difficult.

- *Outputs* Output of service delivery is synonymous with "product" and includes such things as the number of clients served or the units of service delivered. Like inputs, this service dimension is relatively easy to quantify and is often a stand-in for true program results.

- *Outcomes* Outcome is the culmination of service delivery and represents a measurement of the effect or impact that the intervention actually has on the client. Outcomes reflect on the goals of the service and reveal whether the promise made to the client and his or her family has been kept. By and large, quality assurance systems do not yield information about outcomes, in part because of the methodological difficulties involved in such calculations and the problems involved in establishing causality between a particular intervention and a specific result (Ashbaugh et al., 1980). Outcome monitoring on a systematic basis, however, has potential political risks and is more likely to be found in systems under court order (see Lottman, Chapter 13, this volume), or in more mature service systems (see Conroy and Feinstein, Chapter 19, this volume).

Madeleine Kimmich (Chapter 19, this volume) describes how all of these dimensions of quality assurance should be woven into a comprehensive quality assurance system. Specifically, she leads the reader through an explanation of how one state, South Carolina, used these concepts in combination with the quality assurance objectives to create standards for disability as well as human services. Knoll (Chapter 17, this volume) shows how these aspects of service delivery can also be seen as evolutionary stages of concern for the quality of services to people with developmental disabilities.

Michael Kennedy (Chapter 3, this volume), who has been a lifetime consumer of services, provides another perspective of quality assurance. He shows how rigid concerns for the input and process facets of services can constrain the quality of life for people who are trying to lead reasonably normal lives.

COMPONENTS OF QUALITY ASSURANCE

Quality assurance systems are built on three basic elements: standards, monitoring, and response mechanisms. Each of these three components has unique design requirements and criteria. Weaknesses in any one aspect of the foundation will result in a flawed quality assurance system that will leave providers and advocates cynical about the intentions of the overseers. For instance, the presence of comprehensive standards is important, but without rigorous monitoring and response mechanisms, clients will be at risk as surely as if there were no standards at all. Gerald Provencal (Chapter 21, this volume) forcefully shows how real life abuses could have been prevented if the designers and implementers of quality assurance systems had been as careful with the design of measurement, monitoring, and response/control mechanisms as they were with the design of standards. The following discussion suggests some of the criteria by which to judge the effectiveness of these three key ingredients.

Setting Standards

Standards come from a variety of sources including ideology and values, professional theory and practice, and scientific inquiry (Ashbaugh et al., 1980). For instance, the 1987 Standards of the Accreditation Council on Services for People with Developmental Disabilities (ACDD) includes several standards relating to the value of integration of individuals with developmental disabilities into their communities. The following is one example:

Values: Normalization, Age Appropriateness and Least Restriction
People with disabilities should not be segregated solely on the basis of those disabilities. If specialized environments are used for people with special needs, the agency should document the justification for the specialized environments and ensure that those individuals are in as much contact as possible with peers who are not disabled and that they are returned to normal environments as soon as possible. (The Accreditation Council on Services for People with Developmental Disabilities [ACDD], 1987, p. 15)

Kaye Pearce (Chapter 16, this volume) describes how the Commission on the Accreditation of Rehabilitation Facilities (CARF) is grappling with the incorporation of emerging values into the development of standards.

Professional theory contributes much to the standard-setting process including standards having to do with the development of individual plans, staffing standards and staffing credentials, reporting requirements, and so forth. Following is a standard from the *Standards Manual for Organizations Serving People with Disabilities* that is directed at the development of an individual client plan in a residential setting:

Standard B, #18 & #19
A plan should be developed with and for each person served in a residential program. The plan should include:

a. The desires and choices of the individuals including where and how the individual chooses to live
b. The strengths and needs of the individual
c. Where the person will live
d. How friendships and relationships will be continued or developed
e. The services which are to be provided
f. Short-term and long-term goals and objectives which are time-phased, measurable, and functional
g. The methods to achieve the goals and objectives
h. The assignment of responsibilities for implementation
i. The methods which will be used to assess services
j. The methods which will be used to coordinate and integrate the residential services with the family and other available services

Provisions [should be made] for at least semiannual review of the person's plan for services, goals, and progress toward goals. The review should be conducted by appropriate staff members with the involvement of the individual served and family when appropriate. Where changes have been made in plans, goals, etc., there should be evidence of subsequent implementation. (Commission on Accreditation of Rehabilitation Facilities [CARF], 1988, pp. 95–96)

The final source of standards is prescriptions yielded from scientific inquiry. Such standards derive from the results of empirical research and are the smallest components of most standards. Examples of standards based on empirical research have to do with such things as fire and life safety, medication monitoring, oversight of health conditions, and so forth. The following standards from the Minnesota Department of Human Services Licensing Division arguably grows out of empirical knowledge:

Standard III.B

If a psychotropic exceeds a FDA maximum dose, the clinician and provider must document specific reasons and provide evidence that this level is necessary. The general items to look for are as follows:

a) If a blood level test is available for that drug, there is a lab test which shows that the blood level of the psychotropic at normal dosages is below therapeutic levels. This indicates that person metabolizes the psychotropic differently and requires the higher dose to reach therapeutic blood level that other people reach at normal dosages. Additionally, a blood level test at the excessive FDA level shows the level to be within the therapeutic level. (Kalachnik, 1988, p. 8)

In designing standards, there are several criteria that should be adhered to (adapted from Ashbaugh et al., 1980):

Consistency   Can the standards be applied fairly and equitably across programs?

Flexibility   Do the standards allow sufficient flexibility to support innovation and to respond to individual needs?

Clarity   Is the content of the standards easily communicated—especially to direct care staff?

Measurability   Are the standards susceptible to standardized measurement?

Monitoring

This component of a quality assurance system includes the design of measurements to assess the compliance with standards as well as the development of oversight systems including on-site and off-site surveillance. One of the chronic failings at this stage of the design of a quality assurance system is the creation of overly complex and cumbersome measurement schemes. The irresistible urge to know as much as possible about service delivery lures many well-meaning administrators to create data collection schemes that: 1) generate more information than anyone could conceivably use and 2) overwhelm service providers. As a result, such schemes eventually fall of their own weight.

There are a number of questions that designers of quality assurance systems should address as they construct monitoring and measurement schemes (adapted from Ashbaugh et al., 1980):

Cost-Effectiveness   Can the monitoring system be implemented with a reasonable level of resources, and are the data gathered of sufficient interest to justify the expenditure?

Reliability   Does the measurement mechanism ensure inter-rater agreement? In other words, do the ratings of two independent observers of the same phenomenon agree within an acceptable range?

Validity Do the indicators chosen to reflect compliance with standards in fact reflect the phenomenon under observation? (Do the indicators of integration probe for such things as friendships and relationships, community presence, etc.?)

Timeliness Does the monitoring mechanism capture events with sufficient timeliness and proximity to the occurrence to allow for an immediate response?

Feedback Does the monitoring mechanism have built-in means for returning information about performance back to the provider?

Response Mechanisms

This final component of quality assurance is perhaps the most important since it is at this stage that information collected through monitoring scrutiny is assessed and plans of action are generated. The conventional response in most quality assurance systems is to issue sanctions or "punishments." Rarely do systems make provisions for an enhancement response, such as training and technical assistance. Given that many problems uncovered are the result of a lack of knowledge and, in some instances, resources, the more productive response in such situations is to build capacity rather than issue sanctions. Obviously, when the situation is chronic or when there is disregard for the well-being of people with disabilities, swift sanctions are necessary and warranted. However, in a balanced quality assurance system, responses should consist of enhancement as well as enforcement.

One of the responses to quality assurance information should also be to identify needs for systemic reform. Lyle Wray (Chapter 10, this volume) shows how systems can use quality assurance information to improve planning and management. Likewise, James Gardner and Catherine Parsons (Chapter 15, this volume) discuss the ways in which the information gained from accreditation surveys can be utilized in organizational development at the provider level.

Criteria for response systems include the following (adapted from Ashbaugh et al., 1980):

Reasonableness Is the response of the system in proportion to the problem uncovered?

Credibility Are those generating the response to quality assurance information credible to the providers of services?

Constructiveness Does the response contribute to an overall improvement in the quality of the system?

Certainty If a provider jeopardizes the well-being of people with disabilities, is there likely to be a certain and swift response from the formal quality assurance system?

Utility Does the information generated by a quality assurance system circulate back to those within an agency responsible for planning and policy development?

METHODS FOR OBTAINING QUALITY ASSURANCE INFORMATION

Given that quality assurance is a multifaceted activity, no one technique will suffice to collect quality assurance information. A number of techniques are described in this book. For instance, Bersani (Chapter 6, this volume) highlights the benefits of family monitoring of services and focuses on illustrative applications of this technique in Ohio and Michigan. Gardner and Parsons (Chapter 15, this volume) and Pearce (Chapter 16, this volume) all concentrate on the virtues and role of national accreditation. Ashbaugh (Chapter 9, this volume) shows how performance contracting plays an appropriate role in assuring service quality. Dufresne (Chapter 11, this volume) stresses the importance of internal quality assurance mechanisms within provider agencies as a key component to external systems.

Conroy and Feinstein (Chapter 18, this volume) provide a thorough examination of the use of outcome monitoring schemes and the ways in which aggregate outcome data can be used in reporting mechanisms. Gant (Chapter 20, this volume) guides the reader through the multiple methods of quality assurance that are being implemented in Connecticut, and Lottman (Chapter 12, this volume) comments on the methods used by courts to enforce quality mandates.

CONSTITUENCIES OF QUALITY ASSURANCE

As highlighted earlier in this chapter, notions of quality are diverse and quality assurance systems must reflect a consensus of the views of a disparate group of constituencies. It is important to employ each constituency in some phase of quality assurance so that services are viewed from each distinct perspective.

Broadening the number of people involved in monitoring also provides support for the quality assurance enterprise. Given the multiple demands on state developmental disabilities staff, assistance from clients, families, local citizens, and others expands their limited capacity to oversee programs.

CONCLUSION

The following chapters of this volume will both provoke and inform. Together they represent an emerging conception of what is required to ensure the quality of the community system that has been so painstakingly built since the late 1960s. The authors will also introduce the reader to the dilemmas and tensions inherent in developing quality assurance systems including:

The tension between society's responsibility to protect people with disabilities and to oversee their lives in the community and the needs of people with disabilities to exercise personal autonomy and independence

The tension between the need to standardize service delivery around generally agreed-upon conceptions of what constitutes good practice and the need to allow for flexibility, individualization, and continued innovation

The struggle to develop a system that can both enhance service capacity through training and technical support while convincing those who provide services that transgressions against client well-being will not be tolerated

The conflict between the desire to create a dynamic quality assurance system that evolves in response to changes in the state of the art while at the same time giving providers some sense of predictability and stability

The difficulty in balancing the need for strong internal quality assurance systems with external, disinterested monitoring mechanisms

The final challenge will be to design quality assurance systems for programs that look more like people's homes and real jobs. However, the closer society comes to the ideal of community living, the more intrusive and heavy-handed conventional quality assurance systems will appear. The clear goal for the 1990s and beyond will be identifying those quality indicators that capture the goals of integration and personal choice that intrude minimally on the lives of people, and that ensure that the age-old exploitation and abuse of people with disabilities is kept in abeyance.

REFERENCES

The Accreditation Council on Services for People with Developmental Disabilities (ACDD). (1987). *Standards for services for people with development disabilities.* Boston: Author.

Ashbaugh, J.W., Bradley, V.J., Allard, M.A., Reday, M., Stoddard, S., & Collignon, R. (1980). *Overview of methods for assuring the quality of human services currently operating at the state and local levels* (OHDS Grant No. 90-PD-10016/01). Cambridge, MA, & Berkeley, CA: Human Services Research Institute, Urban Institute, & Berkeley Planning Associates.

Bersani, H.A. (1989). *Assuring residential quality: Issues, approaches, and instruments* (NIDRR Grant No. G0085C03503). Syracuse, NY: Center on Human Policy.

Bradley, V.J., Ashbaugh, J., Harder, P., Allard, M., Mulkern, V., & Stoddard, S. (1984). *Assessing and enhancing the quality of services: A guide for the human services field* (DHHS/OHDS Grant No. 90-PD-10016/01). Cambridge, MA: Human Services Research Institute.

Commission on Accreditation of Rehabilitation Facilities (CARF). (1988). *Standards manual for organizations serving people with disabilities.* Tucson, AZ: Author.

Kalachnik, J.E. (1988). *Psychotropic medication monitoring manual and checklist for Rule 34 facilities.* St. Paul: Minnesota Department of Human Services, Licensing Division.

Scheerenberger, R.C. (1983). *A history of mental retardation.* Baltimore: Paul H. Brookes Publishing Co.

Spaar, M.P. (1987, April 29). *ICF/MR: Establishing regulations and enforcement activity.* Presented at the annual conference of the Young Adult Institute, New York.

U.S. Senate Subcommittee on the Handicapped and the Subcommittee on Labor, Health and Human Services, Education and Related Agencies. (1985, April). *Examining the issues related to care and treatment of the nation's institutionalized mentally disabled persons* (Senate Hearing 99-50). Washington, DC: U.S. Government Printing Office.

chapter 2 _____

Developing High Quality Services for People with Developmental Disabilities

_____ *John O'Brien* _____

The following is an example of one person's experiences that illustrates the kind of human services decisions that make a difference in the lives of the people involved.

Brian works in a restaurant cleaning the dining room, stocking the salad bar, and assisting with food preparation. At age 26, it is his first job. His mother says, "He was proud to get a name tag. He is most proud of the idea that he works like everybody else." His co-workers say he enjoys being part of their group. His employer says he does a good job, most of the time. Brian says very little, but most work days he gets up without difficulty and much of the time he does his tasks willingly and capably.

Group home staff recognize that difficult behavior, which led to his institutionalization and which has frustrated their efforts at behavior management, happens less frequently since he has been working. His job coach notices that Brian seldom bites himself, seldom swears loudly, or seldom sucks his thumb at

Preparation of this chapter was supported through a subcontract from the University of Minnesota University Affiliated Facility for the Rehabilitation Research and Training Center on Improving Community Integration for Persons with Mental Retardation. The Research and Training Center is supported through a cooperative agreement #H133B80048 with the National Institute on Disability and Rehabilitation Research (NIDRR). Members of the center are encouraged to express their opinions; these do not necessarily represent the official position of NIDRR.

work and thinks it is mostly because of the influence of his co-workers and his interest in his job.

Brian is not cured. He still has significant difficulty with self-control and he continues to need some extra help from his supervisor, some extra help from his co-workers, and some assistance from his job coach. He still has difficult times at the group home. If he lost his job, he would need a great deal of help to find another one.

Brian does have more satisfying days, the opportunity to be part of a work group, the chance to learn new things and earn a wage, and the status of being a worker. Those close to him have a renewed sense of a positive future for him. As his mother says, "Every year we think he has come to his full potential and he keeps on going." (adapted from Guy, Scott, Hasazi, & Patten, 1989, p. 10)

Brian's changes are a result of changes in the thinking, policies, and practices of the service providers and policymakers he relies on. Because they resolved to make community living possible for everyone, regardless of the extent of disability, Brian returned from the institution to his home community. The unhelpful idea that Brian was not ready to work until his behavior was under control was discarded, and he now has a job. These service providers and policymakers have learned to develop individual jobs that offer people like Brian the opportunity to be part of a work group. Brian spends his work hours and his break times with people who are not disabled in an ordinary restaurant near his home. Since it is possible that Brian might want or need to change jobs, human services providers want to maintain the capacity to support him as his circumstances change. His struggle for effective communication and self-control continues but now in the context of greater participation in community life. With cooperation from the other people he relies on, his life changes, mostly for the better, a step at a time. His mother's life improves, and there are small, mostly positive changes for his employer and his co-workers as they get to know him. Furthermore, service staff feel they have more demanding and satisfying jobs.

Human services designers and providers affect the daily experiences and the future prospects of the individuals, families, and communities who rely on them. Service policies and daily practice influence where a person who depends on service lives, learns, works, and plays; what activities fill the person's days; whom the person gets to know; and even the way the person and others understand exactly who that person is. When someone depends on services for housing, necessary personal assistance, and daily occupation over a long period, as many people with developmental disabilities do, services become life defining.

LEADERSHIP

The fundamental question for those concerned with high quality services for people with severe disabilities is, "How can we use our resources to assist the people who rely on us to live better lives?" As Brian's mother points out, the notion of a better life is ambiguous. Because he has responsive help, Brian keeps outgrowing other people's ideas of what a good life for him will be.

Openness to the question of how to mobilize resources to assist individuals to improve their lives causes uneasiness since human services organizations cannot manufacture better lives. People weave better lives from the resources afforded by individual effort, personal relationships, available opportunities, and help from services. Thus, the outcomes of services to people with developmental disabilities are a result of the collaboration among the person, family and friends, neighbors, classmates, co-workers, employers, and service providers. Frustration awaits those who desire control of services through quantifiable objectives, standard procedures, and well defined lines of accountability and assistance toward better lives for people.

The question of how to assist individuals in improving their lives brings about uncertainty, the possibility of conflict, and the demand for change. However, responsible policymakers and practitioners will not try to dodge the question by reducing the pursuit of service quality to conform with external standards and regulations or by retreating into arguments about the impossibility of doing anything until science produces objective measures of what a "better life is." Avoiding the question reduces decisionmakers' discomfort but at the cost of denying the links between service practice and the realities of life for people with disabilities, their families, and community members. Such denial cuts off policymakers and practitioners from essential information, reduces their options for effective action, and compromises the integrity of their efforts by shifting the whole burden of change to the person with a disability.

The question of how to assist individuals in improving their lives tests and builds leadership. Leadership means mobilizing resources to make progress on difficult problems: problems for which definitions must be negotiated among people with different understandings; problems for which responses must be invented rather than simply selected from a menu of proven solutions; problems for which pressures must be avoided by the people involved since making progress implies personal, organizational, and social learning and change (Heifetz & Sinder, 1988). Leadership is not a position on the organization chart or an expression of personal charisma. Anyone leads when performing the activities that enable people to face and deal with the complex situations that are confronted by a service organization working to learn how to assist people to make better lives for themselves.

This chapter discusses some of the activities of leadership for service quality. These include shaping direction through vision, identifying distinctive contributions by clarifying legitimate purposes of services for people who need long-term assistance, identifying barriers by clarifying and negotiating organizational purposes, and guiding daily work on problems by defining the accomplishments of effective services.

VISION

Vision animates and directs people's action toward a desirable future that is unlikely to become a reality without effort and learning. Such vision describes the community circumstances in which people with disabilities can lead better lives. For example, Judith Snow (1987) spoke powerfully to many concerned people:

> In order to create or expand the capacity of communities to respond to their own members, it is clear that a fundamental activity of change is to welcome people with disabilities into ordinary, rich networks of relationship. To achieve such a welcome, disability and those who carry it must be seen as less threatening and burdensome, if not in fact as unusual gifts to the broader social structure. People must see that disability does not have to be fixed or cured, but accepted and challenged. The individual must be welcomed, celebrated and listened to, challenged and supported in every environment to develop every talent that he or she potentially has, just as ordinary people are. His or her contributions must be facilitated and used for the benefit of the wider group. In short, every citizen must be an ordinary citizen. (p. 1)

This chapter follows Judith Snow's example in seeking a vision of inclusive community. A vision of inclusive community points in a direction different than a vision of human services that meets all needs within its buildings and boundaries. The search for the excellent self-contained service program is a futile effort, but the search for ways to build more inclusive community directs attention to the network of relationships and environments that can lead to opportunities for better lives for everyone (McKnight, 1987).

Expressions of vision arise from careful listening and thoughtful reflection on the experiences and interests of the people concerned. Vision energizes by creating tension with current reality; it communicates how the people involved want things to be different. Statements of vision feel right and vital to the people concerned, even if they may seem strange, impractical, or even foolish to others. Vision can be chosen, but it cannot be coerced. People do not finish with a vision; rather, as they work toward it, their appreciation of its meaning deepens, and the words and symbols that communicate it grow richer and clearer.

A human services organization whose members discover and commit themselves to a common vision has an alternative to bureaucratic control mechanisms. People with a common vision have a sense of direction. They find it easier to face difficult situations, easier to cooperate, easier to deal with conflicts, easier to create innovations, and easier to stick with their work when things get difficult than people controlled only by hierarchical relationships do (Bennis & Nanus, 1985).

The attractiveness of having a vision tempts some managers to counterfeit one by imposing a statement through administrative authority. However, there are no shortcuts. Only listening, reflecting, and testing understanding shape and communicate vision. People involved with the organization—including individuals with disabilities and their family members—contribute to developing vision through these straightforward, but difficult activities:

- Invite a variety of people to describe their sense of a desirable future for people with disabilities, their families, and other members of their communities. Listen carefully and respectfully for the kind of community people want to create to support their search for better lives. Pay special attention to people with disabilities, their families, and their friends.

- Keep the conversation going beyond statements about the internal state of the person with a disability (like "being happy" or "reaching full potential"). Instead, ask, "What would it take to increase the chances of being happy or reaching full potential?"

- Critically study the thoughts of others who have considered the situation of people with disabilities and the question of developing strong communities.

- Reflect on what people say. Think about what social circumstances will make it possible for people with disabilities to pursue better lives. Look for common themes and vibrant images among the different answers people give. Think about whether or not conflicting answers point toward some common intention.

- Practice expressing a vision that captures and vividly communicates what people want to work toward together. Try alternative ways to clearly express vision, and experiment with different symbols and media. Check expressions against other people's sense of a true and exciting direction.

- Ask for agreement about vision, "Is this really what we want to create?" Declare personal commitment to work toward the vision.

- Feel the tension between the vision and current reality by asking, "How does this vision stretch us? Does it test our courage to describe the distance between what we now have and what we want?"

- Scan for opportunities to try behavior consistent with the vision. Keep asking, "How can we respond to this situation in a way that moves us toward our vision?"

- Make time to refresh the vision by renewed listening, reflecting on how working toward the vision deepens or modifies its meaning, reaching out to involve new people, and celebrating.

ORGANIZATIONAL PURPOSES

Vision evokes future social conditions that will make better lives for people with disabilities possible. Organizational purposes specify the distinctive contribution a particular human services program can make to creating those conditions. Additionally, the purposes identify the position the programs seek in the lives of the people who rely on them and in the communities; they delimit organizational contracts by defining the kinds of promises the program can legitimately make; they concentrate energy by ruling out a number of possible courses of action; they promote organizational learning by presenting assumptions about what is possible and what is not and by focusing what the organization needs to learn. Statements of organizational purposes answer the question, "How can you help?" The following purposes of services for people who require long-term support (O'Brien & Lyle, 1987) offer a starting point for understanding, articulating, and negotiating goals.

Move Toward a Desirable Personal Future

One purpose is to assist people with disabilities, their families, and their friends to discover and move toward a more desirable personal future as part of ordinary community life. This implies helping people as necessary to define their interests and capacities, often by helping them discover, try and evaluate a variety of new experiences; assisting in development of opportunities for people to pursue their interests in community settings, including workplaces, schools, and a home of the person's choice; and providing or arranging the assistance, adaptations, systematic instruction, or other supports necessary for the person to use community opportunities.

A human services organization accepting this purpose will move away from a primary focus on people's deficiencies, treatments, and professional-client relationships as well as move away from congregating people with disabilities in human services owned and operated buildings for organizational purposes only. However, an organization accepting this purpose will move toward making alliances with people with disabilities, their families, and their friends; expressing visions of desirable personal futures, even for people who have very limited experiences or great difficulty communicating; incorporating better skilled assistance with health, mobility, communication, learning, and self-control into the routines of ordinary settings; and personalizing support to match individual needs.

Support and Strengthen Community Competence

A second purpose is to offer needed help in ways that support and strengthen community competence. This means to support and not substitute for families and friends who care, to strengthen links to community networks, to expand membership in community associations, to increase the inclusiveness of regular classrooms, to increase the openness of the local economy by developing a variety of jobs for people with disabilities and by increasing the number of adults with disabilities who lease or own their own homes, to improve the effectiveness and inclusiveness of the services and benefits available to all citizens, and to build alliances with people and groups concerned with improving community life.

A human services organization accepting this purpose will move away from all or nothing service designs; the assumption that service providers necessarily know better than people with disabilities, their families, their friends, and ordinary people who share classrooms, workplaces and neighborhoods with people with disabilities; positioning the service as a charity worthy of community support because of the good it does for unfortunates; and staff disconnection from community people, organizations, and activities. Instead, it will move toward sharing responsibility for providing assistance with families, friends, classmates, co-workers, and neighbors; consulting people about how they would define and solve problems for themselves; positioning the service as worthy of support because it builds the inclusiveness of the community; and engaging staff with community people, organizations, and activities.

Protect and Promote Valued Experiences

A third purpose is to offer needed help in ways that protect and promote valued experiences for the people who rely on services. This implies identifying, solving, and evaluating day-to-day problems and long-term investments in terms of their impact on the quality of people's everyday experience.

A human services organization that accepts this purpose will move away from evaluating people in terms of what they must do to get ready for valued experiences, assessing experiences imposed by service providers on groups of people as "for their own good" or "what they choose," and erecting service continuua that require people with developmental disabilities to earn their way to valued experiences. Instead, the organization that accepts this purpose will move toward determining what it would take to offer a person good experiences today; assessing experiences imposed by service providers by asking the people involved for their own evaluations and by asking, "How would this seem to me if I were experiencing it, or if my child were experiencing it?"; and developing policies and services that offer flexible assistance and back-up to people involved in a variety of individually chosen community settings.

What happened to independence as a purpose of human service? Independence cannot be an organizational purpose if it is understood as being able to do for oneself, without extra help. Most people with developmental disabilities need ongoing help, and many rely on human services for at least part of that help. Most people's abilities can be enhanced, and most people can get a substantial part of the extra help they need from family members, friends, classmates, co-workers, and other people. However, a service that identifies its distinctive contribution as helping people so they will do for themselves makes a promise to people with disabilities that existing technology will not allow it to keep. An organization bound to this common understanding of independence will avoid people it is technically incompetent to serve. Of course, people unable to manage without extra help can be in charge of their own lives. Most people with disabilities can set goals for themselves and express preferences about the way they want to live. Many people with developmental disabilities can supervise their helpers. Human services policies and practices can promise these people assistance in pursuing a desirable personal future and support to control their own lives.

BARRIERS TO CLARIFYING AND NEGOTIATING ORGANIZATIONAL PURPOSES

When the people who rely on human services have disabilities, defining and negotiating organizational purposes is problematic for three reasons. First, the effects of available technology are uncertain. Most people with developmental disabilities can expect significant help with mobility, health, communication, productivity, and learning new things; and they can expect the people who assist them in these areas to continuously improve their effectiveness (Snell, 1988). However, a "cure" lies beyond reasonable expectation, and this complicates discussion of purposes. Some people find it hard to value activities that open opportunities and that offer support to individuals without promising some form of medical or behavioral cure. Others find it easier to cope with the impression that a person with a disability should accept fate, rather than face the fact that real change can happen but without cure. Some people with professional skills find it difficult to acknowledge the limits of their expertise and authority.

Second, people with developmental disabilities face ingrained social prejudice that results in their exclusion from everyday life. The prejudices that justify exclusion control many people's thinking about what makes sense for people with disabilities. In an environment shaped by exclusion, it has come to make sense to leave people with disabilities out of ordinary classrooms, workplaces, and homes until their disability has been "repaired" by heroic individual and professional efforts in a succession of carefully graduated service environments (Taylor, 1988). Furthermore, in an environment shaped by exclusion, it makes sense to assign full responsibility for all of the effects of prejudice and service failure to the person with a disability and to redefine collective failure in medical terms as individual chronicity (Ferguson, 1988). Confronting prejudice means challenging and changing arrangements that many people believe make so much sense that alternatives seem absurd or unthinkable. There is no reliable technology for engineering changes in community life or, for that matter, service settings. Shifting the social patterns that exclude and blame people with disabilities requires effort from person to person and setting to setting. Additionally, policymakers and service providers who want change in community practices and attitudes must confront and change themselves as their efforts at changing community members become entangled in the constraints of their own system. Many policymakers and service providers experience understandable reluctance to assume purposes that call for so much change.

Third, most funds are not given to assist people to lead better lives; they are given for slots, seats, beds, placements, active treatment, or preparation for competitive employment. A growing proportion of service providers are virtually wholly owned subsidiaries of federal funding sources that require externally imposed purposes and procedures. Many service managers rightly believe that personal and organizational survival depends on carrying out the intended purposes and requirements of the funds as defined by the appropriate agents and monitors. When expectations vary from local experience, fear of failure drives providers to act ceremoniously. As one residential provider said:

> People are supposed to flow from here to independence because of the training programs we run. That doesn't work for the people here. Just because they need some personal attendant care, they are stuck here. And all the training programs we run aren't going to change that enough to make a difference. But [the system] doesn't care about that. They don't want to hear. All that matters to them is that we are recording enough hours of active treatment every day to keep the money flowing. That makes a big part of our job a joke. (O'Brien, 1987, p. 42)

This leaves policymakers with a distorted picture of the situation they manage and providers with little incentive or energy to explore and negotiate purpose.

Effective leadership clarifies and strengthens purpose by focusing the organization's energy on fulfilling promises it can keep that will assist people to lead better lives. Anyone involved with the organization can exercise leadership in clarifying purpose by assisting people in the organization to deal with these complex issues:

- Spend time thinking about the distinctive contribution this organization can make to building the social conditions necessary for people with disabilities to lead better lives. Consider what people with disabilities and their families and friends want for themselves, and identify how the organization can assist. Gather information about what other organizations are doing to assist the people who rely on them. Think about what is reasonable to expect from the available technology, and clearly describe present limits. Express the results of all this thinking in a clear statement of organizational purpose.

- Select people who are likely to have trouble understanding the organizational purpose statement, and figure out how to explain it to them and get their comments.

- Select people who are likely to oppose the organizational purpose statement, and understand the reasons for their opposition. Look for ways to negotiate their agreement without compromising the organization's purposes.

- Look closely at expectations the organization has for professional people. Avoid pushing professionals into the role of magician by making them responsible for resolving situations that in fact can only be addressed if everyone involved joins in working together. Instances when people feel disappointed with professionals are good times to reconsider ways to take shared responsibility.

- Limit the authority the organization offers professionals to areas of their legitimate competence. Expect professional work to contribute to, rather than control, organizational purposes. Remember, the organization exists to help people define and pursue better lives; professional assistance is one of the means to that end. Expect professionals to join discussions about organizational purposes and individual futures as equals with other concerned people. Expect professionals to sometimes say, "I don't know; let's work on it together." Enable professionals to keep up with the rapid growth of knowledge in their field. Occasions when people feel resentful of professionals are good times to renegotiate expectations.
- Learn to read the purposes the organization communicates through its settings and processes (Williams & Tyne, 1988). Recognize, call attention to, and work to change the ways the organization expresses social prejudices against people with developmental disabilities (Wolfensberger & Glenn, 1975; Wolfensberger & Thomas, 1981).
- Examine the assumptions and procedures that shape the way the organization makes decisions about people with disabilities. Closely challenge the relevance, the limitations, and the costs of testing procedures; entrance and exit criteria that control access to opportunities; and record keeping. Ask, "Does our decision-making focus attention on people's capacities as well as their deficiencies? Does our decision-making value personal knowledge at least as much as professional conclusions? How does decision-making about individuals change the way we use program resources?"
- Pay attention to complaints about the ways funding arrangements, system regulations, and policies block efforts to assist people to lead better lives. Look for ways to satisfy requirements, and do what is necessary; negotiate with funding sources and regulators for waivers or reinterpretations of rules to permit action; improve policymakers' information about system barriers by collecting and communicating information about what people want to do that is otherwise likely to be hidden from them; and support efforts to change counterproductive policies.
- Shift resources toward activities that support organizational purposes as rapidly as possible.

SERVICE ACCOMPLISHMENTS

Vision of an inclusive community sets direction. Organizational purposes identify the distinctive ways a human services program contributes to building inclusive community by assisting people with developmental disabilities to discover and pursue desirable personal futures in ways that support valued experiences. Making progress toward the vision depends on continuous improvement in capacity to manage the problems created by assisting people with disabilities to take their place in community life. Clearly defined service accomplishments guide ongoing work on the stream of problems arising as service resources align with people's desires for a positive future.

Progress comes through a cycle of work in which a person with a disability, his or her family and friends, and service staff define steps toward a desirable personal future, identify opportunities for and obstacles to taking these steps, involve other people as necessary, plan and take action to develop opportunities and supports, negotiate the conflicts arising from action, review what worked and what did not work, and identify the next step. Maintaining and allocating resources through this cycle, over time and in harmony with vision and organizational purposes, creates good quality services (Deming, 1986).

Five closely linked service accomplishments, listed below, focus and guide service staff in their work (O'Brien & Lyle, 1987). These accomplishments do not prescribe how service staff should behave; rather, they describe worthy consequences of service activities and clearly identify results worth the costs of producing (Gilbert, 1978). Each accomplishment supports a vital dimension of human experience that common practice limits for people with developmental disabilities. These interdependent qualities of experience include: growing in relationships, contributing, making choices, having the dignity of valued social roles, and sharing ordinary places and activities. Each accomplishment challenges and strengthens the relationship between people with disabilities and other community members.

Community Participation

A human services program focused on community participation will mobilize its resources to assist people with developmental disabilities to form and maintain the variety of ties and connections that constitute community life. A growing number of people with disabilities will know and be known by nondisabled neighbors, fellow students, and co-workers; will form acquaintances; will contact others who share an interest; will make friends; will share intimacy; will join a variety of community associations and enjoy the responsibilities and benefits of membership; and will participate in civic, cultural, and political life (Ordinary Life Working Group, 1988). People have the help they need to keep in touch with family members or friends from their past. While many people with disabilities will choose friendships and associations with other people with disabilities, services will not impose congregation with people with disabilities as a condition of service. Building community participation challenges all people to live interdependently.

Supporting Contribution

A human services program focused on supporting contribution will mobilize its resources to assist people with developmental disabilities to discover and express their gifts and capacities. A growing number of people with disabilities will contribute to others' learning, enjoyment, and well-being as companions, fellow students, teammates, co-workers, and associates. People will have the help they need to explore their interests and capacities, to develop skills, to preserve health and mobility, to communicate effectively and confidently, and to increase self-control and attention. Facilitating everyone's contribution challenges all people to invest in recognizing and developing human resources.

Promoting Choice

A human services program focused on promoting choice will mobilize its resources to assist people with developmental disabilities to increase control over their own lives. A growing number of people with disabilities will set goals that are personally meaningful, express personal preferences, and manage the assistance they receive. People unable to make decisions for themselves because of age or extent of disability will have a strong personal relationship with a guardian who manages only those areas of life in which the person is incompetent. People will have the help they need to express their preferences, to define personal goals, and to attract the support they need from others to pursue their goals. People will get necessary assistance to interpret their environment, to understand other people's expectations and conditions for cooperation, to figure out satisfying ways to pursue what they want, to communicate effectively, to negotiate conflicts, to limit risks, and to manage the good and bad consequences of their decisions. Promoting choice challenges all people to resolve conflicts creatively.

Encouraging Valued Social Roles

A human services program focused on community participation will mobilize mobilize its resources to assist people with developmental disabilities to experience the dignity and status associated with positively regarded activities. A growing number of people with developmental disabilities will take their place and be recognized as good neighbors, contributing classmates, active members, friends, home owners, productive wage earners, and good citizens. People will get necessary assistance to locate and fill valued social roles in community settings, to meet or change the ordinary expectations of other people in the settings, to deal effectively with prejudiced or stereotyped responses from others, and to present themselves positively. Human services programs will pay rigorous attention to eliminating stigmatizing effects of their own practices (Wolfensberger & Thomas, 1981). Encouraging valued social roles challenges all people to discard stereotypes, see people as individuals, and repair the damage done by past prejudiced treatment.

Community Presence

A human services program focused on community presence will mobilize its resources to assist people with developmental disabilities to share the ordinary places and activities of community life. A growing number of people with disabilities will use a variety of ordinary community settings at the same time and in similar ways as other citizens. People will get necessary assistance to identify useful or enjoyable community settings, to get to and from a variety of ordinary places safely, and to participate effectively. Increasing community presence challenges all people's willingness to include everyone.

LEADERSHIP STRATEGIES

The challenges of assisting people with developmental disabilities to discover, take, and keep their place in community life present problems that require many cycles of action and reflection. These challenges make emotional demands including the demands of close personal contact as well as failure, resistance, rejection, and disappointment. As emotion increases, the pressure grows to avoid work by fragmenting or denying responsibility, blaming, underestimating what is possible, avoiding information about the effects of action, waiting for a magic solution, or ritualizing (Menzies, 1959). As time goes by and complexities and emotional pressures grow, people working on a better future can easily lose track of where they set out to go. In such a complex, highly charged situation, anyone exercises leadership who involves people in the following activities:

- Spend time listening to people with disabilities, their families, and their friends about their past, interests, concerns, and sense of future. Listen to people as individuals and bring them together to talk as a group. Include people who are isolated from family and friends and people who have difficulty communicating. Profile the person's life by describing the way the person experiences relationships, contribution, choice, status, and ordinary community places. Record the images and ideas about the person's capacities and interests, and verify the record with the person, family, and friends. Use such expressions of vision for the person as a guide and a check on the focus of service.

- Develop opportunities for people to pursue their interests in community activities and associations. In developing opportunities, work on offering individuals more of each of the valued experiences. Find opportunities that offer access to more ordinary places, that give individuals the chance to meet others, that offer the individual a choice, that fit the individual's capacities and interests, and that provide a valued social role.

- Practice reversing typical service patterns. Instead of listing ways the person should change, identify opportunities and supports that would offer the person new, positive experiences. Instead of gathering information about the person, gather information about the community; and instead of controlling the person, give the person control.

• Carefully evaluate the organization's capacity from the point of view of the five service accomplishments. Ask the people who rely on the program, their families, and their friends to evaluate the program's effectiveness in promoting choice, status, contribution, presence, and relationships. Plan and negotiate ways to reallocate resources to increase capacity.

CONCLUSION

Developing high quality human services for people with developmental disabilities demands active engagement in complex, emotionally charged, ambiguous situations. It calls for reallocation of service resources, working outside traditional boundaries, and renegotiation of the service's position in community life. This essential work calls for the motivation arising from a vision of inclusive community, the boundaries set by a clear and realistic sense of organizational purpose, and the focus offered by well defined service accomplishments. It requires effective leadership from service workers, people with disabilities, and their families and friends if all concerned are to face the difficult problems of creating high quality services to make progress.

REFERENCES

Bennis, W., & Nanus, B. (1985). *Leaders*. New York: Harper & Row.

Deming, W.E. (1986). *Out of the crisis*. Cambridge, MA: MIT Center for Advanced Engineering Study.

Ferguson, P.M. (1988). *Abandoned to their fate: A history of social policy and practice toward severely retarded people in America: 1820–1920*. Unpublished doctoral dissertation, Syracuse University, Syracuse, NY.

Gilbert, T.F. (1978). *Human competence: Engineering worthy performance*. New York: McGraw-Hill.

Guy, B., Scott, J.R., Hasazi, S.B., & Patten, A. (1989). *Stories of work*. Burlington: University of Vermont, Department of Special Education.

Heifetz, R.A., & Sinder, R.M. (1988). Political leadership: Managing the public's problem solving. In R.B. Reich (Ed.), *The power of public ideas (pp. 179–204)*. Cambridge, MA: Ballinger.

McKnight, J. (1987). Regenerating community. *Social Policy, 17*(3), 54–58.

Menzies, I.E. (1959). The functioning of social systems as a defense against anxiety. *Human Relations, 13*, 95–121.

O'Brien, J. (1987). *Residential services study*. Unpublished field notes.

O'Brien, J., & Lyle, C. (1987). *Framework for accomplishment*. Lithonia, GA: Responsive Systems Associates.

Ordinary Life Working Group. (1988). *Ties and connections: An ordinary community life for people with learning difficulties*. London: Kings Fund Centre.

Snell, M.E. (1988). Curriculum and methodology for individuals with severe disabilities. *Education & Training in Mental Retardation, 23*, 302–314.

Snow, J.A. (1987). *The role of disability in shaping responsive community.* Toronto: Frontier College, Centre for Integrated Education.

Taylor, S.J. (1988). Caught in the continuum: A critical analysis of the principle of the least restrictive environment. *JASH, 13*(1), 41–53.

Williams, P., & Tyne, A. (1988). Exploring values as the basis for service development. In D. Towell (Ed.), *An ordinary life in practice: Developing comprehensive community-based services for people with learning difficulties* (pp. 23–31). London: Kings Fund Publishing.

Wolfensberger, W., & Glenn, L. (1975). *PASS 3: Program analysis of service systems field manual* (3rd ed.). Toronto: National Institute on Mental Retardation.

Wolfensberger, W., & Thomas, S. (1981). *PASSING: Program analysis of service systems implementing normalization goals* (2nd ed.). Toronto: National Institute on Mental Retardation.

section II

CONSUMERS' POINT OF VIEW

chapter 3 ————

What Quality Assurance Means to Me

Expectations of Consumers

———— *Michael J. Kennedy* ————

Editors' Note: *Michael J. Kennedy is a strongly committed self-advocate whose strength and determination have helped him accomplish his most treasured goal—leaving three New York state institutions behind and entering the community as a proud member.*

Michael, who works with the Research and Training Center on Community Integration at Syracuse University's Center on Human Policy as the Self-Advocacy Coordinator, says that he loves his job because he has the opportunity to "give other people with disabilities their deserved right to live like everyone else."

Michael belongs to numerous self-advocacy organizations and is constantly involved with efforts toward making change in the system. Michael has testified before the Senate Subcommittee on the Handicapped and was honored by Governor Mario Cuomo's appointment to the Advisory Council for the Commission on Quality of Care.

Preparation of this chapter was supported by the U.S. Department of Education, Office of Special Education and Rehabilitative Services, National Institute on Disability and Rehabilitation Research (NIDRR), under cooperative agreement #G0085C3503 awarded to the Center on Human Policy. The opinions expressed herein are solely those of the author and no official endorsement by the U.S. Department of Education should be inferred.

My name is Michael J. Kennedy. I was born with cerebral palsy and spasticity of my muscles. I lived in state institutions for 17 years. I worked in a sheltered workshop. This chapter is about what quality assurance means to *me*.

All too often people with disabilities have lives filled with group activities that are not age appropriate or that are not the chosen activity of the individuals involved. They live in dehumanized living conditions and have severely regulated life-styles. Here are some typical examples. Everyone has to be up at the same time; in one institution where I lived it was 5:00 A.M., like it or not. At the staff's discretion half of the group was taken to get showers in the morning, half at night. All residents were thinly dressed with inappropriate clothing; an institutional breakfast was then served to the group. Our toothbrushes were all lined up in a row, and our teeth were brushed. After this we went to the assigned day-care programs. Lunch was provided to take to the day care, and we ate the stuff in shifts. We left day care in the early afternoon and went back to our living units. We were then allowed to watch the programs on television that the staff chose. Dinner was given to the group at about 5:00 P.M. Toothbrushes were lined up again, and we lined up to get our teeth brushed again. We then got ready for bed and sat down to watch TV, or sometimes we went out as a group, then got ready for bed. We were treated as guilty inmates, not individual, free citizens.

When I was 6 years old and living at the West Haverstraw Nursing Home, I had my first experience of advocating for myself. While 6 years old seems young to have to advocate for yourself, it seemed natural to me. It was a natural defense mechanism for me. I needed to protect myself. I advocated for myself by standing up to staff when I felt threatened or deprived of my right to choice. Being that young, of course, we could not make big decisions for ourselves. However, we were given no choices or consideration by the staff, even on small matters such as how to use our free time. We were not allowed to play outside in the dirt as other young kids do. We were not allowed to choose foods to eat or what to watch on television.

From West Haverstraw, I moved to the Rome Developmental Center (New York) where I lived until the age of 18. At Rome, I tried to form a self-advocacy group within the institution. The group failed to materialize because the staff and administration did not support it and, in fact, actively discouraged it. When we tried to exercise our rights, they resorted to physical abuse and drug abuse to keep us passive. They regarded us as "retards" who were not capable of doing anything. In fact, I was misdiagnosed as mentally retarded and labeled as such until I was 18 years old. They tried to keep me passive by abuse such as hanging me upside down in a doorway by tying rope around my ankles. This was retaliation for my complaining to the director about the abuse of another resident who was not able to speak for himself.

At age 18, I moved to the Syracuse Developmental Center (SDC). There I formed a self-advocacy group within the institution. We called ourselves Resident Government. We met once a week and began to discuss advocating for ourselves. We then decided to take further action. We began to stand up as individuals for our rights. We also advocated for those of us who were not able to advocate for themselves.

My stay at SDC lasted 4 years. That entire time I had been pursuing placement in a community residence. I needed to get out of the institution. In 1982, my efforts finally paid off. I was given the opportunity to leave SDC. My choice was between living with the family of my girlfriend or living with United Cerebral Palsy (UCP) Residential Services in a supported apartment. I decided to take whichever became available first. It turned out to be an apartment with UCP that I shared with three other people with disabilities. Shortly after I moved into the apartment, I was offered a position working with the Center on Human Policy as a self-advocacy coordinator. I accepted the position and have been at the Center ever since. It could have been much different. While living at SDC in 1979, I was placed in a sheltered workshop at the Association for Retarded Citizens. They told me I was too disabled to even work in the workshop. So one day I decided to just leave. They told me I could not do that. I just said, "Watch me," and I left. I decided a sheltered workshop was no place for me. With people there making prejudicial, unfounded judgments, how can we guarantee quality? If a person who is not skilled enough to work in a sheltered workshop is skilled enough to coordinate self-advocacy groups and have his talents applied across America, imagine what those people who presently work in sheltered workshops can do.

My job has expanded a great deal since I began in 1983. I have moved into a house that I rent with two friends who do not have disabilities. For recreation I attend parties with my co-workers and other friends of my choice. I also see my family when it is convenient. I go to the neighborhood bars, movies, and sporting events. For the first time in my life I am experiencing the quality of life that is standard for a person without disabilities. I have been given the opportunity to live my life as I choose. I have a good life, not just by the standards for a person with a disability, but by the standards of *any* person. I now realize how good life can be. I have a first-hand experience how a "normal" person lives. I now realize what I have been deprived of and what I can expect in the future. The limits that were placed on me and the quality of my life have been eliminated, although I still have my disability.

I have moved from a developmental center to a supported apartment for adults with disabilities to, finally, a home that I selected, not one that I was selected for. When I moved to the supported apartment, being selected still meant that my roommates and I did not have control of what happened in the house. We were not perceived as the decisionmakers or the heads of the household. While the people from the agency were wonderful and tried to make it as normal a living situation as possible, the fact that it was funded through Medicaid seemed to give people the idea that Medicaid ran the house, not the people who were calling it home.

For instance, during one review of the house by people from Medicaid, we residents of the house were treated with extreme rudeness and with total disregard for our right to privacy, dignity, and respect. I realize these inspections are necessary to a certain degree; however, when they are done, they do not need to be at the expense of the people who live in the residence. These inspections can be performed cordially and respectfully.

In 1987, an inspection of my apartment by people from the Health Care Financing Administration (HCFA) was done with total lack of respect for us residents of the apartment. I described the visit in a letter (see Figure 1) to the chair of the Senate Subcommittee on the Handicapped.

Despite specific requests for a response from the senator on this issue, I received no feedback. So, I wrote a second letter (see Figure 2) on December 8, 1987. Once again, despite requests, I received no response from the senator's office. I was getting to be very angry. On February 25, 1989, more than 5 months after writing the initial letter, I still had received *nothing* from the senator's office. I decided a third letter, worded a bit stronger, was necessary (see Figure 3). I also sent a copy of this letter to a New York senator.

The third letter to the senator produced no immediate response. However, I did receive a response from the New York senator that implied that an investigation into the conduct of the HCFA surveyors was forthcoming.

Following the letter from the New York office, I received a phone call from the office of the senator of the Senate Subcommittee on the Handicapped. They called to say that they had received the letters I wrote concerning the inspection and that they were sorry it had happened. They also assured me they would look into it immediately. They said that if this happened again, we should contact the senator's office while the surveyors are still present in the residence. I was also assured that further action would follow.

There are other problems that detract from the quality of life in a community intermediate care facility (ICF). For instance, ICFs are supposed to be equipped with bright red, lit up exit signs as seen in office buildings or stadiums. I understand that people need to be able to get out in case of a fire, but what good do these signs do? I hope the people who live there are aware of where the doors are. I know one ICF that has these exit signs. Several of the people who live there have visual impairments. Seven of the eight people who live in the house can't see or read well enough to recognize the exit signs; however, they are required for state certification. All the residents do, however, know how to leave the house in a hurry.

I don't think it is right that a person with a disability needs to write a senator three times to get a problem taken care of. I think if I were not

550 South Clinton St.
Apartment 10G
Clinton Plaza Apartments
Syracuse, N.Y. 13202
(315) 478-1060

September 16, 1987

Senator _____
Subcommittee on the Handicapped
United States Senate
Washington, D.C. 20510

Dear Senator _____,

I testified in front of your committee in April, 1985 on my personal experiences in living in the institutions. Now I would like to share with you my personal feelings about a review by representatives of the Health Care Financing Administration (HCFA).

On August 11, 1987, in my home this review was intended to insure that the agency sponsoring my apartment is doing what they are supposed to be doing. I was told by one of the agency's representatives that this type of review was mandated by Congress and specifically your name was mentioned.

Personally, I understand that they're doing their job in making sure our needs are being met, but I don't like the idea that someone can just show up on my doorstep without any notice.

Secondly, I felt they were very rude because when they came in they didn't talk to us (like saying "Hi, how're you doing?").

If I were part of that team, I would give notice to the household because I would not just "show up" at somebody's house, and once I got there, I would knock on the door and would say "Hello, I'm . . . , and I'm from . . ." and would explain why we're here and would apologize to the people living there and say, "I don't really like walking through people's homes because I feel it's an invasion of privacy. Would we be in your way if we just went to one corner of the room and did what we had to do?" Basically they should have had a better attitude about it all—they came across to me as very cold and nasty. They didn't say anything to us (my roommate and I were home at the time), and then one of the reviewers looked at us, and asked the staff, "What are they doing here?" Then I proceeded to answer that question because I feel they should ask us instead of asking the staff because we can talk. Just because we have a disability doesn't mean we can't talk or have feelings. Also, before the reviewers rang the doorbell, one of our staff was in the kitchen doing the dishes. When the reviewers walked in they asked the staff why the kitchen was such a mess. And the staff replied that we had just finished eating breakfast. I feel that this was very rude and usually when someone has just finished breakfast the dishes are generally in the sink waiting to be washed or put in the dishwasher. Also, the guy went in the

(continued)

Figure 1. Letter to senator describing HCFA visit.

kitchen, looked around as I was getting my coffee off the counter and as I was doing this, one of these reviewers stood there, and I felt like he was staring a hole right through me. At first, I didn't say anything to him, but he proceeded to keep staring. Then I proceeded to ask him if I could help him or if he had a problem. He didn't say a word—just walked away from me.

Then the staff person invited him to look into the staff room but not to go into the back bedroom because one of my roommates was shaving and getting dressed. The guy walked back there anyway and walked in my roommate's room without even asking or knocking. They totally ignored my roommate's rights, I feel.

Now I want to ask you—if you were in our position would you want someone to do that to you?

Sincerely,

Michael J. Kennedy

P.S. Please, I would really like you to look over this issue and send a response back to me explaining why this can happen. I really wish to have feedback.

MJK/er

Figure 1. (continued)

disabled and dependent on financial assistance, I would receive a much quicker response. I would only like to be treated as any other citizen. If it is normal for a public servant to receive three requests before responding, then I would send three requests before expecting a response. I am not asking for *better* service because I have a disability; I am asking for *equal* service because I am equally a citizen. **Quality assurance to me means that I will be treated like anybody else.** I need no special treatment.

For a person living in a home that is regulated by some bureaucratic agency, quality assurance is reliant on those people in the agency. Unfortunately, the people who oversee those homes tend to perceive quality assurance in terms of laws and regulations, and they tend to see people with disabilities as objects rather than as people. Laws and regulations are very necessary and serve a purpose; however, the manner in which those laws and regulations are written and put into use is sometimes dehumanizing. For instance, when one lives under the state, regulations such as keeping records of toileting and food consumption are applied to everyone. While some people may require this, others do not, and for some, it infringes on their privacy and rights. Agencies tend to apply all rules and regulations to all people under their care. **Rules and regulations should correspond with the needs of the individual.**

To truly have quality assurance, the individual must be involved. If the individual needs support to become involved, it should be implemented automatically. One should not need to create or refer to a law in order to control another's life.

550 South Clinton St.
Apartment 10G
Clinton Plaza Apartments
Syracuse, N.Y. 13202
(315) 478-1060

December 8, 1987

The Honorable ―――――――――
Russell Senate Office Building
Washington, D.C. 20510

Dear Senator ――――――――――:

   I'm writing this letter to find out if you have had a chance to read
my letter that I wrote to you on September 16, 1987.

   I still wish to have a response because, as I said in the previous
letter, it's an invasion on one's privacy for somebody to walk inside
someone's home without prior notice like the HCFA officials did.

   I don't know if the letter went to you directly or went to your
staff. As I said in my previous letter, I know it is important for people
with disabilities to get the services they're entitled to, but once again
the officials must treat people with disabilities like any other people
because we have feelings too.

   I want to say that I'm not blaming this specifically on you because
you have an administration that dictates rules and you were just
doing what you are supposed to do. But it's important for the
administration to know that we are people and we do have feelings,
just like anybody else.

   So I strongly ask, please send a response to this issue.

                              Sincerely,

                              Michael J. Kennedy

Enc.
cc: Carole Hayes Collier and Sally Johnston
      UCP Residential Services
      1603 Court St.
      Syracuse, NY 13208

      Commission on Quality of Care for the Mentally Disabled
      99 Washington Ave.
      Suite 1002
      Albany, NY 12210

MJK/er

Figure 2.   Second letter to the senator.

   I believe a person should be allowed the opportunity to be as independent
as possible. Being independent does not mean that I should be able to live by
myself and meet all my needs without support. It means I am free to make
choices for myself and engage the supports I choose and to decide what is

550 S. Clinton St.
Apartment 10G
Clinton Plaza Apartments
Syracuse, NY 13202
(315) 478-1060

February 25, 1988

Senator _____
Subcommittee on the Handicapped
United States Senate
Washington, DC 20510

Dear Senator _____,

I have already written two letters to you without a response, though I requested it.

I wrote a letter on September 16, 1987, and another one on December 8, 1987, about HCFA officials reviewing our apartments in a rude and uncaring manner without prior notice. My roommates had asked me if I had gotten any response to my two previous letters to you regarding this matter. I had to reply, "No, I haven't."

Both my roommates and I would like some response. By ignoring my request for a response to my letters, I feel very upset, and I feel that since you are in tune to issues regarding people with disabilities, you should at least give me some kind of response to my letters.

In April, 1985, I came down to Washington to testify in front of the Subcommittee on the Handicapped. I felt that you were really for the rights and the concerns of people with disabilities. But, I begin to feel differently about your views a little bit when you don't respond to this particular issue that concerns many people with disabilities.

I must state again, I know you're very busy, but I would really appreciate some kind of response.

Sincerely,

Michael J. Kennedy

MJK/er

Figure 3. Third letter to the senator on the Senate Subcommittee on the Handicapped and to a senator from New York.

necessary for me. I don't want people to make decisions for me that I can't make alone or to take over certain tasks that I can't complete. I want people to support me in my efforts to complete those tasks and help me make decisions. **All people with disabilities should get the support they need.** Quality assurance means control over the choices in all aspects of one's life.

A person should be allowed to choose where and with whom he or she wants to live. Too often people are grouped together with others who have common handicaps or with whomever makes the living situation most practical to serve. People with common needs are grouped together to make it easier for staff to serve those needs. People should be given the choice of whom they want to live with. It is absurd to force people to be compatible or assume they will be compatible living together solely because they have a common disability. By grouping according to their disability, the chance of permanent living situations is decreased because people's likes and dislikes are not met. If people are grouped according to choice, they will choose to share a home with people who have common likes and dislikes, such as living situations where age, goals, and values are considered. **If people who live together have things they share in common with each other, they will probably be happier living together.** When people are happy together, chances are better that they will remain together. Of course, people will always have problems, but when one is living with a chosen roommate and not a forced roommate, they will probably be more eager to work things out. Therefore, if people are thrown together, often they will not work problems out because they did not choose to be there in the first place. Therefore, I believe for people to be assured of quality living situations, they must be given the choice of whom they live with.

Quality assurance is reliant on people choosing not only whom they want to live with, but also where they want to live. People should not be forced to live in certain places because they need services. **Services should be available to people wherever they want to live.** Too often people are brought to the services, such as institutions, instead of delivering the services to the people. **Services should be made available in all communities, regardless of size.** Too often families with a child with disabilities are forced to leave their neighborhoods and move in order to get the supports they need to keep the child with them. The only alternative to moving is often separation of the child from the family. Families and individuals should be able to choose where they will live and should be able to obtain necessary services.

People want to live in integrated neighborhoods. If given the choice, people with disabilities would choose to live in neighborhoods where they would share the resources with their neighbors without disabilities. They also would probably choose to live in smaller residences with one or two other people, not necessarily with disabilities, as opposed to living in a group home with 12 other adults with disabilities. It is not normal for 12 unrelated people to live together in one house. Nobody who has a choice of living anywhere they like chooses to live with 12 or 15 other people.

Large group residences tend to compromise individual privacy. Residents often share bedrooms, the telephone, the television, the kitchen, and so forth, and don't have opportunities to be alone or to be with another person privately. Relationships of intimacy are very tough to carry on. It is hard for two people to be alone in a house of 12 or 15 people unless all of them leave the house. Everyone needs some time alone. This is no different for a person with a disability. True quality would be for people to have a choice of when and where they want to be, and if they want to be alone, they can be.

Large group residences also limit the control each person will have over his or her life. If a person lives with one or two others, he or she will be able to choose what to watch on television, what to eat, where to go out, who will cook and clean, and what he or she will do at a specific time. When 12 or 15 people live together, it is nearly impossible for each individual to have personal choices. For instance, people can't all eat meals of their choice because the facilities probably are not available. If a person needs assistance to leave the home, sometimes support is not available.

If a person lives in a less populated home in an integrated neighborhood, he or she would have more access to the necessary supports. This is because one or two people living in a home can leave when and go where they like. If a large number of people live together, it is unlikely that support services are available to accommodate the residents. Therefore, either all of the residents stay home or they all go out together. How can anybody call that quality assured service? Recreation and leisure activities must be planned in advance. If one has a sudden urge or need to leave the house, it is often not possible because of the lack of supportive help. For instance, when I lived at the Medicaid funded apartment, I once had to go see a movie that I had already seen and did not want to see again. I had to go because everyone else was going. Situations such as this were a regular occurrence. Occasionally, I did get to leave with only a paid assistant, but that required my speaking to the apartment coordinator. It also sometimes required a staff person to reluctantly come in on a day off.

Large group homes diminish the chance for the residents to be accepted by neighbors and establish relationships with those neighbors. When we first moved into the supported apartment, several people circulated a petition to have us removed. Luckily, it failed. Neighbors are often reluctant to associate with residents of a group home. They sometimes reject those people as a group without even attempting to get to know the individuals. People who live in a small home with two or three people are more likely to be accepted as a part of the neighborhood. A group home with 10 or 12 residents can be intimidating. Residents don't have the opportunity to be recognized as individuals. They are all grouped together.

CONCLUSION

Quality assurance to me means people with disabilities and people without disabilities are integrated into a common community. It means removing limitations and barriers from a person's life. This happened for me when I moved out of the ICF. I am living a life that is *not* typical of a young adult with a disability. I am presently employed by the Center on Human Policy. I work on the Research and Training project. I live in a house on Hawley Avenue in Syracuse, New York, which I share with two friends. In my spare time I go out with friends to do things of my choice. I visit people who I want to. I am living a life that is typical of any 28 year old. At 27, I finally started to live my own life, free and clear. This is why I feel as if I was born at age 27.

chapter 4 ———

Unarmed Truth

A Record of a Discussion

Members of Speaking For Ourselves
——— *as told to Karl Williams* ———

Editors' Note: *Speaking For Ourselves, a self-help and self-advocate group based in and around Philadelphia, began in 1982 and quickly grew to five chapters and 500 members. Publicly the group has sent speakers across the United States and to other countries; they have met with legislators, made presentations at colleges, provided training for the National Park Service, made depositions in court cases, and evaluated programs for quality assurance. However, it is the interactions within the group that have made all of this and more possible. All the members come together for support—to commiserate and to comfort, to coach and sometimes even to cajole.*

Once a year, in the fall, the elected leaders from the five chapters and the elected members of the board of directors meet for a planning retreat. The site for this retreat was Fellowship Farm near Philadelphia. Once the day's work was finished on Saturday, those who had volunteered to work on the chapter for this book sat down to talk about the quality of various programs. Many of them had been with the organization since its inception, but none of them knew that this discussion would turn out to be the most revealing and the most trying one they had yet had.

I believe that unarmed truth and unconditional love will have the final word in reality.

Martin Luther King

At the end of the gravel road there is a block of rooms like a motel; on the second floor the doors open onto a wooden walkway. Up the path to the dining hall there is a barn, and in the yard behind the barn there are sheep and goats. The main house is set back in the trees. A Hispanic family is staying here; the children come into the dining hall at mealtime.

The meeting room is large enough to hold two long tables at its center, and there are couches and chairs around its periphery. On the wall there is a photo of Martin Luther King taken at the old Fellowship House in Philadelphia, where he first learned of Gandhi's philosophy and methods.

The group is made up of various leaders from the five chapters of the organization; the chapters serve the southeastern counties of Pennsylvania, including Philadelphia. Among the guests are two women from Pittsburgh who are interested in starting a chapter there. The group has come here to Fellowship Farm for its second yearly retreat.

In the morning they speak of the events and the work of the past year. When they began to meet in 1982, there were many pauses, much hesitation, and long periods of silence, but now the topic is taken up with vigor. The facilitator writes numbers on the large white sheets of paper he has taped onto the walls, and next to the numbers he records what is said: presentation before American Association on Mental Retardation; speech to a local teachers' group; sixth annual conference; voter registration; march on the state capitol; petition to the court over program funding; training of personnel at Independence Hall; meeting with officials from the local transportation authority; presentations in Pittsburgh, Denver, and London; organizing work in an institution.

In the afternoon they begin to plan. First, they speak of their individual accomplishments and dreams. A man has gotten a job in a restaurant; a woman talks about how good she would feel if she could live in a log cabin in the woods. Another woman wants to go into space; she believes that this would help others like her. A young man has become engaged. One woman says, "When you talk about dreams, I think of myself as a princess for some reason."

They focus then on the year ahead. The facilitator holds four markers between the fingers of his left hand. He writes each line in a different color: stronger chapters; more work in institutions; more presentations in schools, in churches, at conferences, and at colleges; movie, television, and radio spots, and a billboard; a speakers' bureau to coordinate and train; a training program for those who provide services.

At the end of the afternoon, after many comments from the floor, the facilitator writes the final number on the list, and to the right of the number in the center of the page he writes the word "retarded." A man in the back stands and begins to speak but his voice is lost. As if on cue, everyone has begun to talk at once. The facilitator stands next to the sheet of paper and tries to pick out what is being said. He looks for a single person he can focus on and so get on with the discussion. But the jumble of voices from the floor continues and increases in volume, the sound swelling first at the back of the room and then at the front to the right. It is the word itself they object to; they have told him to add it to the list, but seeing it they are inflamed. He looks around the room, listens, and waits. Then he looks down at the markers between his fingers. In response to the emotion in the room, with the red marker he circles the word that has caused the outcry. Again, he looks across the room, and then he turns back to the page. With the red marker he underlines the word and draws a line through the word from top left to bottom right, connecting two points on the circle—meaning not that the people the word refers to, but that the word itself should be outlawed.

Now it is Saturday evening, dinner is over, and they are gathering in the meeting room. The tables have been removed, and the easy chairs converge with folding chairs and wheelchairs in a circle.

Andrea Turner is speaking. She is a thoughtful, middle-aged woman, and when she chooses to speak, her words make a space for themselves, and the space grows until the room is quiet. She sits up straight in a wheelchair.

Andrea Turner: "I think we should do the chapter in the book, but I don't think it's a good idea to use people names, cause somebody could pick it up and say, 'Oh, this person said THAT!' That's the only question I have about it."

Someone suggests that there be a ground rule that nobody's name be used without permission. The topic is the quality of the various programs that provide service and training. A tape recorder lies on the floor in the center of the circle. These questions initiate the discussion: What is most important in your lives? What makes a good community living arrangement? What do you need to make your lives better?

Brian Shaeffer: "As far the group home I live at, OK, I live one that show you how to cook, that show you how to go shopping, and that show you how to wash clothes, how you take the bus by yourself, how you make all the doctor pointments, how you go around the city by yourself. That's called the group home, the place I'm at. But I'm going to be moving pretty soon. I'm going to be by myself; I'm gonna be like Marshall is—go shopping, go to the bank, make your own doctor, and go speech, go to lot of meetings and different places."

Brian Shaeffer is a tall young man with glasses and blond hair. He moves to the edge of his chair as he speaks. The man he refers to is the current president of the organization, Marshall Martin, who sits at the farthest reach of the circle opposite the door.

Dave Pruitt stands to speak. His chair is drawn up just outside the circle. He is wearing a brown suit with a plaid shirt. He gestures with his hands to hold his audience.

Dave Pruitt: "Where I live, I live in a CLA (Community Living Arrangement), a what-do-you-call a SLA (Supervised Living Arrangement), and I live on my own. And what it makes is you get to have your own privileges while you're there. You get to go. (He stops a moment to let the concept of free movement hang in the room.) But, one thing we have to do— every time we have to tell the counselors where you are at all times, every day of the week. And you got to clean up your apartment like you're supposed to do. When you come home from work and you're working hard and every day, somehow you can't always do that part. So, what you got to do is you got to take it one at a time and in the apartment and share the apartment. I share an apartment with another friend of mine that we been together awhile. We cook our own meals. We do what we want. We do what we have to do and have our own privileges. We can go anywhere on our own. We can do things like that. But we still got to ask them before we do that. And those are the good privileges in my book. (This is the end of his speech, but he feels, perhaps, that it has come too abruptly. He goes on.) And everything we have in my apartment is free; we don't have to pay a cent. The only thing we don't have to pay is things like . . . the telephone bill we have to pay, and the rent we have to pay—the rest is covered. It's free; the rest of the stuff we have is free of charge."

Several people start to speak at once. Matthew Bartoli's voice rises above the others, but his thoughts have not yet coalesced; he cannot hold the floor. When the room is quiet again, Gloria Moyer begins to speak.

Gloria Moyer: "Mine's all right too, as long as you do your chores and do your programs. Sometimes, you know, you're not doing everything your best, they might get a little mad at you. Not mad, but upset. But they don't really curse at you or anything like that. They just say, 'Well, you a-posed to do this, you better get this done.' The staff is very, very friendly and very supportive. They help you out in any way they can. I'd say that's a good group home."

Gloria is sitting inside the curve of Hank Lynch's right arm. Hank is tall and thin with a newly grown beard that follows the line of his jaw. He has kept his camel colored top coat on, but a green knit hat rests in his left hand on his knee. His first words are lost; then he finds his voice.

Hank Lynch: ". . . they help me out a lot. (He pauses and looks at Gloria; they enjoy being seen together.) Sometimes I have problems or I'm upset. And if I'm upset, I go for a walk or I call my girlfriend. (Gloria nods her assent; this is a plan they've worked out in which both of them have put their faith and hope.) And if I call my girlfriend, I won't get upset. My girlfriend has helped support me a lot. And she's been supportive after all these years. She's always been my friend. I hope nothing happens to her. (He stops for an instant now, as if he has just realized how many people are listening to him.) This is my first time . . . being up here alone."

Someone asks if anyone lives in a CLA where there is trouble, where things are not always good. Many people begin to speak at once. Again, Matthew's voice rises above the others, but this time he is able to speak.

Matthew Bartoli: "I have trouble all the time. For one thing, the staff don't believe you. When you tell them something, they don't believe you. (He is a compact young man with large glasses and a full mustache. He works with a drill press and has held the job for 4 years. Although he repeats his phrase several times, each repetition seems only to add to the impact of his words. You hear the years and the frustration, but in the end you also hear his magnanimity.) They just don't believe you."

Jeanette Kline: "I do agree what Matthew said. Sometimes they don't believe you, what I'm trying to say to them. It doesn't do any good to tell them ahead of time about upcoming meetings and retreats and all. (She is sitting to Matthew's left. She wears a blue suit with a flowered pin at the lapel. She speaks quietly and slowly and requires your full attention.) They help me on transportation sometimes, but sometimes they don't. . ."

Brian: "OK, the place I lived at had real strict rule. Like Marshall call me on the phone and ask me if I want to come down. I say sure. But I had ask my staff where I'm going. You got to tell them where you're going, all right? If you get hurt, they'll find out where you are. Speaking For Ourselves has a meeting, I had let them know where I'm going. They don't want me to get hurt, and that's what the staff is all about. As you said, the staff trying to show you how you get your own place, and that's what the group home is all about."

Kendall James is sitting in a wheelchair just inside the circle. When he speaks, he commands attention. His manner is like a preacher's; he knows what is right and what is wrong. He speaks slowly, and he does not hesitate to repeat a phrase several times while searching for the proper words to follow.

Kendall James: "I think what Matt was saying was right. A lot of times when we tell our staff something, they act like, they act like they don't care. And I think that if you're going to be working with handicapped people like us, OK, I think you've got to have some type of caring or it just doesn't work. Now in my viewpoint, where I live, I don't get to very many board meetings on time because my staff says, 'Well, there's other people in this group home besides you,' and, 'Why can't you take a cab.' But when I offer to take a cab to get to that meeting, they say no, that they aren't going to put out the money for me to take the cab. So I have to stay home. That's the one thing I hate—when I make a promise to somebody, and then I got to turn round and tell them, 'Well, my staff can't take me because they got to go food shopping,' or 'My staff just won't take me,' or, 'My staff just doesn't drive at night.' And that's just one thing that really gets on my nerves, cause I think if you're going to do a job, you should either do it and do it effectively or you shouldn't be in the job.''

Marshall has just changed jobs. He was working as a janitor at a high school, but he has returned to a job he once had in a cafeteria. The cafeteria is now under new management. He has traveled to several states and to London on behalf of the organization.

Marshall Martin: "The biggest problem of the problems that I have in CLAs is. . . Well, I want to go to, oh, to go to school, to go to the Mayor's Literacy. 'Oh, what are you going there for?' (He mimics the response he has received.) 'What do you want to do that for? Why do you want to do that? You can't, you can't do that.' But I said that it's me, to move ahead, to get some better skills. And they said, 'No, (he laughs) that's what we're supposed to be here for you.' They're supposed to be devoted for you and provide things for you.''

Gloria: "Can I say something? Sometimes I don't really feel that great, you know, and everytime I would say something, well, you know, there's this staff—she's a friend of mine—a good staff, but she said, 'Oh, you're gonna be sick the rest of your life.' And I said, 'No, I'm not—this stuff feels good.' You know I'm on the new medication, but I hate it when staff say things like that. They make fun of you. . . It's been awhile since I didn't stop feeling good. But I don't think she should have said that; I don't think it's fair for her to say I'm gonna be sick the rest of my life. That's not true.''

Matthew: "I'd like to see the staff believe more than not. If they believe us—like me or Kendall over there or Marshall. If we say something, I want them more to believe in us guys. (He pauses as if considering whether or not to go on with the next part.) It makes me feel hurt inside. Like the staff I do live with, they don't believe in me. (He delivers the next line calmly and with resignation.) I just don't say anything now.''

Marshall: "They always say to you that you're niminating these things, you're nimining, you're making up these things—stories. But if the person is telling the truth, you're not making up something that is the truth. You're living it; you're living it.''

There is a pause, and then Kendall speaks again.

Kendall: "I think one of the things I'd like to see is more staff caring about the clients. They tell us all the time they're not getting paid to be a taxi service. They sit up there and they say, 'Speaking For Yourself ain't helping you, Kendall. Is it putting any extra money in your pocket? No. It's not helping you pay these bills. Why do you keep going there? Why do you keep going on all these things? You ain't really getting nothing out of it, you know, so I don't see why you keep going.' So I'd like to see more staff support, more staff caring, and less staff complaining.''

Lawrence Itelli is standing in front of a tall bookshelf next to the door. In the adjoining room a man from a university is conducting interviews with people who once lived at the nearby state institution. When he is finished one interview, the man reads Lawrence the name of the next person he would like to see, and Lawrence escorts that person from the circle.

Jeanette: "I'd like to try to live alone, but my staff doesn't want to give up the money. The group home budget is low. I guess I keep on spending it on things. . . But I'd really like to learn how to handle my finances on my own instead of not having the staff holding onto my finances. I'd like to do that on my own instead of them holding it back from me."

Brian: "One thing I wanted to say, like she said—I forget her name. . ." (He stops, and Jeanette, who is sitting across the room from him, realizes he is speaking about her.)

Jeanette: "Jeanette."

Brian: "Jeanette. Right. Inside your heart, right, inside your body, OK, inside you it tell you—you have a right to do something on your own. You have a right to opinion yourself. There's a lot of stuff I'm hearing tonight that's true things. I'm not trying to throw you off or nothing, but I want to find out how you feel you live you're by yourself, how you feel you get your own place. Inside my heart, inside your body, what I'm trying to say is—you have a right to move out and live by yourself like Jeanette said."

Mary Horter is sitting on a couch behind Matthew; she has come in some time after the beginning of the discussion.

Mary Horter: "There's only one problem with me. (She has graying hair and glasses, and when she makes a point she makes it forcefully.) I'm capable enough to live on my own, but the only problem is, is reading and writing. And right now they don't feel that they should get a tutor for me because they said the reason why not is because that I'm moving. I don't know when, but I know I have to move into a group home."

Now Lawrence has decided to speak. He clears his throat and looks down at his feet as he begins.

Lawrence Itelli: "Brian had asked a question: How it feel to be out of the home, and do you get feeling good about it? Sometimes, yeah, I feel great to be on my own. But sometimes when you don't have nothing to do you get so bored. If you don't have no activities, no TV, and you don't have nobody to talk to, it's bored to be by yourself. OK, I'm by myself, I go out, I'm home around 9; I don't have to tell the staff I'm going out, I'll be back. I'm glad. I'm tired of tell them that because I did that so many times. The staff and I have papers; they help me out plenty. I just don't want no more have people say do this and do that and do that. I can't answer about a group home; I was never in it. I went to (he names a residential facility) one time for the retreat, and I went to another house, it was white, it's a group home. And I said to myself, 'Oh, my Lord, what I'm doing here in this group home? I hate it.' You don't have no feelings. You got to be in certain time, and you got to go to bed when the other person go the bed. I don't like that. I like to go to bed when I feel like go to bed, not for somebody else."

Kendall: "I can only speak for me, but the one thing that I would like to see is I'd like to have more control over my money and how much I decide that I want to spend or how much I decide that I want to keep in the bank. I'm sick of hearing from my staff, 'Oh, you only got $60 in the bank, and you can only take out $15 this week.' Or, when I get this part-time job (he has applied for a job in a movie theater), everybody that's in the office at (he names the agency that operates the apartment program where he lives), they said that I wouldn't last a week. And now they want me to keep going to the workshop and work that part-time job too. So I wish that I had more control over my finances, and when I go for a job interview and if I get the job, I'd like for people just to say, 'Now see what you can do with it and if you can prove to us that you can handle it, then fine.' "

Matthew: "I wish I had control of my own life instead of people running your own, the staff running your own, my own life, telling me what to do. And yelling at yourself, not somebody else. I always yell at myself. I say, 'What'd he do that for?' And not only that, I wish I had more control to have personal friends. And not only me but Lou and Kendall too. Maybe have a housewarming party. But the staff where me and Kendall live don't understand us."

Jeanette: "I wish I had more control over my finances and transportation instead of being told what to do. I like to see what I have done wrong with my own finances and transportation."

Someone asks if she wants to learn by making mistakes.

Jeanette: "No, I don't want to make mistakes. But I like to learn from it on my own instead of having someone else tell me. I'd like to show those people that they don't have no reason to have doubts on me. I want to prove them wrong in some ways, because they don't think I would really make it through my own life on my own."

Someone asks her if she wants permission to make mistakes.

Jeanette: "I like to do it on my own instead of having permission."

Kendall: "Jeanette, I think I know what you're saying. When you make a mistake, instead of having the staff criticize you, if you know you made that mistake. . ."

Jeanette: ". . . say I won't do it again."

Kendall: "And instead of having them harp on you about it and keep reminding you that you made a mistake, you just like to take it and go through what you go through when you make a mistake. . ."

Jeanette: ". . . on my own, instead of. . ."

Kendall: ". . . instead of having somebody harp and keep harping on you about it."

Jeanette: "That's right."

Someone asks if anyone is ever afraid of staff. The room erupts with unanimous but varied assent.

Matthew: "For years. . ."

Dave: ". . . for years . . . we always have. . ."

Matthew: "Imintimination."

When the room quiets, Matthew speaks again.

Matthew: "They threaten you. You don't do what they want, they threaten you. They say for instance, 'Jack, you go the CLA and live.' They threaten you. That's a name out of the, I pulled out of the air, all right? (Pause.) Could they take people's personal property away? The staff? They're not supposed to are they? And they're not allowed to go in our rooms."

Dave: "The staff where I live has threatened me to kick me out my house cause I'm not doing something they don't want me to do. Now that was not my fault. I couldn't clean my room for awhile because I been busy with the job. I can't do it every day of the week, cause I work every day. I work 6 days a week and that's the reason why."

Kendall: "I felt threatened like that. There was a time when my staff wasn't gonna let me go home to visit my dad because they said that they had heard from other sources that I had punched a staff person. And the staff person told me that if I ever hit him again that he was, he was gonna, he gonna come up on his day off and we was just, and we was just gonna fight. (His elbows rest on the arms of the wheelchair; he looks at the floor.) Cause he claimed that I threatened to hit him. And the thing that made me mad—I wasn't even there.

Jeanette: "The staff where I used to live, she said that if I don't shape up I will be sent back to (she names a large private institution). Since I moved, the houseparent I have now says no, I'm not be sending you back. (She gives the woman's name.) She told me that she's a different person; she will not let me go back."

Someone asks if she's still afraid of this and what it is she thinks she might do that would get her sent back.

Jeanette: "Yes, definitely. (There is a long silence.) Lack of communication. That was a home with a lack of communication where I used to live. (Another long pause.) Well, she told me that she can't stand it when I am quiet. I still have some of my quietness, ever since I was a child. I talk to her, she threats me a lot. And if I don't talk to her, she threats me. (Pause.) And I've been through behavior programs too. I don't want to go through the same programs that I was in when I was in (she names the facility again)."

Mary: (She can contain herself no longer.) "They threaten me too—

only they are doing this. They threatened to send be back to a group home (her voice shakes), and they are doing it. They said I had no choice in it. I either had to go back or get out on the street and have no place to live and nobody to help me with anything; that they would refuse to give me any support in anything. So I had to sign the paper. And why I don't want to go back in the group home is because when I was in one I have had very bad experience in them. Everybody out in the community is so afraid of me that I might hurt them because of what I am. (She cries.) And a lot of people are scared and every time I step out of my house I have people watch me like I'm a dog. Anything I do it gets reported—anything. I'm surprised I can go to the lady's room without somebody being on top of me. And it hurts. It really hurts because I don't know what I'm getting into and (she says a woman's name) is one of them that is having me put out. Because they had a meeting on me. . . They had a meeting on me, and I could not go to it because they would not allow it, and I thought that was wrong to have a meeting on me without leave me in there. And then a couple days after they called me to set up a meeting to tell me what was going on."

Someone suggests that, even though there are a lot of problems, each one must have some staff people who care.

Matthew: "Sometimes. . ." (He laughs.)

The question is asked: Who has staff people who care about them?

Matthew: "Present or past?"

Gloria: "I have a lot."

The question is asked: Can't one go for help outside the group home?

Mary: "I'll tell you something else. I have went to meetings, and I have told things, and you know when I got back and they found it out they raised holy h-e-l-l with me. But I'll tell you one thing—I didn't give a damn. Because I was told that I do too much for myself since I learned how to speak up. But I says that is what it's for—to learn how."

Matthew: "You better believe it."

Someone comments that all the stories must have been told by now.

Matthew: (He laughs.) "I got stories that would make your ears grow."

Andrea: "I only have one thing to say. (She waits for their attention.) And it's not a hard thing, and it's not a crucial thing. Everybody in Speaking For Ourselves—and I'm not putting anybody down—but everybody that's in Speaking for Ourselves thinks Speaking for Ourselves can fix all our problems. Well, even though we think each one of these people in here who help us in Speaking For Ourselves, like (she names several people who are present as helpers or advisors to the group), even if they can, they cannot fix all our problems."

Matthew: "I agree."

Lawrence: (He begins to speak and as he speaks he moves into the outer edge of the circle.) "One thing I want to get back to. I heard you say that people are scared of going back to the institutions, correct? When I got out, I was very, very scared. I didn't know nothing. My whole guts came out. I didn't know anybody then. I felt like that I was going back into the institution cause I didn't have the right staff to help me. But my aunt and uncle put me on the right track. I would never be here. And sometimes I hear about institutions, institutions . . . sometimes I feel like I'm going back there. . ."

Someone asks what the advisors and helpers can do, explaining that when they've tried to go into the programs to help in the past, their actions have only made matters worse.

Matthew: "Listen more."

Kendall: "Be supportive. Be supportive of each other. We're here to help each other out. We're here to learn together."

Matthew: "I say call on each person—phone."

Someone asks about the Human Rights Committees.

Mary: "But if we do that, if we do that we get in trouble."

Patty Francis has not spoken at all. She has been sitting in the circle just in front of Lawrence. Her crutches, which fit around her forearms, lie on the floor beside her.

Patty Francis: "Well I'm not living in a CLA, but in the future I would like to be in CLA or a group home. And I think that we should tell our legislators, the people that control our lives, the people that we vote for. Why do we vote, why do we put people in office? . . ."

The room is stirring; the discussion is breaking up. It is not that Patty cannot hold the floor; she is one of the most respected members and the president of one of the chapters. It is the tension in the room that cannot be sustained. Too much has come out; too many stories have been told. And there is nothing anyone can do to put all these things right. Now, everyone is speaking at once.

Andrea makes the last strong statement, as she made the first.

Andrea: (Raising her voice.) "I don't think we should go back and cry what we talked about in here, cause then people are gonna start to worry. . ."

Matthew: "We're done here? . . ." (He moves to the center of the circle and turns off the tape recorder.)

The circle breaks as people stand up and move their chairs out of position. Someone is talking to Mary about her advocate. A wedge forms at the door. Kendall leans forward to move a metal chair out of his way.

Some go now to the dining hall for music, food, and a fire. Some gather in groups of two or three along the path to the hall or in the back of the dining hall itself, and they talk about what has just happened in the meeting room. On Sunday they will finish the business of the retreat. And on Sunday evening, they will return, advisors, helpers, and guests, and each of the members of the organization, to the places where they live and to the people who share their lives—or to people who have control over them.

FAMILIES' POINT OF VIEW

chapter 5 ⸺

Getting What You Want

Expectations of Families

⸺ *Susan Lehr and Robert Lehr* ⸺

In 1988, our son, Ben, was invited to participate in an after-school program at a neighborhood center. Ben, who the school has categorized as severely handicapped, was to be the only "special kid" in the program. The rest of the kids, all in their teens, lived near the center. The program was held 2 afternoons a week, 3 hours each day. A trained support person would be there to help Ben become part of the group, and there would be no charge to us. Transportation from school to the center would be provided free, and a variety of interesting activities were planned, many of which we knew Ben would enjoy. It sounded like a dream come true. We knew that many parents of children with developmental disabilities would jump at this wonderful opportunity for their child to participate. Yet, we hesitated to accept this invitation. Why? The answer is not a simple one, but it does reflect the theme of this book. We wanted to know what the quality of Ben's experiences would be, and we wanted some assurances that his inclusion in this program was really for his benefit.

This chapter begins with a description of what parents of children with developmental disabilities mean by "quality." Also explored are some ways families can recognize and find quality. The final sections discuss the problems families have when they are faced with services that critically limit the opportunity for quality to exist. Throughout this discussion, questions are posed to help parents discover the type of quality that does exist. Concluding this chapter, recommendations are presented to professionals, families, and consumers of service about how they can collaborate to ensure that quality is maintained.

DEFINING QUALITY

Our experiences as parents of a teenage son with autism have led us to believe that, in order to assess the quality of programs or services, parents and consumers generally seek answers to two questions. The first question is, "What does this service or program have to offer?" The second is, "How do they do it?" (That is, what are the underlying values and philosophy supporting this program or service?)

Usually, families look for services and programs that fill a practical need such as respite care, vocational training, or recreation. In our case, since we both work full time, we are always looking for after-school care for Ben. It seems we continuously ask other families what arrangements they have made for their son or daughter. We ask professionals what agencies offer after-school programs. We ask both parents and professionals for recommendations of sitter/companion/respite providers. Once something fits our practical needs, we begin a process for determining if it will also provide the level of quality we expect for our son.

One question families rarely ask is *how* a given service or program will be administered. In order to assess the quality, it is also important to know, on a day-to-day basis, the impact of this program or service on the individual with a disability. How will he or she be treated, valued, and respected? The answer to these questions will reflect both the philosophy and values of the provider.

For families, quality programs and services should be based upon or reflect certain values that are consistent with the family's values. Different families will emphasize different values. Generally, however, when a family finds a program or service that appears to emphasize the same values, they will consider it a quality program or service. Sometimes families are not able to articulate their values, or they are not sure how to recognize whether what they see reflects what they value. Usually, however, they know if it "feels" right or not. That is, they seem to know intuitively whether or not they want their son or daughter to be involved.

How values are translated into practice can vary from one program to another, just as how they are valued can vary from family to family. The point is that for any given family to believe that a program or service is a quality one depends upon whether that family perceives the service or program to meet a practical need, and whether it reflects values consistent with the family's. For example, for one family, a quality program may be one that protects or is safe for their child. Safety can take the form of a high staff to consumer ratio, written safety policies, and so on. For another family, a quality program or service may be one that fosters independence. This could be recognized by the family when their son or daughter is encouraged to make decisions for him- or herself, take planned risks, and so on.

In our case, we took a critical look at what we value as parents for our three children, and we asked ourselves if our values are different for Ben because he is "labeled" autistic. We quickly recognized our values are complex, but in general, they are the same for ourselves and our children. In fact, we believe that our values are consistent with what most people value and especially consistent with the values of other families with children with disabilities. For example, we value people who will engage in sensitive and caring relationships and people who are willing to cooperate and collaborate. We value independence, the ability to make personal choices that gives each of us a sense of control over our own lives. We value honesty, creativity, equality, and fairness. We value diversity, and we appreciate differences. We value education, formal and informal, that allows for a constant exposure to new experiences and ideas. We value an organizational structure that is consistent, yet flexible; one that encourages and appreciates personal freedom of thought and expression. We value freedom; freedom for each of us to be who we think we are. We value other things, but these rank most highly for us personally and as parents.

We also have strong feelings about things we do not value. Any program or service that harms people, physically or emotionally, or is so structured that it is unable to modify or accommodate individual differences, has absolutely no value to us. Other families will have different values or rank these values differently. When we consider programs and services for our son, we use our values as standards of quality. Other families use their values.

RECOGNIZING QUALITY

How do we recognize these values? What are the markers, cues, indicators, signs? In order to answer these questions a personal experience is described that points out the cues or markers we found.

In our ongoing effort to find adequate after-school care, we asked a local respite service agency for help. We knew several other families who had received services from this agency. We were sent an application form and were told it had to be completed and returned before they could proceed with processing our request. It consisted of approximately 15 pages of in-depth questions. We were surprised at the intrusiveness of some of the questions, many of which had nothing to do with routine after-school care, and hesitated to answer them, especially in writing. We were confronted with a dilemma—

we desperately needed after-school care for Ben, but we were not comfortable answering many of the questions. Additionally, we had no idea how long it would take for them to process our application or whether or not we would be eligible to receive services. Because of this dilemma, and because there was no indication how any of the information would be used or who would have access to it, we decided not to submit the application. We asked ourselves, "If this is how they treat us, then how will they treat Ben?"

On another occasion, in late spring, we contacted this same agency, again requesting after-school services for the following September. In the interim, we had talked with several parents who, despite similar initial experiences, claimed that the services they received were very good. Additionally, several professionals whom we respect told us that, in their opinions, this agency was well managed and provided quality services. Assuming that things would be better this time, we decided to apply. Once more we were sent the application form. Since this is the only respite provider in our community and since we knew of no other options, we filled out the application, but answered only those questions that we thought applied. Despite the fact that we had been told a respite worker would arrange for a personal interview and home visit after they had processed the application, we heard nothing for several months. During the summer we made several telephone calls asking if anything was happening. They seemed genuinely amazed that we were calling so far in advance (school started in mid-September), but we explained that we thought it would be good for Ben to get to know his person over the summer so that he would be comfortable with him or her in the fall. We had explained all of this on the application form.

September arrived, school began, and we still had not heard anything from the respite agency. Once again, we were forced to recruit and train our own after-school care for Ben. About early October, we received a handwritten note from the respite care coordinator apologizing for not returning our calls that were made during the summer, saying that she was quite busy finding respite providers for "her" families. She explained that she had been waiting for the university to open for the fall semester in order to recruit special education students as respite providers. Unfortunately, she had not been able to find anyone for Ben, with the exception of one young man whom she named. As it turned out, we already knew the young man the coordinator recommended since he was student teaching in Ben's classroom that semester. We also knew this man worked after school at a group home. It seemed obvious the coordinator had not spoken with him directly or she would have known this.

In a subsequent telephone conversation, we were told that it was really hard to find people who had the skills to be with someone as "difficult" as Ben. We thought this was a curious statement since, on the application form we said that periodically Ben had temper tantrums. No one had asked for clarification, and we had assumed this would be explored during the personal interview. As a result of these experiences, we simply gave up on the agency. We felt they had been totally unresponsive to our needs.

However, we did learn a very important lesson—if parents want quality services and programs for their son or daughter, it is their responsibility to be sure they understand what is being offered, what is not available, and how it will have an impact on the family. This means asking questions and clarifying answers. Additionally, we learned to look for certain cues or markers that reflect the value or quality of the service or program being offered. In summary, these are programs and services that:

- Ask only for information that is relevant to the service requested or that is necessary for improving the quality of a program for a specific person.
- Respect privacy and confidentiality.
- Explain who will have access to information and how this information will be used.
- Explain each of the steps in the process of acquiring the service or program, continually checking with the families to be sure everything is clearly understood and all questions are answered.
- Respond promptly, courteously, and honestly.

Returning to the after-school program at the neighborhood center described at the beginning of this chapter, we were quite surprised to receive a telephone call about 1 year after the last experience from another worker from this respite care agency. This worker said the agency had received some family support money to provide respite services as part of the routine activities of a neighborhood center. She was inviting Ben to join. We were suspicious and hesitant. We loved the idea of Ben being able to go to a neighborhood center, and we were delighted at the prospect of him participating constructively with kids without disabilities. However, we were reluctant to become involved with this agency because of the way in which we had been previously treated. Yet the benefits for Ben seemed very compelling. In an effort to understand what would be best for Ben we knew we needed more information to assure ourselves that this was the type of experience that Ben would benefit from and that he would enjoy.

PINPOINTING QUALITY

In our search for *how* this program would treat Ben, we began by asking what the program proposed to do. The answers were in practical terms of times, locations, amount and nature of supervision, and opportunities for social interaction with teens without disabilities. Since the questions were easy, we expected clear, understandable answers. Also, with each question we probed for the philosophical basis for how people with disabilities were perceived and treated. Basically, we wanted to know if this program was willing and able to accommodate Ben or if they expected him to "fit" into their program. Some of the questions we asked are presented here.

Who Are the Staff?

Who are the staff and how will they translate the philosophy or ideology of the agency into practice? What are their personal values in regards to people with disabilities? We look for staff who show, in various ways, that they enjoy being with people with disabilities. We are encouraged when staff show more interest in talking *with* the person with disabilities, rather than *about* him or her. We are less concerned with professional degrees and more interested in how a staff member sees his or her role. We look for staff who perceive their primary role as facilitators and support persons who offer opportunities for autonomy to develop. We look for good role models. Do they dress appropriately for the tasks? Are they pleasant and courteous? Do they understand the importance of fostering friendships between people with disabilities and people without disabilities? Do they encourage independence or dependence? Do they look for challenges, or do they complain? Are the staff confident of themselves and what they are doing? Have they been provided with continuing in-service education, training, and support that keeps them up-to-date on new issues in the field? Do they seem open to learning?

A physical therapist once told us she "serviced our son in the swimming pool." We were struck first by the fact that she called him "our son," rather than by his name, and the word "serviced" made him sound like a broken car or something that needed repair. In contrast, when Ben missed a day at the neighborhood center because he was sick, it was nice to have the worker call him, and not us, on the telephone to ask how he was feeling. This told us that she really cared about Ben, and that he was more than just a client.

Perhaps most important is whether the staff intend to establish a relationship with the person with a disability, or do they consider it simply a job for which they are being paid? We knew that the respite worker would be paid to provide support for Ben at the neighborhood center, but we did not know how she was going to go about providing this support. We were impressed when she said she wanted to get to know Ben first, before she could determine how best to support him. She went on to say that she had visited the neighborhood center frequently and had already established some relationships with other teens. She thought this would help in getting Ben involved in some of the activities. We were delighted that she had thought about this and had planned for Ben to become part of the group.

It also seemed apparent that she expected to like Ben, even before she had met him. This is very important to us. Later, we learned that she had heard different stories about Ben and that some people were afraid of him. She did not dismiss these comments but felt that she had to get to know Ben herself, before she judged him. She asked us for suggestions of how to approach him initially so that their meeting would be positive for him.

How Are the Participants Treated?

How the participants are treated is a question closely related to the one above, but slightly different in focus. Programs and services that treat people with respect and dignity, in our opinion, refer to the participants by name (Mr. Smith, Mary, Ms. Williams, John, etc.) and not by a label. Such references as the clients, the disabled, the handicapped only serve to demean people with disabilities. The terms consumer and self-advocate have also gained acceptance. However, these are still labels that categorize people based upon their disabilities and, consequently, show little respect for their individual differences. As such, they convey a lack of power or prestige.

Other signs of respect include making eye contact, shaking hands, and routinely including people in conversations and decision-making. While these may seem obvious, they are not always part of the way in which people with disabilities are treated. One of the most offensive habits we have observed involves talking about a particular person in their presence. It is as if the person is an object and not a real person. Ridiculing, restraining, or demeaning a person with a disability indicates total disrespect, as does having them participate in activities that are not appropriate for their age or ability. For us, one indicator of quality is a willingness, on the part of the staff, to learn from the people they are serving. This conveys mutual respect and a belief in each other.

How Is the Program Designed and Administered?

How the program is designed and administered is another consideration. Is there flexibility and a commitment to modify the program to meet the unique needs of each individual served, or conversely, is the person made to "fit" the program?

For example, a family support program that only offers respite care during fixed business hours is not designed to meet the needs of families who seek respite care at other times. The design of such a program has more to do with what is administratively convenient, not what is responsive to family needs. What about families who do not want respite care but need other types of assistance, such as transportation or parent training? An agency that is responsive to the expressed needs of the families it serves will be administered and organized with representatives of its families serving on governing boards, program committees, and as volunteers. Staff, family members, and people with disabilities should be part of the team that designs and monitors all programs and services.

What Information About the Person With a Disability Is Considered Important?

What methods will be used to get to know the person with disabilities? Is there more interest in IQ scores and test and evaluation data than in meeting him or her? We prefer that people who are going to be with our son get to know him before they look at other pieces of information. Tests, evaluations, and information contained in personal files are only a small reflection of the total person, and often they are either incomplete, inaccurate, or misleading. We do not value agencies or services that place a higher priority on formal evaluation measures than they do on how Ben routinely participates in his environment. This applies for schools also.

Suggesting that the after-school program support person and Ben meet at McDonalds (one of Ben's favorite places) in order to get to know each other was an excellent idea. This meeting would give the support person an opportunity to see how Ben handled himself in the community, and we would be able to see how Ben and this person respond to one another. Since one of the values we have is "family," we felt it was important that Ben's two older sisters also be present for the meeting. In part, this was so that the support person could meet them and learn about Ben from their perspectives, but also so that they could "scope out" whether or not his participation in the neighborhood center was something they felt was OK for Ben. We value their judgment and wanted their opinions. We were also interested in how the agency would respond to our request for Ben's sisters to join us. If they had been opposed, we would have been reluctant to proceed.

How Is the Person Valued within the Program?

We value programs that look for potentials, that appreciate people with disabilities for their capabilities, and that enable them to be contributors to society. All too often parents are bombarded by professionals with detailed descriptions of all the needs, problems, deficits, and deviances that their son or daughter has. It can be quite overwhelming and often intimidating. Even the most sensitive and caring professionals can fall into the trap of devaluing a person by noting his or her deficits or needs. Parents are acutely aware of all of these, but they also recognize the positive qualities and potential in their son or daughter that make him or her loved and accepted by the family. A quality program or service should strive to recognize and build upon capabilities and potential, rather than spend time dwelling on weaknesses.

This time, there seemed to be more interest in Ben, his likes and dislikes, his habits and fears, than whether or not we had filled out the proper forms. Additionally, they genuinely seemed to care more about who Ben is today rather than his history or what he did or did not do yesterday or 5 years ago.

How Will Routine Problems Be Responded To?

Many parents of children with disabilities have told us that they are rarely consulted about how to handle a certain situation or how to respond to a problem with their son or daughter. Many parents find that their opinions and information are routinely dismissed by professionals because they are "just parents." It is as if being the mother or father of a child with a disability does not have any value. Gunnar Dybwad, emeritus professor of Brandeis University, cautions parents to never forget that professionals do not have all the answers. After all, they are "only professionals," and as such, they have been known to give bad advice from time to time. Parents also make mistakes and give bad advice on occasion, but they, like the professionals, have valuable information and insights to share. A quality program will seek out the information and experiences that parents are willing to make available and will value these as highly as they value other information received from professionals.

Assuming that Ben would have a problem on occasion (none of us are perfect), we wanted to know how it would be handled. Would he be kicked out? Would professionals be called in, or would the staff of the agency and the neighborhood center look to us for information and assistance? Would they be willing to cooperatively engage in problem-solving and sharing of information, or were they into laying the blame and pointing the finger? Were they going to be interested in what we had to offer as Ben's parents, and would they value this information? We were pleasantly surprised when we realized that what we had to contribute was considered important.

What Happens if There Is a Crisis?

Is there a presumption that when problems arise or crises occur that everyone needs to share in the problem-solving and planning for follow-up? Is the person with a disability blamed as the cause of the problem? One mother told us about receiving a telephone call from the residential manager at her daughter's community residence. In essence, the manager said that the daughter had started a small fire in the basement of the home and was being evicted within the hour. Despite the fact that this woman had lived in this residence for over 3 years and had never had a problem prior to this one, and despite the fact that the original house manager had recently resigned and left, there was no attempt to help this woman express her sad or angry feelings in a more acceptable way. The staff simply were not willing to help problem-solve or to try to understand why she had set the fire. A program or service that blames the victim is not a quality program.

Ben is recognized as a "tough kid," because at times he can get pretty upset. Often, no one knows what the cause is, but everyone who has contact with Ben knows (and probably fears) that when he is upset, he can be self-destructive. For this discussion it is not important what Ben does to express himself, but what is done in response to his actions is important. We value any program that does not blame him for losing control, but one that is willing to look for solutions about how to respond accordingly and how to prevent further outbursts.

How Much Flexibility Is There?

Some programs are so laden with rules that it seems the main agenda is to teach people how to conform and be compliant. We steer away from such programs. We watch out for such statements as, "In _my_ class we do it this way." This indicates to us that following the rules is more important than fostering independence. All too often people with disabilities are placed in situations that appear to be win or lose. A young man in a community residence was told that it was time for him to take a shower. When he refused, two staff physically restrained him. The staff won, the young man lost. In contrast, there was an occasion when Ben was at his job training site and was clearly upset about something, but no one knew what it was. Finally, Ben told the job coach, "No work for today." The job coach recognized that whatever was upsetting Ben was sufficient to make working impossible that day. Ben was asking to leave before he lost control of himself. The job coach recognized this, and they left after explaining to the supervisor that Ben was having a rough day and would finish the work later. In this situation everyone won, and no one lost. Ben was able to control himself and was respected by the job coach for trying. The supervisor maintained a positive attitude about Ben, and eventually, the work was finished.

In summary, families always seek quality. Usually they know how to recognize it. Unfortunately, however, finding quality programs and services can be extremely difficult.

GET WHAT YOU WANT OR TAKE WHAT YOU CAN GET?

The search for quality programs and services can be quite frustrating for families. It is not that quality does not exist, but since there are so few options available, individual, practical needs are not met. Unfortunately, under these circumstances, quality is usually a secondary consideration. Rarely do families have the luxury of measuring their values against an array of service and program options. Instead, they are confronted with limited services, many of which have either long waiting lists or eligibility/admission criteria that limit access. In many cases there simply are no options available. For example, many parents with children still in school would love to have their son or daughter involved in routine after-school activities similar to their typical peers or brothers and sisters. Rarely is this an option, and in those few cases where it is, often it is the responsibility of the family to find and provide the necessary support or supervision. For many families, this is impossible for a host of reasons.

Similarly, the transition out of school offers bleak opportunities. For instance, there seems to be an abundance of sheltered workshops and Medicaid funded day treatment and day training centers. Supported employment, however, is not available except in rare instances. This is especially problematic for families, such as ours, who have strong values about the significance of interaction with people without disabilities. We do not want Ben to leave school, where he has been integrated since first grade, and have, as his only option, placement in some type of segregated, sheltered vocational or residential setting. It seems to us that if quality services were readily available, we would talk more about jobs and homes and less about residential placements and training slots. In reality, these are the only options available for the majority of graduates. No matter how well managed, we do not value these types of settings for Ben because they cannot provide him with integrated experiences. What options do we and other families have?

Most parents are left with the task of either trying to piece together something on their own or not having their son or daughter participate in anything outside the family. Quality is a consideration, but often it is sacrificed for other more pressing concerns. Another factor that prohibits families from seeking quality in programs and services for their son or daughter has to do with knowing or not knowing what is available. Historically, parents have relied upon the professionals to advise them of programs and services that are best for the needs of their child. Since the emergence of parent training and information dissemination, parents are beginning to learn they can question these recommendations.

For example, the way in which children are placed in school programs is usually based on the availability of programs or on a specific classroom for students with similar levels of need. The child has to fit into this program or class, rather than having his or her unique needs met on an individual basis. The majority of families do not know that they can challenge and even refuse this placement recommendation. Even fewer families know they can request services to be provided for their child within the regular school setting. They are often told, "That is not where the program is."

Another example relates to families attempting to find support services. Usually, family support services are based upon the available resources within an agency, not on what any individual family needs or wants. Instead of assisting the family in identifying their unique needs and providing appropriate support (financial and/or programmatic) to enable them to meet those needs, an agency will usually offer family support in the form of discrete programs or services.

One final factor that severely limits the family's expectations is the series of barriers or hurdles they must overcome before they can reach their goal. We think of these almost like an endurance test. We keep trying, and with each try we get a little closer to what we want for Ben. We also get awfully tired, and sometimes we question whether what we gain for Ben is worth what we have to lose.

The problem is, however, that families *do* want quality, and it is terribly painful to have to accept less. We are, as the saying goes, between a rock and a hard place. On the one hand, we want (or desperately need) the services for our child, while on the other hand, we want these services to be quality services. For most families, it is an either/or dilemma. In summary, families always seek quality, but do not always have choices that allow them to eliminate those services that lack quality. Instead, they are forced to take what they can get. When provided with an array of programs and services, however, families will seek the following key elements:

Honesty is reflected in a variety of ways: an honest description of available services (including what cannot be provided); honesty in relaying information to families about their son or daughter's program, behavior, health, well-being, and so on.

Acceptance of the person is translated as a sense of appreciation for the person's capabilities, not his or her deficits, labels, or history.

Respect for the family includes an appreciation of the ethnic and cultural heritage and practices, respect for their knowledge, information, insights, and respect for their privacy.

Confidentiality means that families do not learn about themselves from the information and stories of service providers. We were quite stunned to hear ourselves described as "litigious" parents because we had turned to due process to secure Ben's right to an integrated educational program. Similarly, we were dismayed to learn that Ben's reputation as a person with "challenging behaviors" had spread so far that school bus drivers were afraid to drive him even though they had never met him.

Individuality or autonomy is the right of families to make personal choices and decisions. Likewise, they value programs that encourage autonomy within the framework of the service provided. That is to say, they value services that respect the person with a disability as an individual.

Can parents expect quality? Of course! Can they recognize it? Certainly! Can they find quality programs and services? Yes! Can families demand quality? Always! These are the easy questions. The real problem concerns the lack of options from which families can choose the program or service that best meets their needs and the needs of their son or daughter.

PROMOTING QUALITY

There are good programs in our community and elsewhere that are striving to enhance the quality of services available to families. There are several ways in which agencies can facilitate this. One of the first, and most obvious, is for agencies and service providers to actively recruit parents and consumers in policy development, program planning, and evaluation. Agencies cannot be truly responsive to the needs of families and consumers if they are unwilling or unable to solicit their input. In addition, service providers cannot fully assess the impact of their programs unless they actively involve families and consumers in monitoring and evaluation. Similarly, families and consumers cannot fully appreciate the constraints placed on agencies by local, state, and federal regulations, fiscal limits, staffing shortages, and so on. With a finite amount of resources available in an agency, families cannot expect to have every need met routinely. Involving families and consumers in planning, monitoring, and evaluation will increase this understanding. Only with collaboration and cooperation can agency providers, families, and consumers help each other. Two ways in which this collaboration could happen are as follows:

Family/consumer monitoring of services and programs Teams of family members, consumers, advocates, and agency representatives can become responsible for periodic evaluations of services, including on-site visits, interviews with staff and program participants or their families, and review of relevant materials. We realize that this may be difficult for some consumers and/or family members in terms of time or otherwise, but a stipend or service (such as respite) could be offered. In fact, we suspect that many families would appreciate such an opportunity.

Family/consumer representation on advisory committees and governing boards By having family members and consumers serving on boards of directors, advisory committees, and planning bodies, there will be increased opportunities for assuring quality in program design and administration, in policy development, and in evaluation.

Some communities are aggressively recruiting family members and consumers for county and state planning groups. It is expected that their input will assure that policy decisions and future program development will meet anticipated demands. In Syracuse, New York, there are two committees consisting of agency providers, consumers, and family members who serve in an advisory capacity to the Department of Mental Health. These committees, known as the Rehabilitation and Residential Clusters, are open to anyone for membership and participation. As voluntary bodies, they make recommendations to the county about gaps in existing services, needed development of services, new directions, and trends (i.e., supported employment, individualized family care services, and supportive apartment living). Periodically, they host open forums to discuss a variety of common issues such as how to find more dollars for supported employment, how to transfer dollars away from the institution and into the community, how to offer better family support services, and so on. Family members, consumers, advocates, and service providers participate on an equal level for everyone's benefit. Many families do not have the time nor the inclination to join monitoring teams or to participate in groups such as those described above. They should not be made to feel guilty or be regarded with disrespect because of this fact. Each family member contributes what he or she can, but he or she will always appreciate being invited to become involved and to share in the process.

RECOMMENDATIONS TO PROFESSIONALS

1. Always treat families and individuals with disabilities with respect and dignity.
2. Become aware of cultural, ethnic, or racial practices that may be different from what you know.
3. Be able to clarify the values and principles that underlie the program or service you represent.
4. Use language and terminology that families and consumers can understand.
5. Be honest with families about what you and your agency can and cannot do.
6. Be open to learning from and with parents and individuals with developmental disabilities.
7. Establish working relationships with families and consumers that are based upon mutual respect and understanding.
8. Respect privacy and confidentiality.
9. Never assume anything about parents and their son or daughter, but get to know each unique individual.
10. Do not make parents feel guilty, they already carry enough guilt.
11. Do not blame parents or consumers.

RECOMMENDATIONS TO FAMILIES AND INDIVIDUALS WITH DISABILITIES

1. Treat professionals with respect and dignity.
2. Educate others about your unique cultural, racial, or ethnic practices or beliefs.
3. Remember that professionals are not miracle workers who can meet every need you have.
4. Share information with professionals that will enable them to do a more effective job in meeting your needs.
5. Be honest about your capabilities and limitations.
6. Know what you value and what you want.
7. Know where you are willing to compromise.

RECOMMENDATIONS TO
FAMILIES, CONSUMERS, AND PROFESSIONALS

1. Be honest with each other.
2. Be willing to learn from each other.
3. Treat each other with respect and dignity.
4. Be willing to admit you make mistakes
5. Work collaboratively and cooperatively
6. Be yourself.

CONCLUSION

This chapter explores ways in which families define and recognize quality in the programs and services they select for their sons and daughters with disabilities. Attention is given to the limited options offered to families and the resulting problems in searching for quality. Suggestions are offered for improving the relationship between professionals and families with the intention of improving the quality of life for everyone. In conclusion, a series of recommendations are presented for encouraging professionals, parents, and consumers to listen to each other, respect each other, and learn from and with each other. Out of this foundation, quality emerges and is maintained.

chapter 6 ————

Family Monitoring

Making Sure a
House Is Still a Home

———— *Hank A. Bersani, Jr.* ————

A variety of individuals and groups *may* act as monitors. That is, they have
the authority to monitor—the right to act officially. In addition to the authority
to monitor, they also *should* act as monitors. They have an obligation or a duty
to monitor the quality of services.

AUTHORITY TO MONITOR

The authority to monitor is often vested in a group such as a county, state, or
federal agency that provides all or part of the funding for a service. It is not
unusual for that funding agency to require some level of oversight in return for
their financial support. Similarly, a funding agency has the authority to ensure
that the people who depend on the service are in fact receiving a quality
service or at least some minimally acceptable level of service.

However, the authority to monitor service quality, and some would argue
the obligation to monitor, also comes from a range of personal and/or civic
responsibilities. Parents or family members of individuals with developmental
disabilities often feel it is necessary to monitor service as a means to ensure

quality. However, all citizens in society have the authority to monitoring services. These relationships form the basis of family and/or citizen monitoring.

Parental Authority

Parents often remain as guardians of their sons and daughters with developmental disabilities even after they have reached adulthood. Although formal guardianship has terminated because the family member has reached the age of majority and/or has been declared as his or her own guardian, there is a certain limited prerogative that comes with parenthood. The fact is that all individuals will always be the children of their parents, regardless of age or competencies. Thus, parents have the inherent authority to monitor services.

Consumers' Authority

People with disabilities also have authority to monitor services. As consumers, in a sense, it is their money that is paying for the services that they receive. This is often quite literally true in residential settings where the individual may pay rent or pay for services from their own resources, directly or indirectly, through income supports such as Supplemental Security Income (SSI). As consumers, people with disabilities have both the authority and the right to monitor those services for which they pay. In fact, one could argue that providers have a moral imperative to involve consumers in the monitoring of the services that they receive and for which they pay.

Public Authority

Finally, the general public has the authority to monitor service quality. The public pays for human services, usually through taxes and occasionally through donations. Furthermore, in a very real sense, they are also potential users of the service. In this society, human services workers are employed to provide quality care to members of society, often with the realization that, as Judith Snow so eloquently says, "we are only temporarily able-bodied," and could find ourselves as consumers of such services at any time. As people who use and pay for services for friends, family members, and others, the public has a clear authority to act as monitors.

The purpose of this chapter is to introduce the reader to the dynamics of family monitoring by focusing primarily on the experiences of the Association for Retarded Citizens (ARC) Ohio Monitoring Project, and to extract some lessons that can be expanded to other states and localities. Although this monitoring concept can employ all kinds of citizens, the Ohio project began as an effort of parents. That parental involvement is the focus of this chapter. This author was involved in the development of this project from 1983 to 1986.

THE ARC-OHIO MONITORING PROJECT

In 1983, the state of Ohio was ordered to close one of its large public mental retardation institutions, Orient State School. As several hundred residents were moved into community residences across the state, many family members were concerned that the state did not have sufficient quality assurance mechanisms in place to ensure that each of these individuals would receive good service. In fact, there was concern that services were less than minimally adequate. After several months of meeting, discussing, sharing concerns, and learning about the issues, an ad hoc committee of the ARC-Ohio Board of Directors set out to develop a statewide monitoring effort. By the middle of 1984, they had developed the basis of the system that is still in operation today. Much of this chapter is an attempt to document the efforts of that group and to give other groups the information needed to establish their own family monitoring project.

The ARC-Ohio monitoring project is citizen-based. Although most of the monitors are parents, more specifically mothers, there are several monitors who describe themselves as "just an ordinary citizen." All of the monitors are volunteers, although in some counties there is a paid staff person who coordinates training, supports monitors, negotiates with providers, and so forth. The project is not empowered by the state, and the monitors only have access to those residences where the management has decided to allow them in. Efforts have been made to keep this from becoming just another professional review system. The project prepares monitors by holding a day-long training session and issuing two publications (Bersani, 1984a, 1984b). In addition, the state ARC office maintains a full-time staff member assigned to monitor training and support. Local monitors who complete the training, use the instrument, and operate in accordance with the rules set forth by the ARC are able to identify themselves as participants in the ARC-Ohio monitoring project. This offers a level of assurance to providers that the people who call themselves monitors are not wildcat vigilantes acting on their own.

Why Family Monitors?

When first approached about cooperating with family monitors, many providers responded by pointing out that their services are already monitored extensively. Some services may be reviewed several times a year by the county, state, Health Care Financing Administration (HCFA), local health and fire departments, and so forth. Often, administrators also point out that there are several more informal types of monitoring that they experience, such as citizen advocates, local advocacy groups, regular visitors, and outspoken family members. Some agencies even have resident grievance procedures or some form of resident government. Thus, they ask, "Why do we need yet another form of monitoring?"

Some providers also ask if this type of monitoring could replace one or more other existing forms of monitoring. The ARC-Ohio system is based on the assumption that there is a need for a variety of monitoring efforts and that family monitoring offers a unique perspective that does not duplicate other quality assurance efforts and does not replace other methods.

Consumers, family members, and citizens often see things differently than most professionals do. They approach programs with different expectations and concerns. Volunteer monitors are able to focus on areas that are given little or no attention at all by other types of reviewers because they can leave concerns about minimal standards and firecodes, for example, to those other reviewers. In the terms used by Bradley (Chapter 1, this volume), the family monitors would focus more on "enhancement" rather than minimal compliance. Thus, the purpose of family monitoring is to support and enhance other monitoring forms rather than replace them.

Objectives of the Monitoring Project

From the start, the project was designed to meet five objectives that the committee identified. These objectives are:

1. To assess both the strengths and weaknesses of community residence programs
2. To provide an independent, external assessment of programs by trained citizen volunteers, including parents and consumers
3. To obtain statewide feedback on how services are delivered by providers and how those services are received by individual consumers
4. To develop a constructive method by which concerned family members and service providers could work together to improve the level of services in the state
5. To ensure that the people who depend on such services and supports are able to live in community settings that provide needed levels of support and supervision with a minimum level of intrusion into their lives

Basic Assumptions of the Monitoring Project

In the beginning, the monitoring project was outlined by five basic assumptions for operation. Six years later, the assumptions are still relevant. They are:

Residential services could be better, and good providers want to make them better.

More monitoring is needed in addition to the various licensure, certification, and accreditation schemes that currently exist. Family monitors would augment existing quality assurance efforts, not replace them.

Family monitors can make a significant contribution to professionally provided services by offering a unique perspective.

Family monitors are not to be "professional" review teams, but they will need some minimal amount of training, a monitoring instrument, a handbook of support information, and a statewide network for support.

Family monitors should focus on the *experience* of the consumer, not the *excuse* of the provider.

Qualities and Skills of Monitors

Would-be monitors are often concerned that they do not have the requisite skills to become a monitor. Interested citizens need to know that the skills they bring with them and those that they develop during the training session, which may not be as difficult as they think, are the only skills required. The following are some statements that describe the prerequisite skills of a family monitor. These monitors should:

Be familiar with their community and the various resources available.

Be sensitive to the needs of people, especially people who depend on human services, and should be capable of seeing things from the point of view of the person receiving the service rather than from the perspective of the person delivering the service.

Be committed to high quality living options for all people regardless of their level of disability.

Be committed to the use of typical housing arrangements and "ordinary" residential settings such as houses and apartments.

There are also some basic functional skills for monitors. These are not the professional skills, such as knowing how to write program plans, rather they are the skills of observers and advocates.

Honesty There is no need to set up monitoring visits if monitors are not prepared to be honest. They need to be prepared to give credit where credit is due, as well as speak honestly and frankly about the problems they see.

Aggressive But Polite Monitors need to be polite. They will be working in a sensitive situation; possibly, the presence of monitors is controversial within the agency. Monitors must always remember that they are working in someone's home, and the fact that they are there as monitors does not give them blanket permission to violate people's personal space. Offering criticism of a program is seldom easy, but it is important. As a newsletter article about the ARC-Ohio monitoring system states in the title, "I don't want you to think I'm a trouble maker, but . . ." (Lanning, 1984).

Focused Intention and Purpose When visiting a residential program, there are hundreds of potential questions to be raised. Some bear directly on the purpose of the monitoring visit while others may be of interest to the monitor but will not contribute directly to the evaluation effort. The time of a monitoring visit is usually limited, and the monitors have a great deal of information that they need to collect. Asking tangential questions or pursuing random lines of inquiry may use up precious time and essential information for the review may be missing when the visit is over.

Perseverance Offering constructive criticism, no matter how well done, does not guarantee change. Well meaning, open providers may not be able to respond as swiftly or as completely as the monitors would hope. Less cooperative providers may find any number of excuses to stall even the most basic types of suggestions. "Patience," as such, is not recommended because gentle waiting is not what is needed. "Perseverance" indicates the need to persist day after day, month after month, sometimes year after year. Anyone who hopes to radically change the residential supports in their community with a single monitoring visit should re-examine their commitment to systems change.

Good Observational Skills By the time a monitoring visit is over, monitors will have received a great deal of information. They should also have seen a great deal. One of the tasks of the monitor is to observe as much as possible, to remember key information (or take notes unobtrusively), and to interpret those observations. One woman who was looking for a good child care program for her twins asked a director of an early childhood program how to tell a good program from a poor one. She was instructed to listen for "melodious sounds." At first the mother thought the advice was quite odd. However, after visiting several settings, she was a true believer; she could hear a difference in the sounds, and wanted her children to be in the setting with the melodious sounds. Thus, residential monitors need to be attuned to a variety of information, to "observe" with all their senses, and to not be afraid to discuss their "gut" feelings. Reviewers from HCFA, the Accreditation Council on Services for People with Developmental Disabilities (ACDD), and the Commission on Accreditation of Rehabilitation Facilities (CARF) may not be able to pay attention to the kinds of sights and sounds in the setting the way family monitors can. Other reviewers need to focus on compliance with minimal standards; unfortunately, the monitoring process often assumes that the home is really a rehabilitation facility. However, family monitors can leave the compliance issues to the other reviewers and evaluate the setting as a home.

A Well Developed Value System Remember, monitoring is a form of evaluation. Monitors will apply standards, such as those developed in the ARC-Ohio system. The purpose of using a standard instrument and having uniform training for monitors is to be sure that all of the monitors are measuring the service against the same set of standards. However, in the long run, each monitor is an individual, and in order to best monitor residential services, monitors must have worked out a personal value base that is consistent with the monitoring system in which they participate.

Good Evaluation Skills Once the monitoring visit is complete and the monitors have gathered all of the relevant information, it is time to actually make some evaluative judgments regarding the quality of the service. This task requires that the monitor compare what he or she saw and heard to the monitoring guidelines. The monitor must then evaluate the nature of the discrepancy between the observations and the guidelines and offer recommendations to eliminate or reduce the size of that discrepancy.

Value Base for Monitoring

Monitoring is a type of evaluation. The word in the middle of evaluation is "value." How one monitors a program will be related to that person's values. Some monitoring systems are neutral regarding residential setting, for instance, and focus on the need to assure quality whether people are in institutions, small group homes, or apartments. However, some evaluation procedures begin with the clear value statement that people should live in homes. The standard then is, "Is this a good home?" rather than, "Is this a good group home?" or, "Is this a good institution?" The standards used in monitoring are intimately linked to the spoken and unspoken value assumptions of the monitors. This is why the ARC-Ohio monitoring system started off with a statement of the values that they held. The monitoring materials include statements of values such as various definitions and descriptions of the principle of normalization (Nirje, 1981; Wolfensberger, 1972). Also endorsed is a document titled, *The Community Imperative: A Refutation of All Arguments in Support of Institutionalizing Anybody Because of Mental Retardation* (Center on Human Policy, 1979). An evaluation instrument that reflected these values was then developed.

Levels of Quality

Program evaluators must constantly grapple with the issue of what standards of quality to apply. Some systems, aimed at preventing abuse and neglect, tend to focus on minimal standards and the basic set of requirements that the agency must meet. Other evaluation schemes are based on concepts of adequacy such as "Are people being provided adequate food, shelter, and supervision?" Prior to the closing of Pennhurst, an evaluation was done by David Balla (no date) of Yale University. His report included the following statements:

I found the general quality of care at Pennhurst to be adequate. (p. 8)

I found the health-related nursing care to be quite adequate. (p. 8)

I found the environment at Pennhurst to be generally adequate. (p. 9)

The noise level was well within normal limits. (p. 9)

Privacy curtains and toilet paper are present in most toilet facilities. (p. 10)

The parents and citizens in Ohio decided that their value system was that everyone should live in real homes. They wanted standards that went beyond "adequate" care. A good program was not one where the noise levels were "within normal limits" and where most of the toilets had paper. The standard to be applied was quite simple: "Would I want to live there myself?"

Consumer Experience

When a problem is identified with a service, there is a tendency on the part of professional evaluators and monitors to attempt to understand the situation from the point of view of the administrator or the staff. Comments are made such as, "They are doing the best they can given their funding level," or, "It's not their fault that the state requires them to have so many people living in the house." There may be some value to understanding those explanations. They do help monitors understand the service system; however, when it comes time to offer an opinion on the quality of the setting and to make recommendations, monitors need to focus more on the experience of the consumer. The fact of a state hiring freeze, for example, may be the reason why people are not afforded greater individualization, but it should not change the standards. From the perspective of the consumer, the lack of individualization is experienced regardless of the reason.

Smelling Smoke and Fighting Fires

As the ARC-Ohio monitoring project was developing, the parents and staff had a number of discussions about what was meant by monitoring and what form monitoring should take. Many of the parents and citizens felt that they were not prepared to make specific recommendations to improve service quality. They said that they did not know enough about operating residential services to be able to offer useful suggestions. They had been "taught" by service providers that what was going on was "residential programming," and that a "professional service" was being offered. As nonprofessionals, they had little to contribute. In contrast, the ARC-Ohio value base stated that all people should live in homes.

This discussion eventually led to two very important realizations. First, all family and citizen monitors who are currently living in the community are experts in community living. Each knows the specific signs of success and quality in their own lives and should be able to apply them to the lives of people with disabilities as well. To say that parents and citizens lack the expertise needed to comment on quality is to invalidate their life experiences. To imply that what goes on in the residence is so arcane, so different from the every day experience of ordinary citizens, that a lay person can have little or no insight into the worth of these settings is to miss the point.

Second, it was realized that pointing out a problem has great utility. It is not necessary to also have a solution to the problem to be useful. That, after all, is the responsibility of the staff and the agency. The role of monitors is to watch over or to check on the performance of services. A monitor may be one who advises, admonishes, cautions, or reminds. That is to say, a monitor's job is to voice concern about a problem but not necessarily to offer a solution. As this issue was discussed, it was realized that monitors are human and will make mistakes. The only question is what kind of mistakes will they make? Monitors can either be too cautious, and risk not reporting a serious problem for fear of being wrong, or risk overreacting, and occasionally register concern that is based on a misunderstanding. Given the choice between the two types of errors, and the often vulnerable nature of the people who depend on the services, it was decided that to err on the side of overreporting potential problems is preferable to underreporting.

Finally, a comparison was made between monitoring and a smoke detector. There are two qualities of smoke detectors that are taken for granted: first, the occasional false alarm is far preferable to an alarm failure when there is a fire; and second, the smoke detector specializes in sounding the alarm about the potential problem. The smoke detector is not expected to put the fire out or even to prevent possibly inflammatory situations. Its only job is to sound the alarm, and then the "professionals" (fire fighters) take over. Thus, family monitors are like smoke detectors—risking false alarms and sounding alarms in order to alert professionals to potential problems.

BASIC COMPONENTS OF THE ARC-OHIO MONITORING PROJECT

Written materials were developed to support monitors. These materials include written guidelines and a handbook, *Monitoring Community Residences: Guidelines* (Bersani, 1984a) and *Monitoring Community Residences: Handbook* (Bersani, 1984b). Several basic assumptions were made about the monitoring effort. First, the residential service agency participating in the monitoring system was on a voluntary basis and the individuals who lived in the home had given their permission for the monitors to be there. Second, all family monitors were required to attend a day-long training session prior to making an official monitoring visit. Finally, in order to encourage parents and volunteers to be comfortable with the task, it was assumed that the evaluation could be completed in a 4 hour visit with an additional 4–8 hours to write a brief report.

Guideline areas returned to the original assumption that family monitors could attend to different issues than are likely to come up in more formalized evaluations. Therefore, it was agreed that family monitors should concentrate on six areas of interest: rights, environment, use of community resources, commitment to personal growth, staff, and personal relationships. The *Guidelines* (Bersani, 1984a) contained a one paragraph description of each issue. This description is followed by one to two pages of questions to assist the monitor in evaluating the extent to which that issue is reflected in the residence. The descriptions are as follows:

Rights   Human, civil, and legal rights are held by all persons, and are not forfeited merely by living in a community residence. Service providers are obligated to respect and protect all aspects of the rights of the people who live there. In addition, residential services have added obligations to *teach* people about their rights and to *assist* them in the daily exercise of their full range of rights. (p. 3)

Environment   First and foremost, a community residence is a *home*. Its function as a "program," "service," or "agency" is clearly secondary. Efforts must be made to create a physical and social environment which is "home-like," comfortable, and which asserts the humanity of the people who live there. The residence should not draw any undue attention to the location or the people who live there. The home should blend in with the rest of the neighborhood. (p. 6)

Use of Community Resources   Although living near a resource is desirable, it is even more important that those resources actually be used. The people living in a community residence must have systematic opportunities to use community resources on a regular basis. Resources should be used in small groups (1 or 2) whenever possible. Each individual should have experienced a *variety* of community experiences appropriate to his/her age and interest. The residential provider is required to demonstrate commitment to normalizing uses of community resources and community participation for all people who live in the home. Community resources must be used on a *consistent* basis. (p. 10)

Commitment to Personal Growth   In addition to a place to live, a community residence must provide needed supervision and support in an environment which also provides opportunities for personal growth and development through a variety of experiences. By assuming the responsibility to provide a residential service, an agency also accepts the obligation to provide a diverse range of learning experiences. The experiences must include a *normative* amount of exposure to a *reasonable* level of risks. Learning occurs in an environment with manageable failures and meaningful successes. The commitment to personal growth must include appropriate use of current teaching technologies and adaptive equipment and devices. (p. 12)

Staff   Direct care staff are the individuals who actually provide the service received by the people who live in the residence. Because staff may care for people whose needs are quite challenging, they must be well trained, well supported, and well supervised. The number and type of staff on duty at any given time should reflect the needs of the residents, the number of people being served, and the activities associated with the time of day. (p. 15)

Personal Relationships   Living in the community is a right, and it can provide a better learning environment. Ultimately, the development of strong personal relationships is essential. People who are served in residences should have a variety of social and personal relationships with family members, personal friends, and the general public. The residence must systematically encourage these relationships. (p. 18)

RECOMMENDATIONS

Many evaluation systems focus on specific, concrete recommendations. Often, family monitors have equally specific suggestions. It is important to remember that family monitors do not need to make specific, clinical suggestions in order to make a contribution. (Remember the smoke detector.)

However, to the extent that the monitoring team does have suggestions to offer, it seems to make sense that the recommendations include three types.

The first type of recommendation is one that is easily done and does not require specific permission, authority, or funding. For example, family monitors in Ohio have suggested that an agency use more sensitive language when talking about the people who use the service and that the dishes be washed more often. These suggestions are ones that a sincere agency, or interested staff, can implement immediately at its own will.

The second type of recommendation requires a bit more work before it can be implemented so as not to be controversial. It may require a decision from a board of directors or a funding body. Examples are suggestions to develop a sexuality policy or to include direct consumers in decision-making such as voting on boards of directors or participation in the hiring of new personnel.

The third type of recommendation is one that is much more difficult (maybe impossible) to accomplish or one that the agency is most unlikely to heed. It is important for family monitors to make this kind of recommendation. The recommendation may be a suggestion that the agency go out of business or a suggestion to limit new development of rental units to groups of one or two people even though the funding designates building new housing for groups of eight. Such feedback from family monitors is important because they are in the best position to tell the truth about such matters. It is unreasonable to expect a Medicaid review team to recommend closure of programs that meet minimal standards, and the accreditation groups seem unwilling or unable to state that no one should live in an institution, not even a good institution. If the service system and providers being monitored are ever to get this kind of feedback, it will have to come from family monitors. Sometimes this may mean that their actions are futile, but they fill a very important role by ensuring that at least someone gives that level of feedback to the agency.

LESSONS FOR FAMILY MONITORS

Based on the experiences of family monitoring projects in several states including Michigan, Ohio, Minnesota, and New York, several recurring issues can be identified. There may not be any one solution to these problems, but would-be monitors should give a great deal of thought to how they want to handle these issues, including: sanction and access for monitoring; announced versus unannounced visits; resistance from providers; confidentiality; privacy; and the question of "How good is good enough?"

Sanction and Access

Are the monitors sanctioned by the "system"? That is, does the monitoring project have an endorsement from the state Office of Mental Retardation or other funding body? This would allow for more direct use of feedback and would allow for more direct access to homes. In Michigan, where the Mac-omb-Oakland monitoring project (see Provencal, Chapter 21, this volume) is endorsed by the administration, monitors have guaranteed access to all of the residential services, and they meet with the regional director on a regular basis to discuss needed changes and progress in the programs. In contrast, the Ohio project monitors can only enter programs upon the agreement of the pro-viders. In most cases, the provider agreement stipulates that the results are totally confidential and that the monitors may not even share their concerns with the county Board of Mental Retardation or the state Office of Mental Retardation and Developmental Disabilities.

How do monitors get access to community residences, and what do they do if they are denied entry? When parents in Ohio (prior to the monitoring project) demanded to make an unannounced inspection of a residence, they were denied access by the staff who said that to do so would violate the rights of the residents. The cooperative agreement between monitoring teams and providers now stipulate provisions for emergency unannounced visits.

Announced Versus Unannounced Visits

Should monitors inform the residence in advance of a monitoring visit, or should the visit occur with no advanced warning? Many family monitors feel that they can not get a true picture of the conditions in the residence if they announce their visit. Others are sensitive to the fact that the residence is the private home of the individuals who live there. In a difficult decision, the ARC-Ohio group decided to focus on announced visits for the most part, noting that the kind of problems that they are most concerned with cannot be "swept under the rug" in a week's notice. Several monitors mentioned that they do not appreciate unannounced visitors in their homes and that they all like to clean up a bit before visitors come. The operating style of the monitors should not compromise the very values that are at the heart of the monitoring system.

In contrast, the monitoring program in Michigan made the opposite decision. Monitors are issued identification badges, and upon presenting their identification, a monitor may enter a residence at any time. They point out that by stopping by often enough they become more like a neighbor who drops in, and it is not seen as an "unannounced inspection" in the same light that a HCFA review would be.

Resistive Providers

What do monitors do when a provider does not accept any of their recommen-dations? Again, in Ohio, the monitors enter only with the permission of the providers. Advocates will claim that some of the worst providers do not allow monitors in. Other providers cooperate with monitors (at least on the surface) in order to say that they have participated. However, the providers' commitments are tested by their reaction to unpopular recommendations. Often they are reluctant to implement change. In Michigan, because the monitors have the endorsement of the administration, monitors meet regularly with the administrator and give feedback. They also voice complaints when previous suggestions have not been implemented. This sort of process that closes the feedback loop is quite promising.

Confidentiality

There is concern that monitors may come in contact with confidential information. In both the Ohio and Michigan monitoring projects, monitors sign a confidentiality agreement. In Ohio, monitors do not review any confidential records on residents or staff. That sort of review is left up to other quality assurance groups in the state. The citizen monitors focus on nonconfidential material.

Privacy

How can monitors inspect a community residence and still respect the privacy of the people who live there? Monitors are trained to respect the privacy of the people living in the homes. State ARC staff continually stress to monitors the concern that monitors behave in a manner that is consistent with the values of the project.

How Good Is Good Enough?

One of the areas about which family monitors frequently disagree with professional evaluators and providers is the issue of how good is good enough? When people have been moved out of an institution that is clearly a "snake pit," one standard that might be applied is: "Is the setting better than the institution?" The ARC-Ohio project monitors felt that this was an unacceptably low standard. A setting could be much better than an institution but still not be "good" on any kind of objective scale.

Another standard that is frequently applied is that of "adequacy." Reviewers ask if there is *adequate* food, clothing, levels of supervision, and so forth. Again, the ARC-Ohio family monitors rejected this standard by claiming that most citizens do not aspire to have an adequate life. Monitors want more for themselves and their families, and they should expect no less for people who rely on residential services.

Other standards that are often applied include: "Is the residence the best available locally or nationally?" or, "Is it the best that we can make it right now?" These standards were also rejected by family monitors. They make too many accommodations to the current system and assume that people who are labeled as mentally retarded or developmentally disabled will always have to settle for less than the rest of society; the only question is how much less.

The ARC-Ohio monitors were able to find two standards that they thought were appropriate. Monitors are taught to ask, "Is it as good (or better) than my home?" and, "Would I want to live there myself?" These two questions quickly get to the root of issues like privacy and autonomy. In a "good" home people may have only one roommate. However, few others are willing to share a bedroom with another adult unless they are romantically involved.

SHORTCOMINGS OF FAMILY MONITORING PROJECTS

As stated at the beginning of this chapter, the ARC-Ohio project began in 1983, and the instrument and support materials were written in 1984. As a result, there are some things that would be done differently at this point in time. In addition, the group has years of experience. Since that time, several hundred people have been trained and have monitored settings across the state of Ohio. The ARC-Ohio materials have also been used "as is" or with minor adaptations in several other states. Based on this experience, and reflecting on the changes in the field since 1984, several shortcomings of the ARC-Ohio efforts can now be identified.

Direct Consumer Involvement

At the time the system was being developed, "consumer involvement" all too often meant "parent involvement." Now there is much greater realization of the need to involve direct consumers in the monitoring process. ARC-Ohio has made significant efforts to recruit, train, and support monitors who have various disabilities including mental retardation. Now, a realistic minimum is to have at least one self-advocate on each monitoring team.

Group Home Focus

Although the word "group home" is rarely used in the ARC-Ohio materials, it is clear to the reader that the assumption is that "community residence" means "group home." At the time, it was assumed that 4 to 12 people were living in each residence. Now it is increasingly common to find people being supported to live in their own homes or in apartments shared with one or two roommates. These settings may not be "programs" as such, and occasionally, some of the questions in the current instrument may not fit these more creative and flexible situations exactly.

Lack of Empowerment

ARC-Ohio monitors can only go into residences where the providers have entered into a voluntary agreement with the project. The monitors have no empowerment to enter residences against the wishes of providers. In addition, there is no mandate that recommendations must be followed through. Monitors may occasionally feel that their efforts are futile as they work hard to make responsible recommendations only to learn that the providers disagree with them and have no intention of using any of the feedback.

CONCLUSION

Who benefits from family monitoring? It is clear today that family-based monitoring efforts carry with them at least three levels of benefits. First, there is the benefit to the direct consumer. Family monitoring efforts have increased the quality of life in community residences. In addition, consumers who participate in monitoring efforts reap the added benefit that comes from being directly involved in affecting the quality of the services that they receive (perhaps for the first time in their lives). Second, there is a benefit to the friends and family members of people who use these services. People have greater confidence in the human services system if they are monitors, and they develop an increased sense of self-confidence as they see themselves become effective monitors. Monitoring can be a very empowering experience. Finally, there are the benefits to the general public. Providing better quality care to citizens in need ultimately benefits all of society. The public also benefits as family monitors are an effective, inexpensive component of the quality assurance system. Parents and citizens who participate in monitoring efforts have the added benefit that comes from positive involvement in the lives of people with disabilities and the satisfaction that comes from knowing that they have made a difference.

It is no coincidence that the vast number of monitors in the ARC-Ohio system are mothers of children and adults who have developmental disabilities. They are concerned, interested, knowledgeable, and often more available to participate in training and monitoring visits than are their husbands or other citizens. As one ARC-Ohio mother monitor said: "God could not be everywhere, so *she* created mothers."

REFERENCES

Balla, D. (no date). *An evaluation of Pennhurst Center.*

Bersani, H. (1984a). *Monitoring community residences: Guidelines.* ARC-Ohio. Columbus.

Bersani, H. (1984b). *Monitoring community residences: Handbook.* ARC-Ohio. Columbus.

Center on Human Policy. (1979). *The community imperative: A refutation of all arguments in support of institutionalizing anybody because of mental retardation.* Syracuse, NY: Author.

Lanning, C. (1984, July). I don't want you to think I'm a trouble maker, but . . . *LINKS, 14*(7), 12–14.

Nirje, B. (1981). Normalization. In National Institute on Mental Retardation (Eds.), *Orientation manual on mental retardation.* Toronto: Author.

Wolfensberger, W. (1972). *The principle of normalization.* Toronto: National Institute on Mental Retardation.

GOVERNMENTAL ISSUES

chapter 7

Balancing Quality of Care and Quality of Life

John H. Chafee

The chapters in this book outline many of the problems involved in providing high quality services for people with developmental disabilities. This chapter attempts to frame the issue from the perspective of members of Congress. The context in which congressional decisions are made, as well as efforts at the federal level to provide appropriate, high quality services to individuals with developmental disabilities, is discussed.

In understanding how federal decisionmakers may view this issue, it is important to put it in a proper historical context. The primary source of funding for residential services for individuals with developmental disabilities is the Medicaid program (Title XIX of the Social Security Act). Combined state and federal funding for the intermediate care facilities (ICFs), and waiver programs, equals about $6.7 billion annually. The federal share of this alone is about $3.6 billion. (These figures are for 1988.)

Such federal expenditures are a departure from the past. Until 1971, the federal government had no significant role in financing care for those with disabilities. However, beginning in the 1950s, disturbing revelations of substandard care in state institutions were seen. In 1962, the original President's Panel on Mental Retardation focused on this issue. Throughout the 1960s and early 1970s a series of exposés were published. These chronicled abuse and

Special thanks to Christine C. Ferguson, J.D., for assisting in the preparation of this article.

neglect of individuals with disabilities in large, state funded, facilities, and rocked the foundation of institutional care. The most shocking of these revelations were in *Christmas in Purgatory,* published in 1966.

In response to the failure of states to quickly improve conditions in these facilities, advocacy groups representing those with disabilities went to court. Perhaps the leading decision was *Wyatt v. Stickney* (1971), wherein the U.S. District Court in Alabama held that the constitutional rights of the mentally retarded residents of Partlow State School and Hospital had been violated. The court went even further to define a set of minimum treatment standards that the state school would be required to meet. With this decision, litigation began in earnest over the issue of the treatment and constitutional rights of individuals with disabilities living in state facilities.

Congress also responded to public outrage at the treatment of these vulnerable individuals. In 1971 it voted to expand the Medicaid program to include coverage for residential care provided for certain individuals with disabilities, by creating the Intermediate Care Facility for the Mentally Retarded (ICF/MR) program. Since it involved a major infusion of federal dollars into state services, this was probably the most significant step in improving residential care for individuals with disabilities. Tied to the federal funding, were federal minimum standards that facilities were required to meet in order to receive Medicaid reimbursement. These standards have been updated and revised only twice.

This expansion of the Medicaid program has had a profound influence on the long-term care services provided by the states to individuals with developmental disabilities for two reasons: first, because it was done to resolve a specific problem—substandard care at large state facilities, and second, because it was done through the Medicaid program, which had been designed, when created in 1965 to provide traditional medical services, such as hospital and physician care.

The evolution of the care and services eligible for Medicaid reimbursement has been driven by these two factors. The quality of care standards have been designed to address the problems in large scale residential facilities. The services have focused on the medical needs of the residents, even though over time they have been expanded to include some nonmedically oriented services.

WHAT IS "QUALITY"?

Since its inception in 1972, the ICF/MR program has been constantly scrutinized by those who question whether it is providing high quality services. These concerns were reflected in the development of specialized standards in 1974 that required substantial alterations in the physical environments as well as in staffing and programming. States had deadlines by which to accomplish the major overhaul required in order to continue to receive federal funding. In addition, states were given the responsibility to certify the facilities and to conduct individual program and utilization reviews. The federal government, however, retained the standard setting authority.

Meeting federal standards proved to be difficult and expensive in some states. Delays and extensions of compliance deadlines became the rule rather than the exception. Concerns about quality of care once again came to a head in 1985 when Senator Lowell Weicker conducted a congressional investigation of ICF/MR services. The results were so troubling to Senator Weicker that he introduced legislation to expand quality assurance oversight capacity in the U.S. Department of Health and Human Services (HHS). Though the legislation was ultimately unsuccessful, the issues that were raised led the Health Care Financing Administration (HCFA) to begin an oversight activity, dubbed a "look-behind," in order to validate state quality assurance efforts and to ensure compliance with federal standards. While care in the facilities has improved, significant problems remain.

As Congress is asked to respond to real and perceived abuses of institutional residents, by improving enforcement and raising statutory standards of care, many have begun to question the meaning of quality. Do high quality services simply require that residents have a safe and clean environment, wide hallways, enough space, and proper medical attention, or is something more needed?

New trends are constantly evolving in the field of developmental disabilities. Innovative methods of care and service delivery are being discovered, new technologies and assistive devices are being developed, and there is better understanding of the causes and effects of developmental disabilities and mental retardation. The range of abilities of individuals with disabilities have been recognized. It is being discovered that these individuals should not be removed from society, but rather, allowed to participate in it more fully. In short, society is finding that achieving a high quality of care is inextricably entwined with providing a better quality of life for those with disabilities. What is required is not solely excellent medical services, indeed such services for many individuals with disabilities may be of low priority.

How does one define a good quality of life for those with developmental disabilities? Congress has answered that question in a variety of ways. In the Education for All Handicapped Children Act, enacted in 1975 (PL 94–142), it is clearly stated that those with disabilities have the same right to a proper education as any other citizen. The goal is to ensure that they have the opportunity to learn basic skills to the best of their abilities. In 1984, Congress enacted the Developmental Disabilities Act (PL 98–527) that stated it was "in the national interest to . . . reduce or eliminate the need for institutional care," and the states must work to promote the values of independence, integration, and productivity for all citizens with developmental disabilities. In 1981, when the Medicaid waiver program (PL 97–35) was enacted, Congress was sending a clear sign that the value of family unity and community participation was as important to those with disabilities as to those without.

Nevertheless, because of the way the ICF/MR program evolved, federal Medicaid funds are available almost exclusively in larger, institutional settings. The standards regulating care in residential settings are designed to address large facilities, caring for a variety of individuals in the same fashion, despite their different levels of ability. Community group homes of 12 or less find it difficult, and often inappropriate, to meet standards designed for larger facilities. In addition, most parents who desire in-home assistance find that their child is ineligible for support under Medicaid, even though these same children—if placed in an institutional setting—would be eligible for federal Medicaid assistance.

The Medicaid program remains the last, and most formidable, bastion of segregated care. Quality of life is often sacrificed to what, on paper, appears to be a guarantee of safety and quality services. The way services must be delivered, in order to be eligible for reimbursement, contradicts the philosophies encompassed in the federal programs outlined above that have been associated with a high quality of life. The very structure of the program discourages—or simply prevents—the use of Medicaid funds for in-home care, independent assistance, services provided in small community group homes, and other noninstitutional based services.

IS PROGRESS BEING MADE?

Since 1984, many in Congress have been working to reform the structure of the Medicaid program to better meet the needs of those with disabilities. The main focus of this effort has been to de-emphasize the reliance on large institutional facilities and to develop a comprehensive community-based system of services.

There seems to be general agreement that most of those with developmental disabilities would achieve a better quality of life in smaller, community-based settings, including their own homes or group homes. But again, Congress is faced with the issue of assuring that the care in such settings is of high quality. It is perceived to be much easier to develop, legislate, and enforce standards of care in large facilities. Those facilities are one-stop shopping for surveyors, and there are a circumscribed number of potential problems to anticipate in developing standards.

Thus, one of the most common arguments against moving on a widespread basis to community-based services for this population is the fear that such services cannot be adequately monitored, and therefore, those receiving such services will be at risk of abuse or neglect. Another argument is the difficulty inherent in developing standards for a variety of services provided in a large number of different settings (see Gardner and Parsons, Chapter 15; Pearce, Chapter 16; Provencal, Chapter 21).

In the effort to restructure Medicaid, for the first time, Congress is forced to find a way to balance the need to ensure that high quality services can be maintained with the desire to provide a good quality of life.

A FRAMEWORK FOR QUALITY COMMUNITY-BASED SERVICES

Restructuring the Federal Medicaid Program

Most members of Congress agree that the Medicaid program should address the full spectrum of needs of those with disabilities in order to help them achieve their fullest potential. But what is meant by "fullest potential"? It simply means that each person, regardless of the severity of his or her disability, should have the opportunity to pursue education, recreation, and vocation to the best of his or her ability. The federal Medicaid program should assist them in these endeavors, rather than hinder them.

The Medicaid program should offer a range of services and supports for individuals with disabilities, available in a variety of residential settings— from in-home support such as respite and attendant care, to institutionalization. Most important, these services should be designed to meet each individual's needs rather than requiring an individual to "fit into" a service system or residential program. In short, the program should provide a full continuum of individualized services.

Medicaid restructuring should provide the mechanism to allow individuals with disabilities to live in the community with the security and support they need, along with the opportunity to grow and develop as individuals. It should allow individuals who now live in the community—at home or in some other arrangement—to remain there by giving them and their families the support and services they need.

Any Assurance of Quality Services for Those in the Community?

Once the Medicaid program is expanded to provide funding for noninstitutional services, how is Congress to ensure that those services are of good quality? As previously stated, it is relatively easy to *develop* standards for large facilities. However, it is very difficult to *ensure* that those standards are followed. Knowing this, how can Congress develop standards for a true array of services provided in a variety of settings? Equally important, how can Congress avoid making the mistake of the ICF/MR program in developing standards that inhibit creativity in the delivery of services and stifle individual growth?

There are some members of Congress who insist on stringent federal standards of care and stringent federal enforcement. As outlined above, this approach has not been successful, and perhaps has seriously hampered the ability to provide both quality of life and quality care (see Smith and Gettings, Chapter 8, this volume). Therefore, this author firmly believes that the most effective guarantee of quality services is to provide a multilayered approach to both setting standards and enforcing them. In other words, while vigorous federal participation may be desirable, it is not sufficient. Strong state, local, and individual roles are all essential to success.

The delivery of services should be well structured. Each individual must have an in-depth needs assessment that is updated on a regular basis to reflect progress or regression. The individual and his or her family should participate in this process with an interdisciplinary team that consists of those professionals who will be involved in providing care. This team should also be responsible for making placement decisions. A process should be in place to allow any member of the team, particularly the individual or family, who disagrees with a recommendation to challenge it.

Who Should Set Standards of Care?

The responsibility of setting standards of care must be shared. It may be that there should be federal minimum standards for certain types of services—perhaps to ensure health and safety—while the states should be responsible for other facets, upon which the public would have the right to comment.

There must also be a multilayered system of monitoring to ensure these standards are met. In certain situations, this is a role for the federal government, but states should have primary responsibility for monitoring and enforcement. As a balance against the fear of the "fox guarding the hen house," monitoring boards that consist of parents, individuals with disabilities, and any interested citizen should be required (see Bersani, Chapter 6; this volume). These boards should have an independent ombudsman through which to channel reports of substandard or inappropriate care.

Furthermore, there must be an effective system of protective intervention to remove an individual from a placement in which he or she is being abused or mistreated in some way. Resolution of these situations must be speedy, rather than drawn out.

Perhaps the most important factor in ensuring success is a certain degree of predictability. It is essential that states, as well as those providing care, have some degree of assurance that those who monitor their services will be consistent in how they assess compliance. This will require well-defined standards and well-trained quality assurance monitors. Finally, in the event that all of these safeguards fail, an individual or his or her guardian should have some recourse—perhaps in the court system.

CONCLUSION

Those with disabilities are part of society and have an important contribution to make. Unfortunately, many have not had the option of living in an environment in which they can grow, reach their potential, and contribute to their communities. They deserve the chance to go to work, to take the bus, to go shopping, to eat in a restaurant, to go to a ball game, and to take advantage of the many opportunities that most Americans take for granted.

It is time for Congress to resolve the existing conflict between the straight jacket of institutional life with all of its presumed assurance as to quality on the one hand, and quality of life and the ability to grow that community-based services promise on the other.

REFERENCES

Blatt, B., & Kaplan, F. (1966). *Christmas in purgatory: A photographic essay on mental retardation.* Boston: Allyn & Bacon.

PL 94–142, *Education for All Handicapped Children Act,* 1975.

PL 97–35, *Omnibus Budget Reconciliation Act,* 1981, § 2176 Medicaid home and community-based care.

PL 98–527, *Developmental Disabilities Act,* 1984.

Wyatt v. Stickney, et al. 325 F. Supp. 781 (M.D. Alabama 1971).

chapter 8 _____

Defining a Constructive State-Federal Partnership

Gary A. Smith and Robert M. Gettings

Debates about quality assurance continue to rage in Congress as several legislators attempt to reform the Medicaid program and to ensure that the well-being of people with developmental disabilities and mental retardation is protected in federally funded settings. This chapter presents a critique of federal quality assurance efforts and discusses two proposals submitted to Congress to reform the Medicaid system.

BACKGROUND

Federal Medicaid policies that affect services for people with developmental disabilities should be changed to affirm contemporary service delivery values that are stated in the Developmental Disabilities Act (1987). These values include integration, independence, and productivity. Satisfactory reform demands that policies be recast to permit Medicaid financing to support a diverse range of community services tailored to meet each individual's needs, preferences, and circumstances. Such services must have equal footing with the Intermediate Care Facility for the Mentally Retarded (ICF/MR) program, which in 1988 consumed over $6 billion in state/federal resources to support

The provisions for Medicaid reform that are discussed in this chapter are current and relevant at the time this book went to press.

services in congregate care facilities. Increasingly, the future direction of effective service delivery will emphasize settings and services that are substantially less restrictive and more diverse than the ICF/MR program permits.

While few dispute the need to reform Medicaid policies, there is an intense debate regarding how best to structure such changes. A substantial change in policies will have enormous consequences during the 1990s for shaping publicly funded developmental disabilities services. A variety of issues have proven to be extremely problematic in translating the shared goal of Medicaid reform into specific legislative provisions, thus hindering congressional action. Such issues include whether or not limits should be placed on federal payments to large, congregate care facilities and whether specific types of community services should be authorized for federal financing.

Additionally, the question of the federal government role in assuring the quality of Medicaid-reimbursable services has become a central point of debate. Several questions have been raised:

Should the federal government dictate service delivery standards?
Should the federal government have independent authority to oversee the provision of Medicaid-reimbursable services?
Alternatively, what role should state governments and other service delivery system stakeholders play in protecting the rights and well-being of persons who receive Medicaid-reimbursable services?

How these questions are answered will have enormous consequences for community services.

THE INSTITUTIONAL REGULATORY MODEL

In 1989, the debate regarding Medicaid reform and its implications for the questions above took a new turn. Until 1989, Senator John H. Chafee's Medicaid reform proposals held center stage in the debate concerning federal policies. Since 1983, Senator Chafee has proposed legislation that is aimed at shifting federal Medicaid dollars from large congregate care settings to community services.

Congressman Henry A. Waxman, however, has emerged as a powerful proponent for alternative proposals to broaden Medicaid coverage to include "community habilitation and supportive services" without affecting payments for institutional services. There is no doubt that these proposals are aimed at placing federal financing of community services on more equal footing with the ICF/MR (institutional) program. Any substantive reform of the system must link this change in federal policy to the expectation that federal dollars will be used to assist persons with severe, lifelong disabilities to function as full participating members of society. These key changes, however, would be premised on the adoption of what could be termed the "institutional regulatory" model aimed at improving the quality of community Medicaid services by assigning greater oversight and control over such services to the federal government.

This model asserts that the federal government, as a partner with the states in serving persons with developmental disabilities, has every right to expect that such services will be of high quality and lead to beneficial outcomes. In order to ensure the delivery of high quality community habilitation and supportive services, however, this proposal would institute a federally directed system of standard setting, program monitoring, and oversight. The secretary of the U.S. Department of Health and Human Services (HHS) would be given sweeping powers to specify, in federal regulations, the desired outcomes of such services. The secretary would also be authorized to impose service delivery standards so that each participating state would be obligated to enforce as well as directly survey and monitor community-based programs in order to "validate" state enforcement of federal regulations. Such reform proposals are based on the presumption that federal participation in meeting the cost of community services brings with it the necessity of specifying a wide-ranging role for the federal government in defining what constitutes acceptable service provision practice and in protecting the interests of persons receiving services.

In specifying the federal government's role in quality assurance, the institutional regulatory model would transpose the congressionally-mandated structure for regulating Medicaid-certified nursing facilities (adopted as part of the Omnibus Budget Reconciliation Act of 1987, PL 100–203) to community programs serving persons with developmental disabilities. This structure reserves for the federal government the responsibility of determining appropriate standards of care for nursing facility residents, incorporates an extensive set of penalties to be applied in the event of provider noncompliance, and assigns to HCFA the direct responsibility for determining whether states are adequately enforcing federal regulations. The legislation dictates key protections for nursing facility residents and assigns nursing facilities wide-ranging responsibilities in assessing resident needs and furnishing services within the context of a "comprehensive care" facility.

The institutional regulatory model governs the provision of ICF/MR services. Federal ICF/MR regulations are grounded in the concept that individuals with developmental disabilities must receive comprehensive care and treatment in highly protected environments. Services are expected to be uniform from person to person, facility to facility, and state to state. The institutional regulatory model is premised on a facility's meeting all the needs of each resident in a specialized living arrangement, rather than attempting to support each individual in an integrated setting.

PROBLEMS

In the authors' view, the institutional regulatory model, as it has been proposed, represents a highly inappropriate starting point for designing a balanced, effective approach to assuring and enhancing the quality of community services for persons with developmental disabilities. In fact, the application of an institutional regulatory model would create enormous impediments to achieving the basic statutory aims of Medicaid reform (i.e., promoting community integration, independence, and productivity).

First, community developmental disabilities services are rapidly changing and diversifying. Consequently, progress in community services is highly dependent on fostering an environment in which old service delivery models can be replaced by new approaches. An institutional regulatory model, however, does not tolerate such diversity and, in fact, is premised on achieving a high degree of uniformity and rigidity in service delivery. Adoption of an institutional approach to regulating community developmental disabilities services, therefore, could have a chilling effect on improving both the quality and the effectiveness of such programs.

Second, an institutional regulatory model is premised on the notion that the services provided to recipients should be uniform in every jurisdiction. However, in reality, community services are far from uniform. Indeed, community programs for persons with developmental disabilities vary enormously among the states. This variety is the outgrowth of unique partnerships that have been formed in each state, involving elected officials, state agencies, service providers, advocates, parents, and consumers. The aim of such partnerships is to create service systems that represent the collective views of this diverse constituency. A federally defined, institutionally based regulatory model would be out of place given the diversity of approaches used by the states in organizing and structuring community developmental disabilities services. Evidence suggests that this diversity has positive benefits. Federal policies, therefore, should foster diversity and affirm its legitimacy rather than assume that such diversity is inappropriate or somehow undermines the quality of community services.

One prerequisite of high quality community developmental disabilities services is that they be tailored to each person's unique strengths, needs, and circumstances. The institutional regulatory model, instead, is premised on the delivery of similar services to each resident in a facility. Just as federal policy should accommodate diversity in service alternatives and interjurisdictional differences, it also should foster an environment in which each person is treated as an individual and furnished with services that are molded around his or her strengths, capabilities, and needs. The pathways to integration, independence, and productivity for one individual may be completely different from those of another.

It also is clear that achieving high quality in community services depends on the active involvement and collaboration of responsible state officials, service providers, advocates, parents, and consumers. All interested parties must be committed to solving problems together. A federally driven, institutionally based regulatory model represents the antithesis of this key ingredient in promoting excellence in community services.

Furthermore, to determine whether or not community services are effective in meeting the needs of individuals with developmental disabilities necessitates an assessment of many different dimensions of program performance. Ascertaining consumer satisfaction with services, for example, is as important a quality assurance dimension as determining whether a person's living environment is safe and sanitary. The institutional regulatory model simply cannot encompass the multiple dimensions that contemporary practice suggests are needed to assure the quality of community services. Indeed, such a model would rapidly lead providers to focus on the minimum steps needed to pass a survey rather than on whether the goals of integration, independence, and productivity are truly being achieved.

Finally, high quality community services cannot be maintained over time when the only response to a problem is to take punitive measures. The stability of community services depends upon assisting service providers to improve their performance. However, the institutional regulatory model focuses solely on sanctioning provider agencies for infractions rather than addressing the root causes of such shortcomings.

Obviously, it is legitimate and necessary to be concerned with the health and safety of persons with developmental disabilities as well as the potential for abuse, neglect, and exploitation. Furthermore, the individual rights of program participants cannot be abridged. The credibility of publicly funded services depends on an ongoing demonstration that program participants are afforded such fundamental protections. At the same time, concern for health and safety can result in protectionist policies that impede efforts to achieve greater community integration and independence for program participants. The institutional regulatory model rewards caution and, hence, works against the very aims of Medicaid reform and community development.

A CONSTRUCTIVE PARTNERSHIP

In the authors' view, the institutional regulatory model does not constitute the basis of a constructive state-federal partnership in promoting effective community-based services on behalf of persons with developmental disabilities. The institutional regulatory model of reform that proposes to rigidly control community Medicaid services should be discarded in favor of an approach better suited to the character and nature of community developmental disabilities services. This approach should be based on the principles discussed below.

First, protection of the individual rights of persons with developmental disabilities should be uniformly applied in all parts of the nation; thus, the protection of individual rights is a legitimate area of federal interest. A state covering community habilitation and supportive services should be obliged to safeguard statutorily defined rights.

Similarly, assuring that the environments in which community habilitation services are provided meet basic health/safety standards is the legitimate subject of federal policy. Such standards, however, should encourage integrated housing, rather than forcing provider agencies to operate specialized residences solely for the purpose of meeting institutionally based standards. These standards should not apply to a family's own home or a living arrangement owned or leased by a program participant (as would be the case under institutional regulatory reform). Moreover, such standards must be designed to encourage community integration (e.g., the development of friendships, relationships with neighbors, and the use of natural community supports) and not result in persons with developmental disabilities being isolated from the rest of society.

The responsibility for assuring that health/safety standards and individual rights are observed should be assigned to the states. States, in turn, should be held accountable for carrying out this responsibility. Overlapping federal regulatory activities, however, should not be used as a means of achieving such accountability. Accountability can be best achieved by measuring state performance rather than creating a multiplicity of masters.

Additionally, each state should be required to establish a well-rounded quality assurance system as a condition of covering community habilitation and supportive services. The strategies that undergird such a system should be developed with public input. States should be permitted and encouraged to build upon their quality assurance systems rather than being required to create entirely new processes. There should be ongoing involvement by all key system stakeholders in examining the premises and performance of a state's quality assurance system. This involvement should take the form of a quality assurance advisory council charged with broad responsibilities. Lacking such involvement, there will be no durable commitment to excellence, innovation, and community participation in the provision of developmental disabilities services. Federal policies should specify the required elements of a state's quality assurance system but should not prescribe how a state organizes the activities encompassed with its particular system.

Furthermore, the federal government should not serve as the ultimate enforcer of uniform, nationwide standards. Assigning such a role to the federal government would undermine accountability, not enhance it. Rather, the federal role should be:

To ensure that each state has instituted a quality assurance system that appropriately safeguards vulnerable people without isolating them or otherwise denying them the right to participate, to the maximum extent possible, as fully functioning members of their communities

To facilitate the intrastate exchange of information regarding best practices, including the sponsorship of research, demonstration, evaluation, and technical assistance projects that explore the state of the art in quality assurance

To provide states with additional resources to foster improved practices, including the establishment of intrastate training and technical assistance capabilities

Finally, the effectiveness of each state's quality assurance programs should be periodically assessed and independently evaluated. Failure to comply with basic assurances spelled out in law should be grounds for intervention and corrective action on the part of the state. Assuring accountability on the part of the states, however, can be achieved in a more constructive, effective, and efficient fashion than the approach spelled out in the institutional regulatory reform proposals.

CONCLUSION

The principles outlined for a community development model represent a constructive, well-balanced approach to framing a national strategy for assuring the quality of community programs for persons with developmental disabilities. Under this approach, each state would be allowed to tailor its quality assurance system to best fit the types of services it furnishes to persons with developmental disabilities and assure the participation of key system stakeholders as partners in promoting excellence. Sound, durable quality assurance systems depend on such active participation. The federal role in quality assurance should be to ensure that each state has in place effective systems to safeguard individual rights and health/safety standards and, based on independent assessments, to determine whether a state has an overall quality assurance program that promotes the basic goals of the statute. Finally, the federal government should be an active partner in promoting high quality services by participating in national and statewide efforts to improve services, rather than simply handing out sanctions for substandard performance.

Maintaining high quality community services is not as some members of Congress would suggest, principally a matter of closely policing the provision of services. Good community services emerge only when the aim of promoting excellence permeates an entire service delivery system. If, however, key stakeholders are disenfranchised in favor of the imposition of uniform federal regulations, the prospects for achieving excellence become far less likely. The principles articulated in this chapter attempt to strike a better, more constructive balance among the legitimate interests of the federal government, the states, and other key stakeholders in promoting high quality community services. Medicaid reform based on these principles is more likely to create an environment for excellence in the community than the monolithic, federalized approach that is currently in place. Institutional regulatory practices, therefore, must not be transferred to community services.

REFERENCES

Developmental Disabilities Assistance and Bill of Rights Act and Amendments of 1987, 42 U.S.C. 6012.
PL 100–203, *Omnibus Budget Reconciliation Act,* 1987. (42 U.S.C. 1396r).

MANAGEMENT ISSUES

chapter 9 ————————

The Role of Performance Contracts in Quality Assurance

————————— *John W. Ashbaugh* —————————

There has been an extraordinary growth since the 1970s in the use of contracts to purchase services for persons with developmental disabilities. It follows that performance contracting is being hailed by many as the quality control mechanism whose time has come. Yet, the writing of performance contracts as a quality assurance tool has lagged far behind the writing of contracts in general.

This chapter first identifies important advantages of performance contracting over traditional regulatory approaches. The exponential increase in the use of service contracts for persons with developmental disabilities is described in contrast to the limited use of performance provisos in these contracts. Some explanations are provided for the lag, all relating in some way to the centralized (regulatory) bent of the performance contracting efforts in most states. While recognizing the need for performance data and performance controls, performance contracting advocates are cautioned against setting up systems that compromise case manager and contract manager discretion.

Finally, policymakers are encouraged to think in terms of "full service" agencies and contracts structured to address the range of individual needs, thus opening the door for the writing of truly comprehensive and individualized performance contracts.

BACKGROUND

Performance contracts as described in this chapter refer to legal agreements between the state or local developmental disability authority and service providers. These agreements call for providers to deliver a complement of services to individuals with developmental disabilities for a specified period of time and for an agreed upon amount of funding and other support. The contract may circumscribe the population to be served and it may delimit the type and level of services to be provided. It may include assurances that the provider has the necessary qualifications and capabilities to perform and that the provider abides by specified procedures and constraints. It may identify particular outcomes to be achieved. Incentives and sanctions may be specified. The more performance provisions the contract contains, the more appropriate is the term performance contract.

Contracts have a number of inherent advantages over traditional regulatory approaches to quality or performance control. The range of quality criteria (performance measures) that might be included in a contract can be greater than in regulations because the requirements need not be strictly based in statute. Contracts may be written to address inputs, process, outputs, and outcome dimensions of program performance. They may require minimum staff credentials (inputs), rule out unacceptable practices such as aversive therapies (process), require increases in the number of persons served (outputs), or require that a minimum number of persons be placed in supported work settings during the contract period (outcomes).

Furthermore, the sanctions agreed upon in a contract may be at varying levels of severity. They may provide for nonpayment, partial payment, or full payment for services, or they may provide for no further funding until some corrective action is taken and satisfactory performance is demonstrated. Regulations generally provide for full payment or no payment; discretionary partial payments and other such arrangements are not common practice.

Contract provisions are also more amenable to change than regulatory provisions. Reasonable contract amendments may be granted at almost any time and, at the very least, at the time of contract renewal—usually on an annual basis.

ADVANTAGES OF PERFORMANCE CONTRACTING

Service contract arrangements are hardly new. "Government has promoted human services by contract for over 150 years" (Terrell, 1979, p. 58). "By the 1820's most states had entered into agreements with private residential institutions to serve indigent, deaf and otherwise handicapped children" (Terrell, 1979, p. 72). However, since the 1970s there has been an upsurge in contracting for the delivery of human services to the point where, "by some estimates, contractors have overtaken civil servants in these activities" (Sharkansky, 1980, p. 22). The upsurge can be traced to a variety of factors that have combined to make contracting for services for persons with developmental disabilities an attractive option.

Federal Funding

Important alterations in the character of federal aid (Medicaid) for social services programs served both to encourage and facilitate the purchase of human services.

> Federal legislation encouraging the expansion of social services spurred the growth of purchase. The 1967 Amendments to the Social Security Act authorized public welfare agencies to receive 75% federal reimbursement for expenditures on services that could be purchased from private, nonprofit or proprietary organizations. Previous federal legislation had only provided matching funds for purchase of services indirectly. It permitted welfare departments to buy services from other public agencies. These agencies could then either provide the services directly through their own staff or through purchase of service contracts. A 1969 Department of Health, Education and Welfare regulation, allowing private funds (donated funds) to substitute for state funds in matching federal social services dollars stimulated private organizations to solicit purchase agreements with public welfare departments. (Massachusetts Taxpayers Foundation, Inc., 1980, p. 3)

At the same time, under the Community Mental Health Centers Act of 1967, providing for the development of specialized facilities for individuals with mental disabilities, funds were offered directly to private nonprofit corporations. The 1974 Amendments to the Social Security Act (Title XX) made contracts between service providers and state agencies a condition for federal reimbursement. Also in 1974, the establishment of the Supplemental Security Income (SSI) program raised income maintenance benefits and expanded eligibility among persons with disabilities in many states. SSI payments became the basic funding source for the support of many individuals with developmental disabilities in a variety of private nonmedical residential arrangements.

The advent of intermediate care facilities for the mentally retarded (ICFs/MR) provisions under the Medicaid program in 1974 brought higher staffing and facility standards leading many states to move residents out of large ICFs/MR to avoid decertification and the loss of Medicaid revenues owing to inadequate staffing and facilities. At the same time it permitted states to use federal funds to develop the specialized facilities for persons with mental retardation in the private sector. Although Medicaid funds had been generally available for nursing and medical services for persons with mental retardation, the more programmatic and habilitative thrust of the new regulation made it possible for states to use ICF/MR funds to support more specialized and normalized living arrangements (Bradley, 1980). Then in the early 1980s, through the Home and Community Based Waiver, revenue sharing, and block grants, state and local agencies gained even more freedom to contract for services.

Community Imperative

Also promoting the shift in emphasis to the private sector was an increasing recognition among policymakers and professionals that large state institutions were, by and large, not fulfilling the needs of their residents for active treatment, and furthermore, there was no therapeutic reason or other justification for removing these persons from the community mainstream. In addition, the media exposés highlighted the lack of adequate staffing and substandard conditions in many institutions around the country. Among reformers in the 1960s, institutions became known as warehouses, remote from local communities, for housing individuals whom society wished to forget (Bradley 1980, p. 193).

In devising alternatives to large public institutions, reformers turned to the private sector. At the time it seemed incongruous to build a new community-based system with the same personnel and administrative structure that had contributed to the inadequate conditions in institutions.

> Comparisons between private sector services, both proprietary and nonprofit, and publicly managed institutions inevitably led analysts to affirm the virtues of the former. Such virtues included efficient and economical management, flexibility of programming, capacity for innovation, smaller more homelike settings, variety and richness of service offerings, and the healthy dynamic of competition. (Bradley, 1980, p. 194)

Expediency

In many ways turning to the private sector was also the most expedient way to develop community-based alternatives. Existing grass roots, self-help organizations quickly arose to fill the need. Associations for Retarded Citizens (ARC), United Cerebral Palsy Associations (UCPA) and others set up nonprofit corporations to provide residential care and rehabilitation services for their members. Even when such organizations did not exist, public authorities were able to find experienced entrepreneurs willing to provide these services under contract. Certainly the use of private contractors seemed far easier to tackle than negotiations for the relocation and reorganization of institutional employees and for the waivers necessary to circumvent civil service hiring agreements and hiring freezes. Moreover, through private contracting mechanisms, authorities could stretch limited funds by approving contract budgets or fees built upon staff pay and benefit levels below current civil service levels and by avoiding costly institutional staffing and facility regulations. Essentially, public officials were rejecting the institutional method of service delivery and the rigidity of the state bureaucracy and personnel system in favor of smaller, more flexible, community-based arrangements.

Developmental disabilities authorities also hoped that private contracting would help them to shape the service system insofar as services provided and persons served and to hold providers accountable for their performance. While many program administrators had considerable information on institutional expenses, few could claim much programmatic accountability or control over the nature and quality of services provided. Most institutions operated with considerable autonomy.

ACCOUNTING FOR PERFORMANCE

In spite of the purported interest in holding providers accountable through the contracting mechanism, advances have been slow. In most states service contracts do little more than require that some number of persons be served and that a particular quantity of service be provided at a specified rate or for a fixed sum. A few states go further targeting priority services and subpopulations. One of the most dramatic ways in which such targeting has occurred has been to enhance the development of services for people leaving institutions. Under these arrangements, states contract to pay for community-based residential and day programs and other community support services only if all or a substantial number of persons receiving such services have been previously institutionalized or are at risk of institutionalization (Bradley, Ashbaugh, Harder, & Stoddard, 1984).

Many reasons have been advanced for the sluggish move to more demanding contracts and performance monitoring procedures. One explanation is that the number of providers willing and able to serve individuals with disabilities at a price the state is willing or able to afford is often limited. This in turn constrains the leverage of the public agency to demand high standards of performance. Along the same line, it has been observed that the ability of public monitors to influence performance through the contract mechanism has become increasingly difficult as the political strength of the contractors has grown by virtue of number, experience, and political organization. Still others maintain that authorities do not know what to demand in the way of performance. They "lack a coherent model to say what they are trying to do" (Massachusetts Taxpayers Foundation, Inc., 1980, p. 20).

Probably the explanation most heard is that states have been slow to adapt their monitoring and control mechanisms from those suited to direct service management to those suited to indirect service administration or contract management (Benton, Feild, & Miller, 1978; Harney, 1986; Massachusetts Taxpayers Foundation, Inc., 1980; Wedel, 1976). The result is what Sharkansky (1980) called system "incoherence":

the lack of central records indicating resources or personnel involved in contracting; . . . the lack of program integration [with] different pieces of related activities . . . in the hands of different agencies and contractors; contractor . . . autonomy regarding efforts to standardize reporting or service delivery; the lack of central control over service quality, cost overruns, and prices charged to clients; and overloaded review units incapable of functioning as intended. (p. 23–24)

Often it is in reaction to criticism and pressure from state legislators and others looking for more system coherence and provider accountability that many state developmental disabilities officials have moved abruptly to strengthen their centralized contract management systems by imposing more contract provisions (controls) and information requirements. In so doing, as Sharkansky observed, such officials inadvertently negate the primary advantage of contract mechanisms—flexibility, and thus, the principal value of contracting as a management tool. The need for flexibility is particularly important in the developmental disabilities field where the need to provide services tailored to the special needs of individuals is an article of faith. Yet centralized performance management systems are characterized by a predominance of fiscal as opposed to program performance measures and by limited sets of uniform (as opposed to individualized) performance indices.

Fiscal Performance Orientation

In most states, contractors are still required to report expenditures and to submit to detailed audits. These data are compiled and used to indicate and inform the setting of payment rates and to single out less efficient providers to scrutinize and more efficient providers to emulate. It is, in fact, in the fiscal area of performance measurement that states have attained the most sophistication. Performance measures indicating relative efficiency (e.g., dollars per client or dollars per unit of service) predominate.

The consequent worry and understandable source of contractor resistance to such performance system measures in the labor-intensive developmental disabilities services arena is the absence of more sensitive, programmatic performance measures. The inexorable drive for efficiency can lead to the thinning of service staff to the point where the amount of staff time available per client is no longer of value and may become so diluted as to threaten client health and well-being.

Furthermore, no matter how creative and sophisticated centralized rate setting and payment schemes may be, they are inherently inflexible. They involve categorizing clients and/or providers with different rates or payments set for each category. While these rates may represent the best possible uniform or average rates for some groups of clients or providers, the use of such categorical funding schemes cannot approach the efficiency possible through individualized funding. This is particularly true where funds are not bound to particular services but are free to commit to whatever complement of services are the most practical and reasonable for an individual client (Ashbaugh & Nerney, in press).

In fact, a number of developmental disabilities authorities are now moving toward more individualized, program driven funding arrangements. The Individualized Supported Living Arrangements program in North Dakota operates with no funding rates or caps. The funding for each person is decided on an individual assessment and program plan that specifies service setting, levels of intervention, and other necessary services (Smith & Aderman, 1987). The Personal Care Alternatives program in Colorado also exemplifies an individualized approach to performance assessment and funding. Using Medicaid (Title XIX) Waiver funds, programs are designed based on each individual's habilitation plan with group home arrangements generally giving way to host homes, roommate/peer supervision, and supported apartment assistance programs. This frees up monies for direct service that would otherwise be spent for facility development and maintenance (Ferguson, 1987). Recognizing the efficiency afforded through more flexible, individualized service contracts, the Colorado Division of Developmental Disabilities has proposed to move away from its centralized contracting system that concentrates on line item expenditure controls and elaborate rate setting schemes. It has been proposed that plans allocate funds to the 20 community centered boards around the state that will, for the first time, have the flexibility to establish more client-centered, locally attuned service contracts.

Uniform Versus Individualized Performance Measures

Where efforts have been made to incorporate standard performance measures as part of provider contracts, they have typically met with strong resistance from contractors (Miller & Wilson, 1981). Much of this resistance can be traced to the nature of the performance measures proposed by the "central office" (Massachusetts Council of Human Service Providers, Inc., 1988). They are predominantly nomothetic outcome measures applied uniformly to all clients regardless of their relative potential to change as a result of the particular service intervention. The inclusion of minimum outcome expectations as part of performance contracts might be appropriate where the outcome is of overriding concern. For instance, an employment program may reasonably be expected to secure some minimum number of jobs for clients at a reasonable cost or it is not worth funding irrespective of local circumstances and client potential. Then too, such measures may be appropriate for use at national and possibly state levels where the degree of aggregation is sufficient to overcome differences among providers in terms of the individual potential of their clients. It might also be appropriate to use nomothetic measures in cases where service outcome is relatively independent of client potential. Still, it is difficult to think of human services where the central objective does not involve helping a client change his or her situation and where this change is not, by and large, contingent on the clients' particular situation and potential for change. Thus, for purposes of specific provider performance assessment, many such measures are inherently invalid and unreliable.

In contrast, idiographic outcome measures are by definition sensitive to individual client potentials and situations. There are two basic types of idiographic measures or measurement systems: goal oriented and problem oriented. Goal-oriented measures define the expected outcome in terms of goal achievement; problem-oriented measures define the expected outcome in terms of solutions to specific problems. The primary value of these methods lies in the ability to draw provider and client attention to the achievement of goals or targets agreed upon for problem elimination. With microcomputer-based management systems, the achievement of individual service plan objectives can be easily scored and accumulated. However, the downside of idiographic measures, particularly as centralized performance measures, is their susceptibility to manipulation or gaming. Contractors might be led to document easily achievable objectives or to concentrate on clients or on areas of performance where success is most easily demonstrated (Bradley, 1980).

The Massachusetts Office of Purchased Services (OPS), in its plan for a performance contracting system, allows for both nomothetic and idiographic measures:

> Performance objectives and the criteria to be used to evaluate actual performance must be clearly articulated in RFPs [Request for Proposals] and in contracts. If outcome objectives prove too difficult to articulate, process benchmarks can be emphasized. If quantifiable evaluation criteria are elusive, subjective assessment by department program staff or independent experts will have to suffice. If agreement on standards for programs cannot be reached, then the focus should be on individual client service plans, education plans, etc. Any attention paid to performance, however imprecise or subjective, will be an improvement. (Nessen, 1988, p. 31)

The Massachusetts Council of Human Service Providers is concerned that "because of the individualized nature of the plans and the lack of standardization, it may not be appropriate to compare programs on their [relative progress in achieving service plan objectives]" (Massachusetts Council of Human Service Providers, Inc., 1988, p. 16). Still they are open to the possibility of comparing progress in one program from one year to the next.

CONCLUSION

Most activities reported under the name of performance contracting are actually concerned with the development and implementation of centralized information and control systems. These systems are designed to improve the management of service delivery systems, which in most states happen to be comprised largely of private contractors. In part, they are performance information systems designed to make the delivery system more coherent and manageable from the perspective of public authorities and concerned policymakers. They are also resource allocation systems governing the distribution of funds to contractors along some rational lines.

There has been some success and little disagreement with the use of these systems to inform management and even to target priority clients and services for funding. However, attempts to allocate funds to contractors based on centralized measures of client outcomes have been strongly resisted, slowing the move to full-fledged performance contracting systems appreciably. The point of contention is not with the need to account for performance. The need for standard sets of performance indicators that provide a comprehensive, coherent picture of the service delivery system and contractor performance and that inform system level funding decisions is generally recognized and accepted. The main current of opposition comes from attempts to set up contract management systems that would evaluate, reward, and sanction individual providers on the basis of some limited set of uniform client performance measures. The use of centralized client performance measures, insensitive to local circumstances and individual potentials, gives rise to legitimate questions concerning validity, reliability, and fairness. Moreover, they effectively limit managerially valued discretion. Case managers and local contract managers would be forced to work with contractors driven by measures, only some of which make sense.

Centralized measures of performance, at least those tied to rewards or sanctions, should find their way into contracts only at the discretion of informed contract managers. The contract managers might also include other performance provisos as needed to punctuate or reinforce the importance of particular aspects of provider performance. For example, in the case of a sheltered employment program, one might identify particular clients by name or a minimum number of clients to be placed in supported employment by the end of the contract period. Similarly, a contract with a residential provider might stipulate that the program graduate a particular resident or a minimum number of higher functioning residents from a group home to a minimally supervised arrangement. The contract manager might as easily elect to request performance information only and impose no requirements. This approach would be appropriate where there are too many unknowns to set reasonable performance requirements or where the contract manager senses that the imposition of such requirements would undercut already healthy patterns of provider performance and cooperation.

Most efforts to develop performance contracting systems are tied to central office funding approaches already in existence; they emphasize uniform measures and centralized control. Carried too far, these systems can override the primary virtue of contracting flexibility, giving case managers, providers, and others too little discretion in formulating individualized service plans and performance contracts. A performance contracting system must honor two masters—policymakers, who must have the information and leverage necessary to shape the system of service delivery, and contract managers and case managers, who must retain the flexibility necessary to arrange service contracts that make sense considering individual needs and local circumstances. One need not and should not be satisfied at the expense of the other.

REFERENCES

Ashbaugh, J., & Nerney, T. (in press). Findings and implications of a study of the costs of providing residential and support services to individuals with mental retardation in two substate regions of the United States. *Mental Retardation.*

Benton, B., Feild, T., & Miller, R. (1978). *Social services, federal legislation vs. state implementation.* Washington, DC: The Urban Institute.

Bradley, V.J. (1980). Mental disabilities service: Maintenance of public accountability in a privately operated system. In J. Bevilacqua (Ed.), *Changing government policies for the mentally retarded* (pp. 193–198). Cambridge, MA: Ballinger Publishing Company.

Bradley, V.J., Ashbaugh, J.W., Harder, P.W., & Stoddard, S. (1984). *Assessing and enhancing the quality of services: A guide for the human services field.* Boston: Human Services Research Institute.

Ferguson, L.R. (1987, December). *Personal care alternatives program review.* Denver: Colorado Association for Retarded Citizens and Colorado Association of Community-Centered Boards.

Harney, D.F. (1986, December). A purchasing agent's view of privatization. *Public Management, 68*(12), 16–18.

Massachusetts Council of Human Service Providers, Inc. (1988, September). *Performance-based contracting: A position paper.* Boston: Author.

Massachusetts Taxpayers Foundation, Inc. (1980). *Purchase of service: Can state government gain control?* Boston: Author.

Miller, S., & Wilson, N. (1981). The case for performance contracting. *Administration in Mental Health, 8,* 3.

Nessen, P. (1988). *Progress report to the house and senate committees on ways and means.* Boston: Executive Office for Administration and Finance, Office of Purchased Services.

Sharkansky, I. (1980, Winter). Government contracting. *State Government,* 22–27.

Smith, G., & Aderman, S. (1987). *Community management initiative: Paying for services.* Alexandria, VA: National Association of State Mental Retardation Program Directors.

Terrell, P. (1979, March). Private alternatives to public human services administration. *Social Services Review, 53,* 57–73.

Wedel, K.R. (1976, March). Government contracting for purchase of service. *Social Work, 21*(2), 101–105.

chapter 10 ————

The Role of
Quality Assurance
in Public Agencies

—————————— *Lyle D. Wray* ——————————

Millions of Americans with developmental disabilities and their families depend upon publicly provided services to meet their needs. Social values and a vision of what is both possible and desirable underlie the continuing development of standards for performance that govern these programs. Protection from harm; provision of food, clothing, and shelter; and provision of education and support are only some of the critical areas around which quality assurance standards have been developed within federal and state laws.

Properly designed and implemented, quality assurance systems should involve a continuous quest for information to enhance and improve services. New ways can be found to better serve persons with developmental disabilities by using data to provide for corrective action to remedy identified departures from performance standards, by reducing barriers to effective corrective action, by providing incentives for attaining quality targets, and by fostering innovation and creativity.

This chapter discusses the ways in which quality assurance data can be made useful to program administrators and the ways in which data are linked

The author wishes to express appreciation for helpful comments from Drs. Colleen Wieck, Marcia Tippery, and William Fink.

to public policy-making activities. Although this chapter is primarily directed to issues of internal organizational management within programs or agencies, similar organizational issues apply within federal and state government agencies as well as in the public policy arena.

THE CONTEXT FOR QUALITY ASSURANCE

Quality assurance may be viewed as an agency management activity in which standards are identified or clarified; methods of monitoring are established and applied to assess compliance with these standards; and data are gathered, organized, and acted upon in order to bring actual performance closer to conformity with the identified standards. Quality assurance information arising from these activities can play an important role in a number of areas, such as the processes of policy development, managerial actions, and consumer influence and choice. Targets of change resulting from quality assurance information are varied and include issues in agency management, individual program plans within existing service models, development of a new service model, and changes in funding systems or models of service.

There are a variety of approaches to quality assurance in the developmental disabilities field. These approaches vary depending on what is being assessed and on who, whether professional, parent, or consumer, is carrying out the monitoring activity. In the developmental disabilities field, Bersani (1988) identified eight forms of quality assurance: 1) certification for funding based on federal standards (e.g., standards developed by the Health Care Financing Administration [HCFA] for Intermediate Care Facilities for the Mentally Retarded [ICF/MR], 2) licensure by state departments under established standards for program licensing, 3) accreditation by organizations such as the Accreditation Council on Services to People with Developmental Disabilities (ACDD) and the Commission on Accreditation of Rehabilitation Facilities (CARF), 4) case management oversight, 5) peer review under which reciprocal review arrangements are worked out with other programs, 6) internal review in which the agency reviews its own programs on a regular basis, 7) consumer review by recipients of services, and 8) family/citizen monitoring involving citizen-based visits and a protocol for observation.

Each approach to quality assurance produces information on the degree in which a program or service conforms to identified performance standards. This chapter examines a variety of approaches for making the best use of information derived from the various approaches cited by Bersani. Discussed first is the context in which this type of information is used, and second, a number of steps are recommended that managers of programs or agencies can take to maximize the utility of such information.

Quality assurance activities operate squarely within the public policy context. It is important to understand this in order to identify and address the external relationships surrounding internal quality assurance efforts. These external relationships may influence the development and implementation of quality assurance systems and the rigor in which quality assurance information is transformed into improved practices.

Social policy has been defined as a goal-oriented statement that identifies an existing social problem or need and specifies a future condition in which the problem is reduced or eliminated (Wiener, 1978). A statement of social policy generally leads to one or more sets of activities or programs that are designed to reduce or eliminate the problem. At a broad level, social policies may be viewed as "standards of performance."

To understand the analogies between social policy and quality assurance and their interrelationships, it may be helpful to refer to a model outlined by Chapman (1970). This model for social policy (see Figure 1) identifies six components and three feedback loops that make up the public policy process. These components are: society's values, public needs, public policy, program objectives, practices, and program outcomes. Critical feedback loops extend in three areas: program feedback from program outcomes to program objectives, general public feedback from program outcomes to public needs, and public feedback relating to explicit objectives that address means and costs in relation to program outcomes and society's values. In a sense, the activities of social policy formation and quality assurance are similar in that standards are set, information is assembled comparing standards and actual performance, and corrective action is taken.

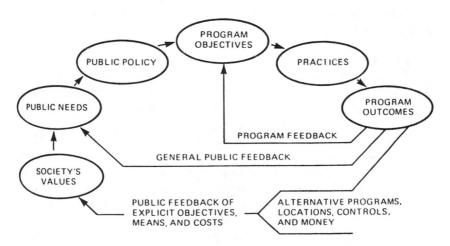

Figure 1. Model for social policy. (From Atkinson, Hargreaves, & Horowitz [Eds.]. [1978]. Evaluation of human services programs. p. 175; Orlando, FL: Academic Press; reprinted by permission.)

Quality assurance operates within a dynamic context of broad social policy that should be understood as monitoring systems that are developed and put in place. There is a link between quality assurance and the social policy field. Quality assurance information can play a role in assisting the public to determine whether a program meets society's values and whether the value of the results equals the money spent. Providing feedback on the effectiveness of programs to the general public as a means of maintaining or generating support cannot be underestimated as one major use of quality assurance data. Failure to do so can contribute to a more gradual erosion of public support for programs. A proactive approach to sharing quality assurance data with the public can form a useful bulwark against erosion of public support. As such, quality assurance is carried on within a complex public policy context and the generation and use of information on programs can have a broader significance beyond program or agency activities. The use of information within the public policy context is another impetus for the development of quality assurance systems.

ACTING ON QUALITY ASSURANCE INFORMATION

"Information" may be succinctly defined as any difference which makes a difference in some later event. (Bateson, 1972)

The suggestions that follow were generated by the author's experiences during the 1980s while serving in a variety of positions representing different vantage points on the system of services to individuals with developmental disabilities. The author's perspective has emerged from the diverse roles held within the service system.

One position held was that of director of mental retardation services for a province in Canada, encompassing both community and institutional services. Another position held was residential program administrator within a state operated facility serving persons with developmental disabilities and a mental health diagnosis. The position of federal court monitor for *Welsch v. Likins* (1974), held for 3½ years, involved oversight of 111 provisions of a consent decree covering all state institutional as well as community services for class members with developmental disabilities. The role as state director of quality assurance for the Minnesota Department of Human Services included responsibility for a 63 component plan covering state operated institutions. Finally, the author has served as county human services director and county administrator for 250,000 persons in Minnesota. The recommendations on generating and using quality assurance information derive, in part, from these varying roles and perspectives. A number of steps are suggested to use the information generated by quality assurance mechanisms to improve services. These steps include: commitment to quality assurance, external pressure and visibility, integration with management control systems, routinization of quality assurance, injection of state-of-the-art knowledge, incentives for action, graphic summaries, packaging of information, appropriate timing of information delivery, skills in problem analysis, and removal of barriers to effective action.

Commitment To Quality Assurance

Support is critical for quality assurance to succeed, not only from the most senior levels of management but from all staff in the organization. If discrepancies are to be promptly remedied, there must be a demonstrated willingness to take issues to the highest level necessary. If there is a lack of commitment, obstacles to implementing change in response to quality assurance information are not overcome, and agency staff may reduce the vigor of their efforts.

Commitment is shown in policy statements and practices of the organization, in the budget priorities, in time priorities of senior management, and in the structure of recognition and rewards within the organization. Commitment forms the foundation for effective use of quality assurance information. It is also important in another respect. If leaders or managers are showing commitment to quality assurance, they often need to build the capacity of an organization to respond to information. The "organizational culture" is built upon what is valued and how change is addressed, how messengers of bad news about the organization are treated, how bad news about quality is acted upon, and how employees are treated during change. These are some of the areas worthy of management attention and effort. While the overall problem-solving abilities of staff and overall agency development are beyond the scope of this chapter, they are likely to be critical for effective utilization of quality assurance information.

There is considerable literature for management on shaping the development of organizations and organizational culture that might be of use in building agency capacity to respond to quality assurance information. Strategies of organizational development may vary from individual skill building and supervision to more general approaches for making an agency more receptive to change. An effective quality assurance program is a prerequisite for any effective organization. Albrecht (1983), for example, proposed a comprehensive strategy for organizational development that could complement quality assurance systems.

External Pressure and Visibility

Quality assurance often needs an outside dimension to support or supplement internal efforts. State agencies such as an ombudsman's office, quality assurance commissions, and consumer advocacy groups illustrate this idea. External systems of quality assurance such as licensing or case management have support from statutes (or regulations) or from a professional community. In addition to their statutory authority, these systems can offer a "bully pulpit" from which issues may be addressed and made highly visible. External groups generally have the flexibility needed to move quickly to raise certain issues that would tend to be buried within organizations.

Since the quality assurance role often involves bearing bad news to managers, internal monitors may require that external support be maintained. Although, ideally, quality assurance mechanisms should generate good news and rewards for exemplary performance, often quality assurance systems—because of the bias built into their design—generate more negative information. Organizations that are not able to function effectively in a problem-solving mode or that employ blaming and scapegoating or information suppression may have a greater need for effective external pressure to underpin internal quality assurance efforts.

In the Minnesota case of *Welsch v. Likins* (1974), there were a number of instances in which the agency was able to use the external role as a platform to highlight serious departures from standards of performance agreed upon in a court sanctioned settlement. Publishing information in a report to the federal court on the proportion of state facility residents receiving psychotropic medications and their relative dosages reinforced an effort to ensure that minimal but effective dosages were provided. Publication of the levels of physical restraint and aversive interventions in various state facilities was followed by greater efforts on the part of the defendants to reduce these levels. Publication of information showing a considerable differential for local governments in the cost of services, with institutional services costing far less than community services, was followed by efforts to find new ways to fund community services.

Consumer advocates and other organizations can apply external pressure for quality services and activities. Consumer advocacy of individual and service system quality issues can offer considerable support for quality assurance functions through informal action, legislative influence, and/or court action. External monitoring and evaluation activities augment the impetus for change initiated by internal quality assurance efforts, sometimes in vitally important ways such as supporting the additional funding necessary to make improvements in the service system.

Integration with Management Control Systems

One of the critical aspects of the use of quality assurance information is that it should be integrated into the ongoing management systems within the agency. Perhaps the most critical aspect of the use of quality assurance information could be described as the three "Fs"—follow through, follow through, and follow through. In this way, data become information by making a difference in subsequent action (Bateson, 1972).

Systems that already exist within the agency should be utilized whenever possible to identify and to make needed changes in staff and managerial behavior. Quality assurance findings and recommended actions that are routinely integrated into position descriptions, annual plans, management objectives, and annual performance reviews of line managers can have a powerful influence on overall system performance.

One approach for integration is management-by-objectives systems that base quarterly goals in staff plans on changes resulting from quality assurance information. (For a general overview of management-by-objectives systems see Albrecht, 1978.) The paper burden of management-by-objectives systems may be minimized if goals are primarily focused on problem-solving and innovative aspects of the organization rather than on routines. By breaking down long-term goals into components of 90 day duration, for example, effective action is made more probable. Inserting the results of quality assurance systems into objectives set for managers, supervisors, and possibly direct service staff can be an effective foundation for an appropriate response to such data. The use of such integration systems recognizes the incremental nature of change in agencies, bounded by resource limits. In many cases, needed changes may take considerable time and require substantial coordination among various participants within an organization. (For a description of how management-by-objectives was linked to an evaluation system in a local government see Elliott and Syfert, 1988.)

A performance review system of employees at all levels is another approach that can be used to support the quality assurance effort. Employee performance reviews should in turn conform with agency planning objectives. Together, all of these internal management systems can be focused to stimulate and coordinate needed systematic changes in staff behavior and improved program effectiveness over short or long periods of time.

Routinization of Quality Assurance

Efforts in monitoring and acting on quality assurance information need to be routinized with a schedule of activities that are tracked. Development of a workplan that identifies the elements to be monitored, defines the monitoring protocol, specifies a monitoring schedule, identifies responsible persons, and reviews dates is an effective first step in fostering compliance. The use of workplans also recognizes the incremental nature of change and the frequent need for coordination across a number of different organizational units. A workplan can also be an effective tool for coordination. It is desirable to build on this foundation to integrate both quality assurance and information resulting from the system into organizational routines and schedules.

Injection of State-of-the-Art Knowledge

Using leading consultants to challenge professionals to do better based on the results of quality assurance data can be a very positive experience, providing both greater motivation for change and providing greater capacity for devising effective solutions to program problems. Data showing that services are not effective should only be the beginning of a process for identifying problems, for generating alternatives, and for planning and implementing improved programs. As an example, a specialist can often be a useful catalyst in this process of devising nonaversive methods for minimizing self-destructive behavior. Such assistance can provide greater responsiveness to quality assurance information in situations where there is a highly specialized or rapidly evolving base of knowledge.

Incentives for Action

The current system of quality assurance is maintained largely through the use of punitive mechanisms geared to the individuals and programs whether through fines, license suspensions, or reprimands and dismissal. Over time, it may be possible to provide a more positive environment for quality assurance by seeking positive incentives for compliance that in turn might lead to greater use of quality assurance information rather than continuing to rely upon a largely punitive system.

Some of the potential steps include providing incentives for programs that show high levels of quality. A proposal has been made, for example, to provide differing levels of reimbursement to nursing homes depending upon the levels of outcomes achieved as shown in quality assurance information (Kane, Bell, Hosek, Riegler & Kane, 1983). While more research is needed on the selection, monitoring, and use of outcome data in reimbursement systems, this field holds promise for fostering creativity and innovation in meeting individual needs.

Less complex positive incentive arrangements could be as simple as lengthening licensing periods for providers who consistently earn high marks on licensing inspection surveys. To better focus limited resources in the licensing function, it might be appropriate to break the process into two stages. In the first stage, a screening for indicators that predict levels of quality could be completed. If these predictors warrant, a second stage of full review could follow. In this context, positive incentives need not use funds and should not adversely affect individuals being served if properly designed and carried out. Similar attention to focusing limited quality assurance resources within organizations may also be mounted. Incentives for effective response to quality assurance information or for achieving high levels of compliance is an area worthy of further investigation and careful application, both from the perspective of external regulatory agencies and internal management efforts.

Graphic Summaries

It is important to display quality assurance data in a form that decisionmakers can readily understand and use. If information is not readily accessible, it is unlikely to be used to remedy compliance issues.

Often organizing such data into graphs can be a useful tool. An approach to identifying key items of data that indicate how well an organization is performing is described by Neves, Wolf, and Benton (1986) with graphic presentations as a center piece of the management indicators strategy. The Washington State Department of Social and Health Services has published a monthly executive management summary report showing key management indicators of agency performance for a number of years. Dakota County, Minnesota, publishes a monthly management indicators report in the Human Services Division containing graphic summaries. In the developmental disabilities services section of this report, the number of persons remaining in state hospitals, the number of children living outside of family care, costs of several types of community-based services, and the number of persons in competitive employment are all graphed. The example presented in Figure 2

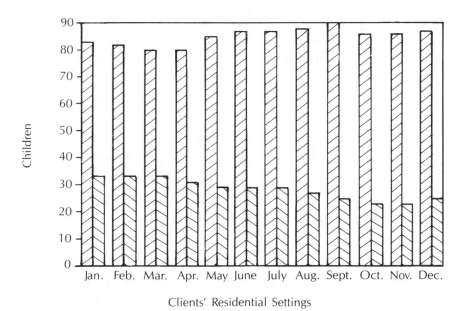

Clients' Residential Settings

Figure 2. Graphic summary of children residing in 24-hour out-of-home care facilities as compared to children residing in their family home. (▨ represents number of children at home, and ▧ represents number of children in placement.) (From Management indicators report, Dakota County. [1988, December]. Hastings, MN. p. 51; reprinted by permission.)

compares children living outside of family care to children living in their family home. The program objective is to maintain or reduce the number of children in long-term placement and to maintain or increase the number of children living at home.

Some concerns about quality assurance information are that the right data are used for decisionmakers, the data make sense, and the data are timely. Another key issue in the use of graphic information is the placement of target lines of performance that provides a standard against which to judge the information. For example, if the goal is to place three persons per month from institutional to community services, one approach would be to structure the graph showing a cumulative placement line of 36 placements per year against which actual monthly data would be plotted. Several other sources of standards for comparisons include performance of comparable agencies against the standard, data from the previous year or an average of a number of previous years against the standard, or performance levels promised within authorized budgets or service contracts against the standard. Providing graphic information on a regular basis sets an impetus for following through on corrective action to remedy problems. Since it has been said that the essence of judgment is comparison, it is very important to provide appropriate comparison with graphic information in addition to identifying the key indicators of performance in the quality assurance area.

Graphic summaries organize information in a manner that makes it easier for decisionmakers to respond, and as such, are an important component of an approach to making information useful. With the rapid rise of availability of microcomputers, graphic presentations are becoming easier to produce.

Packaging of Information

Elliott and Syfert (1988) concluded that "reports presented to decision makers [should be] clear, simple to read, and to the point, concentrating on findings and recommendations. . . . long, complex reports are not read and are therefore not as valuable as summary reports." Reams of unread computer printouts serve little function, and if written reports are to be made, they should generally be short and to the point. Writing short reports that capture the essence of a large amount of data requires substantial effort.

Timing of Information Delivery

In the context of city management, Elliott and Syfert (1988) concluded that ". . . it is more important to have *some* information at the time a decision needs to be made than it is to have a comprehensive evaluation report *after* the decision was made." This is also likely to be true in the area of quality assurance. Often, waiting for complete, highly accurate information may substantially slow the process of improving programs. However, acting on incomplete or inaccurate data may lead to unproductive directions. Timeliness and completeness of information, therefore, must be balanced within a system. Furthermore, concerns over the accuracy of information must be balanced against the level of resources available in the system to make needed changes. These are several important judgments that should be made in dealing with quality assurance information.

Skills in Problem Analysis

Once quality assurance information shows a discrepancy between a standard and actual performance, the next critical step is to identify the nature of the problem and an appropriate course of corrective action. It is often not an easy task to identify the appropriate strategy for change since the appropriate response may vary from a simple to a complex one. A variety of strategies may be appropriate for removing barriers and providing facilitating factors and incentives for change. Staff training and development are likely to be an integral component of many action plans. Mager and Pipe (1970), for example, offered a problem-solving algorithm related to individual performance that might be applicable in organizational settings. It is important to carefully review quality assurance information and to strive to correctly identify both the problem being faced and the most effective strategies to rectify the problem.

Barriers to Effective Action

There are many organizational barriers to responding effectively to quality assurance information. In the developmental disabilities field a major obstacle is the paper burden created by requirements for written documentation. A careful analysis needs to be made of ways to minimize the paper "blizzard," and alternatives, such as using laptop computers, should be explored. A demonstration project is underway in a number of Minnesota counties to provide case managers with laptop computers to more effectively meet their responsibilities in leading team meetings and managing individual service arrangements (Dakota County Human Services, 1988). Technological innovation can be put to work to remove this and other barriers as problems are analyzed and as resources are made available.

CONCLUSION

In order for quality assurance information to be used effectively, many requirements must be met. An external platform from which to disseminate information on broad system solutions and to support internal quality assurance efforts can be vitally important. Effective use of quality assurance information usually requires that attention be paid to the capacity of an organization to respond to information, that consequences for performance be provided, and that the system be installed incrementally so that needed changes do occur over time. The synthesis of data for decision-making in graphic or other summary form and with a clear focus on actual changes required in agency staff behavior is critical. It is necessary to follow through with changes by using all the tools available to the organization. At a broader level, managers have a responsibility to create a climate for change in their organization. Providing leadership by describing a vision for the organization in terms of quality services and creating an organizational climate in which it is possible to seek out and to build upon potentially threatening information is a major challenge.

Beyond specification of some of the key requirements of installing a quality assurance system, it is possible to speculate on the ideal role that such a function should play. Quality assurance may be carried out in different ways depending upon the size of the program or agency in which it is performed. It may be an additional responsibility of a manager in a small operation or the function of an entire department in a larger agency.

When functioning effectively, the quality assurance role of an agency is to appropriately set or interpret standards of performance, set up data collection methods that are effective and efficient in monitoring performance against standards, organize and interpret quality assurance data in a clear and informative manner so that decisionmakers and other staff can readily use it to make needed changes and to correct discrepancies, provide assistance in the formulation of action plans based upon the data, and design and maintain systems that track the results of interventions and assess and report on overall compliance with standards over time.

To establish and maintain an effective quality assurance system, a good deal of clarification or development of standards is usually necessary as a first step. Staff training in data collection and summarization is often needed. Managers are likely to need training in understanding the data in order to use it effectively. They may also need training on how to analyze the underlying problem that is reflected by a performance discrepancy, as well as how to identify an intervention or package of interventions that are likely to be effective in remedying the discrepancy. Is the problem that staff lack knowledge of a potentially effective procedure, is it that staff have failed to implement programs altogether, or is it some combination? The intervention strategies may vary from seeking technical assistance from a specialist in a program area, to better staff training and supervision, to imparting necessary knowledge and skills, depending upon the results of the problem assessment.

As discussed, steps to ensure the effective use of quality assurance information cut across many aspects of agencies providing services and these steps are dependent upon and mutually reinforce effective management practices. The challenge is to work toward a quality assurance program within an effective organization by using a variety of tools at the disposal of leaders and managers. These facts vary from technology to human relations in which a clear vision is needed to better meet the needs of the individuals and families being served.

REFERENCES

Albrecht, K. (1978). *Successful management by objectives: An action manual.* Englewood Cliffs, NJ: Prentice-Hall.

Albrecht, K. (1983). *Organization development: A total systems approach to positive change in any business organization.* Englewood Cliffs, NJ: Prentice-Hall.

Atkinson, C.C., Hargreaves, W.A., & Horowitz, M.J. (1978). *Evaluation of human service programs.* Orlando, FL: Academic Press.

Bateson, G. (1972). *Steps to an ecology of mind.* New York: Ballantine Books.

Bersani, H. (1988, October). Issues in quality assurance in residential settings. *TASH Newsletter, 14*(10).

Chapman, R.L. (1970). Improving driver licensing programs. *Behavior research in highway safety, 1*(3), 172–179.

Dakota County. (1988, December). *Management indicator report.* Hastings, MN, p. 51.

Dakota County Human Services. (1988). *Microcomputer case management preliminary evaluation.* St. Paul, MN: State Planning Agency, Developmental Disabilities Council.

Elliott, N.C., & Syfert, P.A. (1988). Local government evaluation in an executive environment. In C.G. Wyer & H.P. Hatry (Eds.), *Timely, low-cost evaluation in the public sector.* New Directions for Program Evaluation, no. 38. San Francisco: Jossey-Bass.

Kane, R.L., Bell, R.M., Hosek, S.D., Riegler, S.Z., & Kane, R.L. (1983). *Outcome-based reimbursement for nursing home care.* Report prepared for the National Center for Health Services Research (R-3092-NCHSR). Santa Monica, CA: Rand Corporation.

Mager, R.F., & Pipe, P. (1970). *Analyzing performance problems or 'you really oughta wanna'.* Belmont, CA: Fearon Publishers, Inc.

Management indicators report, Dakota County. (1988, December). Hastings, MN, p. 51.

Neves, C.M.P., Wolf, J.F., & Benton, B.B. (1986). The use of management indicators in monitoring the performance of human services agencies. In J.S. Wholey, M.A. Abramson, & C. Bella Vista (Eds.), *Performance and credibility: Developing excellence in public non-profit organizations.* Lexington, MA: Lexington Books.

Washington State Department of Social and Health Services. *Executive Management Summary Report.* Olympia, WA: Office of Research and Data Analysis, Planning, Evaluation, and Professional Development.

Welsch v. Likins, 373 F. Supp. 487 (D. Minn., 1974).

Wiener, M.E. (1978). Application of organization and systems theory to human services reform. *Share Human Services Monograph Series,* (Whole No. 6).

chapter 11 _____

The Role of
Service Providers
in Quality Assurance

_____ *Derrick F. Dufresne* _____

The issue of quality assurance is widely discussed. Often this topic is looked at from the viewpoint of external monitoring processes that assist to ensure the quality of life for people with developmental disabilities. The provider is seen as the recipient or subject of this information that highlights both strengths and weaknesses in the service delivery system. The role of such quality assurance systems is to ascertain whether the services provided are in keeping with the mission statement, public declarations, and promulgated standards.

Often overlooked, however, is the importance of making quality assurance mechanisms and approaches responsive to needs of providers. There has been little discussion about the benefit that providers enjoy for implementing quality assurance programs. Until this issue receives full review, one key component in establishing a good quality assurance system is missing.

OVERVIEW

As executive director of New Concepts, a community residential program of services for individuals with developmental disabilities in the state of Wisconsin, this author is fully aware of the benefits to providers. New Concepts operates by contracting with purchasers (counties) who pay for delivery of high quality, cost-effective services to people referred to the program. In exchange for the dollars received through the contractual process, New Concepts must provide assurances to the counties, who in turn provide assurances to the state of Wisconsin, that the services they are paying for are in fact received. Depending upon the type of program (residential group home, apartment, foster care), various types of regulation, licensing, and quality assurance mechanisms are required. All of these different types of services have different external quality assurance mechanisms that are put in place by the purchaser. In addition, New Concepts has put into place its own internal quality assurance processes that differ greatly from the external reviews and mechanisms.

There are several important distinctions between internal and external quality assurance that need to be explored. While on the surface it may appear that external quality assurance mechanisms are the most valid and provide a greater degree of oversight than internal systems, this is not always the case. Experience shows that much of what is touted as both "quality" and "assurance" in external systems is neither quality nor assurance. Instead, standards and regulations often set up *minimum* guidelines that providers must meet to continue to receive funding.

This approach allows providers to make one of two mistakes. First, if there are no deficiencies found on the external survey of quality assurance, providers can be lulled into believing they have quality programs. Second, providers may assume that external quality assurance mechanisms are irrelevant and therefore tend to ignore the outcomes. In reality, provider responses are probably somewhere in the middle. The critical fact remains that many current quality assurance mechanisms are woefully inadequate and, because they are standards-based, often miss the point. By focusing on *standards* (i.e., input and process indicators) rather than *outcomes* (i.e., increased productivity, autonomy, and integration), they are neither responsive to consumers' needs and wishes, nor do they affect the ability of the provider to meet such needs. Thus, when quality assurance is said to meet provider needs, there is a danger in assuming that if it meets the agency's needs, it is also meeting the individual consumer's needs. Simply put, the purpose of the agency is to bring about results for people with developmental disabilities. Therefore, any discussion of meeting provider needs should presume that consumer needs are inextricably related. The remainder of this chapter outlines some of these issues from the provider's perspective and discusses ways in which quality assurance mechanisms can be beneficial to providers of services.

THE IMPORTANCE OF MISSION

One of the emerging concepts in the developmental disabilities field is the notion that people can and should speak and advocate on their own behalf. This is evident in the growth of such self-advocacy groups as People First and

Speaking for Ourselves (see Chapters 3 and 4, this volume). In addition, it is becoming more common for consumers to speak at conventions on their own behalf and sit as representatives on boards.

While in principle most providers welcome this development, in more candid moments, many would admit that it is sometimes disconcerting, if not downright irritating, to have consumers criticize them for not providing what they really want. This highlights one of the major areas that providers must address in establishing quality assurance guidelines. Often there are times when one person tells another what he or she wants when in reality that person doesn't want it. For example, a wife may tell her husband that he needs to lose a little weight but he may not want to. As a result, the wife can say or do little to motivate her husband to do things that she says. This difference causes dissonance in discussions with people and creates varying levels of expectations.

In providing supports to people with disabilities, it has been the author's experience that providers many times do the same thing to their consumers. People with disabilities are often regarded as if they are a homogeneous group and not individuals. (This author finds himself guilty—even in this chapter.) While one type of service may truly enhance the quality of one consumer's life, the very same approach may be inadequate for another consumer in that same program. In order to deliver quality services, the provider must never lose sight of the individual being served. One way of making sure this happens is to develop provider-based, internal quality assurance systems.

Therefore, it is important for the provider to answer the question: *What is the purpose of this business?* Why does the agency receive money and why is it still in existence? The driving force of any agency concerned with quality of life must be its mission statement. The mission statement must define why the business operates and address quality of life issues. The personhood, dignity, and personal choices of consumers must be taken into account when determining the mission statement. After the agency has decided on its mission, the next step is building ownership of the mission throughout the agency. Until this ownership of the agency's mission and principles is clearly articulated, it is not really possible to set internal agency standards of excellence or to clearly enunciate expectations of the role of staff. In addition, without such attention to these details, it is virtually impossible to determine whether or not the agency is providing quality services *from the viewpoint of the consumer.* Ultimately, any quality assurance mechanism put in place by the provider must make the consumer perspective paramount.

THE ROLE OF INTERNAL AND EXTERNAL QUALITY ASSURANCE

As previously mentioned, almost every provider must meet some sort of regulations, licensing requirements, and in some cases, accreditation standards in order to continue to receive funding. These are all external quality assurance mechanisms. The first two mechanisms tend to be state or federal minimum requirements that assure that there is some sort of a "floor" that services will not fall below. Accreditation, in most cases, is a voluntary effort on the part of an agency to do more than the minimum. In fact, most accreditation standards profess to be the highest award that an agency can receive.

Accreditation certainly has its place in quality assurance. It can be responsive to providers' needs as part of a total system of quality assurance that includes both external and internal assurances. However, accreditation in whatever form should not be used by a provider as a badge to wear or a plaque to display signifying the achievement of the highest plateau.

Providers can fall into the accreditation trap and believe that if they are accredited, they are meeting the needs of those they serve to the greatest extent possible. It may be possible for accreditation to be responsive to providers' needs, and yet the aforementioned issues of quality of life for the consumer may not be fully addressed.

How can this happen? It is possible for the Accreditation Council on Services for People with Developmental Disabilities (ACDD) and the Commission on Accreditation of Rehabilitation Facilities (CARF) to fully accredit both a 600 bed institution and a two person home using the same tool. Accreditation, while speaking to the values of normalization and community integration, still has not come to grips with the fundamental issue that the same quality of life cannot exist for a consumer in a 600 bed institution as for a consumer in a two person program. Thus, as long as both of these programs continue to be accredited using the same mechanism, providers will mistakenly believe that accreditation is not only responsive to their needs but embodies the most current values of service delivery. Whether it be through licensing, regulation, or accreditation, providers should receive assurances that the following needs will be met by the external review process.

Standards Should Be Outcome-Oriented

It is not the role of external reviewers to dictate the process by which services are delivered. Such prescriptive process standards tend to be geared to the "composite" persons with developmental disabilities. They reward standardization and require an array of services whether clients need them or not. Furthermore, they reward paper compliance that can result in a mad rush to spruce up the program and to ensure paperwork is caught up in the days and hours before a survey is to be conducted. These standards are responsive to neither the provider's needs nor the needs of the individuals with disabilities.

By taking an outcome approach, the standards to be achieved clearly focus on the outcomes desired and not the processes to be used. This allows for individual agency creativity and assumes that approaches to quality assurance vary by size of agency, location of service (rural or urban), and other unique characteristics that do not lend themselves to a prescriptive approach to service delivery.

Standards Should Be Reviewed By Surveyors

Surveyors in the area of quality assurance can, at times, be incompetent and insensitive to the service delivery system. This author has found that the quality of a surveyor is directly related to the quality of the survey experience. Too little time and attention has been paid to the education, training, and support of the people who do quality assurance surveys. In some cases, it resembles the abused child who as an adult does the abusing. Many surveyors are overworked, underpaid, and receive little support. As a result, they sometimes take it out on the providers. Consumers clearly do not benefit from such behavior either.

Surveyors should be demanding and unyielding in the requirements for evidence that the quality of life for consumers is enriched by the provider's service delivery system. It has been this author's experience that some of the best surveyors are those that are the toughest in such areas of quality. They are surveyors who realize the importance of paperwork but who spend most of their time observing staff-consumer interactions, looking for evidence of community integration opportunities, and challenging providers to set even higher goals for the coming year.

Technical Assistance and Education Should Be Provided

Meaningful external quality assurance must document areas that providers meet or do not meet with regard to specific standards in a review of the agency. True quality of life for consumers is enhanced when the provider's opportunities for technical assistance and training explore new methodologies, ways of thinking, and various "cutting edge" approaches to service delivery.

One of the biggest obstacles for providers is that they are so busy *doing* that their knowledge may be frozen at a point some years earlier. Many providers forget that in this high-tech age, new discoveries are being made all the time. They may sometimes "con" themselves into believing that they are being paid to manage. This misstates the role of the provider. Training, technical assistance, and education can all help providers achieve a higher degree of sensitivity and knowledge about important concepts. Providers have a need to see that if they are committed to the highest quality services, then funds will be available to meet the needs identified.

It is frustrating for providers to attempt (and in many cases deliver) quality services and see no change in funds for the increased supports certain individuals need. New Concepts, along with other programs, has determined that an important element of the mission is to serve those individuals requiring more intensive supports. If somehow the enhanced quality of life for the individuals served does not translate into additional funding, providers often feel as if their efforts are unrewarded.

Increased funding alone is not the only indicator of support for quality. However, when purchasers endorse external quality assurance and state in their own principles the importance of normalization, community integration, and respect for the individual, it is ludicrous at best and hypocritical at worst to expect that providers can attain these high goals when they are not given the resources necessary to do the job.

Providers Need to Feel Respected

Most providers of services really do want what is best for persons with developmental disabilities. While providers may differ about proposed goals and, at times, the potential of the people being served, it is a valid assumption that they do have what is best for consumers in mind.

Providers often have disheartening and frustrating feelings that they are being clubbed into submission or that watchdogs are needed in every program to ensure that standards are maintained. They need to hear about the programs that are running well and the positive steps that have been taken as well as the mistakes, the gaps, and the problems that will inevitably exist.

Providers Should Welcome Parent/Citizen Monitoring

In addition to the traditional external quality assurance mechanisms (licensing, regulation, accreditation), a new development has emerged—parent/citizen monitoring. Parent/citizen monitoring has great potential for enhancing the quality of services; yet if not implemented well, it can be perceived by providers as another layer of regulation and as someone else telling them how to do their job.

The field of human services is a highly regulated industry, and such regulation appears to have increased. The federal government has deregulated certain industries, which has led to those industries making record profits. At the same time, regulations have increased tenfold in the field of human services while funding has been cut in some states. It certainly defies logic.

The desire for parents and citizens to take a more active role in the monitoring of services certainly has its advantages (see Bersani, Chapter 6, this volume). However, there are costs. This additional involvement requires extra staff time, issues of confidentiality are raised, and the desired outcome of such monitoring is in question. Candid discussions in which the providers and the monitors can discuss what each others' needs are and what their specific agendas are in such an effort are a necessary part of the process. By doing so, the quality of life for persons with developmental disabilities will certainly be enhanced, which is the ultimate goal of both parties.

Providers Need Assurance That the
Persons They Serve Are Not Overburdened By Regulations

It is the responsibility of regulators, licensors, and those doing accreditation and monitoring to ensure that their quality assurance reviews do not impinge upon the privacy rights and personal space of persons being served. While visiting Seguin Services, an agency serving those with developmental disabilities in suburban Chicago, this author had the following experience:

> While touring the facilities, several times we passed a woman who seemed to be troubled. The third time we passed, the woman asked, "Sue, are they going to come back and visit me?" Sue answered, "The survey is almost over. They should be out of your place tomorrow."

At that moment it was realized that this woman was distraught at the fact that there were surveyors coming into her home. She lived with two or three other women, and it was very upsetting to her to have these surveyors coming in and out of her home and being there at all hours observing her. Any quality assurance mechanism must respect the rights and dignity of persons with disabilities. It is perhaps an unalterable dichotomy that a place is called "home" and at the same time intruders are allowed in these people's lives.

INTERNAL PROVIDER QUALITY ASSURANCE MECHANISMS

There is a tendency to think that if external quality assurance mechanisms are made responsive to providers' needs then the task is finished. This, however, is only the beginning. The true test of a provider's commitment to quality assurance is not how well he or she does on external mechanisms, but what types of review processes he or she sets up internally.

There is no way that external quality assurance can achieve the depth and breadth of review that an agency's own system can achieve. Additionally, there is a tendency to think of external quality assurance as a goal to achieve (i.e., accreditation), rather than as an ongoing process.

It is vitally important that providers set up their own internal quality assurance mechanisms. These mechanisms should be based on the provider's mission statement and should list specific operating principles that the provider wishes to see implemented throughout all of the services in the agency.

The ultimate responsibility in any agency for ensuring the quality of services lies with the executive director. The degree in which he or she espouses and lives the principles is the degree in which the agency will implement them. Phil Crosby (1984), author of *Quality Without Tears,* stated:

> As a general malaise sets in, someone in management decides that the employees need some better communication and support. This is usually a genuine approach with the theme of "making this a great place to work." A search is conducted for programs to use so that the employees can be trained to communicate.

The result of this search is "quality of work life" or "quality circles" or productivity improvement or something similar. There is nothing wrong with these programs except that they are all aimed at the bottom of the organization. (p. 15)

Crosby is saying that in order to achieve quality, the top management must be adamantly committed to ensuring that these principles of quality are in place throughout the organization.

At a conference of the National Association of Private Residential Resources, Jim Cashen (1988), who is involved in quality assurance efforts in the state of New York, described five qualities that he saw in exemplary quality programs. They provide an excellent yardstick for which agencies can implement quality assurance mechanisms. According to Cashen, exemplary programs are those programs that exhibit the following:

1. A clear mission statement
2. Staff who are immersed in the lives of the persons they serve
3. A high degree of staff-to-staff and staff-to-consumer interaction
4. Respect for cultivation of innovation, flexibility, and the encouragement of improvisation
5. An agency director who demonstrates personal leadership qualities, takes personal responsibility for the agency meeting its goals, and does not blame regulation and bureaucracy for shortcomings or inability to achieve goals

Cashen has succinctly defined qualities that all providers should strive for. These five qualities offer providers a measure in which to evaluate their abilities to implement their vision of quality for the people they serve.

PROVIDER BENEFITS OF QUALITY ASSURANCE MECHANISMS

How can quality assurance mechanisms benefit providers? Why should providers insist upon quality in the programs they offer to those whom they serve? The rewards for adherence to standards of excellence are many.

A Better Quality of Life for People with Developmental Disabilities

At its core, the issue for providers is to assist in enhancing the quality of life, personal choices, and community integration opportunities for the people they serve. The degree to which these goals are met cannot be determined by providers alone. Quality assurance mechanisms can assist by providing feedback regarding program strengths and weaknesses.

The importance of seeking feedback, direction, and involvement from people with developmental disabilities in reviewing the quality of programs cannot be stressed strongly enough. An entire chapter could be devoted to interdisciplinary team process and how it should be restructured to better listen to the needs and wants of the people served. Simply stated, at the heart of quality assurance is respect for the dignity, individuality, and uniqueness of each person who is receiving services.

Early Warning Signals That Provide Feedback About Programs

In addition to licensors, surveyors, and others who conduct formal review processes, there must be an opportunity for informal, unstructured feedback on the quality of services. Particularly in a decentralized environment where there are multiple sites at which individuals with developmental disabilities are served, the importance of natural interaction and ongoing feedback is crucial. Unresponsiveness in this area has been a focus of criticism from parents and those who believe that institutions provide a safe place to monitor the quality of service. Mechanisms, both formal and informal, that can provide feedback on the quality of services should always be readily available.

Visibility of Programs and Recognition and Financial Support for Efforts

As previously mentioned in this chapter, increased quality does not necessarily guarantee increased funding. It is probably a certainty, however, that lack of quality will reduce funding. Yet, if providers enhance the quality of their programs, it is possible they will be able to concretely demonstrate to purchasers, the general public, and various constituencies that because of their adherence to quality standards their programs deserve additional support.

Commitment to Quality Can Have an Impact on the Service Delivery System

The more committed providers are to their mission and the more they listen to the needs and wants of their consumers, the more it is possible to not only enhance the quality of life for the people being served, but also to serve a unique role in the service delivery system. Providing quality services makes it possible for a provider to be a leader in the field of developmental disabilities and speak forthrightly with clear enunciated values that demonstrate to skeptics and supporters alike that true community integration for all people, regardless of length or severity of disability, is possible.

Providers make it possible for purchasers (states, counties, etc.) to implement their visions of community integration. If providers can demonstrate that they are on the cutting edge of adherence to quality assurance principles, then they will have a stake and a voice in molding the future of the service system for people with developmental disabilities. This is both an exciting and refreshing challenge.

Commitment to Quality Can Work for Organizational Change

If providers truly believe and listen to the feedback that they receive regarding quality, it is possible for them to change their organizations to respond to the needs and wants of consumers. Organizational change is never easy, and there are many obstacles that need to be overcome. However, if providers are committed to quality of life for the persons they serve, then they must be in the forefront of proposing the organizational change necessary to meet those needs.

CONCLUSION

There has never been a more exciting time to be a provider in the field of developmental disabilities since the early 1970s. Sometimes it seems that the burdens of funding, finding and retaining quality staff, and excess regulation may be overpowering; however, there is a resurgence of grass roots efforts and natural supports to enhance the lives of people with developmental disabilities. Providers who embrace quality assurance can be in the forefront of the effort to improve the community integration opportunities for the people they serve. It is not a question of whether or not things will change, it is a question of whether providers will manage change or change will manage them.

REFERENCES

Cashen, J. (1988, January). *Setting the stage for ideas of excellence.* Paper presented at a conference of the National Association of Private Residential Resources (NAPRR), Fort Lauderdale, FL.
Crosby, P.B. (1984). *Quality without tears.* New York: McGraw-Hill.

ADVOCACY ISSUES

chapter 12 ————

Quality Assurance and the Courts

———— Michael S. Lottman ————

Editors' Note: *The following chapter is based on the varied experiences of the author with major class action lawsuits brought to vindicate the rights of people with developmental disabilities and mental retardation. These experiences in- clude serving as Associate Director of the Office of Special Litigation in the U.S. Department of Justice, (Civil Rights Division), founding and editing the* Mental Disability Law Reporter *for the Commission on the Mentally Disabled of the American Bar Association, and monitoring implementation of federal court or- ders as Member and Counsel of the Willowbrook Review Panel, Hearing Master in the* Halderman v. Pennhurst *case, and Executive Director of the Mansfield Class Panel of Monitors in Connecticut. The author has also been counsel for the plaintiffs or the United States in numerous landmark cases, including* Wyatt v. Stickney, New York State Association for Retarded Children v. Carey/Cuomo, *and* Society for Good Will to Retarded Children v. Cuomo.

Although federal courts have been closely involved with state mental retar- dation and mental health systems since the early 1970s, a cautious, almost hesitant, approach has characterized judicial actions in the area of quality assurance. Even in early decisions that advanced a "right to treatment" for residents of state institutions, the standards actually imposed by the courts reflected no more than minimally adequate habilitation or treatment (*Wyatt v. Stickney,* 1972). A decade later, this reserve seemed even more evident as the focus of judicial inquiry was limited to whether a challenged practice or decision "is such a substantial departure from accepted professional judgment, practice, or standards as to demonstrate that the person responsible actually did not base the decision on such a judgment" (*Youngberg v. Romeo,* 1982, pp. 322–323). Such deference to the state's professional judgment has been applied not only to determinations of liability for damages or injunctive relief, but also to the remedial phase of mental disability litigation (*New York State Association for Retarded Children [NYSARC] v. Carey,* 1983).

In truth, however, whether the standard was minimal adequacy or deference to professional judgment, judges have always been reluctant to impose detailed programmatic requirements of their own. Although many people still believe that judges make up these orders more or less on the basis of their own personal predilections, or (to be only slightly more realistic) on the basis of the evidence in the record, judicial rulings almost never evolve this way. In fashioning and enforcing remedial orders, the courts have relied (probably more than they should have) on the views and concerns of the professionals, administrators, and bureaucrats who were responsible for the situations that brought the case to court in the first place. For example, in the *Wyatt* litigation involving the Alabama mental retardation and mental health systems, some serious pressure from the court led the parties generally to agree on the parameters of a right to habilitation or treatment; on the mental retardation side of the case, the resulting orders strongly resembled what were then the standards of the Joint Commission on Accreditation of Hospitals (Herr, Arons, & Wallace, 1983; *Wyatt v. Stickney,* 1972).

Indeed, lack of confidence in the ability or willingness of courts to discern and impose meaningful standards of performance has often forced class-action plaintiffs, even those armed with powerful evidence of sustained abuse and inadequacies, to negotiate consent decrees that would be acceptable to state defendants. Examples have included the Willowbrook case (*NYSARC v. Carey,* 1975) and the *Lelsz* case in Texas (*Lelsz v. Kavanagh,* 1983). These decrees have had a way of unraveling when the bloom of amity faded and the difficulties of implementation became apparent (*NYSARC v. Carey,* 1980, 1983; *Lelsz v. Kavanagh,* 1987). In *NYSARC* and *Lelsz,* the evisceration of earlier settlements also had something to do with changes in the law and the conservatism of the appellate courts.

Similarly, courts are and always have been reluctant to hold state defendants accountable for their seemingly inevitable failures to carry out remedial orders. Judges are extremely sympathetic to bureaucratic and fiscal obstacles to compliance, and they seem reluctant to challenge excuses for inaction if the slightest patina of clinical plausibility can be found. The attempt of one judge, John R. Bartels, to expose the shallowness of pseudo-professional justifications and excuses (*NYSARC v. Carey,* 1982) resulted only in a reversal by the

Court of Appeals (*NYSARC v. Carey*, 1983). The message of this highly visible case was presumably not lost on other judges. As one legal scholar has aptly observed:

> No judge is likely to decree more than he thinks he has the power to accomplish. . . . The judge will seek to anticipate the response of others, and though he may try to transcend the limits imposed by that response, he is likely to accept the reality of those limits and compromise his original objective in order to obtain as much relief as possible. (Fiss, 1979, pp. 54–55)

Given these attitudes, it is not surprising that there have been very few findings of contempt of court in the major mental retardation class actions. Those that have been issued have often been based not on clinical concerns but on administrative or fiscal issues (e.g., *Halderman v. Pennhurst State School and Hospital,* 1981, 1982). One significant exception should be noted, however. In *Lelsz v. Kavanagh* (1987), the court found state defendants in contempt with respect to conditions, which were beyond any defense or justification, at the Fort Worth State School. The court's findings so embarrassed Texas officials that they agreed to sweeping statewide relief that had seemed unattainable after an appellate court decision only months before.

Even as great a judge as Frank M. Johnson, Jr., who heroically oversaw the desegregation of many of Alabama's schools and other public facilities, insulated the *Wyatt* (1972) mental retardation and mental health defendants from serious scrutiny for many years (Lottman, 1976). When Johnson finally acted in the face of conceded noncompliance, he placed the mental retardation system in the receivership of the governor—not a very big step, at least from an outside vantage point (*Wyatt v. Ireland,* 1979, 1980). Such decisions should not be seen as instances of lack of resolve or commitment, but rather of judicial reluctance to intrude too far into the mysterious realm of professional practice. So it has always been and is likely to continue.

If the courts are in fact operating in a range between minimal adequacy and professional acceptability, and if class-action defendants (even those found guilty of repeated transgressions) have a vote in determining their own punishment, then an obvious question arises: What does any of this have to do with quality assurance? The answer, *sometimes,* is not much. But the courts *can* play a role in upgrading programs and services, provided that the enterprise proceeds with a sane conception of "quality," an appreciation for the limits of judicial competence (and patience), and careful structuring of remedial orders and compliance mechanisms. The chances for real progress are greatest when the system on trial—not the court or some court-created superstructure—is recognized as the only entity that can bring about the desired kinds of changes.

QUESTIONS FOR JUDICIAL CONSIDERATION

Almost any class-action court order, regardless of what it says or how it is enforced, will have some *gross* effects on the system it seeks to regulate. An order to close an institution or to place specified numbers of class members into community programs will produce, if not the required result, at least some movement in the direction indicated (Bradley & Allard, 1983; Conroy & Bradley, 1985; *NYSARC v. Carey*, 1982, 1983). An order to increase institutional staffing will almost certainly result in the hiring of more people, if not better care (*NYSARC v. Carey*, 1982). Almost all court orders, and the attendant publicity, have led to significant infusions (or at least reallocations) of funds for mental retardation or mental health services (Bradley & Allard, 1983; Herr et al., 1983). Furthermore, states usually find it politically impossible to limit the benefits of a class action solely to members of the class (typically, residents of the particular institution under suit). While it may be legally possible to grant benefits to a favored class and not to others (*Philadelphia Police and Fire Association for Handicapped Children v. City of Philadelphia*, 1989; *Society for Good Will to Retarded Children v. Cuomo*, 1983), state officials almost always say they do not want to create a dual system of entitlements. And once changes have been made in response to litigation, it is difficult to envision systems returning to their former ways even when the case is over (Rothman & Rothman, 1984). It should be pointed out, however, there is scant evidence on this point. Lawsuits in this field tend to go on for years, even decades. The Willowbrook litigation, filed in 1972, was extended in the last settlement [*NYSARC v. Cuomo*, 1987] until at least 1992.)

While these gross, not to say cosmetic, improvements would not be considered sufficient by plaintiffs in class litigation, or by most defendants for that matter, they are nonetheless important indicators of what can reasonably be expected from judicial intervention. Courts work best at the macro-issue level, rather than at the micronic level where litigants often take them. (For example, a court would be far more comfortable, and on safer legal ground, in ordering implementation of a statewide policy for administration of psychotropic medication than in requiring a change in a particular person's prescription.)

In terms of the kinds of issues it ought to be addressing under a remedial decree, the court should be viewed as the peak of a pyramid. At the base are the professionals of the system and the interdisciplinary teams, the initial decisionmakers on most issues; on the next level are the area or facility administrators who oversee, regulate, and manage the implementation of these decisions; and just below the courts are the commissioners of mental retardation or mental health and other state officials responsible for overall direction, policy-making, and allocation of resources.

Disputed issues rising through this structure, or introduced by plaintiffs, parents, and advocates from outside the structure, may be suitable for court intervention if resolution at a lower structural level cannot be achieved. Especially if a system has its own responsive grievance and appeal mechanisms, issues reaching the court should have sufficient breadth and importance to justify a judge's intervention. In this regard, it is essential that the court have assistance in the form of a monitoring body to ensure that people at various levels of the pyramid are performing their appropriate roles, to see that the decision-making processes are operating as intended, to resolve minor matters for which guidance or precedent already exists, and to package unresolved issues in a manner that is amenable to judicial resolution. Without such a monitoring mechanism, the burden falls on plaintiffs' attorneys to perform many of the foregoing functions, especially that of framing issues for the court. For many reasons, including overloaded work schedules, their adversarial perspective (albeit appropriate to their role), and their often unavoidable focus on problems instead of solutions, plaintiffs' lawyers are not in the best position to process issues for the court. A monitoring body can therefore be helpful (see discussion later in this chapter) and need not detract from plaintiffs' indispensable participation in the ultimate resolution of the issues. (Of course, the presence of both a monitoring body and active plaintiffs' attorneys can lead to serious tensions as to whose agenda should be pursued. But such a development is wholly consistent with the maxim that if court monitors do their job, they will eventually earn the enmity of everyone else involved in the litigation [Rothman & Rothman, 1984]. Plaintiffs' lawyers, nonetheless, are well advised to keep one eye on the defendants and the other on the court monitors.)

Regardless of who presents the issue and the form it takes, the court should be concerned with three overarching considerations in any systemic reform litigation:

1. Do adequate procedures exist, and are they being used, to make and review programmatic decisions for individual members of the class?
2. Are these decisions being properly implemented?
3. Are class members protected from abuse and neglect, unsafe conditions, unwarranted or punitive treatment techniques, and other forms of harm?

In seeking to verify that these conditions are met, the court will be undertaking virtually all of the quality assurance of which it is institutionally capable. However, to ensure that judicial entitlements reach down to individuals and to specific programs and that the positive results of the litigation outlive the case itself, there should be a fourth area for serious judicial concern:

4. Do adequate mechanisms exist (apart from the court) for enforcing the

above entitlements and furthering the legitimate policy goals of the system?

Lately, litigants seem to have discovered, often in the course of trying to get out of cases that have dragged on for years (*Halderman v. Pennhurst*, 1983, 1985; *NYSARC v. Cuomo*, 1987; *Welsch v. Gardebring*, 1987), that an essential part of the court's quality assurance function is (or should be) ensuring that the system under suit is developing adequate quality assurance mechanisms of its own.

Since courts can be forced to resolve questions that no one else wants to face, they will frequently be led away from the main issues in a systemic reform case to areas where they may become mired in technical detail or left without a mandate. If nothing else, involving the judge in each little (or even large) issue that comes along, despite the attendant satisfaction and the "victories" that may be won, will only exhaust the court's political capital over time and threaten its very legitimacy. As Owen Fiss (1979) has written, a structural remedial order (the kind this chapter discusses) "places the judge in an architectural relationship" with the system being reformed, so that the judge "is likely to lose much of his distance from the organization" and begin to identify with it instead: "[T]his process of identification is likely to deepen as the enterprise of organizational reform moves through several cycles of supplemental relief, drawn out over a number of years" (Fiss, 1979, p. 53).

At the same time, according to Fiss, judges want their decrees to be "efficacious," which often requires negotiation with or manipulation of social and political forces far outside the formal structure of the case. Some judges are remarkably successful in this regard, but

> the issue is not . . . the capacity of judges to devise strategies for dealing with these limiting forces, but rather the very need to devise these strategies and what the perception of this need does to their sense of independence. (Fiss, 1979, p. 54)

Thus, the court in the Willowbrook case, after such exciting sidetracks as deciding how many consumer advocates the state ought to fund (*NYSARC v. Carey*, 1979) and whether the New York City schools could exclude or segregate carriers of hepatitis B (*NYSARC v. Carey*, 1978, 1979), finally foundered when forced to decide how many individuals with multiple handicaps should be allowed to reside in a single community residence. The backlash against this decision—the court actually engineered a three- to six-bed compromise—eventually led to the dissolution of the monitoring body, the deterioration of institutional conditions, a virtual halt to all placements of the types of clients involved, and finally the approval by an appellate court of the state's desire to create "community placements" of up to 50 beds (*NYSARC v. Carey*, 1979, 1980, 1982, 1983; Rothman & Rothman, 1984). Indeed, the indirect effects of luring the court into treacherous currents and the direct effects of the appellate court decision are still reverberating throughout New York and have tragically distorted a once admirable community system. The point is not that the three- to six-bed limit was wrong (it was not) but that its embodiment in an order unleashed forces that the court ultimately could not control.

Thus, a court, especially in an era of so-called judicial restraint, would do well to confine itself to the basic elements of judicial quality assurance (listed above) as much as possible and rely on the system's own quality assurance mechanisms for an extension of its efforts. Some of the ways the court can maintain this kind of effective focus are suggested in the remainder of this chapter.

FORMULATING THE REMEDIAL ORDER

All court orders, of course, cannot be alike. What the order includes depends upon the characteristics of the state system and the institution on trial, the shortcomings sought to be remedied, the personal biases of the attorneys involved, and the patience (and, some would say, relative foolhardiness) of the judge. Theoretically at least, the order should bear some relation to what is in the trial record (if there was a trial). Early remedial orders tended to be voluminous: the original *Wyatt* orders contained 35 detailed standards (with numerous substandards) for Alabama's mental hospitals and 49 standards for the Partlow State School, covering a total of 13 densely printed pages in the *Federal Supplement* (*Wyatt v. Stickney,* 1972). The landmark Willowbrook consent judgment consisted of 29 single-spaced typewritten pages, 27 of which set forth largely unreachable institutional standards and little of which addressed the lawsuit's primary goal of community placement, other than requiring reduction of Willowbrook's population from 3,300 to 250 (*NYSARC v. Carey,* 1975). The orders in both of these cases were loaded with specific and numerical requirements. Indeed, the *Wyatt* staffing standards became benchmarks for many other lawyers and judges (*Connecticut Association for Retarded Citizens [CARC] v. Thorne,* 1984; *Davis v. Watkins,* 1974), even though the mental health ratios now seem unbelievably low and many of the mental retardation ratios are completely inapplicable to institutional populations of the 1990s. These excruciatingly detailed decrees reflected the belief, still held by many, that enforceability depended upon the objective measurability of the standards imposed (Lottman, 1976). As one commentary offered, "courts have made some effort to design objective standards based on quantitative criteria. This approach relieves courts from making detailed and frequent subjective judgments on the quality of treatment offered . . . in the compliance phase" ("Implementation Problems," 1977, p. 438).

It may, or may not, be instructive that the *Wyatt* orders went largely unimplemented for at least 7 years (*Wyatt v. Ireland,* 1979, 1980) and that the Willowbrook litigation is still going strong 14 years after the judgment was entered. Increasingly, it seems that effective judicial quality assurance involves more than adding up the numbers, and that other ways need to be found to articulate the goals of reform litigation. In evaluating accomplishment of the purposes of a decree, courts cannot and should not avoid making subjective judgments, but they need to enlist the aid of others in the process of doing so. A master or monitor is essential in enabling the court to make qualitative evaluations of compliance, and the defendants can be required to evaluate themselves through development of a quality assurance system. If the court does not wish to appoint a monitor or master (*Society for Good Will to Retarded Children v. Cuomo,* 1983), however, then the judge might be unwise to undertake a subjective or qualitative approach and should probably adhere to a "by the numbers" remedial approach.

Input-Based Orders

Despite the obvious surface appeal of objective or input-based orders, such as *Wyatt,* there are built-in drawbacks to this sort of remedy. As much as plaintiffs' lawyers tire of hearing defendants' pleas for flexibility, a rigid set of input standards can tie all parties to a particular configuration for a system that soon becomes inapplicable or outmoded, as the *Wyatt* standards have. Constitutional minima quickly evolve into practical maxima (or, even worse, merely aspirations), and the game then becomes one of seeing how far below the standards the defendants can fall without getting into serious trouble. Yet another problem with input-based orders is that to the extent they are later seen as usurpations or preemptions of professional judgment, they are likely to be reversed on appeal either immediately or years later when the defendants begin to find them onerous. Orders mandating specific numbers of community placements, for example, have not fared very well in recent years (*Halderman v. Pennhurst,* 1979; *Lelsz v. Kavanagh,* 1987; *Society for Good Will to Retarded Children v. Cuomo,* 1984). While other orders requiring community placement have occasionally been upheld, these decrees were based upon long-standing professional judgments affecting individual clients, rather than unidentified numbers of class members (*Clark v. Cohen,* 1985; *Savidge v. Fincannon,* 1988; *Thomas S. v. Morrow,* 1986). Class-action defendants might more successfully be ordered to evaluate all class members for placement (without preordained results), and then to carry out their own professional recommendations.

Some class-action decrees, especially more recent ones, have not been so voluminous or prescriptive. The first remedial order regarding Cambridge State Hospital for the mentally retarded in Minnesota went into exacting detail as to staffing and other inputs, but was only eight pages long (*Welsch v. Likins,* 1974). Unfortunately, the *Welsch* case later proliferated with new orders, expanded orders, and modified orders to such an extent that only an insider was likely to comprehend the proceedings (*Welsch v. Likins,* 1977;

Welsch v. Noot, 1980; *Welsch v. Gardebring,* 1987). The early *Welsch* orders, however, at least had the virtue of realism. While some scoffed at their modest staffing ratios and community placement goals, the *Welsch* orders may have reflected a more pragmatic assessment of what was possible than most other decrees in this field. Court orders that seek to do everything, without establishing priorities or considering fiscal realities, are doomed to failure ("Implementation Problems," 1977). Such failure will be compounded when those subject to the order realize how hopelessly behind they are in all respects and essentially give up. This caveat is applicable to all forms of quality assurance.

In light of these concerns, the *Pennhurst* decision in Pennsylvania was one of the more sensible orders that has been entered (*Halderman v. Pennhurst,* 1978). The 1978 order focused on the goal of closing Pennhurst through community placement and the process by which that would be accomplished, and included only bare-bones protections and requirements for what remained of the institution. Even as later embellished, it posed the kinds of quality assurance questions—Were the class members moved to the community or not? Was the placement process established or not?—that a court could suitably address, particularly with the aid of a monitoring arrangement that was probably more intricate than necessary for the type of relief involved. Even though the mandate to close Pennhurst was modified in the first appellate decision (*Halderman v. Pennhurst,* 1979), the placement process and protections remained in place. Furthermore, as might have been expected, once Pennsylvania felt it was no longer required to close the Pennhurst institution, it proceeded to do just that (*Halderman v. Pennhurst,* 1985; Woestendiek, 1987).

Process-Based Orders

The negative experience in earlier cases with rigid requirements (e.g., *Wyatt*-type standards), coupled with an overall conservative trend in constitutional doctrine, may counsel a shift from particularized, input-based quality assurance at the judicial level to court decrees that emphasize process and values. Enforcing such decrees may involve more difficult judgments, but they are judgments that courts can make with proper assistance. And they are judgments that courts ought to make.

A prototype for future system reform decrees may be the consent agreement approved and entered by the court in the suit against Mansfield Training School in Connecticut (*CARC v. Thorne,* 1984). This decree—agreed upon by the plaintiffs and the state after 5 years of bitter pretrial proceedings, challenged at various points by pro-institution parent groups, the employee union, and the U.S. Justice Department, and subjected to 31 days of arduous "fairness" hearings—may actually have benefited from all the adversity. It emerged as 12 short pages of tightly written process and safeguard requirements (plus five more pages dealing with monitoring and procedural matters) that, at first glance, do not seem to demand very much of the defendants but in fact call upon the service system to transform itself radically.

Most of the *CARC* decree is concerned with establishment of an interdisciplinary process, involving clients and their representatives as well as professionals, for determining on an individual basis what placements and programs are appropriate for each member of the class. No specific numbers of placements are required, although the decree makes it clear that "developing quality community placements is central to [its] implementation." The decree also characterizes itself as "mandat[ing] programs and placements based on individual need and . . . not . . . closure of Mansfield Training School as a residential facility for retarded citizens." The order further requires processes for appealing interdisciplinary team decisions and, more importantly, for carrying them out. Sections of the decree place strict procedural limits on the use of restraints and psychotropic medication, prohibit physical and psychological abuse and neglect, and impose some basic staffing and safety requirements on the institution.

In terms of former notions of measurability, the main numerical requirements in the *CARC* order apply to institutional staffing: the federal intermediate care facility (ICF/MR) standards for direct care in all units and for clinical staff in units certified (or those supposed to be certified) as ICFs/MR, and the *Wyatt* ratios for clinical staff in non–ICF/MR buildings. Almost everyone involved with the case would now agree that these earlier "objective" standards are inappropriate. As a measure of direct care staffing levels, the ICF/MR standards fall far short of adequacy and are at odds with enhanced expectations in other parts of the decree. Mansfield has generally met the ICF/MR standards in non–ICF units and substantially exceeded them in certified buildings. The ICF/MR standards for professional staffing have proved so inherently immeasurable that the *Wyatt* standards have been used by default for the whole institution, and they too have had to be amended (Mansfield Class Panel of Monitors, 1985).

As for the balance of the decree, a judge can evaluate compliance with *CARC*-type process requirements but will need to look beyond plans, policies, and procedures in order to determine whether the processes are actually functioning in an acceptable manner. For this purpose, unless the court intends to be in virtually continuous session, it needs assistance in the form of a monitoring body, which is included in the *CARC* decree. Furthermore, unless the court monitors are intended to be a mammoth and eternal bureaucracy, the system must be required to monitor itself in ways that will advance the aims of the decree. This aspect of the *CARC v. Thorne* litigation has been one of the most painful—and potentially the most productive.

The *CARC* decree required, in no great detail, that the defendants develop a quality assurance system that performed the following functions:

Ensure that class members "live, work, learn, and recreate in a humane physical and psychological environment which affords each the opportunity to interact with and participate in the community."

Guarantee that class members are protected from harm.

Review individualized habilitation plans and their implementation.

Ensure that case managers and service providers are properly trained. (Staff training per se is not a quality assurance function and has not been viewed as such in the *CARC* case. Checking to see that the training has been provided, of course, is a valid quality assurance activity. However, those responsible for quality assurance should avoid being drawn into operational matters.)

Determine whether or not class members are benefiting from required programs and services.

Report to the public on the results of the foregoing.

This unexceptionable language lay dormant for many months, until a not totally fortuitous chain of events brought it to the fore. The court monitors, tracking implementation of the defendants' quality assurance plan, noted a lack of activity. The issue came to the court's attention at more than one informal status conference, and the question soon became not how the defendants should be doing quality assurance but whether they were doing it at all. The state, in an effort to demonstrate good faith, announced the hiring of a recognized national figure to be quality assurance director; before even beginning full-time work, the new director presented the court with a startlingly ambitious plan for meeting the quality assurance mandate (Connecticut Department of Mental Retardation, 1986). Nevertheless, another year went by with little progress. The state became increasingly defensive toward any suggestion of systemic problems, even denying the results of its own initial reviews. Finally, the court monitors formally advised the commissioner of their dissatisfaction, and the plaintiffs moved to cite the commissioner for contempt (*CARC v. Thorne,* 1988).

In the end, the matter was settled out of court with an agreement that, if implemented, gives Connecticut a state-of-the-art system of quality assurance and translates the quality assurance principles in the decree into concrete monitoring mechanisms (*CARC v. Thorne,* 1988). As a result of the settlement and related developments (see Gant, Chapter 20, this volume, for a discussion of the Connecticut quality assurance system for people with mental retardation), the system includes the following:

Licensing of private residential programs and an equivalent process for state-run facilities

Medicaid ICF/MR compliance surveys and strengthened independent professional reviews for public and private intermediate care facilities

Interagency agreements to apply the court decree to class members in nursing homes and health-related facilities

National accreditation for sheltered workshops

"Program quality review" (i.e., program enhancement) for residential and day service sites

Quarterly individual client review with a "red flag" (potential crisis situation) process for corrective action

Continued longitudinal study of client growth or regression

Monitoring and trend analysis of unusual incidents, abuse and neglect allegations, and use of medication and restraints

Mortality review

A "quality assurance implementation group" with external and internal representation to review and evaluate the quality assurance system and recommended necessary changes

An annual quality assurance report compiled by the defendants and an annual outside audit of the quality assurance program

Publication of the longitudinal study, the annual report and audit, and other quality assurance information

Continued oversight of all the above by the court monitors, augmented by an expert consultant (*CARC v. Thorne*, 1988; Connecticut Department of Mental Retardation, 1988.)

The point of this extended recital is not to glorify Connecticut's progress or the brilliance of the *CARC* litigants since, at the time of this writing, it will be several years before the results of either can be assessed. Rather, the point is to show what forces are set in motion when a judge simply orders that there be quality assurance and refuses to answer questions that should not be asked of him. A judge is normally not equipped to include the "how to" of quality assurance in an initial decree; nor are the professionals involved likely to be responsive to such a frontal assault. Indeed, such an initial order, if appealed, would probably be reversed on sight, whereas a decree like *CARC*'s—creating a framework and a process in which the defendants, with considerable external prodding, can eventually write their own rules while the court's role remains exceedingly limited—is in nearly all respects virtually unassailable on appeal. Furthermore, the quality assurance system that eventually evolved provides an important means of narrowing the issues that may be presented to the court in the future and of framing the issues in a way that is susceptible to judicial resolution.

Conceptually similar to the *CARC* decree, although it could not look more different, is the "Court Plan and Order of Deinstitutionalization" entered in the contested case against the Hissom Memorial Center in Oklahoma (*Homeward Bound Inc. v. Hissom Memorial Center,* 1987). Despite a length of more than 60 pages, including job descriptions, projected budgets, and numerical placement requirements, the order is mostly concerned with process and leaves most of the planning to defendants. It envisions the resulting system not only in terms of process but also, almost elegiacally, in terms of outcome:

> As Americans and citizens of Oklahoma, we believe in rugged individualism, the sanctity of our family and in taking care of our own. We admire those who work and we work hard so that our children can have the best life and education possible. We have sacrificed to maintain our freedom and a life which is nonrestrictive. These values are our heritage which we preserve so that it can be passed down to our children—all of our children.
> The quality of life made available in the United States as a result of this value base is the best in the world for those who are allowed to share in it. The "American Dream" rests at the foundation of the values we defend. (*Homeward Bound Inc. v. Hissom Memorial Center,* 1987, pp. 1–2)

Though as noted above, numerical placement requirements have not been popular in other cases, there is nothing wrong with a court's articulating a set of values and "guiding principles," posing questions that need to be answered, and setting up a process in which the aims of the decree can be actualized through choices made by the state. Whatever else this unusual order may be, it is not intrusive. The court would be in its proper role in evaluating defendants' performance in light of the core values of American society, which judges, as much as anyone, have been responsible for articulating (Fiss, 1979).

COURT MONITORING METHODOLOGY

The most important observation to make about judicial monitoring mechanisms is that there must be such a mechanism in a case of structural reform. Courts commonly retain jurisdiction over the implementation of remedial orders and require, at a minimum, periodic reports by defendants on the status of compliance (*Society for Good Will to Retarded Children v. Cuomo,* 1983; *Wyatt v. Stickney,* 1972). They usually, though not always, grant plaintiffs' attorneys broad access to clients, programs, and records during the period of implementation (*Welsch v. Likins,* 1974). However, these minimal devices are never sufficient to enable the court to evaluate compliance with its orders, unless the decree's requirements are all narrow and numerically based. The defendants' reports, if not counterbalanced by a less partisan observer's, are inevitably going to be self-serving and selectively accurate; and plaintiffs' lawyers, regardless of how smart they think they are, will have neither the time nor the skills to compete with the state's flow of paper.

In *Society for Good Will to Retarded Children v. Cuomo,* a suit against the Long Island Developmental Center, the court entered an extensive and detailed order, largely suggested by the defendants, but refused to appoint a monitor or master (or to grant plaintiffs access to the facility) and relied on compliance information solely from biannual reports submitted by a facility employee. (State officials appealed the order anyway and won at least partial reversal, but then agreed to carry it out "voluntarily" [*Society for Good Will to Retarded Children v. Cuomo*, 1984]. Unfortunately, they reneged [*Society for Good Will to Retarded Children v. Cuomo*, 1987].) The facility's reports were invariably positive and eventually ceased altogether. Then in 1986 and 1987, the Center was threatened with Medicaid decertification by the federal government and even sanctioned for noncompliance by the state Medicaid agency—a rare occurrence anywhere and almost unheard of in New York. This discouraging result was all but inevitable once the court declined to provide for ongoing judicial monitoring.

Types and Forms of Monitors

Court-appointed monitors have had many titles and have taken many shapes: ombudsmen (*Morales v. Turman*, 1973), human rights committees (*Wyatt v. Stickney*, 1972), expert consultants (*Lelsz v. Kavanagh*, 1983), monitors (*Welsch v. Noot*, 1980), review panels and panels of monitors (*CARC v. Thorne*, 1984; *NYSARC v. Carey*, 1975), masters and special masters (*Davis v. Watkins*, 1974; *Halderman v. Pennhurst*, 1978; *Michigan Association for Retarded Citizens v. Smith*, 1979; *Wuori v. Zitnay*, 1978), and receivers (*Wyatt v. Ireland*, 1980). Most of these titles do not have any fixed meaning (although people seem to think they do), and it is not the title that determines the success of the effort. In general, ombudsmen and human rights committees can raise issues but not resolve them, expert consultants and monitoring bodies specialize in more systematic compilation of information, and receivers simply are not going to be appointed very often because of the gravity of such a remedy.

Much of the scholarly discussion (Fiss, 1979; "Implementation Problems," 1977) and many plaintiffs' hopes and threats seem to focus on appointment of a special master who, under Rule 53 of the Federal Rules of Civil Procedure and the court's equity jurisdiction, can be given extensive power and authority, including the ability to hold hearings and issue orders appealable to the judge (*Halderman v. Pennhurst*, 1980). But while special masters have been used with some success in at least one education case and several prison cases (Cornwell, 1988; "Implementation Problems," 1977), they have not been much help to date in structural mental disability litigation (Cornwell, 1988).

The special master in the *Pennhurst* case was given a host of responsibilities and a budget of nearly $1 million per year, but no commensurate authority to enforce her decisions; even when she filed reports with the court (not as a result of Rule 53 hearings), there was no mechanism for enacting her recommendations into law. Compounding this absence of actual power, the perception of the special master as a potential rival to the existing bureaucracy made cooperative efforts almost impossible (Bradley & Allard, 1983; Conroy & Bradley, 1985). The *Pennhurst* case also featured a "hearing master" (this chapter author), whose powers were more like those of a special master than the special master's were, but who was limited to a narrow range of issues and to deciding one class member's case at a time (*Halderman v. Pennhurst,* 1980, 1983). The hearing master was accused, quite rightly, of trying to exceed his limited authority (Temple University & Human Services Research Institute, 1983).

One specific power granted to the *Pennhurst* special master was that of drafting implementation plans for community placement and program development for each of the five counties in the Philadelphia area (*Halderman v. Pennhurst,* 1978). It was a tribute to the master's patience and wisdom that she never tried to exercise this authority, as she had neither the detailed information nor the resources required for the task and recognized that she had no business writing plans for local governments to implement (Conroy & Bradley, 1985). Even if the plans had been written, those charged with putting them into effect would have felt no ownership of them and no great sense of loss if they failed. When a sole master (or receiver) is given this type of responsibility—but sits outside a bureaucracy of thousands, all of whom are answerable to someone else—the most likely outcome is that nothing will happen and the master will be identified as the problem. For this and other reasons, court monitors are better off without many of the powers that a special master can be given.

Among these powers best forgone is, perhaps above all others, the power to hold hearings and issue orders. Hearings and orders are what the judge is for; in systemic reform cases, court monitors have more important roles than to play People's Court—among them interpreting and applying the decree's provisions, fact-finding, prodding the system to perform, facilitating communication, providing technical assistance, settling disputes as they arise, presenting unresolved issues to the court in a proper form for decision, and assisting the court in assessing the overall status of compliance.

In discharging these various tasks, the form of the monitoring entity, like the title, is not particularly important. Certain elements, however, must be in place if the monitor is to be an effective adjunct to the court. First, the monitoring entity must be a full-time presence on the scene of the implementation activity. One cannot be a participant-observer in planning exercises, policy development, interdisciplinary team proceedings, and other less formal but significant events if one is following the case from a distance and juggling other full-time responsibilities.

In a panel-staff or master-staff monitoring arrangement, where the court designees are experts from other places, it is sufficient if the staff is a constantly visible and available presence. Staff members do not usually need to possess any particular clinical credentials, but they must be generally knowledgeable in the field, of sufficient personal or professional stature to deal with those they are observing, and capable of making judgments without becoming judgmental. Ideologues have no place in the monitoring business; the only ideology that counts is the one expressed in the court order.

Personally or through staff, the monitor must be omnipresent, seeing that court-related procedures are followed and that the relevant actors are aware of their new roles. He or she needs to be available when interpretations of the decree are required or a dispute needs immediate resolution, and it is a full-time job (and more) to develop the network of clients, parents, advocates, program staff, low- and mid-level bureaucrats, legislative staff, and others through whom the monitor finds out what is really occurring. Relatives of class members or institutional staff are not going to make many long-distance telephone calls to ask some remote figure for help or advice. As a corollary to this point, the monitor should also have unquestioned access to all clients, staff, programs, facilities, and documents related to implementation of the decree.

Next, the monitoring entity must possess an independent legal capacity, in order to provide interpretations of decree provisions, identify legal issues, negotiate with the other lawyers in the case, and ensure as much as possible that questions reaching the court are those that a judge ought to address. (The court should not be forced into making professional judgments or expending its limited reservoir of persuasion on relatively trivial matters; nor should questions be presented to the court in most situations without a proposed response. A surprising number of litigants, including experienced attorneys, think that the court is all-powerful and all-knowing and has nothing else to do but worry about the class action.)

If only one person is going to be involved in the monitoring effort (not a preferable arrangement), that individual almost has to be a lawyer. Monitors cannot, for obvious reasons, rely on the parties' counsel for legal advice, and they should not seek it from the court, although many have. Asking the court for advisory opinions may seriously compromise the judge's ability to deal with the issue later. In fact, even though monitors are often referred to as an arm of the court, substantive ex parte communications between the arm and the head (outside the presence of the parties) should be avoided altogether. They create an image of unfairness and reduce the distance the judge should maintain from the messy details of implementation (Fiss, 1979). Monitors, by the same token, should not ask the judge how to oversee the case; judges do not known how to monitor and should not want to know.

Functions of the Monitor

In interpreting and applying decree provisions, it is especially important that a monitor set the proper tone from the outset. Under a new order, questions of interpretation and application are likely to arise that are what clinicians call "testing" behavior, designed to see if the monitor is serious about his or her role. For example, in the Mansfield Training School case in Connecticut, one of the first skirmishes took place over whether transfers to 17- and 11-bed facilities complied with the decree's stipulation that most community residences be designed for eight persons or fewer (*CARC v. Thorne*, 1984). This question does not seem to pose any knotty legal problems, but the state badly wanted to move the clients and earnestly argued that they would be better off than in their current institutional placements. The monitoring panel held firm; if it had not, the case might have been over before implementation had really begun. Monitors have to realize that much of their job consists of telling people what they already know—and taking the blame for it.

A monitoring body's role and its authority from the court similarly put it in a position to resolve many disputes that arise during the implementation of a decree. The monitor should take care not to preempt the decision-making processes the court is trying to create, but he or she can perform a great service to the judge (and the parties, although one side or both may not concur) by heading off many issues before they become matters for further litigation. If numerous disputes cannot be resolved short of court action, the judge will soon be overwhelmed and the entire implementation process may be clogged with issues waiting to be decided. Protecting the judge from overexposure is part of the monitor's role. As Owen Fiss put it, somewhat skeptically:

> The special master [or monitor] is the judge's appointee, but the hope is that once the authority is infused, the judge will be able to stand in the background, return to his position of independence, judging rather than wheeling-and-dealing. (Fiss, 1979, p. 56)

In refereeing disputes, and promoting compliance generally, the monitor need not—in fact, should not—follow a rigid adjudicative course that leads almost inevitably to the judge's doorstep. The novelty of going to court wears off very quickly for all concerned. Rather, the monitor should take advantage of what Fiss calls "the ambiguity of his status, judge and non-judge" and whenever possible simply assert the authority necessary to resolve the situation. In many cases, nobody (including the monitor and sometimes the judge) is really sure what the monitor can or cannot do; in that position, one should not be in a hurry to have the matter clarified.

In the long run, of all the monitoring functions listed above, probably the most important is fact-finding: building through various means the body of information that shapes the way the case is perceived by the parties and the way issues are presented to the court. A successful monitoring effort will produce a written record related to the provisions of the decree that can be drawn upon by the parties or related to the court as needed. This record will consist, in part, of the monitor's own observations and the results of his or her inquiries, and eventually, in equal or greater part, of information collected by the system itself, pursuant to a quality assurance program mandated in general terms by the court and developed with the input of the monitor and the parties. Courts and monitors are wise to avoid construction of massive and competing information systems or of convoluted monitoring procedures that require enormous expenditures of time and energy to establish the simplest facts.

In the Willowbrook case, the special master named in 1982 usually conducted "joint audits" with the state and employed other means of avoiding factual disputes (*NYSARC v. Carey*, 1982), but the office also expended extensive resources on developing its own computerized data system and attempting to make it compatible with the defendants'. In the *Welsch* case in Minnesota, not only was a single monitor expected to keep track of at least eight institutions and hundreds of community placements in that vast state—with a budget that never exceeded $120,000 and was usually much less (Bradley & Allard, 1983)—but he also had to grapple with a fact-finding procedure that was an example of due process run amok. As described by the court:

> If [the monitor] determined that the Department was not in compliance with the Consent Decree, a notice of non-compliance was sent to all interested parties. Resolution of the matter was attempted first through an informal meeting of the parties. If this was unsuccessful, the parties met formally with the monitor. If a formal meeting did not result in a resolution of the matter, the monitor or a qualified hearing officer conducted an evidentiary hearing and based on this hearing, the monitor submitted recommendations regarding appropriate corrective action to the Court. These recommendations could be implemented upon motion of either party or the court. (*Welsch v. Gardebring*, 1987, p. 7)

It is difficult to see how such laborious approaches to fact-finding and dispute resolution can advance multifaceted structural reform. The monitor is supposed to be the "eyes and ears" of the court; while striving to be fair and readily admitting to mistakes, the monitor should rely for fact-finding primarily on his or her own observations, plus the state's quality assurance reports (which the defendants presumably will not be able to challenge). Thus, one of the first rules of judicial quality assurance is to make the defendants do most of the work.

ELEMENTS OF STATE QUALITY ASSURANCE SYSTEMS

Although the subject is thoroughly dealt with elsewhere in this book, some observations are in order here as to the characteristics of a state quality assurance system that a court or monitor can trust. First, the quality assurance function should be vested in a person who ranks high enough in the defendant organization to deal directly with the commissioner and the court, who has the requisite authority over other agency officials, and who is not answerable to anyone (except the commissioner) in control of the programs being evaluated.

There should be a clear line of demarcation between quality assurance and operational functions, so that the quality assurance director, as with monitors or masters, is not held accountable for things beyond his or her control. Quality assurance is a means of evaluating programs, not fixing them. Advocates frequently argue that the quality assurance system should be located outside the operating agency altogether. Outside watchdogs can serve a valuable function (after all, that is what the court monitor is), but the organizational and bureaucratic obstacles inherent in a "department of quality assurance" (who reports to whom? how can anyone make anyone do anything?) are truly daunting. Once the court, with the kind of coercive power it represents, is no longer part of the equation, whatever changes have occurred are more likely to be sustained from within.

There should be a purpose for every piece of data the quality assurance system collects, and the monitor should ensure that the data include the kind of information that will shed light on decree implementation. Where possible, the system should seek to collect positive as well as negative information, in order to avoid an unfair impression of unrelieved problems and failures. The system should have the capacity to manage the data it generates, and above all there must be a process for using the information to secure corrective action.

At least theoretically, licensing and certification programs effectively "close the loop" by noting deficiencies, requiring plans of corrections, verifying implementation of those plans, and imposing sanctions if violations continue. These quality assurance methods also have the virtue of specifying standards in advance, so that failure to meet them is per se evidence of inadequacy without further debates over "professional judgment." But licensing and certification programs are notoriously unable to recognize that some things are more important than others. In particular, perhaps because they are so often applied to empty buildings, they tend to emphasize extreme fire safety measures and other physical plant requirements for handicapped persons that no "normal" home could hope to meet and that in many cases are thoroughly unnecessary. These well-intended excesses are in reality a form of discrimination and have denied or delayed many people's access to the community (*NYSARC v. Carey,* 1982). In any case, despite what can be learned from some licensure and certification methodologies, much more is required in order to ensure quality programs and quality lives.

Quality assurance data and reports should be available in unexpurgated versions to the court and members of the public (who, after all, are paying for all of this), but advocates and monitors then need to respond reasonably to the identified problems. The system should not be punished for finding deficiencies but for failing to correct them.

CONCLUSION

There are those who will say one cannot rely on state mental retardation and mental health systems to report accurately on themselves or to take action in response to what they find. It is true that many states have not distinguished themselves in this area, or in mental disability services generally. But state systems are the major provider of services and only they—not a small and short-lived court bureaucracy—can do the job that needs to be done. Most state administrators and professionals, whatever their initial resistance to change, will eventually feel the empowerment implicit in a well-constructed court decree and will use that power in a creative way. Every effort should be made to see that the case unfolds in this manner. For if a state bureaucracy channels its collective strength into frustrating the purposes of a decree, all the courts in the world are unlikely to make much of a difference.

REFERENCES

Bradley, V.J., & Allard, M.A. (1983). *Longitudinal study of the court-ordered deinstitutionalization of Pennhurst, implementation analysis #3: Issues affecting complex litigation.* Boston: Human Services Research Institute.

Clark v. Cohen, 613 F. Supp. 684 (E.D. Pa. 1985). *affirmed* 794 F. 2d 79 (3d Cir. 1986), *certiorari denied* 479 U.S. 962 (1986).

Conditions of Participation for Intermediate Care Facilities for the Mentally Retarded, 42 *Code of Federal Regulations* §483. 400 *et seq.* (formerly 42 Code of Federal Regulations §442.400).

Connecticut Association for Retarded Citizens (CARC) v. Thorne, No. H-78-653 (D. Conn., April 9, 1984); Motion for Contempt, February 2, 1988; Order of August 11, 1988.

Connecticut Department of Mental Retardation. (1986). *A plan to assess and enhance the quality of services.* East Hartford, CT: Author.

Connecticut Department of Mental Retardation. (1988). *Statewide quality assurance methods.* East Hartford, CT: Author.

Conroy, J.W., & Bradley, V.J. (1985). *The Pennhurst longitudinal study: A report of five years of research and analysis.* Philadelphia: Temple University Developmental Disabilities Center. Boston: Human Services Research Institute.

Cornwell, J.K. (1988). "CRIPA: The failure of federal intervention for mentally retarded people," 97 *Yale Law Journal* 845–862. New Haven, CT: The Yale Law Journal Co., Inc.

Davis v. Watkins, 384 F. Supp. 1196 (N.D. Ohio 1974).

Fiss, O.M. (1979). "Foreword: The forms of justice," 93 *Harvard Law Review* 1–58. Cambridge, MA: Harvard Law Review Association.

Halderman v. Pennhurst State School and Hospital, 446 F. Supp. 1295 (1977, 1978), *affirmed in part, reversed in part* 612 F. 2d 84 (3d Cir. 1979), *reversed* 451 U.S. 1 (1981), *on remand* 673 F. 2d 647 (3d Cir. 1982), *reversed* 465 U.S. 89 (1984); Order of April 24, 1980; 533 F. Supp. 631 (E.D. Pa. 1981), *affirmed* 673 F. 2d 628 (3d Cir. 1982), *certiorari denied* 465 U.S. 1038 (1984); Order of August 26, 1983; 610 F. Supp. 1221 (E.D. Pa. 1985).

Herr, S., Arons, S., & Wallace, R.E. (1983). *Legal rights and mental health care.* Lexington, MA: Lexington Books.

Homeward Bound, Inc. v. Hissom Memorial Center, No. 85-C-437-E (N.D. Okla., July 24, 1987).

Implementation Problems in Institutional Reform Litigation. (1977). 91 *Harvard Law Review,* 428–463. Cambridge, MA: Harvard Law Review Association.

Lelsz v. Kavanagh, No. S-74-95-CA (E.D. Tex., July 21, 1983); 807 F. 2d 1243 (5th Cir. 1987), *rehearing denied* 815 F. 2d 1034 (5th Cir. 1987), *certiorari dismissed* 483 U.S. 1057 (1987); 673 F. Supp. 828 (N.D. Tex. 1987).

Lottman, M.S. (1976). "Enforcement of judicial decrees: Now comes the hard part," 1 *Mental Disability Law Reporter* 69–76. Washington, DC: American Bar Association Commission on the Mentally Disabled.

Mansfield Class Panel of Monitors. (1985). *Annual report, May 1984–June 1985.* Hartford, CT: Author.

Mansfield Class Panel of Monitors. (1985). *Audit report: staffing at Mansfield training school.* Hartford, CT: Author.

Michigan Association for Retarded Citizens v. Smith, No. 78-70384 (E.D. Mich., August 30, 1979).

Morales v. Turman, 364 F. Supp. 166 (E.D. Tex. 1973).

New York State Association for Retarded Children (NYSARC) v. Carey, No. 72-C-356/357 (E.D.N.Y., April 30, 1975); 393 F. Supp. 715 (E.D.N.Y. 1975); 446 F. Supp. 479 (E.D.N.Y. 1978); 466 F. Supp. 487 (E.D.N.Y. 1979), *affirmed* 612 F. 2d 644 (2d Cir. 1979); 596 F. 2d 27 (2d Cir. 1979), *certiorari denied* 444 U.S. 836 (1979); Order of October 22, 1979; 492 F. Supp. 1110 (E.D.N.Y. 1980), *reversed* 631 F. 2d 162 (2d Cir. 1980); 551 F. Supp. 1165 (E.D.N.Y. 1982), *affirmed in part, reversed in part* 706 ꞏF. 2d 958 (2d Cir. 1983), *certiorari denied* 464 U.S. 915 (1983); Order of July 13, 1982; NYSARC v. Cuomo, No. 72-C-356/357 (E.D.N.Y., February 25, 1987).

Philadelphia Police and Fire Association for Handicapped Children v. City of Philadelphia, 874 F.2d 156 (3d Cir. 1989).

othman, D.J., & Rothman, S.M. (1984). *The Willowbrook wars.* New York: Harper & Row.

Rule 53, *Federal Rules of Civil Procedure.*

Savidge v. Fincannon, 836 F. 2d 895 (5th Cir. 1988).

Society for Good Will to Retarded Children v. Cuomo, 572 F. Supp. 1300 (E.D.N.Y. 1983), *vacated and remanded* 737 F. 2d 1239 (2d Cir. 1984), *on remand* 103 F.R.D. 168 (E.D.N.Y. 1984); 652 F. Supp. 515 (E.D.N.Y. 1987), *reversed* 832 F. 2d 245 (2d Cir. 1987).

Temple University & Human Services Research Institute. (1983). *Pennhurst longitudinal study 1979 to 1983: Fourth year summary.* Philadelphia: Temple University Developmental Disabilities Center. Boston: Human Services Research Institute.

Thomas S. v. Morrow, 781 F. 2d 367 (4th Cir. 1986).

Welsch v. Gardebring, 667 F. Supp. 1284 (D. Minn. 1987).

Welsch v. Likins, 373 F. Supp. 487 (D. Minn. 1974); No. 4-72-451 (D. Minn., October 1, 1974); Order of December, 1977.

Welsch v. Noot, No. 4-72-451 (D. Minn., September 15, 1980).

Woestendiek, J. (1987). "An emotional closing ceremony for Pennhurst," *The Philadelphia Inquirer,* December 10, 1987.

Wuori v. Zitnay, No. 75-80-SD (D. Maine, July 14, 1978).

Wyatt v. Ireland, No. 3195-N (M.D. Ala., October 25, 1979); Orders of January 15, 1980.

Wyatt v. Stickney, 344 F. Supp. 373 and 387 (M.D. Ala. 1972), *affirmed* 503 F. 2d 1305 (5th Cir. 1974).

Youngberg v. Romeo, 457 U.S. 307 (1982).

chapter 13 ———————

Elements of an Effective Governmental Watchdog Agency

———————— *Nancy K. Ray* ————————

The struggle to ensure the quality of care and protection from harm for persons with developmental disabilities has a long history in New York and the nation. Although standards and expectations have evolved and radically differed over time, one can essentially plot the history of developmental disabilities and mental retardation services worldwide by tracing public scandals and the government response.

In New York, as in other states, the government's responses to scandals in the field of disabilities have frequently been marked by the establishment of independent oversight bodies within government. The Utica Act of 1842, establishing the state's first public institution for the mentally ill, the State Lunatic Asylum at Utica, also authorized the appointment of nine lay persons to serve as the board of managers for the institution.

A quarter of a century later, in 1873, the New York Legislature augmented the oversight of boards of managers by creating the Office of Lunacy, empowered to visit and inspect institutions, and in 1902 the office was renamed the Commission on Lunacy and was authorized to oversee the boards of managers.

Despite the early precedent of lay oversight of public institutions in New York, the authority and influence of these lay overseers waned in the early part of the twentieth century. Statutory changes in 1927 renamed the lay boards "boards of visitors" and stripped them of their management decision-making authority but continued to afford them broad investigatory and advisory authority over the institutions. The statutory functions, powers, and duties of boards of visitors remained essentially unchanged for the next 50 years; but as New York continued to expand its number of public institutions for people with developmental disabilities to over 50 facilities, which served 93,000 individuals at their peak in 1955, the actual performance and activities of individual boards of visitors varied. At their worst, they were no more than a nice group of men and women who met periodically with the institutional superintendent over tea and cakes.

THE WILLOWBROOK SCANDAL

In 1972, the public disclosure of the horrors of the Willowbrook State School in New York by Geraldo Rivera in nightly ABC news broadcasts raised the curtain on another era of scandal in New York's mental retardation system. The exposé resulted in major changes in the administration of human services in the state, the most dramatic of which was splitting the state's mammoth Department of Mental Hygiene into three separately administered agencies— the Office of Mental Health, the Office of Mental Retardation and Developmental Disabilities, and the Office of Alcoholism and Substance Abuse Services. (In actuality, the latter office has functioned as two separate agencies, the Division of Substance Abuse Services and the Division of Alcoholism, although there have been stirrings within state government to forge the two agencies into a single office.)

The scandal also brought to light the relative ineffectiveness of boards of visitors as independent watchdogs of the state's public mental institutions. As well documented in David Rothman's (1984) historical account, *The Willowbrook Wars,* the board of visitors at the Willowbrook State School had been virtually moribund for years. Furthermore, such inactivity was the norm among boards of visitors across the state.

There was also little objective evidence that the governor (who appointed board members) or the state Senate (which confirmed them) actually anticipated that boards of visitors would be vigorous advocates for the residents of the institutions for which they were watchdogs. In many areas, appointments to the boards were strictly political, and many members had literally stayed on boards for decades, often forming close allegiances with superintendents and public developmental disabilities officials. Most critically, there was virtually no training for board members, and whatever technical assistance new or old board members received was usually provided by institutional officials.

Indeed, there was wide recognition that boards of visitors had largely lost their essential independence and that most board members were neither knowledgeable of their responsibilities nor skilled to carry them out. Additionally, many voices in and out of government questioned whether the broad investigatory and advisory responsibilities of boards of visitors could realistically be carried out by lay, volunteer members. In particular, many state legislators did not have confidence that board members could thoroughly and competently address their constituents' complaints.

CREATION OF A NEW WATCHDOG AGENCY

These concerns, together with the fear that individuals with multiple disabilities (historically poorly served by the state's unified Department of Mental Hygiene) would be even more likely to fall between the cracks of the now separate offices, contributed in 1977 to the creation of a new watchdog agency for developmental disabilities and mental retardation services in New York, the Commission on Quality of Care for the Mentally Disabled. Modeled in part after the state's newly created Commission on Corrections that was designed to oversee prison and jail services, the Commission on Quality of Care was armed with broad statutory responsibilities and powers that allowed investigation of virtually any policy, programmatic, or fiscal issue and allowed access to any relevant facility, its records, and staff.

The Commission's statute also extended its jurisdiction across state-operated treatment facilities and programs to those operated by local governments, voluntary agencies, and private corporations or entities. Additionally, the Commission's legislation assured a specific statutory responsibility to train boards of visitors and to provide them other technical assistance, as needed.

Thus were the stormy origins of New York's new watchdog agency. Despite its broad mandate, it is also probably fair to say that few within the halls of government or state human services communities had great expectations for the new commission they had created. In the first year or two of the Commission's existence, its three commissioners and staff traveled the state announcing that the agency would respond to complaints, investigate unusual deaths, examine reports of abuse, and train boards of visitors. The commissioners and staff also frequently deflected criticisms that as an agency within the government, its independence was too compromised and that it, too, would not be a strong voice for reform and change.

Since 1977, the New York State Commission on Quality of Care for the Mentally Disabled has grown from a small, vaguely acknowledged watchdog agency to a prominent state agency, frequently called upon by the state Legislature and the governor for policy, program, and fiscal advice and for immediate investigatory response to specific incidents and situations. This characterization should not imply that the Commission is universally successful in its advocacy, that reforms and changes always occur as promptly as the agency would like, or that serious systemic problems do not continue to exist in New York's services to persons with developmental disabilities. The Commission's influence and opinions are, however, well recognized, and its credibility to provide objective investigations of issues and problems, as well as constructive recommendations, is well-respected both in and out of government.

The purpose of this chapter is not to chronicle the Commission's growth, but to reflect on the factors that have contributed to its effectiveness and, in so doing, to lay out the essential attributes that make it an effective internal quality assurance watchdog agency in government. This delineation appears especially relevant since many states are contemplating or just beginning to form similar watchdog agencies. New York has 13 years of experience with an internal watchdog agency that can be shared with other states.

At the outset, there are certain caveats that should be noted. First, most of these observations are derived from the author's personal observations as an insider and staff to the Commission, although travels and consultancies in other states, including Tennessee, Texas, Connecticut, and Louisiana, have had a definite balancing influence on perspectives. Second, an insider's perspective is always somewhat clouded. Suffice it to say there is more than a measure of truth that watchdogs perceive themselves somewhat differently than those who are watching them.

THE BASIC STATUTE

From the beginning, the Commission profited from its broad statutory mandate, which assured sufficient universal language to allow the agency to approach almost any issue or concern and adequate concrete responsibilities and powers to provide a clear framework for its basic tasks and duties. As noted previously, the Commission's statute provided broad advisory and investigative authority that extended from specific incidents and situations to statewide or regional issues involving fundamental policy and the programmatic and cost effectiveness of services. Equally important, however, the Legislature's delineation of specific responsibilities for the agency—to investigate complaints, to ensure the effective investigation of allegations of abuse and neglect, to review all patient/client deaths and investigate those that appear to be due to unnatural causes or unusual circumstances, and to train members of boards of visitors—provided a focus and central mission for the Commission's activities.

Along with these responsibilities, the Commission was also blessed with ample access rights and other authority to carry them out. By statute, Commission staff may visit any state operated or licensed developmental disability and mental retardation facility or program, day or night, announced or unannounced. The Commission also has access to all documents, data, and information, including patient records, relevant to carrying out its responsibilities.

Employees of facilities and programs, as well as personnel assigned to the state or local administration of developmental disability and mental retardation services, are also obliged to cooperate with Commission investigations and to submit to individual interviews as warranted. The Commission is also explicitly afforded subpoena powers should any employee resist cooperation with an investigation or should any specific data, document, or record be withheld. The Commission is also authorized to speak with any individual receiving services.

The Commission is also authorized to issue its findings and recommendations directly to facility directors and the commissioners of the three state offices, *and* the statute requires these individuals to respond to the Commission's recommendations within 90 days. Although the statute affords the Commission no enforcement authority, this language has assured formal status to Commission findings and recommendations, and it has guaranteed a level of public accountability and governmental response.

Additionally, and not inconsequently, this language implicitly requires public access to Commission findings and recommendations through state and federal freedom of information laws. In keeping with this public access, the Commission has, as a matter of operating policy, been diligent in publicly reporting its findings and recommendations in formal reports, in its newsletter, in letters of findings, and in public legislative hearings and other forums. Increasingly, advocates, family members, legislators, and representatives of the media have also taken advantage of the freedom of information laws to request Commission findings and documents that have not routinely been made public.

The central underlying attribute of the Commission's statute, however, is its allowances for considerable administrative discretion in the actual choice of priorities and the specific activities undertaken. For example, although the Commission has broad authority to investigate complaints, allegations of abuse or neglect, or unusual or unnatural deaths, it also has discretion to develop criteria for shaping and setting priorities in each of these areas. Particularly in such a large state as New York, this allowance for administrative flexibility has been invaluable; it has ensured that the scope of agency responsibilities do not overwhelm its resources, and it has provided essential leeway for Commission leadership to allocate resources where they are needed and most likely to yield constructive reform and change.

This litany of the statutory authorities, responsibilities, and powers of the Commission may appear quite basic, but it is remarkable how many watchdog agencies are circumscribed and substantially limited by less adequate statutes. Not uncommonly, responsibilities of watchdog agencies are tailored by bureaucratic categories that may make sense in governmental terms, but do not facilitate monitoring the quality of care for real people whose problems and disabilities may not be so easily categorized.

The Commission's access to facilities and programs, and their staff's and clients', as well as access to all documents, data, and records, is also not enjoyed by many watchdog agencies. Without this access to facilities, programs, people, and information, many watchdog agencies have been compelled to let important issues and concerns go unaddressed.

The Commission's authority to issue recommendations and require timely responses has also been universally afforded to (or capitalized upon by) many governmental watchdog agencies. As a result, their activities have often been orchestrated within the soundproof walls of government with little public scrutiny or accountability for their recommended reforms or changes.

Perhaps most critically, public advocates and state legislators, in their desire to craft the "most effective" watchdog agency, often err in specifying responsibilities so precisely that there is little room for agency administrators to make essential decisions in allocating resources among many competing priorities. Without this flexibility many watchdog agencies lose their effectiveness as they drown in mandates and responsibilities that far exceed their resources.

ATTRIBUTES OF A WATCHDOG AGENCY

Leadership

Notwithstanding the critical underpinnings of their statutory base, the lifeblood of effective watchdog agencies is without question its leadership. Advocacy, oversight, and analysis are not clear-cut tasks; along the way there is much need for wise and often difficult decision-making. There are always more problems and concerns than available resources, and few of the issues actually confronted present black and white profiles of available alternatives or needed reforms and changes. Just as critically, watchdog agencies by their nature are often the bearers of "bad news." It requires a certain strength of character to convey these messages.

These essential attributes of the leaders of watchdog agencies are not easily quantified or measured. Such leaders are characterized by certain intangibles of integrity, the strength of their convictions, the ability to focus on the most critical priorities, clear thinking, and the capability to ensure an efficient and effective operation. While these characteristics are not ones that are easily assessed by appointing authorities, conscious commitment to them often marks the difference between oversight agencies of meager or substantial effectiveness.

By statute, the Commission was also designed with certain safeguards for sound, protected leadership. First, the Commission is headed by three commissioners, and despite inevitable operational difficulties of this tripartite administration, it has assured representation of more than one single voice.

Each commissioner is appointed for a 5-year term, and removal can be effected only by the governor for a specific cause, thus assuring explicit protections from political retribution for Commission members.

Additionally, at its creation, the three commissioners had staggered terms of 1, 3, and 5 years to ensure that there would not be a complete turnover of commissioners (or a clean sweep of the agency) in any one year. Finally, actual appointments to the Commission are also jointly made by the executive and legislative branches of government. The governor nominates, and the state Senate confirms.

In addition to the safeguards in statute protecting the Commission's leadership, there have probably been other equally, if not more important, attributes of the actual men and women who have assumed these roles. These individuals have represented divergent backgrounds and experiences in developmental disabilities services. These individuals who have served in these positions have brought strong backgrounds in state and constitutional law; in the financing of public services; in the administration of governmental and voluntary not-for-profit agencies; as well as in developmental disability, education, and health services. They have also held strictly to the principal of nonpartisanship. Early on, the commissioners, and especially the chairman, established a reputation of not doing business along political party lines.

The Commission has also been markedly blessed by the stability of its leadership. The chairman of the Commission has served with the agency since its origin, completing an initial 3-year term, and serving a second 5-year term. The other two commissionerships have each turned over once, but in each case, the initial appointees stayed on through the agency's first 5-years.

Finally, and not inconsequentially, the Commission has enjoyed active support from the governor and the state Legislature. This leadership support for the Commission at the highest levels of state government has also been invaluable.

In its early formative years, then Governor Hugh L. Carey, a strong proponent of developmental disability reform and of the presence of a vigilant independent watchdog capacity over developmental disability services, set a tone within government for responsiveness to Commission concerns. Later, Governor Mario M. Cuomo continued this support early in his first term by reappointing the agency's first chairman to an additional 5-year term.

Additionally, especially as the agency established its credibility through actual work efforts and products, support for Commission concerns, as well as recognition of its value within government, was also forthcoming from the state Legislature. Increasingly, legislators call on the Commission for specific advice and assistance, both in directly responding to constituent complaints and in addressing systemic policy issues. Since 1984, the Legislature has specifically requested that the Commission examine and report upon such wide ranging issues as support services for families caring for relatives with developmental disabilities, basic living conditions in public institutions, the incidence of offenders with developmental disabilities in state prisons, mental health outpatient services, and conditions in adult boarding homes serving persons with developmental disabilities. Most importantly, the Legislature has been supportive of Commission recommendations, often providing needed legislation to encourage and enforce their implementation.

Relevant Priorities

Early in the Commission's life it became apparent that there were many more problems and concerns warranting the agency's attention than resources to address them. Determining which priorities to select has been an ongoing process that has required time, decision-making, and most critically, many open channels for communication with various constituent groups. One of the first activities of the Commission was to hold public forums across the state, both to announce the agency's mission and responsibilities and to hear from constituents. Since that first year, the agency has repeated this activity many times, and each time it has proven to be immensely valuable in keeping the agency's priorities closely in tune with concerns of consumers, families, and managerial and direct care staff of the service delivery system.

The Commission also recognized early on that formal mechanisms for its own staff to influence agency priorities are essential. In addition to many ongoing informal ways that staff can bring concerns directly to Commission members and midlevel managers, more formal efforts, including staff retreats and full-day staff meetings to discuss agency priorities and to evaluate the effectiveness of the agency's oversight strategies, have been an important part of the agency's overall process for selecting its agenda of priorities and for designing its specific interventions.

Early in 1984, one of these meetings surfaced significant staff frustration with the agency's piecemeal approach to overseeing inappropriate institutional conditions. This led to the planning of comprehensive unannounced institutional reviews across the state. After an initial pilot effort in the spring of 1984, the effectiveness and need for a systemic approach was also recognized by the state Legislature, which provided increased fiscal support to enable the agency to continue this effort on a broader scale. Since then, staff concerns have focused on the agency's handling of specific complaints of abuse and neglect in treatment facilities, and they have spurred the agency to reorganize and allocate more resources toward these problems and also to address these issues from a more systemic perspective.

While the Commission's continued use of public and staff forums has helped to ensure that the agency is kept informed of issues needing its attention, it has also increased the complexity of priority decision-making. Over the years, the Commission has never written down explicit guidelines to direct this decision-making process, nonetheless, certain principles have clearly had a longstanding and entrenched influence.

The first of these is that the agency should be responsive to concerns of individual consumers, their families, and other client advocates. Resource allocation at the agency has always reflected this choice, and over half of the agency's professional staff have been reserved for individual advocacy of one type or another (e.g., complaint investigations, death investigations, abuse and neglect investigations, information, and referral.

A second and equally important principle is that the agency should focus on the "basics." Although the agency has frequently intervened on peripheral issues, there has been an overriding bias that core issues of safety, humane care, protections from specific harm for persons with developmental disabilities, and the essential cost-effective delivery of quality services should be on the agency's main agenda. Rooted in a recognition that violations of these primary precepts are still all too common in New York, as well as a belief that higher expectations can be assured only once these violations are rectified, this principle has helped the agency to keep to the main course and not drift off to less consequential issues.

Additionally, the agency has historically chosen those issues for systemic studies where reform was both needed and likely to be achieved. In actualizing this premise, the Commission's leadership has always been astutely sensitive to political and public sentiment, as well as the adequacy of its resources to do the job well. This has not meant that the agency has stayed away from controversial and highly charged issues, but it has ensured that before embarking on any issue of concern, it has carefully assessed the likelihood of constructive outcomes from its efforts. More importantly, it has meant that the agency's leaders have been keenly aware of critical windows of opportunity, often created in the wake of a particular crisis or fiscal situation, that allow an opening for clear and practical policy recommendations for change and reform.

At times, adherence to this principle has also meant that the agency has steered away from issues where staff expertise and/or numbers would not be sufficient to explore the issue competently or fully. For example, in its early days, the Commission chose its cost-effectiveness issues carefully. The agency's fiscal staff was small, and the Commission members were sensitive to the powerful forces that could coalesce around issues of fiscal accountability in government. Gradually, however, through the careful selection of these issues and the thoroughness of the agency's work, the Commission's efforts in cost-effectiveness studies and fiscal fraud investigations gained respect within state government. In 1985 and 1987, the state Legislature increased the agency's appropriation to ensure its fiscal oversight role.

Another important but less tangible principle that has guided the Commission's selection of priorities and activities has been a prejudice in favor of flexibility. Thus, although the agency annually projects both a short-term and a long-term agenda, it has also been receptive to changing agendas. By the nature of its work, the Commission is continually confronted with emerging crises. Additionally, in the course of its own activities, previously unrecognized issues often surface. As a result, the Commission has always valued flexibility and recognized that shifting gears and priorities midstream is both a necessary and desirable attribute of a watchdog agency.

Fairness and Objectivity

Another essential cornerstone of an effective watchdog agency is its credibility across many different constituent groups. It's inevitable that any watchdog agency will be viewed with some anxiety and even trepidation among providers. Yet, despite this likelihood, it is imperative that the service system also views the watchdog agency as a fair and objective observer and investigator of its activities and operations.

There is no magic formula to ensure this public image, but there are clearly several factors that can contribute to it. First, the agency's staff must be able and experienced, and their activities in the field must be well-directed and carefully supervised. Commission staff, since its earliest hires, have been largely selected from among men and women who have worked on the front lines of service delivery. These staff members have assumed different types and levels of positions in the service system, and the Commission has encouraged its staff not to forget their roots.

This hiring principle has ensured that staff not become zealot critics, unmindful of the difficult jobs and sensitivities of the men and women who still work on the front lines. Furthermore, it has encouraged staff to investigate complaints objectively and fairly with a strong underlying belief that quality care and treatment is also crucially dependent on a quality workforce whose efforts are recognized and respected.

Second, and equally important, the Commission has always set a premium on a front-line presence in treatment facilities and service programs. The number of on-site visits and meetings with providers, staff, consumers, and their families that the Commission achieves each year has always been a matter of record, and it has been carefully monitored as a statistic of primary value. Additionally, as the agency has gained more expertise in systemic studies, its methods have increasingly relied upon client-centered data collection. Thus, as the Commission reviewed the availability of family support services, the appropriateness of discharge planning, or the treatment and experience of criminal offenders with developmental disabilities, for example, it has sought to explore issues by tracing the actual experiences and outcomes for individual clients.

This bias toward direct observation has not only ensured a greater validity to Commission findings, but it has also promoted the agency's credibility with the field. It is hard to contest actual empirical data, and it is difficult to dismiss a watchdog who frequently shows up on the doorstep eager to see personally what is going on.

The Commission's reputation for fairness and objectivity has been immeasurably enhanced by its own internal diligence in checking preliminary findings and in requiring careful, detailed documentation of any concerns or problems. The Commission has also been willing to share preliminary findings and recommendations with providers and the relevant state agency(ies) prior to making them final and public. These operational practices have, without doubt, often caused delays in the release of public reports that have sometimes caused both the Commission and the public to be impatient.

Sometimes delays in provider or state agency responses to draft reports have added to the impatience, but these delays seemed to have some purpose. Thus, the process step of allowing comment on draft reports has been helpful overall. Although the Commission has rarely received substantial criticism of its basic findings in the review of draft reports, the process has ensured an essential measure of fairness and an important safeguard for accuracy that has been invaluable. Finally, the Commission's fairness has probably been most often judged by its commitment to present both the good and the bad. It is often tempting for watchdog agencies, seeking to mobilize support for their proposed reforms, to fail to present a balanced picture. At the same time, yielding to this temptation is a critical pitfall. In failing to recognize and highlight good performance, watchdog agencies not only betray their public mission, but they also overlook the likely possibility that a few words of well-deserved praise may be far more motivational in effecting needed reform than tracts of criticism.

Consumer Accountability

Perhaps the most essential attribute of a watchdog agency is its consumer accountability. Few paid advocates in this field will not honestly admit that, at times, they have become frustrated working directly with consumers and their families. Sometimes they seem overzealous, sometimes intolerant to concerns of others, and sometimes simply very confused and mixed up about what they really want.

Fundamentally, however, most paid advocates, like this author, are products of their own upbringing and the longstanding prejudice against the capacities of people with disabilities to speak wisely for themselves. Historically, this prejudice against persons with disabilities often has spread to their families, who have alternately been blamed for their children's handicaps and simultaneously cruelly chastised for their deep concern for their children's care and well-being. To be sure, most fight these prejudices, nonetheless, they can influence one's basic responsiveness to consumers and their families.

The Commission, too, has been threatened by these prejudices, and it is perhaps the most enduring and valued attribute of the men and women who have led the Commission that they have been ever vigilant in combating this threat. This fight has not been carried out as any planned action, but it has been won by many subtle day-to-day activities. For example, letters of concern from consumers and family members are frequently received by Commission members, and they always receive a prompt reply and often a personal telephone call. These letters are also commonly circulated to Commission staff.

Consumers and family members routinely receive stipends to attend Commission conferences; they assume valuable positions on various agency advisory boards, and they are often called upon individually or in small groups to provide the Commission with advice in planning major studies and projects. In fact, Michael Kennedy (Chapter 3, this volume) serves on an advisory committee to the Commission. Equally important, at agency affairs the commissioners take the lead in soliciting consumer and family member participation and, when necessary, assuring needed interference to guarantee that their voices and concerns are not dismissed.

However, the Commission has fostered consumer accountability by directly and personally rewarding individual staff efforts that endorse it. Working out difficult and trying situations with individual consumers and families is highly respected, and new staff soon learn that even if solutions cannot be readily tailored, an important component of their job is to be there to listen.

Another aspect of consumer accountability for a watchdog agency is its responsibility to ensure with diligence that government funds allocated to its operation are well spent. To this end, it is essential that watchdog agencies are scrupulously and publicly accountable for their use of resources and the outcomes of their activities. It is, in many ways, a paradox that in the early days of the Commission, many engaged in seemingly endless debates about how the agency's placement within government may short-circuit its effectiveness. Now, notwithstanding continued respect and periodic envy for truly external advocates, the Commission recognizes that the agency's place within government responds to a vital public mission and that the agency's ultimate success must be measured against the fundamental benchmark of public accountability.

This last point now appears almost self-evident, but in the early days of the Commission, many staff (mostly products of the college campus protests of the 1960s) hardly reflected on the agency's own public accountability. Fortunately, they grew up quickly and learned that executive, legislative, and judicial oversight of the agency's accomplishments would be routine and vigorous. Furthermore, they came to recognize that this oversight—in contrast to their early fears—would not, at least in the presence of strong and capable leadership, be constraining of the agency's efforts. Quite the contrary, the agency has generally found government oversight to be reinforcing and supportive of their efforts.

This reinforcement has been more visibly apparent in the Legislature's increasing fiscal support for Commission operations. Since its first full year of operation in 1978, state funding for the Commission has increased fourfold. Additionally, the agency's cognizance of its responsibility to ensure public accountability has fostered its very public profile. Commission public reports, its newsletters, its regular press conferences, as well as the frequent presentations by its commissioners before state legislative committees and the governor's Human Services Sub-Cabinet have all taken substantial resources, but at the same time, these efforts have assured public accountability and public awareness, and they have been critical to the agency's ongoing effectiveness.

CONCLUSION

It is not easy to provide a concise recipe for an effective governmental watchdog agency for developmental disability services. It is not that it is hard to identify particular factors that can contribute and alternatively limit their effectiveness (at least over the short term), or contribute to their downfall. From these examples, many more lessons can be drawn.

Instead, the dilemma is that there are so many lessons and so much need for a watchdog agency to keep learning and growing. Effective internal watchdog agencies have both demanding and ever-changing agendas, and they do not have the luxury of operating in an ivory tower where learning can take on a gentle and rhythmic pace.

Cast in the midst of constantly changing political environments, as well as ongoing changes in clinical and rehabilitative service approaches, governmental watchdog agencies must learn, adjust, and adapt new strategies quickly. Most critically, they must maintain the courage and motivation to take the risks often inherent in new approaches, to avoid complacency with the status quo, and to recognize with humility that however much they have learned, each day will bring new insights, new missions, and new challenges.

REFERENCE

Rothman, D. (1984). *The Willowbrook wars*, New York: Harper & Row.

ACCREDITATION ISSUES

chapter 14 ⎯⎯⎯⎯

Accreditation
of Developmental
Disabilities Programs

⎯ *Richard Hemp and David Braddock* ⎯

Editors' Note: *Accreditation is a major element in the array of mechanisms available to assess the quality of services to persons with developmental disabilities and mental retardation. The following discussion provides the reader with an understanding of the utility of accreditation as well as a sense of history about the evolution of the principles that underpin national accreditation approaches. Although accreditation is a key ingredient in quality assurance, very little basic analysis or research has been done on the results of accreditation, the patterns that emerge from accreditation surveys, and the relationship of deficits uncovered in accreditation surveys and negative outcomes for clients. What analysis and research that does exist, however, is the work of Richard Hemp and David Braddock. This chapter is a presentation of an article by Hemp and Braddock that appeared in* Mental Retardation, *(1988), Vol. 26, No. 5, pp. 257–267. Their research and analysis is based on ACDD accreditation reviews from*

The Accreditation Study was supported in part by grant #90 DD 0047 from the Administration on Developmental Disabilities (ADD), Office of Human Development Services, U.S. Department of Health and Human Services, and we are grateful for the support of former ADD Commissioner Jean K. Elder. We also acknowledge the assistance of Glenn T. Fujiura, Tamar Heller, and research assistants Steve Garcia, Lynne Mock, and Larry Prebis. Kenneth Crosby, the former executive director of the ACDD and Mary Cerreto, former chief executive officer, as well as the ACDD Executive Committee and Council staff provided valuable cooperation essential to the successful completion of the study.

1980–1984, and is not a reflection of experience with more current standards. However, the study still stands as one of the only systematic reviews of its kind and the issues that the authors raise—both for further research and for quality assurance policy—are still current and thought provoking.

Residential program standards with national impact originated with the American Association on Mental Deficiency (now called the American Association on Mental Retardation—AAMR) in 1952 (Crosby, 1973; National News, 1979). A grant from the National Institute of Mental Health supported the publication in 1964 of *Standards for State Residential Institutions for the Mentally Retarded* (American Association on Mental Deficiency, 1964), and these standards were presented by the Accreditation Council for Services for Mentally Retarded and Other Developmentally Disabled Persons (ACMRDD) (1984) as "minimal . . . generally attainable within 5 to 10 years" (p.v). Grants from the Mental Retardation Branch of the United States Public Health Service in 1965 and subsequently from the Division of Mental Retardation in the Social and Rehabilitation Service, United States Department of Health, Education, and Welfare (HEW) in 1966 supported the development of accreditation instruments. By 1969, the instruments were utilized to evaluate 134 state institutions for individuals with mental retardation. These surveyed facilities constituted 75% of all such institutions and 90% of total residents (Accreditation Council for Services for Mentally Retarded [ACMRDD], 1984, p.vi).

In 1969, a Memorandum of Agreement was completed with the Joint Commission on the Accreditation of Hospitals (JCAH) that established the Accreditation Council for Facilities for the Mentally Retarded (ACF/MR) as a JCAH component (ACMRDD, 1984; Orlans, 1975). The first edition of the ACF/MR accreditation standards (Accreditation Council for Facilities for the Mentally Retarded [ACF/MR], 1971) focused on large residential programs. In 1973, ACF/MR standards were adapted for use by the HEW for certification of Intermediate Care Facilities for the Mentally Retarded (ICFs/MR) (Boggs, 1976). Reflecting the increasing numbers of community-based alternatives to institutions, the Council published standards specific to community agencies (Accreditation Council for Facilities for the Mentally Retarded [ACF/MR], 1973). The separate institutional and community services standards were consolidated in 1977, and new editions were published in 1981, 1984, and 1987 (Accreditation Council on Services for People with Developmental Disabilities [ACDD], 1987). In 1979, the JCAH terminated affiliation with four accreditation councils, including the ACF/MR, and the Council was then established as an independent, not-for-profit corporation (National News, 1979). [The independent organization is known as the Accreditation Council on Services for People with Developmental Disabilities—ACDD.]

Accreditation by the Council has been generally acknowledged to be an important process for monitoring services (Boggs, 1976; Braddock, 1977; Butterfield, 1976; Epple, Jacobson, & Janicki, 1985). For a number of years, California, Illinois, and Tennessee have used accreditation standards as goals for state-operated residential facilities, and South Dakota has utilized ACDD accreditation in lieu of licensure or other program review for community programs. Maryland mandated in 1982 that private organizations undergo accreditation survey (Hemp & Braddock, 1985) and Montana (R. B. Offner, Director, Montana University Affiliated Program Satellite, personal communication, December 10, 1986) and North Dakota (North Dakota Department of Human Services, 1986) adopted ACDD accreditation standards for all community-based developmental disabilities programs. States that utilize ACDD standards for components of their service systems include Colorado (day programs), Iowa (community residential), Massachusetts (Medicaid Waiver services), and Washington (vocational rehabilitation) (C. Hayes, Director of Operations and Development, ACDD, personal communication, September 23, 1987).

The Health Care Financing Administration (HCFA) in its proposed rules for the ICF/MR program stated: "We based our proposal, particularly the Active Treatment Services section . . . primarily on the accreditation standards published in 1983 by the ACDD" (Health Care Financing Administration [HCFA], 1988, p. 20448). Moreover, the American Association on Mental Retardation "encourages accreditation and monitoring of programs by ACMRDD and other commonly recognized and accepted entities that adhere to the highest professional standards" (Legislative Goals, 1987, p. 54). The AAMR (Legislative Goals, 1987) has further recommended that "facilities accredited by the ACMRDD should be deemed to be in compliance with state and federal certification requirements" (p. 54).

In a discussion of accreditation as quality assurance, Ross (1980) concluded that "what is an acceptable level of service quality is a judgment call . . . debates and disagreements tend to promote reliance on accreditation as the foremost quality assurance device" (p. 36). Boggs (1976) and Bradley, Ashbaugh, Allard, and Liegey (1977) discussed the difference between accreditation (evaluation by a nongovernmental agency), licensure (government, usually state, granting permission to operate), and certification (for reimbursement with federal funds). Boggs (1976) stressed that accreditation and licensure should be complementary: "The role of voluntary nongovernmental bodies [is] improving standards, securing consensus, and assisting providers to improve their performance . . . Public licensure . . . responds to the ultimate demand for public accountability" (p. 366).

Bradley, Ashbaugh, and Harder (1984), citing evidence that formal, bureaucratic mechanisms are often ineffective, suggested that "persuasion of peers rather than administrative coercion is . . . the most effective means of controlling human services practice" (p. 167). Bradley et al. (1984) reviewed 22 nongovernmental evaluation systems, including citizen evaluations with Program Analysis of Service Systems (PASS) in Pennsylvania and parent monitoring at the Macomb-Oakland Regional Center in Michigan. Besides accreditation by the ACDD, quality assurance approaches that have been widely used include federal and state licensure and certification, accreditation by the Commission on Accreditation of Rehabilitation Facilities (CARF), and PASS.

In 1985, the federally mandated ICF/MR survey activity affected 140,000 individuals in 2,911 facilities (HCFA, 1986, pp. 7520, 7528). Although 70% of these facilities were 15 beds or less in size, they served only an estimated 19,900 individuals (Braddock, Hemp, & Fujiura, 1987). Over 100,000 individuals resided in ICF/MR units in large public residential facilities in 1983 (Epple et al., 1985). Generally, ICF/MR certification surveys have been conducted by state health department staff, utilizing the federal regulations. The Secretary of the Department of Health and Human Services, following provisions in Section 1910(c) of the Social Security Act (amended by PL 96–499 in 1980), however, has also instituted federal "validation" surveys or "look-behinds." Federal "look-behind" surveys in 1984 conducted at 17 facilities previously approved by state health department surveyors resulted in the citing of serious deficiencies in many of them and the withdrawal of Federal Financial Participation for one facility (Gettings & Salmon, 1985; Subcommittee on the Handicapped, 1985).

State and local governments are also engaged in numerous licensure, monitoring, and/or certification activities. State, county, and city health departments often require that a nursing home or other long-term care facility be licensed prior to opening, whether or not the facility is ICF/MR certified or accredited by a voluntary organization. O'Connor (1976) classified 733 weighted community residential facility respondents and found that three quarters had state licenses, usually focusing on fire and health regulations; a third had city licenses or certificates; and 14% had county licenses (some facilities had more than one type of license). State licensure requirements have often replicated substantial portions of the ICF/MR and ACF/MR standards (Allard & Toff, 1980; Repp & Barton, 1980).

Accreditation by the Commission on Accreditation of Rehabilitation Facilities is often recognized by state departments of rehabilitation in connection with funding of vocational services. Hemp, Fujiura, and Braddock (1986) inspected 500 developmental disabilities surveys conducted by the Commission in 13 states during 1982–1984. They noted that over 90% of the organizations surveyed provided vocational or other day services, and 2% provided residential services. An estimated 1,100 of those surveyed organizations provided developmental disabilities services in 1984, constituting 85% of the 1,351 organizations accredited by the Commission that year (Commission on

Accreditation of Rehabilitation Facilities [CARF], 1985). Alabama and Massachusetts also mandated that Commission standards be applied to Medicaid Waiver programs (Commission on Accreditation of Rehabilitation Facilities [CARF], 1987).

The Program Analysis of Service Systems (Wolfensberger & Glenn, 1975a, 1975b), a voluntary evaluation system embodying the normalization principle (Wolfensberger, 1972), was utilized to assess community programs in five states (Ross, 1980). Flynn and Heal (1981) reported its use in Canada, England, Australia, Holland, and Israel. The program analysis system has also been utilized as a measure of environmental quality in research (Eyman, Demaine, & Lei, 1979; Hull & Thompson, 1980; Lei, Nihira, Sheehy, & Meyers, 1981). Flynn and Nitsch (1980) reviewed PASS evaluations of residential, vocational, and special education services.

ANALYSIS OF ACDD SURVEYS

An analysis of surveys was designed to summarize basic information about ACDD accreditation and the agencies ACDD surveyed. The analysis included all 296 surveys conducted from July 1980 through December 1984. Utilizing the Council's numerical coding system to maintain confidentiality of individual agency survey results, a computer data base was established at the Institute for the Study of Developmental Disabilities/School of Public Health at the University of Illinois at Chicago. The data included number of individuals served, number of staff, ownership (governmental, private not-for-profit, and private proprietary), length of time in operation, primary program focus, and number of residential sites with number of residents per site.

Data about individuals served included number with mental retardation; functioning levels; presence of additional disabilities, including autism, cerebral palsy, mobility limitations, seizure disorders, and hearing or vision impairment; sex; and age (0–6 years, 7–17 years, 18 years and older). The data were obtained from three separate ACDD survey documents: 1) the Application of Accreditation Survey; 2) the Survey Report documenting Category A standards with which the agency was in less than full compliance and stating the Council's accreditation decision; and 3) the agency compliance sheet, which summarized the number of Category A standards applicable during the survey.

A classification system was based on survey research on community residences and public residential facilities (Epple et al., 1985; Hauber et al., 1984; Rotegard, Bruininks, & Krantz, 1984; Scheerenberger, 1983). The six agency categories that were developed covered ownership, basic programs offered, and size of residential programs—large public residential, the majority of individuals served by the agency resided in larger (16 beds or more) residential sites; large private residential; small public residential, the majority of individuals served by the agency resided in sites of 15 beds or less; small private residential; public nonresidential, the majority of individuals served by the agency resided in residential sites other than those operated by the agency being surveyed; and private nonresidential.

Four types of accreditation outcomes were identified: 2-year accreditation, 1-year accreditation, accreditation deferred, and not accredited. With minor exceptions, the standards contained in the 1984 edition (ACMRDD, 1984) were applicable throughout the 1980–1984 period considered in the study. There were 1,478 standards, of which 794 (54%) were considered the most important requirements and were designated "Category A" by the Council. An agency was eligible for accreditation if surveyors found evidence of noncompliance with no more than 15% of the Category A standards. If the Council's Accreditation Committee found no major inconsistencies with the intent of the standards, such as "technically sophisticated but abusive behavior management practices" (K. Crosby, [former ACDD] Executive Director, personal communication, November 22, 1985), then 2-year or 1-year accreditation was granted.

Because the agencies in this sample were self-selected, causal inferences about agency characteristics and accreditability have been withheld. Limits in the generalizability of the data are discussed in the concluding section of this paper.

Basic Characteristics of Agencies

Table 1 presents information on the number of agencies surveyed by ACDD by type of agency and by state. The private agencies providing residential or day services constituted the largest group being surveyed by ACDD in 1983–1984, representing a major change from earlier years when nearly all agencies surveyed had been large public institutions. Seventy-four privately operated agencies were providing a variety of services other than residential care—such as vocational or habilitative services, family support, or case management. No small public residential agencies were surveyed during 1980–1984. Illinois, Maryland, South Dakota, and Tennessee had the largest numbers of surveyed agencies.

Table 2 presents characteristics of residential agencies surveyed by ACDD in 1983 and 1984. These data were compared to data on all residential facilities in the United States in 1982 (Hill, Lakin, & Bruininks, 1984). In Table 2 small private residential facilities and number of residents obtained from Hill et al. (1984) were for "group residential 1–15" (p. 247) and therefore included some publicly operated facilities. The ACDD surveyed 28 small private residential agencies; altogether, these agencies operated 210 facilities serving 1,018 individuals, and they served an additional 317 individuals in nonresidential programs. *Individuals living in large public institutions surveyed by ACDD constituted over 25% of the total population served*

Table 1. Number of agencies surveyed by ACDD in 1983–1984

State	Residential Public Large[a]	Residential Private Small	Residential Private Large	Nonresidential Public	Nonresidential Private	Total
AZ	2					2
AR	1					1
CA	8					8
GA	4					4
IL	12					12
IA		2			1	3
KY			5			5
LA	1					1
MD	2	11	2		34	49
MI	6			1		7
MN	3					3
MO	2		1	2	2	7
NE			1	2		3
NM	1				2	3
NY	1	1				2
NC	2					2
ND		2	1	3	1	7
OH	3		2	1	1	7
PA	2		2			4
SC				1		1
SD		8			5	13
TN	5	4			25	34
TX	1				2	3
VA	4					4
WV					1	1
Total	60	28	14	10	74	186
	(32%)	(15%)	(8%)	(5%)	(40%)	(100%)

Note: ACDD - Accreditation Council on Services for People With Developmental Disabilities.

[a]There were no surveys of small public agencies.

in large public facilities throughout the United States in Fiscal Year 1984 (Braddock, Hemp, & Howes, 1986).

Accreditation Outcomes

The 296 surveys considered included 107 repeat surveys for some agencies. One large private residential agency and two private nonresidential agencies did not seek repeat survey. Thus, there were 186 agencies that, as of De-

Table 2. Basic characteristics of residential agencies surveyed compared to national data

Agency/characteristic	ACDD surveyed[a]	National data[a]	ACDD % of national
Large public residential			
No. of agencies	60	369	16
No. of residents	28,657	134,943	21
Mean no. of residents	478	366	
Standard deviation	412	384	
No. of MR residents	27,561	122,971	22
No. of MR residents	27,561	109,827[b]	25
% severe/profound	81	80	
% nonambulatory	18	26	
% under 18 years	18	—[c]	
% under 22 years	—[c]	22	
Large private residential			
No. of agencies	14	886	2
No. of residents	1,807	46,068	4
Mean no. of residents	129	52	
Standard deviation	131	56	
No. of MR residents	1,788	40,347	4
% severe/profound	60	43	
% nonambulatory	17	14	
% under 18 years	31	—[c]	
% under 22 years	—[c]	32	
Small private residential			
No. of agencies	28	6,414	.4
No. of residents	1,335	43,588	3
Mean no. of residents	48	7	
Standard deviation	35	3	
No. of MR residents	1,259	42,018	3
% severe/profound	30	33	
% nonambulatory	2	5	
% under 18 years	10	—[c]	
% under 22 years	—[c]	20	

[a]The Accreditation Council on Services for People With Developmental Disabilities surveyed agency data (1983–1984) are from Hemp and Braddock (1985); national data (1982) (with noted exception) are from Hill, Lakin, and Bruininks (1984).

[b]Source for 1984 national data, Braddock, Hemp, and Howes (1986).

[c]Not applicable.

cember 1984, were operating with an accreditation status or had been surveyed and an accreditation decision was pending. Table 3 summarizes accreditation outcome rates for three survey groups: those 48 agencies surveyed by ACF/MR in 1973–1974 (Braddock, 1977), the 110 surveyed during 1980–

Table 3. Outcome rates for accreditation surveys in three time periods

Type of agency	No. of surveys 1973–1974	% accred.	No. of surveys 1980–1982	% accred.	No. of surveys 1983–1984	% accred.
Large public residential	45	27	39	97	60	78
Large private residential	3	33	7	71	14	64
Small private residential	—[a]	—	13	77	28	61
Public nonresidential	—	—	3	100	10	80
Private nonresidential	—	—	48	81	74	68
All surveys	48	27	110	86	186	70

Note: There were no surveys of small public residential agencies.
[a]Dash indicates that there were no surveys of these types of agencies.

1982 considered in the present study, and the 186 agencies surveyed during 1983–1984.

Accreditation rates (accredited for 1 or 2 years) improved for all types of agencies surveyed during 1980–1984, compared to the low overall rate of accreditation in 1973–1974. The 48 large residential agencies surveyed in 1973–1974 constituted 63% of the accreditation decisions that had been made on residential facilities by ACF/MR as of May 1975 (Braddock, 1977).

Table 4 summarizes accreditation success for agencies undergoing multiple surveys. This table represents 398 surveys, including 102 surveys conducted by the Council prior to the 1980–1984 analysis period. Only one of the five agencies that the Council had surveyed six times was successful on its first survey, but through five subsequent surveys all agencies in this cohort maintained accreditation. Of the 81 agencies that had initial surveys in 1983–1984, nearly half were successful. Overall, nearly two thirds of the 186 agencies surveyed in 1983 and 1984 had been successful on their first survey, and the proportion improved to over 90% as of the second survey undergone by 105 agencies. Continuing accreditation by ACDD was not guaranteed,

Table 4. Percentage of agencies accredited on a series of surveys

No. of agencies	% accredited per survey					
	1st	2nd	3rd	4th	5th	6th
5	20	100	100	100	100	100
9	78	100	100	100	89	
18	78	94	100	89		
24	92	100	92			
49	73	82				
81	49					
% accredited on successive survey	65	91	96	94	93	100
No. of agencies	186	105	56	32	14	5

Note: In 1983–1984, 186 agencies were surveyed.

however. One agency with five total surveys and two pairs of agencies with three and four surveys, respectively, were *not* successful on their most recent surveys.

Critical Standards Identified

Consistent with Braddock (1977), a standard for purposes of this analysis was defined as "critical" if 40% of the agencies surveyed failed to comply with it. Table 5 identifies the critical standards by type of agency, providing an indication of the most important program issues in different service settings. Virtually all of the large congregate settings were found by surveyors to be in less than full compliance with standards related to normalization (Nos. 2.1.7; 2.5.1.3.4; 2.5.1.3.10.1; 4.1.1.1; 4.12.4). Small residential agencies and agencies providing day services, case management, and other nonresidential programs were frequently found to be in less than full compliance with standards on assessments of individuals served, record-keeping, professional services (particularly interdisciplinary team formation), and evacuation procedures.

DISCUSSION

Additional Research

The present study was an initial effort to report on the extent of ACDD accreditation activity and the basic characteristics of agencies surveyed and to focus on the need for additional research on the impact of accreditation. No causal inferences were made in this descriptive analysis regarding the relationships of survey results to the basic characteristics of agencies. Agencies voluntarily elected when to undergo an accreditation survey, and this introduced unknown selection biases in the study sample. In addition, there were many potentially important determinants or confounding variables (e.g., reimbursement rates, salaries, and other measures of staff qualifications) that were not available. The *n* in some of the agency categories defined for the study was quite small, and continued analysis of ACDD survey results beyond 1984 would yield valuable data on small residential agencies in particular. The recommendation by Hemp and Braddock (1985) that the Application for Accreditation Survey form be modified so that more comprehensive data can be collected about surveyed agencies has been addressed by the Council.

Criticisms about the accreditation process are related to general evaluation design problems and, thus, are not limited to ACDD accreditation. These problems include the creation of a superstructure of documentation and basing evaluation on "paper goals" and "processes" as opposed to outcomes (Weiss, 1972, cited in Rowitz, 1979). A related problem concerns the manner in which an agency can prepare for a preannounced survey and then revert to

Table 5. Critical standards for 186 agencies surveyed in 1983–1984

Standard number, type, and percent cited[a]				Summary of the critical standard
Individual program planning and implementation				
1.1.1	L(55)	—	—	ID[b] team identified for each individual
1.1.2	—	S(57)	N(54)	ID team properly constituted
1.2.8.2	—	—	N(40)	Assessment includes dental evaluation
1.2.8.3	—	S(57)	N(64)	Assessment includes medication history
1.2.8.4	—	S(86)	N(81)	Assessment includes nutritional status
1.2.8.5	L(57)	S(57)	N(58)	Assessment includes visual screening
1.2.8.6	—	S(54)	N(57)	Assessment includes auditory screening
1.2.8.7	—	S(46)	N(46)	Assessment includes speech and language screening
1.2.9.2	L(76)	S(71)	N(68)	Assessment includes visual and auditory acuity
1.2.11	—	S(46)	N(51)	Assessment completed within 30 days
1.2.12.4	—	S(46)	N(65)	Health assessments at least annually
1.3.1	L(64)	—	N(48)	Individual has program plan
1.3.2	L(95)	S(86)	N(96)	Program plan developed by appropriate ID team
1.3.3	L(91)	S(93)	N(93)	Plan states objectives
1.3.3.1	L(64)	S(64)	N(75)	Plan's objectives reflect individual's needs
1.3.3.2.1	L(70)	S(57)	N(67)	Plan's objectives are stated separately
1.3.3.2.2	—	S(50)	N(45)	Plan's objectives assigned completion dates
1.3.3.2.3	L(70)	S(68)	N(77)	Plan's objectives in behavioral terms
1.3.7	L(77)	S(79)	N(81)	ID team reviews plan monthly
1.3.7.1	L(80)	S(79)	N(81)	ID team records individual's response monthly
1.3.7.3	L(50)	S(46)	N(44)	ID team reviews plan when problems occur
1.3.8.1	L(54)	S(50)	N(49)	Plan review assesses individual's response

(continued)

Table 5. (continued)

Standard number, type, and percent cited[a]			Summary of the critical standard
1.4.1.5.3.4	L(51)	—	—	Support plan specifies reason, situation, and time
1.4.1.7.2.1	—	S(61)	N(63)	Modified diets prescribed by ID team
1.4.1.10	—	—	N(54)	Individual's weight recorded quarterly
1.4.1.14	—	S(75)	N(65)	Prescription drug orders review by date
1.4.1.19.2	L(76)	S(82)	N(90)	Each medication record has current profile
1.4.3.2.3	—	—	N(43)	Training program specifies training schedule
1.4.3.2.5	L(53)	S(46)	N(61)	Training program specifies assessment data
1.4.4.3.1	L(72)	S(79)	N(55)	Agency determines work interests
1.4.4.3.2	L(69)	S(79)	N(61)	Agency measures individual's work abilities
1.4.4.3.3	L(69)	S(75)	N(60)	Agency measures individual's task performance
1.4.4.3.5	L(53)	S(46)	N(42)	Agency assesses attitude for employment
1.4.4.4	L(77)	S(79)	N(58)	Agency has work evaluation in employment program
1.4.4.4.2	—	—	N(44)	All work performance records are organized
1.4.6.1.4	—	S(46)	—	Individual participates in behavior management policies
1.4.6.8	L(47)	S(61)	N(56)	Behavior modification plan teaches appropriate behavior
1.4.6.8.2	L(49)	—	N(45)	Restraint, medication, and behavior modification only if less restrictive options documented
1.4.6.9.1	L(41)	—	—	Restraint used only as part of ID team's plan
1.4.6.9.1.2.1	L(43)	—	—	Restraint plan approved by behavior management committee
1.4.6.9.1.2.2	L(42)	—	—	Restraint plan approved by rights committee
1.4.6.10.1	L(61)	S(71)	N(80)	Behavior management drugs only as integral to plan
1.4.6.10.1.1.1	L(50)	S(64)	N(83)	If drugs, MD signs; time and data collection specified
1.4.6.10.1.2	L(74)	S(61)	N(81)	Plan weighs potential harmful effects
1.4.6.10.1.4.1	L(74)	S(64)	N(81)	Behavior management committee reviews each drug plan

Code				Description
1.4.6.10.1.4.2	L(74)	S(61)	N(82)	Rights committee reviews each drug plan
1.5.2.1	L(93)	S(100)	N(95)	Individual's program coordinator attends to needs
1.5.2.2	L(62)	S(82)	N(74)	Individual's program coordinator obtains services
1.6.5.1	L(49)	—	—	Individual's record is legible
1.6.5.2	L(58)	S(89)	N(76)	Individual's record is dated
1.6.5.3	L(46)	S(64)	N(65)	Record entries authenticated by signature
Alternative living arrangements				
2.1.6	L(53)	—	—	Living areas give access to service and activities
2.1.7	L(93)	—	—	Living arrangements integrated in community
2.1.10.3.5	L(62)	—	—	Resident provided with appropriate furniture
2.1.11	L(45)	—	—	"Rhythm of life" in accordance with norms
Alternative living arrangements				
2.1.11.2	L(50)	—	—	Resident has access to quiet, private area
2.1.11.9.1	L(78)	—	—	Residents have individual toilet articles
2.1.13.4	L(47)	—	—	Storage space provided for each resident
2.5.1.1.1	L(66)	—	—	Living unit assures development of relationships
2.5.1.1.4	L(69)	—	—	Different ages, levels not housed together
2.5.1.3.4	L(89)	—	—	Interior design of unit simulates a home
2.5.1.3.7	L(62)	—	—	Furnishings safe, comfortable, and homelike
2.5.1.3.10.1	L(88)	—	—	Toilets, baths approximate normal home
2.5.2.8	L(57)	—	—	Appropriate title for living-unit staff
Achieving and protecting rights				
3.1.4	L(72)	S(61)	N(81)	Rights not limited without due process
3.1.12	—	S(57)	N(57)	Individual's record is confidential
2.1.13	L(46)	S(46)	N(50)	Record has appropriate authorization and consents

(continued)

Table 5. (continued)

Standard number, type, and percent cited[a]			Summary of the critical standard
Individual program support			
4.1.1.1	L(97)	S(71)	N(68)	Agency implements principle of normalization
4.1.1.2	L(46)	—	—	Agency uses least restrictive alternatives
4.1.6.1	L(47)	S(46)	—	Contracts stipulate quality as do standards
4.6.1	L(45)	—	—	All receive professional services needed
4.6.2	L(41)	—	—	Agency professional services of equal quality to all
4.7.1.1	L(61)	—	—	Agency has sufficient staff
4.10.1.13	—	S(57)	N(43)	Agency has continuing management audit
4.10.4.2.2	—	S(50)	N(46)	Record documents characteristics, contains photograph
4.10.4.4	—	S(54)	N(61)	Record includes AAMR[c] diagnosis
4.11.1	—	S(71)	N(46)	Agency annually evaluates goals and objectives
4.11.3	L(53)	S(79)	N(55)	Effect measured by objectives in plan
4.12.4	L(88)	—	—	Dining areas pleasant and normalizing
Safety and sanitation			
5.3.3	—	S(61)	—	Quarterly evacuation drills each shift
5.3.3.5	—	S(50)	N(43)	Written reports assess each evacuation drill
5.5.5	—	S(46)	—	Buildings free of insects, rodents, and vermin

[a]L = large residential, S = small residential, N = nonresidential. Number in parentheses is % of agencies in that category cited on the standard.
[b]Interdisciplinary team.
[c]American Association on Mental Retardation.

inadequate programming (Bible & Sneed, 1976; Repp & Barton, 1980). Conroy and Bradley (1985) noted that a 323-item version of the ACMRDD standards employed preliminarily in the Pennhurst study failed to show a relationship to client developmental progress. They also acknowledged, however, limitations in the study's methodology, including use of the standards as a scale (for which they were not designed), small sample size (one facility unit), and the employment of inappropriate statistics.

It is important to explore in greater detail the relationship of ACDD accreditation to more direct measures of program quality and effectiveness, both in terms of validation of the standards (concurrent and predictive validity) and to gain a better understanding of the ways in which accreditation affects programs (construct validity). One useful outcome measure is individuals' "movement through the system" toward independence (Schalock & Harper, 1981, p. 317). Uniform data reporting systems (Rowitz, 1984, 1985) could track the progress of individuals, and several states have implemented systematic client information systems, such as the Minnesota Developmental Programming System (Bock & Weatherman, 1976). With such an instrument, statewide client data bases could be coupled with accreditation results, thus enabling exploratory studies of the relationship between accreditation and client behavioral gains.

Although some programs and residential sites should emphasize intensive training programs and movement to less restrictive settings, residential stability and the opportunity to develop social relationships with peers (Heller, Berkson, & Romer, 1981; Romer & Berkson, 1980a, 1980b) are also important program criteria. Landesman (1986) suggested using ICF/MR and ACDD survey data in defining procedures for monitoring "quality of life" in service programs. Case studies of sites undergoing ACDD surveys could yield important qualitative data on client, staff, and organizational outcomes. These studies should include staff ratings of the agency's performance, of the impact of accreditation, and of progress and adjustment of individuals. Naturalistic observations and personal interviews with clients should also be an integral part of these case studies.

The importance attached to the interdisciplinary team process in accreditation (ACDD, 1987; Crosby, 1976) suggests a special research focus. For example, Glaser and Morreau (1986) described how an interdisciplinary team helped to assure that physicians would not over-prescribe potentially dangerous psychotropic medications, and additional research could explore which specific standards have the most impact on professional performance in other disciplines. Differential weighting of standards was addressed by the Council in the most recent edition (ACDD, 1987) in that the total number of standards was reduced from 1,478 to 689. As the ACDD surveys additional programs and service systems, the standards' applicability to various settings can be further examined. For example, should surveys of small residences stress the interdisciplinary team or focus on a client program coordinator assuring that each individual has access to necessary generic services?

"Deeming" ACDD Accreditation

Redundancies between government certification and accreditation have been described by Repp (1976), and Covell (1980) maintained that "annual [Medicaid] reviews of excellent facilities waste staff resources that could be devoted to more marginal facilities" (p. 117). Recently, there were 75 facilities that were both ACDD accredited and ICF/MR certified (W. Smith, Health Care Financing Administration, personal communication, December 8, 1986). There should be concern about this redundancy of effort, and the recommendation of the AAMR (Legislative Goals, 1987) that federal/state governments "deem" ACDD survey outcomes in lieu of licensure and certification seems reasonable. Agencies initially licensed or certified by the appropriate federal or state mechanisms could, in subsequent reviews, be "deemed" to be in continued compliance if they received 1- or 2-year ACDD accreditation. If not accredited, they might have 3 to 6 months, assuming that no life-safety or other serious deficiencies were present, in which to acquire the appropriate governmental licensure/certification.

Relinquishing direct survey activity in favor of the "deeming" of accreditation need not necessarily mean less governmental accountability. The implementation of outcome oriented systems discussed previously (qualitative reviews, including systematic monitoring by parents and citizen advocates, client information systems, and repeated formal surveys of staff and clients), all contribute to monitoring the quality of programs. Annual or biennial accreditation by the private sector should be coupled with governmental evaluations of these multiple sources of quality assurance data. Unannounced government site inspections, when necessary, would therefore occur within a broader context of quality assurance measures.

In conclusion, it has been suggested that research on the role of accreditation in developmental disabilities programs is important. Community-based alternatives to institutions in this country are rapidly expanding, and voluntary accreditation is fulfilling a larger quality assurance role in these settings. Continuing analyses of accreditation survey results are therefore needed to enhance understanding of accreditation as a quality assurance methodology.

REFERENCES

Accreditation Council for Facilities for the Mentally Retarded (ACF/MR). (1971). *Standards for residential facilities for the mentally retarded.* Chicago: Joint Commission on the Accreditation of Hospitals, The Council.

Accreditation Council for Facilities for the Mentally Retarded (ACF/MR). (1973). *Standards for community agencies serving persons with mental retardation and other developmental disabilities*. Chicago: Joint Commission on the Accreditation of Hospitals, The Council.

Accreditation Council for Services for Mentally Retarded and Other Developmentally Disabled Persons (ACMRDD). (1984). *Standards for services for developmentally disabled individuals: 1984 edition*. Washington, DC: The Council.

Accreditation Council on Services for People With Developmental Disabilities (ACDD). (1987). *Standards for services for people with developmental disabilities: National quality assurance program*. Boston: The Accreditation Council.

Allard, M.A., & Toff, G.E. (1980). *Current and future development of intermediate care facilities for the mentally retarded: A survey of state officials*. Washington, DC: The George Washington University, Intergovernmental Health Policy Project.

American Association on Mental Deficiency. (1964, January). *Standards for state residential institutions for the mentally retarded*. Springfield: Illinois Department of Mental Health.

Bible, G., & Sneed, T.J. (1976). Some effects of an accreditation survey on program completion at a state institution. *Mental Retardation, 14,* 14–15.

Bock, W.M., & Weatherman, R.F. (1976). *Minnesota Developmental Programming System*. Minneapolis: University of Minnesota.

Boggs, E.M. (1976). Quality control of community services. In M. Kindred, J. Cohen, D. Penrod, & T. Shaffer (Eds.), *The mentally retarded citizen and the law*. New York: Free Press.

Braddock, D. (1977). *Opening closed doors: The deinstitutionalization of disabled individuals*. Reston, VA: Council for Exceptional Children.

Braddock, D., Hemp, R., & Fujiura, G. (1987). National study of public spending for mental retardation and developmental disabilities. *American Journal of Mental Deficiency, 92,* 121–133.

Braddock, D., Hemp, R., & Howes, R. (1986). Direct costs of institutional care in the Unites States. *Mental Retardation, 24,* 9–17.

Bradley, V.J., Ashbaugh, J.W., & Harder, W.P. (1984, May 15). *Assessing and enhancing the quality of services: A guide for the human services field*. Washington, DC: Human Services Research Institute.

Bradley, V.J., Ashbaugh, J.W., Allard, M.A., & Liegey, A.L. (1977). *Deinstitutionalization of developmentally disabled persons: A conceptual analysis and guide for state officials*. Washington, DC: Human Services Research Institute.

Butterfield, E. (1976). Some basic changes in residential facilities. In R.B. Kugel & A. Shearer (Eds.), *Changing patterns in residential services for the mentally retarded* (pp. 15–34). Washington, DC: President's Committee on Mental Retardation.

Commission on Accreditation of Rehabilitation Facilities (CARF). (1985). *Operations analysis of 1984 survey activities*. Tucson, AZ: Commission on Accreditation of Rehabilitation Facilities.

Commission on Accreditation of Rehabilitation Facilities (CARF). (1987, September). *CARF report*. Tucson, AZ: Commission on Accreditation of Rehabilitation Facilities.

Conroy, J.W., & Bradley, V.J. (1985, March). *The five year longitudinal study of the court-ordered deinstitutionalization of Pennhurst: A report of five years of research and analysis*. Philadelphia: Temple University, Developmental Disabilities Center.

Covell, R.M. (1980). The impact of regulation on health care quality. In A. Levin

(Ed.), *Regulating health care: The struggle for control* (pp. 111–125). New York: Academy of Political Service.

Crosby, K.G. (1973). Additions and revisions to Standards document (memorandum). Chicago: Joint Commission on the Accreditation of Hospitals/Accreditation Council for Facilities for the Mentally Retarded.

Crosby, K.G. (1976). Essentials of active programming. *Mental Retardation, 14,* 3–9.

Epple, W.A., Jacobson, J.W., & Janicki, M.P. (1985). Staffing ratios in public institutions for persons with mental retardation in the United States. *Mental Retardation, 23,* 115–124.

Eyman, R.K., Demaine, G.C., & Lei, T. (1979). Relationship between community environments and resident changes in adaptive behavior: A path model. *American Journal of Mental Deficiency, 83,* 330–338.

Flynn, R.J., & Heal, L.W. (1981). A short form of PASS 3: A study of its structure, interrater reliability, and validity for assessing normalization. *Evaluation Review, 5,* 357–376.

Flynn, R.J., & Nitsch, K.E. (Eds.). (1980). *Normalization, social integration, and community services.* Baltimore: University Park Press.

Gettings, R.M., & Salmon, S. (1985). *Federal administrative constraints on state Medicaid outlays for mentally retarded and other developmentally disabled recipients: A state-by-state survey report.* Alexandria, VA: National Association of State Mental Retardation Program Directors.

Glaser, B.A., & Morreau, L.E. (1986). Effects of interdisciplinary team review on the use of antipsychotic agents with severely and profoundly mentally retarded persons. *American Journal of Mental Deficiency, 90,* 371–379.

Hauber, F., Bruininks, R., Hill, B., Lakin, K.C., Scheerenberger, R., & White, C. (1984). National census of residential facilities: A 1982 profile of facilities and residents. *American Journal of Mental Deficiency, 89,* 236–245.

Health Care Financing Administration (HCFA). (1986, March 4). Medicaid program; standards for Intermediate Care Facilities for the Mentally Retarded. *Federal Register, 51*(42), 7520–7538. Washington, DC: Health Care Financing Administration, U.S. Department of Health and Human Services.

Health Care Financing Administration (HCFA). (1988, June 3). Medicaid program; conditions for Intermediate Care Facilities for the Mentally Retarded; Final rule. *Federal Register, 53*(107), 20448–20505. Washington, DC: Health Care Financing Administration, U.S. Department of Health and Human Services.

Heller, T., Berkson, G., & Romer, D. (1981). Social ecology of supervised communal facilities for mentally disabled adults: VI. Initial social adaptation. *American Journal of Mental Deficiency, 86,* 43–49.

Hemp, R. & Braddock, D. (1985). *ACMRDD accreditation: Analysis of nationwide survey results.* Chicago: University of Illinois at Chicago, Evaluation and Public Policy Analysis Program, Institute for the Study of Developmental Disabilities.

Hemp, R., Fujiura, G., & Braddock, D. (1986). *CARF accreditation: Summary of 500 surveys, 1982–1984.* Chicago: University of Illinois at Chicago, Evaluation and Public Policy Analysis Program, Institute for the Study of Developmental Disabilities.

Hill, B.K., Lakin, K.C., & Bruininks, R.H. (1984). Trends in residential services for people who are mentally retarded: 1977–1982. *Journal of The Association for Persons with Severe Handicaps, 9,* 243–250.

Hull, J.T., & Thompson, J.C. (1980). Predicting adaptive functioning of mentally retarded persons in community settings. *American Journal of Mental Deficiency, 85,* 253–261.

Landesman, S. (1986). Quality of life and personal life satisfaction: Definition and measurement issues. *Mental Retardation, 24,* 141–142.

Legislative Goals, 1987. (1987). *Mental Retardation, 25,* 47–54.

Lei, T., Nihira, L., Sheehy, N., & Meyers, C.E. (1981). A study of small family care for mentally retarded people. In R.H. Bruininks, C.E. Meyers, B.B. Sigford, & K.C. Lakin (Eds.), *Deinstitutionalization and community adjustment of mentally retarded people* (Monograph No. 4., pp. 265–281). Washington, DC: American Association on Mental Deficiency.

National News: Accreditation Council Formed. (1979). *Mental Retardation, 17,* 219.

North Dakota Department of Human Services. (1986, December 12). Correspondence from Patricia Nygaard, Administrator, Quality Assurance, Developmental Disabilities Division.

O'Connor, G. (1976). *Home is a good place: A national perspective of community residential facilities for the mentally retarded.* Washington, DC: American Association on Mental Deficiency.

Orlans, H. (1975). *Private accreditation and public eligibility.* Lexington, MA: Lexington Books.

Repp, A.C. (1976). A tracking system for resident's records designed to meet JCAH standards and ICF/MR regulations. *Mental Retardation, 14,* 18–19.

Repp, A.C., & Barton, L.E. (1980). Naturalistic observations of institutionalized retarded persons: A comparison of licensure decisions and behavioral observations. *Journal of Applied Behavior Analysis, 13,* 333–341.

Romer, D., & Berkson, G. (1980a). Social ecology of supervised communal facilities for mentally disabled adults: II. Predictors of affiliation. *American Journal of Mental Deficiency, 85,* 229–242.

Romer, D., & Berkson, G. (1980b). Social ecology of supervised communal facilities for mentally disabled adults: III. Predictors of social choice. *American Journal of Mental Deficiency, 85,* 243–252.

Ross, E.C. (1980, October). *Accreditation and programs for persons with developmental disabilities: A search for compatibility and coordination.* Unpublished doctoral dissertation, George Washington University.

Rotegard, L.L., Bruininks, R.H., & Krantz, G.C. (1984). State operated facilities for people with mental retardation: July 1, 1978–June 30, 1982. *Mental Retardation, 22,* 69–74.

Rowitz, L. (1979). The importance of client/program impact measures in evaluation designs. In P. Sanofsky (Ed.), *Evaluating program effectiveness: The administrator's dilemma* (pp. 15–25). Watertown, MA: SPS Communications.

Rowitz, L. (1984). The need for uniform data reporting in mental retardation (Editorial). *Mental Retardation, 22,* 1–3.

Rowitz, L. (1985). Proposal for information networks in mental retardation (Editorial). *Mental Retardation, 23,* 1–2.

Schalock, R.L., & Harper, R.S. (1981). A systems approach to community living skills training. In R.H. Bruininks, C.E. Meyers, B.B. Sigford, & K.C. Lakin (Eds.), *Deinstitutionalization and community adjustment of mentally retarded people* (pp. 316–336). Washington, DC: American Association on Mental Deficiency.

Scheerenberger, R.C. (1983). *Public residential services for the mentally retarded, 1981.* Madison, WI: National Association of Superintendents of Public Residential Facilities for the Mentally Retarded.

Subcommittee on the Handicapped. (1985, April). *Staff report on the institutionalized mentally disabled requested by Senator Lowell P. Weicker, Jr.* Washington, DC:

Subcommittee on the Handicapped, Committee on Labor and Human Resources and the Subcommittee on Labor, Health and Human Services, Education and Related Agencies, Committee on Appropriations.

Weiss, C.H. (1972). *Evaluation research*. Englewood Cliffs, NJ: Prentice-Hall.

Wolfensberger, W. (1972). *The principle of normalization in human services*. Toronto: National Institute on Mental Retardation.

Wolfensberger, W., & Glenn, L. (1975a). *Program analysis of service systems (PASS 3): A method for the quantitative evaluation of human services (Vol. 1): Handbook*. Toronto: National Institute on Mental Retardation.

Wolfensberger, W., & Glenn, L. (1975b). *Program analysis of service systems (PASS 3). A method for the quantitative evaluation of human services (Vol. 2): Field manual*. Toronto: National Institute on Mental Retardation.

chapter 15 ————

Accreditation as Synthesis

James F. Gardner
and Catherine E. Parsons

The Accreditation Council on Services for People with Developmental Disabilities (ACDD) is an organization uniquely dedicated to the promotion of quality services for individuals with developmental disabilities. It assists agencies providing services to engage in the complex process of identifying, embracing, and expressing values shared by consumers, their families, and providers. The ACDD provides a method in which agencies can assess their performance against external standards and accords recognition (i.e., accreditation) to those agencies that achieve a certain level of success as measured by an independent third party evaluator. The accreditation process and the establishment of standards represents a synthesis of emerging values and technologies with traditional norms and practices. The dynamic integration provides an evolving consensus model of quality.

The steps leading to accreditation also present the service agency with the opportunity to combine diverse tasks and activities into a coherent process. These steps bring together elements of strategic planning, organizational development, program evaluation, and staff orientation and training. Accreditation combines these elements and grounds them into the collective needs of individuals with developmental disabilities. Accreditation, then, can benefit the agency by providing significant outcomes in terms of strategic planning, organizational capabilities, and quality assurance programming.

This chapter provides an overview of the ACDD (also known as the Accreditation Council). The quality assurance program of the ACDD is discussed as well as the values and evolution of its standards. Additionally, the benefits of accreditation to both the individuals served by the agency and the direct care staff are identified. Finally, the accreditation process is described within the context of strategic planning, organizational development, and program evaluation.

OVERVIEW OF ACDD

During the period from 1952–1969, organizations serving persons with mental retardation and professional associations began the movement to develop a set of standards to measure the quality of services to people with mental retardation and other developmental disabilities. These efforts led to the formation of the National Planning Committee on Accreditation of Residential Centers for the Retarded, which in 1969 affiliated with the Joint Commission on Accreditation of Hospitals as the Accreditation Council for Facilities for the Mentally Retarded (ACF/MR) (Accreditation Council on Services for People with Developmental Disabilities [ACDD], 1987, p. 99 ff).

In 1971 the Accreditation Council published its *Standards for Residential Facilities for the Mentally Retarded.* The following year, a federal district court took an unprecedented step and adopted the recommendation of the U.S. Justice Department to require the state of Alabama to comply with the 1971 standards at the Partlow State School and Hospital. In 1974, the Medical Services Administration of the federal government used the 1971 standards as the basis for the federal regulations for the Intermediate Care Facilities for the Mentally Retarded (ICFs/MR) program.

In 1979, the Accreditation Council left the Joint Commission on the Accreditation of Hospitals and re-established itself as an independent, not-for-profit corporation with a board of directors representing professional, consumer, and service provider organizations. (For a more detailed history of the Accreditation Council see Hemp and Braddock, Chapter 14, this volume.) The organizations represented on the board of directors in 1989 were:

American Association on Mental Deficiency
American Occupational Therapy Association
American Psychological Association
Association for Retarded Citizens of the United States
Council for Exceptional Children: Division on Mental Retardation
Epilepsy Foundation of America
National Association of Private Residential Resources
National Association of Social Workers
United Cerebral Palsy Association

ACDD QUALITY ASSURANCE PROGRAM

The Accreditation Council offers a range of services to assist agencies in providing quality programs.

Development of Standards and Guidelines

The Accreditation Council develops and improves standards that will result in effective services for those individuals and their families who are served. The ACDD revises its standards periodically. Major revisions have occurred in 1981, 1984, and 1987, and on each occasion sponsoring agencies, affiliates, agencies that have participated in the accreditation process, professional organizations, government agencies, and other interested persons were given the opportunity to review the proposed standards and provide comments. The standards committee of the Accreditation Council reviewed the comments, sought additional advice, and eventually recommended new standards to the board of directors for approval. Over 2,000 copies of the draft on the *1987 Standards on Services for People with Developmental Disabilities* were distributed (ACDD, 1987). (Preparation of the 1990 standards began in 1987.)

Since the early 1970s, the Accreditation Council's standards have consistently focused on the experience of the individual served and the manner in which services promote the quality of that experience by both advancing his or her intrinsic capacities and assuring access to physical and social environments that support his or her efforts. Thus, ACDD standards are client centered. In the 1987 standards, the ACDD took a final logical step by eliminating categorical references to agencies (e.g., schools, vocational programs, and health care providers). Standards now emphasize that each of the agencies that may be contributing to the achievement of an individual's goals (as well as the individual himself or herself and, where relevant, his or her family) must be concerned holisticly with the individual's needs as comprehensively assessed. Additionally, each agency's agreed-upon role in developing and implementing the individual's plan consistently in all environments must be understood by all concerned.

ACDD does not have separate standards for different types of facilities or nonfacility based programs. However, not all standards will apply to all agencies. The applicable standards are selected as appropriate to each agency. The 1987 standards listed 610 separate standards. The number applicable to individual agencies tends to run between 400 and 600. The majority of standards are applicable to agencies that provide a single service to 10 individuals as well as to facilities that provide multiple services to as many as 1,000 individuals.

Development of Training Materials

The Accreditation Council has published many resources for those interested in quality assurance programs, including *An Effective Habilitation Planning*

Process, The Manager's Guide to Program Evaluation; Standards Interpretation Guidelines: A Companion to the 1987 Standards; and _The 1990 Standards on Services to People with Developmental Disabilities—Field Review Edition._

Provision of Training, Technical Assistance, and Consultation

Training workshops include an _Introductory Workshop, Individual Habilitation Plan Workshop, Self-Survey Workshop, 1987 Standards Workshop, Self-Assessment Accreditation Workshop,_ and a _1990 Standards Workshop._ Special workshops, such as these, and individualized technical assistance and consultation can be tailored to the specific needs of organizations. The training is provided to assist agencies in program design and delivery and to strengthen internal quality assurance efforts.

Accreditation Surveys

ACDD staff survey agencies using the applicable standards. Standards are generally of two types—those that reflect organizational characteristics or practices, such as the use of accepted fiscal controls or the presence of a mission statement; and those that relate directly to individuals, such as the use of age-appropriate clothing or prompt provision of needed treatment. The former type is relatively easy to verify accurately while the latter requires more extensive examination.

VALUES, SYNTHESIS, AND THE EVOLUTION OF STANDARDS

The standards that are developed and published by the Accreditation Council represent a contemporary consensus among the members of the board of directors in consultation with senior field staff. The consensus reflects a mainstream point of view of requirements for quality services to persons with developmental disabilities. The standards deliberately reflect a middle ground position; they are not as close to the cutting edge as some would wish nor are they as deeply rooted in past practice as others would prefer.

The assumptions about the quality of services for people with disabilities rest on shared values. The standards change over time as the assumptions of what constitutes quality evolve. The shared values of society evolve over time and shape the behaviors and attitudes of its citizens. Shared values govern behavioral norms and shape and preserve diverse cultures. In a society that values diversity, standards will show respect for diverse cultures and for the rights of individuals to express their uniqueness.

Different sub-groups can subscribe to different values, and those values may change over time. For example, in 1972, students at the University of California at Los Angeles identified the following values in order of importance (Rubinstein, 1975):

1. Love
2. Self-respect
3. Peace of mind
4. Sex
5. Challenge
6. Social acceptance
7. Accomplishment
8. Individuality
9. Involvement
10. Well-being (economic and health)
11. Change
12. Power (control)
13. Privacy

In a similar exercise, the American Academy of Arts and Sciences (Rubenstein, 1975) identified a different set of values expected to be most important in the year 2000. The identified values were:

1. Privacy
2. Equality
3. Personal integrity
4. Freedom
5. Law and order
6. Pleasantness of the environment
7. Social adjustment
8. Efficiency and effectiveness of organizations
9. Rationality
10. Education
11. Ability and talent

There is no universal set of values or assumptions in the fields of human services or developmental disabilities. Individuals with disabilities, service providers, advocates, families, government agencies, and professionals often have divergent points of view. The ACDD attempts to give each the opportunity to participate in identifying what is desirable. Thus, the ACDD standards represent the shared values for human services programs for people with developmental disabilities.

The evolution of the ACDD standards reflects both an attachment to traditional values and a recognition of changes in the field of developmental disabilities. This metamorphosis can be seen in the changes in the language of the standards over time. The 1973 standards for community agencies reflected the following assumptions (Accreditation Council for Facilities for the Mentally Retarded [ACF/MR], 1973):

1. The person with mental retardation or other developmental disability is first of all a person who has the same basic rights as other persons, plus the special right to adequate treatment and habilitation.
2. The most useful way to view mental retardation and other developmental disabilities is within a "developmental model" in which each person is considered to be capable of learning, growing, and developing no matter how severely disabled he may be.
3. Services can and must be provided to meet the developmental needs of the disabled person throughout his life span, so as to maximize his human qualities, increase the complexity of his behavior, and enhance his ability to cope with his environment.
4. Programs and services should be conducted in accordance with the principle of normalization, defined as the use of means that are as culturally normative as possible to elicit and maintain behavior that is as culturally normative as possible.

The Accreditation Council acknowledged the previous statement of assumptions in the introduction to the 1984 standards, but noted in the Fundamental Principles of the Standards and Requirements for Accreditation (Accreditation Council for Services for Mentally Retarded and other Developmentally Disabled Persons, 1984) that:

> The primary mission of each agency serving developmentally disabled individuals must be to provide and promote services that enhance the development of such individuals and maximize their achievement of self-determination and autonomy. Programs for individuals with developmental disabilities must be:
>
> > interdisciplinary in their approach to identifying the needs of the individuals and devising ways to meet them,
> > based on developmental principles, and
> > provided within an environment that is normalized and normalizing.
>
> Services for each individual must be provided as part of a process of developing, implementing, and periodically re-evaluating an individual program plan. The individual program plan must:
>
> > be based on a relevant assessment of the individual's needs;
> > reflect the participation of the individual and, as appropriate, the individual's family;
> > provide for the coordination of the individual's total program; and
> > incorporate a continuous and self-correcting process for reviewing the individual's progress and revising the plan and program accordingly.

The 1987 standards reflected a new format as standards were grouped under one of four headings: values, agency, habilitation, and environment (ACDD, 1987). The section on values stressed:

Achieving and protecting rights of individuals (47 standards)
Normalization, age-appropriateness, and least restriction (23 standards)

The 1990 standards continued the new format of values, agency, habilitation, and environment (ACDD, 1988). In the introduction to the values section, the standards state:

There are a number of values that shape contemporary service delivery and that are reflected in these standards:

(1) the family is the primary social environment for children with developmental disabilities and the basis for lifelong personal relationships for adults;
(2) the community is the natural environment in which individuals should live, work, and play;
(3) the fabric of social relationships supports individuals in that environment;
(4) individuals with developmental disabilities have the same rights as those who do not have a disability; and
(5) the individual and, where appropriate, the family should have some control over the individual's participation in services received.

We also espouse:

(1) the principles of normalization;
(2) the principles of age-appropriateness; and
(3) the principles of least restriction.

The values section of the 1990 standards is divided into the following categories:

Consumer empowerment and decision-making (5 standards)
Community integration and social relationships (28 standards)
Affirming and protecting rights of individuals (51 standards)
Normalization, age-appropriateness, and least restriction (24 standards)

The 1990 standards and the 1973 standards reflect a different set of assumptions about services for individuals with developmental disabilities. However, throughout the series of revisions the ACDD has continued to stress attention to individual needs and outcomes and integrity, continuity, and consistency of the individual's comprehensive service plan, which usually includes several different providers and environments.

The Accreditation Council has continually re-examined its standards to ensure that the values and assumptions remain current without being trendy. As a measure of change in the field of development disabilities, the ACDD standards have represented a synthesis of multiple, and often diverse, points of view since the early 1970s, as well as reflected the findings of ongoing research.

BENEFITS FOR INDIVIDUALS

Increasingly, agencies participating in the ACDD accreditation process must develop an "open systems" view of services. Agencies can no longer operate as closed, self-contained units. The community agencies that the ACDD surveys often offer one or several but not all services required by an individual, and they may not have the power to procure or provide some component needed. In many instances, the agency being surveyed does not control the individual's interdisciplinary team or the case management function. The obligation of the agency then becomes one of active participation *with others* in identifying goals and achieving the desired outcomes for the individual. This responsibility may include systems advocacy efforts to create new needed resources for that community.

The 1990 standards move a step further by recognizing that some individuals, usually adults, have progressed to the point where they no longer require a *comprehensive* plan but should still have access to some specialized supports or services that the agency seeking accreditation may wish to provide. In such situations a less complex plan will suffice. These standards recognize the possibility that a person with a disability may be able and willing to assume responsibility for his or her own case coordination, and this can be viewed as a successful individual outcome.

The accreditation process is designed to provide direct benefits to individuals served by the agency. By focusing on a strong interdisciplinary team process in which the individual participates (or is represented), the standards encourage individuals to make decisions for themselves. The team decision-making process is designed to assist people with disabilities (or their advocates) to determine the outcomes they want and expect from the service provider.

The accreditation standards encourage the service provider to develop services around individual need rather than "fitting" the individual into the best available bundle of services. When the single individual is the focus of services, various relevant systems are expected to respond to his or her needs and aspirations.

BENEFITS FOR STAFF

The benefits for staff who have direct contact with individuals served are similar to those reported in strategic planning and organizational development programs. When such staff members are involved in the accreditation process they are more likely to "buy" into the agency mission and values. Their commitment is strengthened, both to the organization and to individuals with whom they work.

Staff members also benefit from training in the best practices as delineated in the standards. The preparation for the accreditation survey often involves participation in seminars and workshops. Becoming familiar with the standards and the guidelines also provides staff exposure to contemporary trends.

Finally, workers at all levels are better able to implement agency policies and procedures because they understand the underlying values and assumptions. Many staff members report that they feel more competent and confident after participating in the process because they understand the reasons for policies and procedures. They are better able to analyze the impact of their actions on the lives of the individuals with whom they work.

ACCREDITATION PROCESS OUTCOMES

The outcome of the accreditation process is usually associated with the resulting status of the accreditation survey. Yet the benefits and outcomes of the process extend beyond the 1 or 2 years accreditation or reaccreditation. The accreditation process involves an agency in strategic planning, organizational development, and monitoring and evaluation. The process of ACDD accreditation is an integrating and synthesizing force that leads the key staff through the fundamentals of management, administration, and leadership.

Strategic Planning

Strategic planning refers to the process of determining what an organization is going to be in the future. Strategic planning addresses the mission and values of the organization, the opportunities and threats in the external environment, and the strengths and weaknesses of the organization (Daft, 1989; Steiner, 1979; Tichy, 1983).

From the analysis of the external environment, management can define the current emerging and probable future trends and demands in the field of developmental disabilities. These efforts to scan the organizational boundaries include an exploration of new program directions, financing and funding opportunities, and changes in state and federal priorities. The scan of the environment is directed to the future and attempts to identify a position the agency must occupy in the next 3 to 5 years. The American Management Association identified a strategic planning process (Birnbaum, 1987) that began as follows:

1. Situation analysis
   a. Internal—strengths and weaknesses
   b. External—opportunities and threats
   c. Trends
2. Assumptions about the future
3. Mission definition

Strategic planning also includes an assessment of particular strengths and weaknesses in the organization. This assessment should enable the agency to identify distinctive competencies and the specific types of services it proposes to offer people with disabilities. The identification of weaknesses can lead to a priority for improvement or the conclusion that the agency does not have (or want) the capability of providing a particular service. The agency may conclude that other providers are better situated to provide a specific service such as supported employment or respite care.

The final step in strategic planning takes place after the analysis of the internal and external environment. The final step is to identify the overall goal and mission for the agency given the internal capabilities, the external demands and needs, and a set of values and assumptions about services for people with developmental disabilities.

Strategic planning and accreditation begin with an identification of values. The focus of strategic planning is on the "should" and "ought" rather than on the "is." In contrast, long range plans begin with the "is" and project the given across a future time span. Therefore, the key questions for the strategic planner begin with the individuals served and grow outward to the organization:

What does the individual want to do in the future?

Where does the individual want to live in the future?

How can the organization assist individuals to achieve future goals directly or through system advocacy?

What is the organization going to be in the future?

The strategic planning consideration of values and assumptions about services for people with developmental disabilities forms the link with the process of accreditation. The ACDD accreditation process requires that strategic planning be governed by values and assumptions that continually relate to individual outcomes. In other words, the accreditation process grounds the organization in activities that are client-centered rather than organizationally based. The accreditation process assists the agency to formulate strategic plans of "what" the agency should be in 3 to 5 years based on "what" individuals need and "where" they should be in 3 to 5 years.

Unless they incorporate individual needs and futures in the strategic planning process, organizations can easily become more efficient and effective in accomplishing the wrong ends. They become better at meeting agency goals and objectives, and more efficient and effective in complying with policy and procedure without ensuring that the organizational activity is grounded in individual needs and aspirations.

The ACDD's role is to ascertain whether the individual's needs are being met (ACDD, 1987, 1988). The foundation of this outcome is a strategic planning process, and the resulting organizational culture is derived from and depends upon the aggregate of individual needs and aspirations.

ACDD accreditation also influences strategic planning because it requires agencies to focus on individuals across programs (Accreditation Council for Services for Mentally Retarded and other Developmentally Disabled Persons 1984; ACDD, 1987, 1988; ACF/MR, 1973). In today's society no single agency provides the full range of services needed by an individual. Service systems rather than agencies must be comprehensive. To achieve accreditation by the ACDD an agency must promote individual interaction with a variety of different specialized and generic service agencies. Accreditation in the 1990s increasingly moves agencies in the direction of open systems models focusing on social integration and community participation. Thus, the pursuit of quality for individuals it serves requires an agency to engage in organizational development.

Organizational Development

Organizational development refers to the direction of planned change. French and Bell (1984) defined organizational development as an effort that is: 1) planned, 2) organization wide, 3) managed from the top, to 4) increase organization effectiveness and health, through 5) planned interventions in the organization's processes using behavioral science interventions.

Organizational development efforts stress the process of individual motivation, goal setting, problem-solving, group and intragroup relations, and team building. Planned interventions typically consist of exercises and experiences to assist individuals and groups manage work against a set of goals (Golembiewski, Proehl, & Sink, 1982). Organizational development efforts stress that individuals are guided by internalized meanings, values, and habits. Changes are alterations in normative structures and in established roles and relationships as well as cognitive and perceptual orientations (French & Bell, 1984).

The ACDD accreditation process contributes to organizational development efforts. Accreditation is:

A planned effort to improve the system
Endorsed by the organization
Accomplished through a facilitator
A re-examination of assumptions and values
A joint examination, diagnosis, and problem-solving experience by the agency and the Accreditation Council

The organizational development aspect of the accreditation process is best illustrated by self-assessment. Self-assessment generally begins 18 to 24 months prior to a site survey with a thorough review of the definitions and principles in the *Standards Manual* (ACDD, 1987). These definitions and principles describe the values upon which the standards are based.

The examination and discussion of the value base enables the agency's board and administration to reaffirm or redefine its values and mission. To the extent that all individuals served by the agency and staff participate in the consideration, an agencywide norm will emerge to guide future organizational behavior.

The self-assessment process also combines elements of strategic planning with organizational development. The self-assessment process allows an agency to do the following:

Identify areas of strength.
Identify areas of need.
Identify staff training needs to achieve future goals.
Identify policies and procedures that need to be written or rewritten.
Identify policies and procedures that are not being implemented.
Identify practices that are or are not consistent with the agency's values, policies, or procedures.

Repeatedly, agencies involved in the accreditation process report that the self-assessment phase is the most beneficial aspect of the accreditation process. In general, the payoff and utility of organizational development efforts increase when staff at all levels are involved because it increases sensitivity and understanding of the standards and agency mission. The self-assessment phase usually results in greater agency cohesion around identified group and agencywide norms. Specific comments about the benefits of self-assessment include:

> "The self survey helped identify where systems break down and helped establish some safeguards because of early warning signs."
> "Focused staff attention on the provision of quality services . . ."
> "The process provides focus and direction for the agency."
> "Preparing for and going through the survey provides good training for new administrative and support staff."

Program Monitoring and Evaluation

Program evaluation is a judgment about an agency's performance against its stated goals and objectives (Fitz-Gibbon & Morris, 1978). The most important measure of that performance is the extent to which the agency is assisting people with developmental disabilities to achieve life objectives.

The self-assessment and the survey processes can be used as part of an agency's program evaluation and quality assurance effort. The results can direct the establishment of organizational goals and objectives. Goals may exist at the individual, agency, or service system level. The ACDD standards require that the agency have its own internal program evaluation process that can provide frequent feedback in the following areas:

1. *The Benefits to Individuals Served* The agency examines the extent to which individuals are making progress toward achieving outcomes identified in their individualized habilitation plans.
2. *Program Delivery Through the Service System* The agency examines the extent to which the agency works within the larger service system to provide needed services.
3. *Staffing* The agency looks for evidence that staff tasks and performance are directed toward achievement of agency goals.

4. *Space and Equipment* The agency examines the extent to which the space, facilities, and equipment are directed toward the accomplishment of agency goals.

5. *Cooperation* The agency measures the extent to which it works cooperatively with other agencies in the service delivery system.

The self-assessment process provides a beginning point for designing and implementing an evaluation or quality assurance system unique to the agency. Self-assessment causes an agency to measure what it does against external norms and how it accomplishes its ends. It identifies inconsistencies between the agency's mission, values, and actual operations and provides the opportunity to begin an ongoing evaluation process. Self-assessment is an ongoing process and provides the agency with a longitudinal view of its services.

The accreditation process provides the organization with the opportunity to obtain an independent assessment of whether it is in substantial compliance with the quality assurance standards set by the Accreditation Council. Accreditation, however, is but one component of an organization's ongoing monitoring and evaluation process.

CONCLUSION

The Accreditation Council has provided a national quality assurance program evolving from the 1950s. The underlying values and assumptions in the accreditation standards reflect a synthesis of past traditions, current practice, and innovation. The synthesis provides a coherent force in the field of developmental disabilities that unites the diverse coalition of individuals with developmental disabilities, their families, advocates, service providers, professionals, regulators, and financiers and funding agencies.

The accreditation process provides direct benefits to both the individual with developmental disabilities and the staff. This results from the application of the standards and from the participation in the process of accreditation. Individuals with developmental disabilities determine service outcomes they want and expect from the agency. Staff at all levels are brought into the team process through the standards and through participation in the accreditation process.

The process of accreditation provides many of the benefits to agencies that are commonly associated with strategic planning, organizational development, and monitoring and evaluation. The accreditation process provides incentives for the synthesis of organizational resources toward a common future based on shared values and expectations. The accreditation standards and process offer a framework for accomplishing that common future. The benefits of accreditation for the individual with developmental disabilities, the staff, and the organization are maximized when the standards are utilized as milestones in the strategic planning, organizational development, and monitoring and evaluation efforts. Organizations that approach accreditation as self-directed growth and development generally achieve compliance with standards more easily than organizations that view accreditation as a demonstration of the ability to comply with a certain percentage of 611 individual standards.

REFERENCES

Accreditation Council for Facilities for the Mentally Retarded (ACF/MR). (1973). *Standards for community agencies serving persons with mental retardation and other developmental disabilities.* Chicago: Joint Commission on Accreditation of Hospitals, The Accreditation Council on Service for People with Developmental Disabilities.

Accreditation Council for Services for Mentally Retarded and other Developmentally Disabled Persons. (1984). *Standards for services for developmentally disabled individuals: 1984 edition.* Washington, DC: The Accreditation Council for People with Developmental Disabilities.

Accreditation Council on Services for People with Developmental Disabilities (ACDD). (1987). *1987 standards on services for people with developmental disabilities.* Boston, MA: Author.

Accreditation Council on Services for People with Developmental Disabilities (ACDD). (1988). *1990 standards for services for people with developmental disabilities: Field review edition.* Boston, MA: Author.

Birnbaum, W.S. (1987). *Strategy implementation.* New York: American Management Association.

Daft, R.L. (1989). *Organization theory and design.* St. Paul, MN: West Publishing Company.

Fitz-Gibbon, C.T., & Morris, L.L. (1978). *How to design a program evaluation.* Beverly Hills: Sage Publications.

French, W., & Bell, C. (1984). *Organization development: Behavioral science interventions for organizational improvement* (3rd ed.). Englewood Cliffs, NJ: Prentice-Hall.

Golembiewski, R.T., Proehl, C.W., & Sink, D. (1982). Estimating the success of OD applications. *Training and Development Journal, 36,* 86–95.

Rubenstein, M.F. (1975). *Patterns of problem solving.* Englewood Cliffs, NJ: Prentice-Hall.

Steiner, G.A. (1979). *Strategic planning: What every manager must know.* New York: Free Press.

Tichy, N.M. (1983). *Managing strategic change: Technical, political, and cultural considerations.* New York: John Wiley & Sons.

chapter 16

Building Values into Accreditation Practices

C. Kaye Pearce

Persons with developmental disabilities are individuals with worth and value. This is a simple statement, but one that is still not fully realized. The very simplicity of the statement masks the complexity of making such a concept reality. One of the dynamics that has increased the day-to-day consciousness of this concept is the evolution of society's perspective toward standards for services for people with developmental disabilities.

In reviewing changes in service perspectives, specifically the accreditation standards and practices that embody them, it is more appropriate to talk about a metamorphosis than a change that has been built incrementally. Building, as a metaphor, connotes putting one thing on top of the other. When building, of necessity, some things must be on top and some things must be on the bottom. It is a hierarchical symbol that creates separation. Building also implies denuding the landscape and starting from scratch. Metamorphosis, by contrast, is a gentler, more evolutionary process that is creatively oriented. Metamorphosis also implies a continuum of growth and change with the new entity incorporating the old.

Society is now seeing the continuing evolution or metamorphosis of a set of values regarding people with developmental disabilities. As with any aspect of an evolving system, standards and accreditation should ultimately reflect changes in values. This chapter looks at the accreditation practices that are reflective of this evolution and speculates about the value-based issues that accreditation faces in the future.

BACKGROUND

When the Commission on Accreditation of Rehabilitation Facilities (CARF) was founded in 1966, the human services field was not bereft of values. In fact, values were inherent in the service delivery system of the late 1960s and shaped the standards that the system reflected. People with developmental disabilities were, for the most part, considered as "others." Not only were they denigrated, they were disenfranchised and segregated from the community-at-large through placement in institutional settings. Probably the most insidious aspect of this particular era was that the values that drove the system were essentially unconscious. People designing the institutional service system of the 1950s and 1960s viewed themselves as well meaning providers of care. Yet, the unconscious values of "otherness" inherent in the institutional design provided fertile ground for the institutional atrocities that have been so well documented.

The early phases of the metamorphosis of the values underlying the institutional model were beginning to evolve at the time that CARF came into being. In fact, by the late 1960s the voices for community placement were beginning to be heeded. Thus, CARF's development closely paralleled the growing national movement to relocate people with developmental disabilities from institutions into communities. The Commission was created when community providers of vocational rehabilitation and medical rehabilitation programs and services came together to address the need for standards for those types of programs. Although the first CARF standards were not designed for people with developmental disabilities, the value of community was a major underpinning of the standards that were developed. Since the founders of CARF were rooted in the community, a community bias in the very first CARF standards was inevitable.

As more people with developmental disabilities moved out of institutional settings and as fewer people were placed in institutions, one of the major community resources that was available for these people was the vocational rehabilitation system. Thus, during the 1970s more vocational programs accredited by CARF were serving persons with developmental disabilities. In turn, these organizations looked to CARF to develop standards that were responsive to the unique needs of this population for habilitation rather than rehabilitation.

At this point, it is important to underscore the fact that in order for any standards to achieve the goals for which they are intended, it is essential that the development process include an explicit examination of values. The values that are ultimately espoused provide the measure against which the adequacy and the appropriateness of a standard can be measured. These named values have the most profound effect on human interactions between providers of services and recipients of services; and the unnamed values, as in the case of institutions, have the potential for allowing humanity's darker side to surface.

CARF, given that its history coincides with the deinstitutionalization movement and its initial commitment to community services, has had to confront the issue of the metamorphosis and the naming of values head-on in its standards setting process. Through a process that has taken place since 1984, and that has involved consumers, advocates, and national organizations as well as providers and other professionals, CARF has named one primary value that forms the underpinnings of all of its standards. That value says that people with developmental disabilities have, first and foremost, the right to have maximum control possible over their own lives. A corollary of that value is that people with developmental disabilities also have the right to live their lives maximally integrated into the fabric of the community within which they reside.

The values of personal empowerment and community integration are amplified in the CARF standards through the requirement that services provided within the community must contribute to the enhancement of the individual's potential for growth and development and to the maximization of their interactions in the community, including their relationships with family, friends, co-workers, and others. Accreditation standards, however, must go beyond statements of philosophy and values and must set forth requirements for service providers that translate values into day-to-day practice.

For CARF, the following values must be reflected in practice for a provider of programs and services to people with developmental disabilities to be eligible for accreditation. Persons served must be offered the opportunity to:

Receive services in an environment that promotes integration, self-sufficiency, and productivity.

Receive programs that maximize their functioning.

Determine the direction of their own lives through involvement in planning, decision-making, and implementation of their programs.

Maximize their developmental potential through individual program planning that is goal-oriented, coordinated, interdisciplinary, and subject to time-based review.

Move among various programs and levels so as to ensure that services are provided in the most integrated, least restrictive environment possible.

Be supported in their struggle for independence in an environment that promotes social and economic opportunities in the community through the removal of attitudinal, architectural, and other barriers.

These statements clearly reflect one step in the metamorphosis of values that regard people with developmental disabilities as important, valued, and worthwhile members of the community. The next section focuses on the three major areas of accreditation that have evolved in services for people with developmental disabilities and their interest in the values discussed.

VOCATIONAL AND EMPLOYMENT PROGRAMS

CARF has long been recognized as the leader in the accreditation field in terms of vocational and employment programs. The emphasis that has been placed on standards for vocational and employment programs around the country is reflective of the extremely high value placed on work in American society. People in this society have long defined "who they are" by "what they do." For people with developmental disabilities to be accepted as part of American society the importance of work cannot be ignored.

The first CARF standards for vocational programs reflect an early phase in the process of metamorphosis. People with developmental disabilities were once viewed as capable of some level of productivity within a work environment. It was also felt that sheltered workshops provided an appropriate environment for training that would ultimately lead to employment. The value of integrated work had not yet become a part of the professional consciousness in the 1960s. Thus, CARF's first vocational standards were designed for sheltered workshops. These programs were developed by vocational rehabilitation professionals to meet the needs of people with disabilities by providing both training and employment in the same location, the rehabilitation facility.

The rehabilitation facility movement can be viewed as a critical transition point in the metamorphosis of values from isolation and otherness to integration and togetherness. It provided and, in some cases, continues to provide an environment of learning and productivity that has not been available through any other service mechanism.

Creative forces, however, began to envisage an approach to vocational and employment services that would provide a blending of the values related to work and the values related to integration. This approach led to the next phase of the metamorphosis of values—supported employment. The success of the supported employment effort, which was initiated at the federal level and implemented at the state and local levels, has created an enthusiasm and zest in the field that has not been seen since the deinstitutionalization efforts of the 1970s.

Thousands of people with developmental disabilities who would have had only one employment option—sheltered employment—are now able to find a place in the world of work alongside workers who do not have disabilities. The result is increased productivity, increased independence, and certainly increased opportunities for community integration.

Along with the obvious successes and positive outcomes, concern has been raised, especially by parents, advocates, community-based providers, and others. The concern is not with the concept of supported employment or with the values that it upholds, rather it is for the potential abuses inherent in the underlying values of a capitalistic system—well known abuses that have manifested through time from the sweatshops of the 1880s to the questionable ethics of the inside traders of the 1980s.

In profit-oriented businesses, most people with developmental disabilities, like other workers, find employment, which is the fundamental value that drives the system's "Has a profit been turned?" attitude. Fortunately, most such businesses also operate according to an industry code of ethics and according to federal, state, and local laws and regulations. However, the sad fact is that there are employers throughout this country that take every advantage they can of those they perceive as vulnerable, including women, illegal aliens, the poor, and people with developmental disabilities.

Community providers of supported employment are rightly held in esteem for their accomplishments. However, just as there have been historical abuses in institutions and facility-based programs, providers of supported employment are not immune to ineptness, insensitivity, or, at worst, abuse. Given these concerns, it is necessary to look at accountability from the perspective of the needs of persons with disabilities who are working in a supported employment position. There are a variety of approaches that can be considered in the accountability issue: vigilance by managers of supported employment services, input from those served and their family members, and standards applied by third party funding agencies. Another option that funding sources are turning to more often in terms of accountability for supported employment programs is independent third party accreditation. The reasons for using national accreditation standards for supported employment duplicate those that motivate funding agents to use such standards in other program areas. These include independent and unbiased reviews, standards that are current and reflect a national consensus, enhancement of resources available for quality assurance, and cost effectiveness.

In 1985, in response to these concerns, CARF established the first national standards for programs in industry that were designed to enable people with disabilities to obtain, retain, and/or upgrade employment in the community. In response to the constituency that is specifically concerned with supported employment, CARF subsequently developed standards within the category of programs in industry.

The discussions among national experts that resulted from the supported employment standards reflected the need to have a system of accountability that was reflective of the needs of people with developmental disabilities, but that was not so intrusive that the private sector would slam the door on such programs if CARF's standards were required. These discussions resulted in a consensus that certain values must be explicitly addressed in the standards:

Those working in the private sector have every opportunity to be integrated into the community work setting.

The decisions affecting the person served should be reflective of both the person's needs and desires.

There are a variety of activities that need to take place to ensure that there is a common set of expectations on the part of the person served, the provider, and the private business.

Knowledge of functional teaching techniques and behavior management are critical for staff who work directly with the person with developmental disabilities and the private employer.

Training does not need to proceed placement.

Assessment can take place at the worksite and does not need to meet CARF's standards for vocational evaluation.

Where appropriate, the family is a part of the decision-making process and receives ongoing communication from the supported employment provider regarding the employee's status.

Appropriate follow-up services should be provided.

Given the health and safety requirements that most businesses must now meet, issues of safety should be approached on a common sense basis.

Career ladders should be a part of planning for individuals so that the supported employment placement is not viewed as "terminal" or "the end of the road."

Such discussions, which shaped CARF's standards for supported employment, reflect the unique three-way relationship involving the person served/employee, the community-based provider, and the private business that is found in the supported employment environment. As shown in Table 1, each interest has distinct needs and each has specific objectives. Accreditation standards strive to ensure that the most desirable outcome, a "win-win"

Table 1. Members of the three-way relationship found in the supported employment environment and their individual needs and objectives

Members of the relationship	Needs and objectives
Employee	Work, income, status in the community
Provider	Work, outcomes
Business	Productive employees, profits

situation, is the ultimate outcome for everyone. In a competitive society, "win-win" is rarely even thought about, much less sought after as a valued outcome. Yet, the consensus of those who shaped CARF's standards for supported employment is that "win-win" is the only acceptable outcome— the only outcome that will assure that supported employment will continue to be a successful model. Perhaps the ultimate irony is that, as more people with developmental disabilities find competitive employment in the community, those who historically have been among the most devalued will demonstrate, as they become valued, productive members of society, that the greatest successes of all come from cooperation, equitable human interaction, and respect for individual empowerment.

RESIDENTIAL SERVICES

The first standards for residential programs for people with developmental disabilities were for institutions, the primary out-of-home setting. These early standards were much like licensing requirements and reflected the assumption that good quality was good caretaking. Thus, measures of quality were essentially of the "brick and mortar," "yardstick and thermometer" variety. They certainly were neither programmatic nor people-oriented in their design or application.

The next phase in the metamorphosis of values related to residential services was to view people with developmental disabilities as capable of growth and development. This rather significant leap forward from the caretaker model to a model that embraced the values of growth and development required a different perspective on the worth and humanity of those served. People with developmental disabilities were deemed to have an attribute of some significance in this society—they had the capacity to learn. Thus, standards evolved that stressed program planning and training for the developmental model.

At this stage of the values metamorphosis, persons served were no longer perceived as objects of care but as recipients of professional intervention. This perspective reflected a value base rooted in a professional service orientation that, though decently motivated, was still supported by a belief system that assumed that persons with developmental disabilities should be "acted upon." Programs were something done "to" rather than "with" people. It was believed by many that professionals were in the best position to determine the direction of the lives of people with developmental disabilities.

Additionally, as a part of the "new" approach, the rights of persons served were recognized as important and in need of protection. Thus, when the deinstitutionalization effort began in full force, there was a model of expectations, both in terms of program and in terms of client rights, that was transferred from the institution to the community setting. State and federal standards for community residences, specifically group homes and later the Intermediate Care Facilities for the Mentally Retarded (ICFs/MR), soon reflected these new values.

Those who were concerned with accountability, whether in an institutional or community setting, took the concepts of behaviorally oriented programming and client rights and translated them into various standards. Accreditation standards embody this "great leap forward" in terms of services to people with developmental disabilities. There is not a set of accreditation standards for developmental disabilities programs that does not address individual program planning, interdisciplinary team concept, behavioral programming, coordinated service delivery, client rights, and so forth.

Both in the work setting and in the residential setting it was recognized that the individual program planning and client rights standards served as a prologue to the next stage. Two values, integration and involvement of persons with developmental disabilities in the day-to-day decision-making of their own lives, began to appear in society's consciousness and subsequently in the literature, and finally in practice.

Here again, a major step in recognizing the total worth of people with developmental disabilities was taken. Not only were people with developmental disabilities viewed as capable of learning, they were viewed as worthwhile and contributing members of their communities, capable of some degree of self-determination. Such values incorporated into practice moved members of society closer to recognizing the true reality that people share this planet together and that there is no such thing as "us" and "them," only the human "we."

As the values of community integration and self-determination began to take form in terms of practice, they were then translated into standards, including accreditation standards. The power of accreditation standards, because of their national visibility, lies in their widespread impact, both numerically and geographically. Accreditation standards, in fact, serve as a vehicle for the dissemination of both the values and attendant practices.

These notions of integration and self-determination have clearly had an influence on the standards for residential services. This phase of the metamorphosis placed the concept of "home" inside rather than outside of the community. The resulting practices emphasize the importance of both where and how a person lives and now form an integral and basic part of CARF's standards for residential services. The CARF definition for residential services crystallizes the value base discussed:

> A residence is a place where a person lives. The goal of a residential program is to enable those served to have the best possible quality of life through a program which is integrated into the community. Toward that end, services are typically provided in houses or apartments which provide a personalized living environ-

ment. (Commission on Accreditation Rehabilitation Facilities [CARF], 1989, p. 97)

In addition, the standards that CARF-accredited residential providers must address not only include generally accepted principles of program planning, normalization, training of those served, staff requirements, environment, and health care, but also an array of values that include the following:

Opportunities for input include provisions for meetings of those served, the inclusion of client satisfaction in the measures of program success, opportunities for consumers to influence the program design, and so forth.

Community integration includes utilization of generic community resources; utilization of community cultural activities; homes whose designs fit the neighborhood; promotion of positive relationships with friends, neighbors, staff, and other individuals in the community.

Individual rights include provisions for information regarding rights, preservation of rights, the right to appeal decisions such as those made by the interdisciplinary team, and so forth.

Support of individual decision-making and choices includes incorporation of individual desires and choices into program planning; training in contingency planning, problem-solving, and decision-making; opportunities for individual choices in all aspects of daily living, and so forth.

Any individual in this society, including individuals with developmental disabilities, need not just shelter but a home. The meaning of home goes much beyond meeting basic needs of protection from the elements. These homes are stamped with individual identities. The challenge to both providers and standards setters, such as accrediting bodies, is to ensure that all of the skill-learning activities that occur in the home of a person with developmental disabilities, activities that support the person's right to develop and grow, are in balance with the need to see the home not as a training site but as an extension of the energy, the persona, and the inner being of the person served. This most effectively happens when those whose home it is not, most typically the staff, focus on the person and the values discussed above rather than on simply "running the program."

PERSONAL AND SOCIAL ADJUSTMENT SERVICES

The evolution of this set of standards provides another useful parallel reflecting the metamorphosis of values. When CARF first established what are called personal and social adjustment standards, they were titled, using the common terminology of the time, "work activity standards." The work activity standards were rooted in the belief system that said many people with developmental disabilities were so limited in their work capacity that a quasi-work, quasi-habilitation program design was the most appropriate, and the only way for a person with developmental disabilities to reach his or her destination, that is competitive employment, was to pass through a graduated hierarchy of programs of which work activities were frequently seen as the first step.

The next turn of the evolutionary wheel in terms of values, driven by the developmental model and the professionalization of services, resulted in replacement of CARF work activities standards with standards for activity services. These standards were defined as "developmental and therapeutic services" focusing on enhancing independent functioning in a variety of skill areas. The standards themselves provided a framework upon which professional staff could produce well designed training programs for individuals who needed such training. The activity service standards were also viewed as taking the first step away from a hierarchical, lockstep approach to programming. Activity services, as opposed to work activity, could be provided in concert with other vocational programs. In addition, the standards for activity services did not completely ignore the concept of community. For instance, goals were to be established that took into consideration the person's functioning within the community, from his or her own point of view. However, the primary focus of the standards was a training/habilitation model controlled, for the most part, by professionals within a facility context.

As with the vocational and residential standards, the human services field expressed concern about the implications and impact of the changing value base on the area of activity services. After major rewriting, a set of standards for activity services emerged that still focuses on increasing independent functioning and on skill training, but now with an emphasis on functionality and on providing broad opportunities for valued, nonwork roles in the community.

The values of input from those served, community integration, individual rights, involvement of persons served in decision-making, and choices that are found in the residential standards are duplicated in the personal and social adjustment standards. Particularly stressed are:

1. The training of functional skills within the community context
2. The provision of training in and opportunities for decision-making
3. The inclusion of individual preferences and desires in the program planning, especially in the goal setting aspects of that planning

These new standards also took another step away from the hierarchical model in that they are defined as alternatives to employment programs for those not yet employed or those currently unemployed, as supplements to part-time employment, or during transition to employment. By defining personal and social adjustment services in relation to employment, rather than as preparatory to employment, these standards round out the holistic approach to meeting the array of needs of people with developmental disabilities within the community context.

SUPPORT SERVICES

In keeping with the values discussed throughout this chapter, the utilization of generic support services should be encouraged, rather than services provided by a developmental disabilities organization. If this is the appropriate direction, it is legitimate to question whether accrediting bodies should even address standards for support services. The response of CARF to this question has been no. CARF's standards, like other accreditation standards, are focused on services that are driven by the individual habilitation planning process. The field is still reflecting the consensus that vocational, residential, and personal and social adjustment programs need to be supportive of individual growth and learning through utilization of a structured program planning process involving multiple disciplines working together with the person served. Support services frequently do not require that level of structure or intensity. Therefore, except for organizationally based respite programs, CARF does not have standards for support services.

FOCUS ON OUTCOMES

Concomitant with the evolution of values, there has also been a shift in focus from process to outcomes. Since 1973, CARF has been involved in assisting the human services field to measure the success of its programs based on results rather than inputs, processes, or other measures. Clearly, if desired results are defined as community integration, employment, and self-determination, then the value base will be operationalized into everyday practice. In this way, the values become conscious and will drive both overall service design and individual program planning.

CONCLUSION

However, the metamorphosis of values is not complete. The inexorable demands of a metamorphosis in process is already forcing the human services field to recognize the progress that has been made in establishing people with developmental disabilities as valued citizens. It is recognized that as important as value-based program standards are, as critical as client rights standards are, as significant as standards relating to community integration, personal relationships, and consumer involvement are, they are not enough. In relation to the ultimate values—the essentialness of self-worth, self-direction, and the value of the human spirit—such standards still miss the mark. An awareness is necessary that the transformation process that has moved society from the institutional, caretaker model to the community, and from the professional model to a community integration model, also carries with it its own potential "dark side" of power and control.

The field of developmental disabilities, like any other part of the social fabric of American society, mirrors the larger world. One has only to read the paper, watch the news on TV, deal with one's boss, or interact with family members to know that the issue of control is one that still creates vast difficulties for most Americans. Every individual feels a need to be in charge, resulting in the inevitable conflicts in "power over" and "power under" relationships. Certainly those most vulnerable to suffering from "power over" are those who by dint of economics, sex, race, or intelligence are not deemed worthy of having power of their own. People with developmental disabilities frequently are subject to such "power over" relationships.

"Power over" relationships have at their root the need to control. At the root of the need to control is fear. If fear can be surrendered, then there is an ability to let go and allow others to be exactly who they are, which means, most frighteningly of all, not like oneself. Leaders in the field of developmental disabilities simply cannot ignore the implications of this. The successful evolution to the next stage of metamorphosis requires the examination of one's fears and one's need to control. Can the choices made by people with developmental disabilities be truly accepted when others are fearful that these individuals may not make the choices others feel they "should" make? Can input and feedback from people with developmental disabilities be truly accepted when others are afraid these individuals may tell them things they do not want to hear? Can there be interaction with people with developmental disabilities without fear and the resulting discomfort? Can others look at a person with developmental disabilities and know they are truly one with that person? Such questions are exactly the ones that must be asked if each person concerned with developmental disabilities is to be a facilitator, rather than an inhibitor, of the next stage of the metamorphosis. If allowed to evolve, the next stage will lead to the true actualization of who each person is, including people with developmental disabilities.

REFERENCE

Commission on Accreditation of Rehabilitation Facilities (CARF). (1989). *Standards manual for organizations serving people with disabilities*. Tucson, AZ: Author.

A RESEARCH PERSPECTIVE

chapter 17 ————

Defining Quality
in Residential Services

———— *James A. Knoll* ————

There is a school of thought that says that all policy and programmatic decisions should be clearly reasoned and empirically validated before they are fully implemented (Butterfield, 1985). From this perspective problems in the definition of concepts like "program quality" and "quality of life" can be resolved by rigorous scientific inquiry. Burton Blatt, one of this century's leading advocates for people with developmental disabilities, used to illustrate the fallacy in this point of view with a parable that had immediate relevance to the junior faculty members and doctoral students in his audience.

> It could undoubtedly be demonstrated that most junior professors would have a better shot at tenure and certainly would develop impressive publication lists if they were restricted to a dormitory, the classroom, and the library. We could show that empirically. But even the experiment would be considered immoral because we have some basic social values which preclude us from doing such things. So we have to leave these people out in the world where they have to deal with spouses, lovers, children, financial problems, and so forth. As a result some of them never make it. But, after all, that's life. (B. Blatt, personal communication, 1984)

The point is, of course, that in the definition of program standards and quality is a process that transcends empiricism. This process ultimately appeals to the fundamental values of a society.

A review of the various standards applied to residential programs for people with developmental disabilities clearly demonstrates that these standards are the result of an ongoing dialectical process in which research evidence is but one contributor to the dialogue. The driving force in this process has been the day-to-day experience in service settings that is challenged by the developing perspective on what constitutes quality. This evolutionary process has gone through three distinct phases. In the first phase, the era of institutional reform (roughly 1965–1975), the mandate was for protecting individuals from harm and a need for the development of minimal standards of care. This phase was followed by the era of deinstitutionalization (1976–1986) that was marked by the development of community services and by emphasis on defining the characteristics of quality programs. The third and current phase, the era of community membership, is marked by an emphasis on community integration, quality of life, and the development of individualized support systems. Standards developed during each of these periods bear the distinctive stamp of a particular series of historical events.

This chapter examines the types of standards that have been articulated during each of these phases in an effort to demonstrate how they are reflective of certain historical circumstances. The central assertion of this analysis is that standards are an outgrowth of the predominant attitudes and values that characterize each phase. In other words, the delineation of appropriate standards is not only a product of advocacy, research, or good administration, it is an interactive evolutionary process driven by the growing experiences of people with developmental disabilities and their service providers interacting with the demands of daily life in the community.

INSTITUTIONAL REFORM

Not long ago the issues surrounding quality assurance in services for people with developmental disabilities were pretty clear cut. In a decision on conditions at the Willowbrook Developmental Center on Staten Island, New York, the District Court declared it was not a case of quality services but one of "protection from harm" (*New York State Association for Retarded Children* [*NYSARC*] *v. Carey, 1975*). As a journalist covering the case reflected, the idea of quality of life at such places was a cruel joke.

> Willowbrook is atrocious—an exercise in surrealism that seems to have sprung full blown from one of the inner circles of Dante's Inferno. To label Willowbrook "a developmental center" is to mutilate the phrase beyond recognition . . . there were children lying on floors . . . abandoned in shower stalls . . . sitting in pools of urine . . . beds were crowded head to head, side to side in some wards, only inches separating them . . . there were broken windows . . . the overall pattern from floor to floor, building to building, was one of repetition . . . no supervision, no structured activities . . . the only forms of "recreation" [were] a television set . . . or a blaring phonograph. ("Action Not Words," 1975)

From the sound of life at Willowbrook, one might think it was an extremely unfortunate anomaly. However, nearly identical accounts of abuse surfaced at Partlow in Alabama, Beatrice State Hospital in Nebraska, Sandhaven in North Dakota, Pennhurst in Pennsylvania, Solomon State Hospital in Maryland, Cloverbottem in Tennessee, and Belchertown in Massachusetts. The conditions of institutional life across America were shockingly similar. The response to a nationwide tide of exposés and litigation in the late 1960s and through the 1970s was the development of standards to govern services for people with developmental disabilities and the growth of a wide range of new community-based services that were seen as measures to avoid the pitfalls of the old isolated institutional model.

In many of the court cases that were filed in response to the deplorable conditions in many mental retardation institutions, courts imposed comprehensive minimum standards of care (see for example, *NYSARC v. Carey,* 1975; *Wyatt v. Stickney,* 1972). These standards were an effort to ensure that the physical, social, and psychological deprivation witnessed in these settings would be corrected (see Lottman, Chapter 12, this volume). Often the court decrees offered very specific guidelines articulating such things as staffing ratios, daily schedules, professional qualifications, number of residents per toilet, and nutritional content of meals. While some standards responded to specific issues in a particular court case, most represented an effort to bring these facilities in line with minimal care standards as articulated by expert witnesses in the case. Needless to say, these individual witnesses had personal opinions about what constituted programmatic quality, but more often than not, they cited the consensus of the professional community as expressed in the standards articulated by what was then called the Accreditation Council for Facilities for the Mentally Retarded (ACF/MR) (see Gardner and Parsons, Chapter 15, this volume).

During this same period, the Health Care Financing Administration (HCFA) was in the process of establishing standards for nursing homes and Intermediate Care Facilities (ICFs) that were eligible for reimbursement under the Medicaid and Medicare programs. These standards, like the court cases, were largely motivated by media exposés of abuse found in long-term care settings and the resulting public outcry. Not surprisingly, the HCFA standards, as they affect people with developmental disabilities and mental retardation as well as Intermediate Care Facilities for the Mental Retarded (ICFs/MR), are based on the same body of professional opinion as the court imposed standards. Based on the assumption that they would generally be used in large public institutions, the ICF/MR standards, issued in 1974, essentially echo the voluntary 1971 standards of the ACF/MR (Health Care Financing Administration [HCFA], 1988).

These regulations had a profound impact, directly and indirectly, on the shape of residential services. As of 1988, 49 states participated in the ICF/MR program providing residential services to over 154,000 people in 3,600 sites that ranged in size from 4 to almost 1,500 persons (HCFA, 1988). In addition to the direct affect this program has on all of the people living in large institutional ICFs/MR and small (less than 16 persons) community-based ICFs, these standards have also shaped many community-based programs that do not provide Medicaid reimbursed services. Many states, sensitized by the threat of litigation and of advocates and parents concerned about the quality of dispersed community programs, modeled their regulations for group homes and other community programs on the federal ICF/MR standards.

What was often lacking in the adoption of these standards was a critical analysis of the primary motivation underlying the initial preparation and whether or not the focus of such standards was fully compatible with the intent of settings that were usually described as "small homelike group living arrangements." In other words, little consideration was given to how the dominant concern for protection from harm and minimal programmatic standards could be integrated with the principle of normalization (Wolfensberger, 1972) that had become the guiding philosophy of the reform movement within services for people with developmental disabilities and mental retardation.

An example of this potential for conflict on a minor, but not inconsequential, matter was commented on by a program supervisor during an observational study of life in a community residence certified as an ICF/MR.

> Yes, we really try to create a homelike environment and at the same time remain in compliance with the state's regulations. They constantly are trying to get us to run an institution-like environment. But, we think we do a pretty good job of trying to keep an atmosphere that is pretty close to what someone's home should be like. . . . As it is they have all these silly rules about keeping things—so called dangerous substances, like dish soap—under lock and key. So we defeat that regulation by giving all the residents their own keys to everything in the apartment. After all it's their home! They can't have part of their own home inaccessible to them. (Biklen & Knoll, 1987a, p. 20)

Similar concerns were voiced in the early 1980s by some critics who seriously questioned what the long-term impact of the ICF program would be on community-based services for people with developmental disabilities and mental retardation. They felt that the institutional orientation of the regulations would cast a pallor over many programs that were intended to provide quality community living experiences for people (Taylor et al., 1981). Indeed, one study that examined a range of residential programs including small ICFs on the campus of an old institution, a community ICF, a state licensed group home, a small family-scale community residence, and a supported apartment found that the more rigorously the site conformed to an ICF or ICF-like standards, the more likely they were to limit the participation of residents in the activities in the house and community. The application of such standards fostered practices such as restricting residents' access to the kitchen thereby excluding them from even rudimentary participation in meal preparation, all in the name of protection from potential harm (Lutfiyya et al., 1987).

The changing perspective on program quality, the fact that so many of the ICF programs are community-based, and the reaction to criticism such as that just reviewed led HCFA to revise the ICF/MR standards in 1988. Even with these revisions, ICF standards continue to have an emphasis on minimal standards of program quality and protection from harm.

In summary, this era, to use Bradley's conceptual framework (see Chapter 1, this volume), largely put in place many of the basic *inputs* to be examined by evaluators of residential services. It should be stated that even the critics of how such standards have been implemented do not question the need to have such basic protections in place. The problem arises when measures of quality go no further than this basic floor or when these basic standards are used to define the character of a setting.

DEINSTITUTIONALIZATION

The second phase in the development of standards for residential programs saw the emergence of the concept of quality enhancement as a step beyond mere protection from harm in an effort to define a true "quality" program (Bradley, Allard, Mulkern, Spence, & Absalom, 1984). Efforts to delineate these enhanced standards turned to the burgeoning research literature on community programs for guidance. Here the concentration was on identifying those program characteristics that influenced resident progress; thus, they were seen as indicative of high quality. In this regard, this phase of development articulated standards that primarily focused on the *processes* involved in residential services.

While the research literature does offer some rather clear directions in identifying the best program practices, there are major limitations. For the most part, the lessons about the design of quality programs must be drawn indirectly since most researchers during the period were caught up in addressing another more general question: Are traditional institutions or community-based programs the most appropriate setting for people with developmental disabilities? Most of the contributors to this volume are clear in responding to this question by affirming the appropriateness of the community and also realizing that such a position is as much a value judgment as it is an empirical question. Yet, in some quarters this is still regarded as an open research question (Landesman & Butterfield, 1987; Larson & Lakin, 1989).

Just as in the first phase where the issue of reforming institutional abuse clouded any discussion of health and safety standards, the institution/community debate continues to obscure a clear focus on what the research has uncovered about the characteristics of quality programs. But, before attempting to delineate some of the characteristics that can be identified, general research approaches that have led to these findings will be reviewed.

Research Approaches

Research on community living can be sorted into five broad groupings: 1) individual characteristic studies, 2) outcome studies, 3) comparison studies, 4) community environment studies, and 5) qualitative studies. While this research has provided valuable information on the development of community programs, most of it cannot be translated into program design or evaluation. The potential utility of the results is very closely connected to the way in which the researchers framed their principal research question.

Individual Characteristic Studies Many of the early studies of community residential settings (Heal, Sigelman, & Switzky, 1980; Sutter, Mayeda, Call, Yanagi, & Yee, 1980; Taylor, 1976) concentrated on the characteristics of individuals—IQ, adaptive behavior score, age, sex, length of institutionalization, and so forth—that were found to be associated with successful or unsuccessful (i.e., return to the institution) community placement. The usual conclusion drawn from this work was that individuals had to be prepared to live in the community, or, in other words, a person had to earn the right to live in the community by learning the required skills. In addition to the intrinsic contradiction of having someone earn that which is their birth right, the position espoused in this body of literature is a classic example of "blaming the victim" (Ryan, 1972). It places all responsibility on the person with a disability to overcome a handicap and fails to look at the characteristics of the environment that can either ameliorate or amplify the disability. As such, these studies offer little useful information regarding the design or evaluation of quality programs.

Outcome Studies The largest group of studies related to the design of community programs (Larson & Lakin, 1989, identified over 50 studies in this group) were concerned with examining the effect of placement in a small community setting of previously institutionalized individuals (Aanes & Moen, 1976; Bell, Schoenrock, & Bensberg, 1981; Bradley, Conroy, Covert, & Feinstein, 1986; Close, 1977; Conroy & Bradley, 1985; Conroy, Efthimiou, & Lemanowicz, 1982; Eastwood & Fisher, 1988; Kleinberg & Galligan, 1983; Schroeder & Hanes, 1978; Thompson & Carey, 1981). Usually this effect is defined in terms of some readily quantifiable variable such as increase in IQ, adaptive behavior score, or number of new skills demonstrated. These studies typically use either a longitudinal tracking of subjects before and after deinstitutionalization or a contrast group strategy in which individuals placed in the community are compared with a twin group remaining in the institution. While these studies as a group clearly affirm the positive outcomes associated with community placement, their general focus means that they provide little information for use in program design or evaluation.

Comparison Studies   The studies in this group (Balla, 1976; Hemming, Lavender, & Pill, 1981; King, Raynes, & Tizard, 1971; MacEachron, 1983; McCormick, Balla, & Zigler, 1975) compare traditional institutional settings with more "normalized" units or community residences. For the most part these comparisons used one of two measures. One comparison measured the degree to which an environment was characterized by institutionalized practices, such as group treatment, rigidity of routine, and depersonalization (*Revised Resident Management Profile [RRMP]*, King, Raynes, & Tizard, 1971). Alternatively, a measure of the level of environmental normalization (*PASS-3,* Wolfensberger & Glenn, 1975) was used as the independent variable and compared to a measure of resident change, such as score on the adaptive behavior scale, as the dependent variable. On the whole, these studies come down strongly in support of the advantage of more normalized living situations, but individually, this finding is often obscured by discussions of some peripheral issues such as the importance of size of living unit as opposed to size of total facility. However, these studies do provide the program planner and the evaluator the general guideline that good program practice, when defined in terms of change in adaptive behavior, is associated with increasingly normalized environments and less rigidity of routine, less block treatment of residents, and more personalized care.

Community Environment Studies   An awareness of the limitations of the earlier research on community living has fostered a growth to examine the characteristics of community-based residential programs. This investigation breaks down into two distinct groups. The first group uses pre-existing environmental measures such as *PASS-3* or the *RRMP,* which are known to be associated with higher quality care, as the dependent variable and seeks to explore what specific environmental characteristics are associated with better scores on these measures (Hull & Thompson, 1981; Pratt, Luszcz, & Brown, 1980). The second group uses time sampling, environmental questionnaires, or structured observation to examine life in community residences (Landesman-Dwyer, Sackett, & Kleinman, 1980; Landesman-Dwyer, Stein, & Sackett, 1976; Willer & Intagliata, 1981). This ecological perspective, which concentrates on seeing behavior as a function of the environment rather than as a characteristic of the person, now defines the state-of-the-art research on community living arrangements (cf. Rotegard, Bruininks, Holman, & Lakin, 1985). On the theoretical level this approach is a vast improvement over much of the earlier community living research and has the potential for addressing the gap between research and practice. However, thus far this research approach remains dependent on predetermined instruments and/or analytical techniques that greatly restrict its utility to service planners and evaluators. For example, it has identified interesting but not very practical (for design purposes) variables, such as a service provider's degree of religiosity, that are associated with more personalized community settings.

Qualitative Studies   A small group of researchers have used holistic techniques to examine the community living experiences of people with developmental disabilities. These studies break into two subgroups. The first of these concentrates on describing the experience of previously institutionalized persons now living in the community and emphasizes understanding how they think about their experiences (Bogdan & Taylor, 1982; Edgerton, 1967; Edgerton & Bercovici, 1976; Edgerton, Bollinger, & Herr, 1984). The second group of qualitative studies uses a case study methodology to provide descriptive analyses of life within group homes or other community-based programs (Bercovici, 1983; Biklen & Knoll, 1987a; Heshusius, 1981; Kielhofner, 1983; Rothman & Rothman, 1984). In general, qualitative studies attempt to understand how the people living and working in community homes think about their experiences. The questions are endless and extremely complex, for example, "What do you like/dislike about the group home setting? What do you think about the resident/staff relationships? How do the residents see the employees?" When dealing with these complicated issues, researchers tend to emphasize the experience of individuals rather than the characteristics of programs. However, as the definition of quality becomes increasingly sensitive to the experience of the individual, these studies and this approach to research may have increasing utility in design and evaluation.

Landesman-Dwyer (1985) provided a relevant conclusion to this general review of research literature on residential services that speaks directly to the limited utility of this material as a guide in evaluating program quality:

> . . . simply knowing that someone lives in a foster home or a group home may convey virtually no meaningful information about the physical or functional qualities of his or her environment. If the nature of these programs is not carefully investigated in each locality, erroneous conclusions could be drawn about the impact of these environments on individuals. In fact, the majority of empirical studies about different types of residential programs fails to provide enough descriptive information to determine reliably what the program itself is like. (p. 191)

Lessons from Research

There are many restrictions that inhibit the research literature from assisting with the efforts of program planners and evaluators. These restrictions stem directly from the intent of the research enterprise to develop generalized findings. As a result, the research lessons tend to be rather broad in nature. For example, research on the ability of community settings to handle a whole constellation of problems, which at one time was used to justify the need for some individuals to remain in more restrictive settings, highlights the need for a good planning process. The primary factor influencing success seems to be the careful matching of the individual with an environment or with a service provider who is attuned to the needs of that individual (Willer & Intagliata,

1982). It is known, for example, that when people with disabilities have advocacy and support services they tend to achieve success in community residential placements; this is often true even when the residents exhibit "maladaptive" behavior (Schalock, Harper, & Genung, 1981).

Nor surprisingly the research shows that when support services and programming are unavailable in the community, residents of group homes are more likely to be institutionalized or reinstitutionalized (Polivka, Marvin, Brown, & Polivka, 1979). The complement of this is also true:

> When residential environments [community residences] are more normalized along the lines of increased training opportunity, increased opportunity to assume responsibility for in-house tasks, more autonomy, clearer expectations on the part of staff members, and increased access to resources, residents are more likely to perform mastered skills and be satisfied with the residential setting. (Seltzer, 1981, p. 629)

Another look at some of the early studies of community life is instructive since it reminds researchers that none of the recent findings should come as a surprise. Two such studies (Edgerton, 1967; Fernald, 1919) on deinstitutionalization suggested that people with developmental disabilities tended to succeed in community living arrangements when they enjoyed the assistance of benefactors or, as known today, support networks. Without such support, these people were assumed to be incompetent to achieve independence. This early finding would seem to support the importance of citizen advocacy and other support programs.

However, research now suggests the difficulty of predicting precisely those factors that influence success in community living. When Edgerton and Bercovici (1976) did a follow-up study 12 to 14 years after Edgerton's original *Cloak of Competence* (1967) study, many of those deinstitutionalized persons who had been expected to successfully adjust in a conventional sense (jobs, friends, family ties, increased steady income, etc.) had not. Yet, they lived in and seemed to prefer the community to the institution. Others who had been predicted to fail succeeded. In other words, Edgerton and Bercovici found that it was difficult, if not impossible, to tell who would successfully adapt to community life. In a second, albeit less extensive follow-up study—it is becoming increasingly difficult to locate the original research subjects— Edgerton and his colleagues (Edgerton et al., 1984) found that their notions of success, as they themselves readily admit, were often inconsistent with the perspectives of the individuals with disabilities. Invariably, despite terribly difficult conditions and seemingly quite limited life opportunities, the deinstitutionalized individuals regarded their own adjustment to community living positively and had a remarkably optimistic outlook. It might be concluded then, in regard to adjustment to community living, that whatever measures are used, whether the client's own perspectives on happiness, satisfaction, or other externally devised measures, the consistent pattern is one of moderate, though unpredictable, success.

This expectation seems to be justified in light of findings that residences in more populated areas and ones that offer "socially integrated vocational, educational, recreational, and social activities" (Hull & Thompson, 1980, p. 260) tend to promote more culturally normative appearance and behavior (including social interaction) than those that are more isolated or less promoting of social integration. It is clear that all people seem to benefit from small homelike placements, but the benefits are greatest for those with more severe disabilities (Conroy et al., 1982; Hemming, Lavender, & Pill, 1981; Keith & Ferdinand, 1984; Raynes, 1980). This finding stands in sharp contradiction to the claim that institutions are needed to serve individuals with the most severe disabilities.

Due to the direct implication for service design, the issue of what constitutes the appropriate size of a "small" community program has generally dominated much of the research. Although the research seems to indicate that "smaller is better," the question continues to reappear. In 1980, Baroff examined 8 major studies available at that time that related size to behavior and found: "Seven of them show some advantage to the smaller settings and one shows no difference. None show any advantage to the larger one" (p. 116). However, size continues to resurface in the literature as a key variable, probably because these findings challenge the potential survival of larger settings (e.g., institutions and large "community" residences), and possibly due to stereotypes about "the retarded."

Perhaps some of the compelling evidence regarding the value of small size is found in the limited number of studies that provide descriptive information about the quality of life within various living arrangements (Bercovici, 1983; Rothman & Rothman, 1984). A sense of this type of research and the value of direct, informed, observation as a quality assurance strategy is conveyed in this excerpt from the observational study cited earlier (Biklen & Knoll, 1987a):

> Morey and a staff person had together made dinner for everyone—six regulars [4 residents, 2 staff] and one guest [the observer], not the 15 people we observed in a larger "small" community residence. Everyone, including George, was part of the conversation, which took place in a nice pleasant tone of voice. There was no need to speak up to be heard over the din of clashing dishes. Nor was there the deadly silence of a rushed meal where the only aim is to empty the serving dishes as quickly as possible. The staff made a conscious, but natural, effort to insure this was a relaxed social occasion. They were able to do this at the same time they were attending to special needs or problems, such as Morey having difficulty pouring. The staff had to assist only four people, not ten. It was striking that throughout this mealtime, one staff person was able to devote most of his efforts to assisting George eat. This is a long process which continued for well over an hour. George was able to pace his own meal. The staff person did not rush him.

The three other residents were able to see to their own needs. In other words, apart from the small size of this residential group, the heterogeneous nature of the people living here means that the special needs of the more severely handicapped person can be seen to in an individualized manner. (p. 17)

Life in this home differs markedly from situations where the numerous demands of a homogeneous grouping of people with severe disabilities tend to create or are associated with an environment and care that is "characteristically unstimulating, undifferentiated [not individualized], depersonalized, and rigid" (Raynes, 1980, p. 220).

Perhaps the most frequently cited research on the size of community residences is the work of Landesman-Dwyer et al. (1980). This work is distinctive because it is the only research to date that purports to find clear benefits for residents in larger community settings. Needless to say, this has become a favorite citation of those who are looking for support for their attempts to build large "institutional" community residences (e.g., *NYSARC v. Carey*, 1982, p. 41). These researchers found:

residents in [a] larger group home [18–20 persons] interacted with more peers, were more likely to have a "best friend" [i.e., a peer with whom a person was observed with more frequently than any other person], and spent more time with their best friend than did residents in smaller group homes. . . . Clearly, the smallest facilities did not foster better interpersonal relationships than did the larger facilities. (Landesman-Dwyer et al., 1980, p. 14)

A moment's reflection makes it clear that Landesman-Dwyer's findings are not the unqualified endorsement of larger settings that they are presented to be. As with all research, any generalization of the findings is constrained by the limitation inherent in the method. In this case the focus is on providing a quantifiable picture of life within the walls of 20 community residences. The fact that the essence of community living involves integration into the larger community outside the walls of a person's abode is ignored. Indeed, these findings on relationships are consistent with other research (Willer & Intagliata, 1983) that found that residents of larger homes tended to have more of their social needs met within the place of residence while individuals who lived in smaller settings had a broader network of relationships and social activities in the community. From this perspective the most that can be said about Landesman-Dwyer's research is that it provides a great deal of information about how people occupy themselves within their place of residence, but it really does not address the qualitative differences among the social relationships of individuals living in settings of various sizes.

In summary, the research literature explores the question of size and the relative merits of traditional institutions and community residences. Yet direct service providers need answers to questions like: "How do you run a service setting with paid employees and still assure that it feels like the residents' homes?" It appears that the rapid growth of a system of community services has passed the research establishment by. Some researchers continue to examine questions that are largely irrelevant to the lives of real people. Trained as they are in the traditional practice of social science and the study of individual differences, most researchers seek generalizations in a system that is defined by its diversity. They continue to approach the collage of residential settings—this basically unknown and ever changing quantity—with methods that are predicated on the assumption that the researcher has some idea of the right questions to ask. This issue of the relationship between research and practice becomes even more strained as the questions asked by service providers begin to focus more acutely on the quality of life of the people they are serving.

COMMUNITY MEMBERSHIP

As seen in the 1970s and early 1980s, the major issue that dominated the field of developmental disabilities was the issue of institutions versus community. This issue is still provoking debate. With over 100,000 people with developmental disabilities living in public institutions (Braddock, Hemp, & Howes, 1986), it would be misleading to suggest that the institution versus community debate has been resolved. Yet the state-of-the-art services for people with developmental disabilities has moved beyond this issue. It is not just a theory that people with severe disabilities can live in the community. It is a reality in a growing number of places across the country. The critical issue of the 1990s has to do with how people with disabilities, including individuals with severe or multiple disabilities, challenging behaviors, and complex medical needs, should be served in the community and what arrangements foster the greatest degree of community membership.

In general, community services, as developed during the era of deinstitutionalization, are based on the continuum model and are often described as offering residents a range of "residential settings" that are "homelike" and "normalized," primarily because they are smaller and geographically less isolated than the large institutions of the past. The major emphasis of this era has been on the development of a limited array of programmatic options. The concept of community integration offers an alternative to the continuum of services with its emphasis on program slots. Rather than focusing on putting people into community programs, the developing concept emphasizes building a network of formal and informal supports that a person with a disability needs to meet the day-to-day demands of their homes and communities (Ferguson & Olson, 1989; Taylor, 1988; Taylor, Racino, Knoll, & Lutfiyya, 1987).

This shifting away from deinstitutionalization and the establishment of community-based programs to community membership and meeting the support needs of individuals in their homes presents new challenges to the service planner and evaluator. Providers are increasingly concerned with the degree to which true social integration in the community is taking place and how that can be facilitated. Unfortunately, the literature lags far behind the most advanced thinking in the field (Research and Training Center on Community Integration, 1989). While there have been some efforts to articulate the components of quality services as they relate to the process of individual planning, the idea that some of these same components are a necessary part of quality assurance is rather new to the field.

Much of the work in the area of community integration, which has implications for service quality, places an emphasis on liberating people with disabilities from the stigma of "clienthood" and providing supports that are in line with typical expectations concerning freedom and control over one's own life (Biklen & Knoll, 1987b; McKnight, 1987). The central idea seems to be assuring people with disabilities a quality of life that is congruent with how that concept is defined by society in general. An important consideration is that the concept of quality of life is such a pervasive one that even individuals who have reservations regarding the "community integration" movement recognize it as a crucial element to be included in program evaluation (Landesman, 1986; Robinson, 1987). The third phase, then, is focusing on defining the appropriate *outcomes* to be explored by evaluators of residential services.

At this point, there have been a number of efforts to conceptualize those aspects of life that should be examined when the focus is on quality of life. Indeed, some of the authors who emphasize the need to refocus quality assurance efforts on issues such as community membership do not like to articulate a list of crucial components for fear they will be directly translated into a checklist that will be completed in a perfunctory manner, rather than being used to guide efforts to support individuals (Bersani & Salon, 1988). These authors generally show a preference for qualitative evaluation strategies that emphasize direct observation and interviewing in an effort to understand a setting from the perspective of the individuals living there, while simultaneously calling on evaluators to clearly articulate their own preconceptions regarding quality of life.

Certainly the subjective perception of quality of life is a crucial consideration and is central to one group's thinking about services for people with developmental disabilities. Unfortunately, this group has had very little influence on the agenda of researchers, program planners, and evaluators because in many ways they are the least powerful people in the service system. They are people with developmental disabilities. However, in the late 1960s some people with disabilities articulated a vision of quality of life for themselves even though they required some form of support in their daily lives. In 1970, a group of people with developmental disabilities issued a statement of "beliefs, questions, and demands" that was drafted by retarded adults at a conference sponsored by the Swedish Association for Retarded Children. Among the demands made at the national conference in Malmö, Sweden, were the following:

> We wish to have an apartment of our own and not be coddled by personnel; therefore, we want courses in cooking, budgeting, etc.
>
> We want the right to move together with the other sex when we feel ready for it, and we also want the right to marry when we ourselves find the time is right.
>
> We want to have more personal freedom, and not as it is now in certain institutions and boarding homes where you have to ask permission to shop for fruit, newspapers, tobacco, etc.
>
> We who live at home have found that: it is largely good, but one ought to move out when the time is right to a sheltered apartment or hostel; one cannot for his whole life be dependent on his parents. We want, however, to have our own key when we live at home.
>
> We demand more training in a wider range of vocational fields so that we can have larger freedom of choice in determining our vocations.
>
> We want to choose our vocations ourselves and have influence over our education.
>
> We demand more interesting jobs.
>
> We do not want to be used on our jobs by doing the worst and the most boring tasks we do at present.
>
> We demand that our capacity for work should not be underestimated.
>
> We think that we should be present when our situation is discussed by doctors, teachers, welfare workers, floor men, etc. Now it feels as if they talk behind our backs. (cited in Wolfensberger, 1972, pp. 190–193)

The message was clear. People wanted support to achieve independence, dignity, and personal fulfillment.

In retrospect, it should come as no surprise that when this statement is read in its entirety the demands essentially parallel the major components of a quality life as defined by the general public. Flanagan's (1978) extensive research in this area identified 15 life domains that contribute to quality of life. These include: 1) material well-being and financial security, 2) health and personal safety, 3) relations with a spouse, 4) having and raising children, 5) relationships with other relatives, 6) relationships with friends, 7) helping others, 8) citizenship, 9) intellectual development, 10) self-understanding and planning, 11) job role, 12) creativity and personal experience, 13) socializing, 14) passive recreation, and 15) active recreation. The message is that people want enduring relationships, security, dignity, and personal fulfillment. It is important to note that the issue of freedom, autonomy, or independence does not come up in Flanagan's classification of quality of life. These rights are taken for granted in regard to the general public, but in the case of people with developmental disabilities who are involved with the service system these basic rights need to be asserted.

It has taken 20 years, but the improvements in the field of services for people with developmental disabilities have finally come to the point where the professional providers and evaluators can hear the statement made in Malmö. Quality of life as a primary consideration in the design and evaluation of services is finally beginning to get the attention it deserves; quality assurance is focusing on the heart of the process—the experience of the person who is receiving services.

The focus on quality of life as a crucial component in quality assurance is only now emerging. There have been a few efforts in the field for people with developmental disabilities to organize quality of life factors, but as yet there have been no systematic presentations of the topic. As a contribution to the dialogue on this issue and to aid planners and evaluators in thinking about quality of life, the range of topics that a number of authors have suggested as necessary considerations in assessing quality of life are presented in Table 1.

A diverse range of resources was consulted to compile the information in Table 1 in order to cover the spectrum of actors concerned about quality of life issues. Flanagan's (1978) life domains have been included to provide a baseline for comparison with topic areas identified by people who largely come from within the human services field. In addition, the topics in the matrix come from a framework for individualized service planning (O'Brien, 1987), quality of life scales to be used with residents of community programs (Baker & Intagliata, 1982; Bersani & Salon, 1988; Schalock, Keith, Hoffman, & Karan, 1989), state quality assurance guidelines or measures (Connecticut Department of Mental Retardation, 1986; Pennsylvania Department of Mental Retardation, 1986; Washington Division of Developmental Disabilities, 1985), quality of life checklists developed by or for program residents (Allen, 1981; Allen & Gardner, 1983; People First of California, undated; People First of Washington, 1985), and professionally developed lists of quality of life indicators for service providers (Biklen & Foster, 1985; Callahan, undated; Donnellan, 1987; Knoll & Ford, 1987; Options in Community Living, 1987). The topics in Table 1 are organized in the order of the frequency in which they were identified. The sources, listed at the head of the columns, have been arranged in order of the number of quality of life variables that each identifies.

While the information in Table 1 is drawn from resources that are nominally concerned with the issue of quality of life, the variation in the topics highlights the divergence in definition of this concept. Only the first 11 topics are identified by the majority of the sources, while 39 of the 96 topics are suggested by only one or two sources. This diversity seems to be related to two factors. First, the topics identified by each source reflect the target audience or purpose for which it was prepared. This is clearest when the differences between the quality components identified by Donnellan, which have a strong focus on quality enhancing professional practice, are compared with those suggested by People First of California to assist people with disabilities in evaluating their own living situations. Thus, while there is some agreement

Table 1. Factors contributing to quality

Suggested quality of life topic:	O'Brien (1987)	Donnellan (1987)	WA Dept of MR (1982)	Baker & Intagliata (1982)	Biklen & Foster (1985)	Options (1987)
Real choices in all aspects of daily life	X					X
Functional skills		X	X		X	
Interaction with a variety of people		X	X	X	X	
Use of "generic" services			X		X	
Access to community resources			X	X	X	
Age appropriateness		X	X		X	
Use of a range of community environments		X	X		X	
Living in typical neighborhood			X	X	X	
Meaningful daily activity	X			X		X
Nonaversive interventions		X			X	
Relationships with friends				X		X
Relationships with family				X		X
Respect	X					
Skill development						
Typical daily routine						X
Active participation	X					
Adult relationships supported						
Personal appearance				X		X
Relationships with neighbors						X
Safety within the home			X	X		X
Working in integrated worksite			X		X	
Access to medical care						X
Client input in program decisions						
Coherent planning process		X	X			
Personal sense of competence	X					
Freedom of movement						X
Good health			X	X		
Individualization		X			X	
Personal responsibility fostered						
Privacy						
Public education					X	
Secure/sufficient income				X		X

Allen & Gardner (1983)	Knoll & Ford (1987)	Flanagan (1978)	Schalock et al. (1989)	PA Dept of MR (1986)	Callahan (undated)	People 1st of CA (undated)	Bersani & Salon (1988)	Allen (1981)	People 1st of WA (1985)	CT Dept of MR (1986)
X	X		X	X		X	X	X	X	X
X					X	X	X	X	X	X
		X			X	X	X		X	X
	X		X	X	X	X	X		X	X
	X			X			X	X	X	X
X	X				X			X	X	X
	X			X		X	X		X	X
				X	X		X	X		X
X		X	X		X					X
	X			X	X	X			X	X
	X	X	X				X		X	X
	X	X					X		X	X
X					X	X		X	X	X
X	X	X				X		X	X	X
X	X				X		X	X		X
X	X			X			X		X	X
X		X			X		X	X	X	X
X						X			X	X
	X		X				X		X	X
		X		X						X
				X	X		X			X
			X			X		X		X
X					X			X	X	X
					X			X		X
		X	X						X	X
						X		X	X	X
		X		X				X		
							X		X	X
X						X		X	X	X
	X					X		X	X	X
X						X	X			X
		X	X							X

(continued)

Table 1. (continued)

Suggested quality of life topic:	O'Brien (1987)	Donnellan (1987)	WA Dept of MR (1982)	Baker & Intagliata (1982)	Biklen & Foster (1985)	Options (1987)
Community participation	X					
Exercising citizenship						
Reliable, accessible transportation						
Clear agency priority on integration						
Client options actively sought						
Good nutrition				X		X
No restrictions on visitors						
A range of recreation opportunities				X		
Personal growth						
Personal satisfaction						
Relationships with housemates				X		X
Relationships with staff						X
Resident chooses to be here						
Secure/attractive home				X		X
Service coordination		X			X	
Access to educational opportunity						
Assistance in accessing community						
Assumption of competency						
Choice-making actively taught						
Competent managers						
Data-based decisions		X			X	
Informed consent						
Preparation for future demands		X			X	
Respect for individual rights			X			
Visitors treated with respect						
Ready access to mail and phone						
Active recreation				X		
Active role of family/advocates						
Being treated as an adult						
Channels for complaints						
Control over medication						
Freedom of assembly						
Full access within the house						

Allen & Gardner (1983)	Knoll & Ford (1987)	Flanagan (1978)	Schalock et al. (1989)	PA Dept of MR (1986)	Callahan (undated)	People 1st of CA (undated)	Bersani & Salon (1988)	Allen (1981)	People 1st of WA (1985)	CT Dept of MR (1986)
	X						X		X	X
		X		X		X	X		X	
			X					X	X	X
					X		X		X	X
X								X	X	X
							X			X
			X				X	X	X	
		X						X	X	
X	X								X	
	X		X	X						X
	X		X							
								X	X	X
						X		X	X	X
								X		X
			X		X					
			X			X			X	
							X		X	X
					X				X	X
							X		X	X
				X		X		X		
										X
						X			X	X
										X
								X	X	
							X	X	X	
							X	X	X	
		X								
				X						X
									X	X
X										X
			X			X				
						X				X
			X						X	

(continued)

Table 1. (continued)

Suggested quality of life topic:	O'Brien (1987)	Donnellan (1987)	WA Dept of MR (1982)	Baker & Intagliata (1982)	Biklen & Foster (1985)	Options (1987)
Generalizable skills		X				
Individual adaptations		X				
Life-long supports if needed						
Meaningful assessment						
New experiences encouraged						
Opportunity to help others						
Outside advocates						
Religious expression supported						
Small-size living arrangements						
Staff accountable to residents						
Ongoing staff training		X				
Annual evaluation						
Caring staff						
Citizen monitoring						
Confidentiality respected						
Consistent organizational structure			X			
Personal control over finances						
Cost effectiveness			X			
Growth in creativity						
Disagreement respected						
Due process procedures in place						
Full access to files						
Having and raising a child						
Heterogenous groupings						
Information sharing						
Personal memories nurtured						
Reasonable risk encouraged						
Resident prepared for emergencies						
Residents hire staff						
Residents train staff						
Zero rejection due to level of disability					X	

Allen & Gardner (1983)	Knoll & Ford (1987)	Flanagan (1978)	Schalock et al. (1989)	PA Dept of MR (1986)	Callahan (undated)	People 1st of CA (undated)	Bersani & Salon (1988)	Allen (1981)	People 1st of WA (1985)	CT Dept of MR (1986)
										X
										X
					X					X
					X					X
							X		X	
		X				X				
			X							X
						X				X
			X				X			
								X	X	
							X			
				X						
						X				
				X						
										X
			X							
		X								
									X	
										X
										X
		X								
					X					
				X						
									X	
										X
									X	
									X	
									X	

among all the sources, the different focus of each is reflected in what the authors saw as priorities in defining quality.

The second consideration that accounts for the diversity seems to be the authors' varied perspective on whether to provide broad topic areas to be examined or to provide a comprehensive list of specific points to be reviewed. On one extreme, there is O'Brien's effort to provide a broadly stated general framework for planning, which would certainly encompass many of the specific items identified by other sources. On the other extreme, there are the guidelines developed by People First of Washington (49 items) and the Connecticut Department of Mental Retardation (60 items). Both of these attempts to provide a comprehensive guide, one from the consumer perspective and one from the provider perspective, cover all the bases in assessing quality.

One final consideration in reviewing the contents of Table 1 merits a brief discussion. While these authors are all concerned with the issue of quality of life, it is important to note that they almost all give some consideration to the inputs and processes seen in residential services. This highlights the fact, at the heart of the quality assurance process, that there is a hierarchy in evaluating residential services just as there is in all human life. People have to be clean, healthy, and safe from harm before they can learn and grow. Quality of life is only possible when people have a home and the basic services they need to support them. All those in the human services field can now begin to explore the meaning of quality of life because the precautionary measures to assure health, safety, and basic services have been taken.

CONCLUSION

As stated in the beginning of this chapter, the process of quality assurance seemed easy when the major charge facing the evaluator was to ensure that people had at least a minimal level of service and were secure from harm, but the intervening years have raised expectations on the part of service providers, parents, advocates, and people with developmental disabilities. Now the demands of safety and security must be balanced with demands for good programmatic practice and a good quality of life for individuals supported by services.

At the heart of the developmental process reviewed in this chapter lies the tension between the rights of people with developmental disabilities and the need that many of them have for assistance in dealing with the challenges of everyday life. In earlier periods this tension was captured in concepts like "the right to treatment" and "the least restrictive environment." Now this challenge is reflected in terms like community integration with the mandate to support individuals as full members of their communities. The service provider, the advocate, the researcher, and the evaluator must all work together to figure out what this means in the lives of real people.

Once the enormity of this challenge dawns on those who wish to elaborate standards of performance for a system of services, they can then begin to appreciate the complexity of this evolutionary process. Furthermore, they can begin to understand that the swirl of competing priorities is not a symptom of a field lapsing into incoherence; at this moment in the history of services for people with developmental disabilities, it is the dress rehearsal for the comprehensive, individualized, community-based support system that has been in the making since the 1960s. Finally, service providers, parents, advocates, and people with disabilities are getting their act together. The real show begins once all the standards for quality of life, so systematically defined, are balanced.

REFERENCES

Aanes, D., & Moen, M. (1976). Adaptive behavior changes of group home residents. *Mental Retardation, 14,* 3–40.

Action not words needed at Willowbrook. (1975, May 5). *Albany Times Union.*

Allen, W.T. (1981). *Housing checklist.* Napa, CA: Area IV Developmental Disabilities Board.

Allen, W.T., & Gardner, N.E.S. (1983). *ANDI for consumers.* Lawrence, KS: Center for Mental Retardation and Human Development.

Baker, F., & Intagliata, J. (1982). Quality of life in the evaluation of community support systems. *Evaluation and Program Planning, 5,* 69–79.

Balla, D.A. (1976). Relationship of institution size to quality of care: A review of the literature. *American Journal of Mental Deficiency, 81,* 117–124.

Baroff, G. (1980). On size and the quality of residential care: A second look. *Mental Retardation, 18,* 113–117.

Bell, N., Schoenrock, C., & Bensberg, G. (1981). Change over time in the community: Findings of a longitudinal study. In R.H. Bruininks, C.E. Meyers, B.B. Sigford, & K.C. Lakin (Eds.), *Deinstitutionalization and community adjustment of mentally retarded people* (pp. 195–206). Washington, DC: American Association on Mental Deficiency.

Bercovici, S.M. (1983). *Barriers to normalization: The restrictive management of retarded people.* Baltimore: University Park Press.

Bersani, H.J., & Salon, R. (1988). *Personal integration inventory.* Syracuse, NY: Syracuse University, Research and Training Center on Community Integration, Center on Human Policy.

Biklen, D.P., & Foster, S.B. (1985). Principles for integrated community programming. In M. Brady & P. Gunter (Eds.), *Integrating moderately and severely handicapped learners: Strategies that work* (pp. 16–46). Springfield, IL: Charles C. Thomas.

Biklen, D., & Knoll, J. (1987a). The community imperative revisited. In J.A. Mulick & R.F. Antonak (Eds.), *Transitions in mental retardation: Vol. III. The community imperative revisited* (pp. 1–27). Norwood, NJ: Ablex.

Biklen, D., & Knoll, J. (1987b). The disabled minority. In S.J. Taylor, D. Biklen, & J. Knoll (Eds.), *Community integration for people with severe disabilities* (pp. 3–24). New York: Teacher's College Press.

Bogdan, R., & Taylor, S. (1982). *Inside/out: The social meaning of mental retardation.* Toronto: University of Toronto Press.

Braddock, D., Hemp, R., & Howes, R. (1986). Direct costs of institutional care in the United States. *Mental Retardation, 24*, 9–17.

Bradley, V.J., Allard, M.A., Mulkern, V., Spence, R.A., & Absalom, D. (1984). *Assessing & enhancing the quality of services: A guide for the human services field.* Boston: Human Services Research Institute.

Bradley, V.J., Conroy, J. W., Covert, S.B., & Feinstein, C.S. (1986). *Community options: The New Hampshire choice.* Cambridge, MA: Human Services Research Institute.

Butterfield, E.C. (1985). The consequences of bias in studies of living arrangements for the mentally retarded adult. In D. Bricker & J. Filler (Eds.), *Severe mental retardation: From theory to practice* (pp. 245–263). Reston, VA: Division on Mental Retardation of the Council for Exceptional Children.

Callahan, M. (undated). *Values which enhance integrated working and living.* Syracuse, NY: Marc Gold & Associates.

Close, D.W. (1977). Community living for severely and profoundly retarded adults: A group home study. *Education and Training of the Mentally Retarded, 12*, 256–261.

Connecticut Department of Mental Retardation. (1986). *A guide to program quality review of day programs.* Hartford, CT: Author.

Conroy, J.W., & Bradley, V.J. (1985). *The Pennhurst longitudinal study: A report of five years of research and analysis.* Philadelphia: Temple University Developmental Disabilities Center. Boston: Human Services Research Institute.

Conroy, J., Efthimiou, J., & Lemanowicz, J. (1982). A matched comparison of the developmental growth of institutionalized and deinstitutionalized mentally retarded clients. *American Journal of Mental Deficiency, 86*, 581–587.

Donnellan, A. (1987). Criteria for best professional practices. In C. Wieck (Ed.), *Resource materials: A variety of approaches to outcome evaluation.* St. Paul, MN: Governor's Planning Council on Developmental Disabilities.

Eastwood, E.A., & Fisher, G.A. (1988). Skill acquisition among matched samples of institutionalized and community-based persons with mental retardation. *American Journal of Mental Deficiency, 93*, 75–83.

Edgerton, R.B. (1967). *The cloak of competence.* Berkeley: University of California Press.

Edgerton, R.B., & Bercovici, S.M. (1976). The cloak of competence: Years later. *American Journal of Mental Deficiency, 80*, 485–497.

Edgerton, R.B., Bollinger, M., & Herr, B. (1984). The cloak of competence: After two decades. *American Journal of Mental Deficiency, 88*, 345–351.

Ferguson, P.M., & Olson, D. (Eds.). (1989). *Supported community life: Connecting policy to practice in disability research.* Eugene, OR: University of Oregon, Specialized Training Program, Center on Human Development.

Fernald, W. (1919). After-care study of the patients discharged from Waverly for a period of 25 years. *Ungraded, 5*, 25–31.

Flanagan, J.C. (1978). A research approach to improving our quality of life. *American Psychologist, 33*, 138–147.

Heal, L.W., Sigelman, C.K., & Switzky, H.N. (1980). Research on community residential alternative for the mentally retarded. In R.J. Flynn & K.E. Nitsch (Eds.), *Normalization, social integration, and community services* (pp. 215–258). Baltimore: University Park Press.

Health Care Financing Administration (HCFA). (1988, June 3). Medicaid program: Conditions for intermediate care facilities for the mentally retarded. *Federal Register, 53*(107), 20447–20505.

Hemming, H., Lavender, T., & Pill, R. (1981). Quality of life of mentally retarded adults transferred from large institutions to small units. *American Journal of Mental Deficiency, 86,* 157–169.

Heshusius, L. (1981). *Meaning in life as experienced by persons labeled retarded in a group home.* Springfield, IL: Thomas.

Hull, J.T., & Thompson, J.C. (1980). Predicting adaptive functioning of mentally retarded persons in community settings. *American Journal of Mental Deficiency, 85,* 253–261.

Hull, J.T., & Thompson, J.C. (1981). Factors contributing to normalization in residential facilities for mentally retarded persons. *Mental Retardation, 19,* 69–73.

Keith, K.D., & Ferdinand, L.R. (1984). Changes in levels of mental retardation: A comparison of institutional and community populations. *Journal of The Association for Persons with Severe Handicaps, 9*(1), 26–30.

Kielhofner, G. (1983). "Teaching" retarded adults: Paradoxical effects of the pedagogical enterprise. *Urban Life, 12,* 307–326.

King, R.D., Raynes, N.V., & Tizard, J. (1971). *Patterns of residential care: Sociological studies in institutions for handicapped children.* London: Routledge & Kegan Paul.

Kleinberg, J., & Galligan, B. (1983). Effects of deinstitutionalization on adaptive behavior of mentally retarded adults. *American Journal of Mental Deficiency, 88,* 21–27.

Knoll, J., & Ford, A. (1987). Beyond caregiving: A reconceptualization of the role of the residential service provider. In S.J. Taylor, D. Biklen, & J. Knoll (Eds.), *Community integration for people with severe disabilities* (pp. 129–146). New York: Teacher's College Press.

Landesman, S. (1986). Quality of life and personal life satisfaction: Definition and measurement issues. *Mental Retardation, 24,* 141–143.

Landesman, S., & Butterfield, E.C. (1987). Normalization and deinstitutionalization of mentally retarded individuals: Controversy and facts. *American Psychologist, 42,* 809–816.

Landesman-Dwyer, S. (1985). Describing and evaluating residential environments. In R.H. Bruininks & K.C. Lakin (Eds.), *Living and learning in the least restrictive environment* (pp. 185–196). Baltimore: Paul H. Brookes Publishing Co.

Landesman-Dwyer, S., Sackett, G.P., & Kleinman, J.S. (1980). Relationship of size to resident and staff behavior in small community residences. *American Journal of Mental Deficiency, 85,* 6–17.

Landesman-Dwyer, S., Stein, J., & Sackett, G.P. (1976). *Group homes for the mentally retarded: An ecological and behavioral study.* Olympia, WA: State of Washington, Department of Social and Health Services.

Larson, S., & Lakin, C. (1989). Deinstitutionalization of persons with mental retardation: The impact on daily living skills. *Policy Research Brief, 1*(1), 1–5.

Lutfiyya, Z.M., Moseley, C., Walker, P., Zollers, N., Lehr, S., Pugliese, J., Callahan, M., & Centra, N. (1987). *A question of community: Quality of life and integration in "small residential units" and other residential settings.* Syracuse, NY: Syracuse University, Center on Human Policy, School of Education.

MacEachron, A.E. (1983). Institutional reform and adaptive functioning of mentally retarded persons: A field experiment. *American Journal of Mental Deficiency, 88,* 2–12.

McCormick, M., Balla, D., & Zigler, E. (1975). Resident-care practices in institutions for retarded persons. *American Journal of Mental Deficiency, 80,* 1–17.

McKnight, J. (1987, Winter). Regenerating community. *Social Policy,* 54–58.

New York State Association for Retarded Children (NYSARC) v. Carey, 393 F. Supp. 715 (E. D. NY 1975); 72–C–356/357 (E. D. NY 1982).

O'Brien, J. (1987). A guide to life-style planning. In G.T. Bellamy & B. Wilcox (Eds.), *A comprehensive guide to the activities catalog: An alternative curriculum for youth and adults with severe disabilities* (pp. 175–189). Baltimore: Paul H. Brookes Publishing Co.

Options in Community Living, Inc. (1987). *Options policy on quality of life.* Madison, WI: Author.

Pennsylvania Department of Mental Retardation. (1986). Quality assurance in community mental retardation programs. *Mental Retardation Bulletin, 99,* 1–9.

People First of California. (undated). *Your rights and responsibilities.* Sacramento, CA: Author.

People First of Washington. (1985). *What we want from residential programs.* Tacoma, WA: Author.

Polivka, C.H., Marvin, W.E.C., Brown, J.L., & Polivka, L.J. (1979). Selected characteristics, services and movement of group home residents. *Mental Retardation, 17,* 227–230.

Pratt, M. W., Luszcz, M.A., & Brown, M.E. (1980). Measuring dimensions of the quality of care in small community residences. *American Journal of Mental Deficiency, 85,* 188–194.

Raynes, N.V. (1980). The less you've got the less you get: Functional grouping, a cause for concern. *Mental Retardation, 18,* 217–220.

Research and Training Center on Community Integration. (1989). *From being in the community to being part of the community.* Syracuse, NY: Syracuse University, Center on Human Policy, School of Education.

Robinson, N. (1987). Direction for person-environment research in mental retardation. In S. Landesman-Dwyer & P. Vietze (Eds.), *Living environments and mental retardation* (pp. 477–486). Washington, DC: American Association on Mental Deficiency.

Rotegard, L.L., Bruininks, R.H., Holman, J.G., & Lakin, K.C. (1985). Environmental aspects of deinstitutionalization. In R.H. Bruininks & K.C. Lakin (Eds.), *Living and learning in the least restrictive environment* (pp. 155–184). Baltimore: Paul H. Brookes Publishing Co.

Rothman, D.J., & Rothman, S.M. (1984). *The Willowbrook wars.* New York: Harper & Row.

Ryan, W. (1972). *Blaming the victim.* New York: Random House.

Schalock, R.L., Harper, R.S., & Genung, T. (1981). Community integration of mentally retarded adults: Community placement and program success. *American Journal of Mental Deficiency, 85,* 478–488.

Schalock, R.L., Keith, K.D., Hoffman, K., & Karan, O.C. (1989). Quality of life: Its measurement and use. *Mental Retardation, 27,* 25–31.

Schroeder, S.R., & Hanes, C. (1978). Assessment of progress of institutionalized and deinstitutionalized retarded adults: A matched-control comparison. *Mental Retardation, 16,* 147–148.

Seltzer, G.B. (1981). Community residential adjustment: The relationship among environment, performance, and satisfaction. *American Journal of Mental Deficiency, 85,* 624–630.

Sutter, P., Mayeda, T., Call, T., Yanagi, G., & Yee, S. (1980). Comparison of successful and unsuccessful community placed mentally retarded persons. *American Journal of Mental Deficiency, 85,* 262–267.

Taylor, J.R. (1976). A comparison of the adaptive behavior of retarded individuals successfully and unsuccessfully placed in a group living home. *Education and Training of the Mentally Retarded, 11,* 56–63.

Taylor, S.J. (1988). Caught in the continuum: A critical analysis of the principle of the least restrictive environment. *Journal of The Association for Persons with Severe Handicaps, 13,* 41–53.

Taylor, S.J., Brown, K., McCord, W., Giambetti, A., Searl, S., Mlinarcik, S., Atkinson, T., & Lichter, S. (1981). *Title XIX and deinstitutionalization: The issue for the 80's.* Syracuse, NY: Syracuse University, Center on Human Policy, School of Education.

Taylor, S.J., Racino, J., Knoll, J., & Lutfiyya, Z. (1987). *The nonrestrictive environment: A resource manual on community integration for people with the most severe disabilities.* Syracuse, NY: Syracuse University, Community Integration Project, Center on Human Policy.

Thompson, T., & Carey, A. (1981). Structured normalization: Intellectual and adaptive behavior changes in a residential setting. *Mental Retardation, 18,* 193–197.

Washington Division of Developmental Disabilities. (1982). *Conceptual basis for community services.* Seattle, WA: Author.

Willer, B., & Intagliata, J. (1981). Social-environmental factors as predictors of adjustment of deinstitutionalized mentally retarded adults. *American Journal of Mental Deficiency, 86,* 252–259.

Willer, B., & Intagliata, J. (1982). Comparison of family-care and group homes as alternatives to institutions. *American Journal of Mental Deficiency, 86,* 588–595.

Willer, B., & Intagliata, J. (1983). *Promises and realities for mentally retarded citizens.* Austin, TX: PRO-ED.

Wolfensberger, W. (1972). *The principle of normalization in human services.* Toronto: National Institute on Mental Retardation.

Wolfensberger, W., & Glenn, L. (1975). *PASS 3: A method for the quantitative evaluation of human services.* Toronto: National Institute on Mental Retardation.

Wyatt v. Stickney, 344 F. Supp. 387 (M. D. Ala. 1972).

chapter 18 ———

A New Way of Thinking About Quality

James W. Conroy
and Celia S. Feinstein

In the field of developmental disabilities, the individuals with disabilities are the consumers of services and the quality of services, therefore, should be judged *primarily* from the viewpoint of the consumer. The best way to do this is to measure the well-being of the consumers who are receiving the services, aggregate the measures of well-being, and compare these measurements to those of prior years and to those of consumers of other services. This orientation for assessment of quality is called the outcome orientation.

The purpose of this chapter is to translate the authors' experiences with outcome orientation into perceptions about quality. Specifically, the authors provide their sense of what aspects of services are associated with positive outcomes. Since 1975, these authors have been designing, conducting, analyzing, and reporting on outcome-oriented studies of quality. These studies have involved many thousands of people with developmental disabilities. The work has included public and private service systems, institutional and community-based models, and has often focused on changes in outcomes when people move from an institution to the community.

INTRODUCTION

In Pennsylvania, beginning in 1979, the quantitative, "Are people better off?" portions of the Pennhurst longitudinal study were conducted. Every one of the more than 1300 Pennhurst class members are still visited every year. A range of quantitative measures are collected about the class members' well-being, comparing their current well-being to that of the year before and a decade before. (There is now no question whatsoever that the Pennhurst class members *are* better off in their new community settings than they were at Pennhurst, and they continue to make progress every year.)

In addition to the massive data base that was created in response to the deinstitutionalization of Pennhurst, an outcome-oriented research and quality assurance mechanism has also been implemented in Connecticut. This system covers more than 1300 Mansfield class members, and data have been collected annually since 1985. In New Hampshire, the phasedown of Laconia State School was monitored by applying the outcome-oriented methodologies to more than 600 people over a 3-year period. In Louisiana, the progress and the outcomes of nearly 400 young people were tracked for a 4-year period. These young men and women had been placed in institutions in other states. Under court order they were brought back to Louisiana and moved into community settings.

Similar but smaller outcome and quality assessment projects have been conducted in California, Colorado, Georgia, Hawaii, Illinois, Minnesota, and Texas. The authors have tried to learn how one can visit a service program and, in a relatively short time, collect scientifically reliable and valid information about individual well-being. It is believed that, to a large extent, these authors have succeeded.

Quality services produce results. It is important to note that the "end" does not justify the "means"; there are inhumane behavioral technologies available that clearly produce results, but those technologies could never be called quality. Results are therefore a necessary, but not sufficient, indicator of quality. The results must be carefully defined with constant input from consumers and with continuing refinement. It seems clear that there is considerable consensus about quite a few results that are important for consumers, families, advocates, and even for service providers and government officials.

A few of these results are: people should grow and learn constantly, unless an overriding health or physical issue takes precedence over developmental progress; people should have things to do during the day that are dignified and useful; people's daily lives should include contact with ordinary citizens; people (and for those people who do not communicate, their loved ones) should be satisfied with the services and supports they receive; and people should have a voice in deciding what they receive and how it is delivered.

These areas of consensus were summarized in national legislation. The Developmental Disabilities Assistance and Bill of Rights Act as amended in 1987 stresses the same "results" as those given above: independence, productivity, integration, satisfaction, and consumer empowerment. These "results" are measurable, and they should be considered as the primary criteria of service quality.

PROCESS-ORIENTED VERSUS OUTCOME-ORIENTED

The conceptual approach of measuring results is different from the generally accepted approach in the human services field. The most widely understood and accepted approaches have always focused on the service delivery *process*. Falling into the process half of quality assessment are local or state licensing, local or state standards, federal certification programs (such as Intermediate Care Facilities for the Mentally Retarded [ICFs/MR]), ideologically grounded assessment systems (such as Social Role Valorization [SRV]), and national accreditation (such as the Accreditation Council on Services for People with Developmental Disabilities [ACDD] and the Commission on Accreditation of Rehabilitation Facilities [CARF]). Given constraints in methodology, all of these approaches are inevitably focused on the service process rather than on the results.

Methodologically, process-oriented quality assessments are all characterized by the slice-of-time approach. Whether the evaluation is conducted by a team or by one person, whether it lasts a day or several weeks, process assessments are directed at what is right now, rather than what has changed since last year or 10 years ago. This makes it difficult to look at improvements over time, either in the program or in the lives of the consumers.

The process-oriented assessments are also constrained by their emphasis on program level concerns rather than individual level concerns. Process evaluations simply cannot include a review of the life situations of a statistically valid sample of the people receiving the service. This means that the process level assessments tend to emphasize management-oriented, rather than individual-oriented, measures.

In an ICF/MR program survey, for example, a small number of individuals are sampled for intensive records review, observation, and/or other analyses (U.S. Department of Health and Human Services [HHS], 1988). Table 1 lists the sample size of individuals seen by a survey team for different sizes of facilities. This strategy does not reflect any kind of scientific sampling theory (Sudman, 1976). The phrase "representative sample" is used in the *HHS State Operations Manual,* but the text of the representative sample section notes that " . . . it is not designed to be a 'statistically valid' sample . . ." If the sample of people seen by an ICF/MR survey team is truly not representative of the life experiences of all people in the facility, then the

Table 1. Number of individuals sampled in an ICF/MR survey

Number of individuals in facility	Number of individuals in sample
Up to 16	4
17–50	8
51–100	10
101–500	10%
Over 500	50

survey is severely flawed. From the sampling theory point of view, the findings generated by the ICF/MR sample have a high probability of being misleading.

It is believed that, in reality, this kind of individual sampling procedure reflects what is feasible given limited survey resources. With hundreds of process-oriented items in the ICF/MR checklist, surveyors simply cannot devote too much time to the situations of individuals. They are there to certify a facility, not to ascertain the well-being of every person receiving services. The outcome-oriented approach is just the opposite. No one "falls through the cracks;" the intention *is* to ascertain the well-being of every person. All resources are devoted to the people rather than the facility.

However, it is suggested that the use of the words "outcome-oriented" are misplaced when applied to the ICF/MR program survey approach. The process-oriented approaches used by organizations such as ICFs/MR, ACDD, and CARF have made considerable progress toward the individual and outcome concepts since the early 1980s. They are using the terminology of outcomes, and have increased their emphasis on direct observation of individual situations. However, there is no substitute for seeing every person (or valid samples of persons). Furthermore, the notion of outcomes must also include tests of whether people are "better off" than they were the year before. None of the standards or accrediting approaches include any requirement for demonstration of that value.

In the outcome-oriented approach the major focus is on individual consumers as well as on changes over time. Every person is included so the validity of the sample is not an issue. (Alternatively, when the resources for 100% coverage are absolutely impossible to find, a valid sample of enough consumers to produce high confidence in the findings must be designed. Usually, this means at least 300 consumers. The validity of any sample is primarily a function of the size of the sample, not on the proportion of the population included in the sample.)

It is believed that scientifically valid sampling is essential when the issues are so important: quality of life, prevalence of abuse or neglect, funding decisions, and service configuration decisions. These issues should never be based even partially upon a very small sample of consumers since small sampling has a high probability of being misleading. In some cases, such as the 1988 Health Care Financing Administration's (HCFA) review of community services funded by the Medicaid waiver in Philadelphia, the process approaches do not choose consumers at random. In the case in Philadelphia, a multimillion dollar service system serving nearly 400 persons in residential settings was evaluated on the basis of scrutiny of 16 individuals, 4 of whom were selected specifically because other parties had identified them as being in distress. This made the sample even less representative.

Outcome assessments are not terribly costly to implement. The highest cost for the most intensive system the authors have assisted in creating is roughly $200 per person per year (Pennsylvania). This system includes a "red flag" (potential crisis situation) procedure, 24-hour notification of emergencies, a series of brief reports on topics of special interest, and comprehensive reports on the progress and well-being of the consumers as compared to the previous year and any year since the system was implemented. Individuals who have regressed behaviorally are pulled out and identified for further case management attention.

Systemic areas in need of attention are easily identified. For instance, service providers with a number of out-of-date individual plans that exceed the norm can be highlighted. Providers who excel, such as those who serve people with severe disabilities and achieve high levels of social integration (as measured on a scale), are also highlighted for special attention and replication.

Dozens of behavioral measures have been reviewed and tested. There are several that are simple, highly reliable, and easy to administer (e.g., short versions of the American Association on Mental Retardation [AAMR] Adaptive Behavior Scale [1975], the Behavior Development Survey [Evaluation and Research Group, 1982], the Client Development Evaluation Report of California's Department of Developmental Services [1979], the Minnesota Developmental Programming System [Bock & Weatherman, 1979], and the Instrument for Client and Agency Planning developed by Bruininks, Hill, Weatherman, & Woodcock at the University of Minnesota [1986]).

Most of what is important for an enhanced quality of life is in principle reliably measurable. Thus, measures have been developed to assess day program/employment, residential social integration, consumer satisfaction, family satisfaction, consumer choice-making, consumer health, service or "programming" intensity, and so on. To be sure that setting-level variables are not ignored, dozens of environmental scales have been tested, and eight have been used extensively. Elementary safety, comfort, individualization, and normalization are the setting-level issues usually selected for community programs. The reliability of these measures have been carefully established and are continually checked.

These outcome-oriented methods have been applied in service systems in many states and have been used in tens of thousands of one-on-one site visits to the homes and day programs of people with developmental disabilities. From this cumulative experience with the outcome perspective, a few conclusions and principles about quality have been made. These remarks are divided into two sections: what is known and what is not known about quality variables. They are offered, not as scientific conclusions, but rather as the impressions of two researchers who have been observing almost solely from the perspective of "what produces results."

WHAT IS KNOWN ABOUT QUALITY VARIABLES

Case Management

Case management is often viewed as the foundation upon which good service delivery rests. Based on the authors' experience, case management can make or break the quality of the services individuals receive. The case manager is the person responsible for coordinating and monitoring services that are delivered to individuals. In the best of situations, case managers can be among the best advocates that individuals have. The major impediments to the success of case management include large caseloads and lack of independence from the service delivery system.

Requirement 1: Reasonable Caseloads In many cities and states the average caseload for a case manager may be in excess of 100 individuals. The expectation is that case managers are responsible for planning, coordinating, monitoring, and advocating for services, but it is impossible to accomplish these tasks for 100 individuals. At any point in time some individuals will be receiving poor case management, some will be receiving excellent case management, and some will be receiving mediocre case management. A caseload of this size often leads to "crisis case management," where only those individuals with the most immediate needs are served. Once their immediate needs are met, they too will sink to the bottom of the pile as the critical needs of another individual are met. Two ways in which this situation can be avoided are to assign manageable caseloads from the beginning, and assign caseloads in a way that individuals are responsible for people with needs that vary in intensity and type.

In terms of caseload size, there is no empirical evidence that supports an optimal caseload size for a case manager. However, the broad parameters have become clear. For instance, managing 10 cases is too small a load because as size becomes too small returns begin to diminish. In other words, the case managers begin case managing one another. Conversely, 100 is definitely too large a caseload. Even when caseloads exceed 50, regular monitoring is constrained.

One of the expectations of case managers is that they visit and become familiar with the individuals they monitor. In some states such as Pennsylvania, where a court order mandates case management visits to each individual's residence on a monthly basis and the day program every 6 weeks, large caseloads would preclude case managers from performing their court ordered functions. Given a caseload of 50, a case manager in Pennsylvania would have to visit at least two individuals each working day to meet the court's requirements. Therefore, caseloads in Pennsylvania for Pennhurst class members cannot exceed 30.

Thus, work done in Pennsylvania and many other states suggests that certain caseload parameters can be set. These parameters establish a reasonable and manageable caseload to include 30–50 individuals.

Requirement 2: Independence from Service Delivery System Case managers, in addition to being service coordinators and monitors, are consumer advocates. It is often the case manager who succeeds in getting someone a job or forcing the local school to allow an individual to attend in spite of the severity of his or her disability. In order for a case manager to perform the role of advocate, it is best that he or she operate in a conflict free environment. In other words, the case managers must not be compromised by their paycheck. One might make the argument that a case manager can never really be conflict free. In a situation where the state contracts with a not-for-profit agency that provides no services other than case management, the agency is not totally independent because the state is funding the program. To what extent state expectations may compromise the case managers depends on the local political context, but even at this level the potential for conflict does exist.

The most conflict laden systems are those in which the case manager works for the same agency that provides residential and/or day services. Clearly the case manager working in that system would have a difficult time "blowing the whistle" on the residential provider if such a situation came up. Many states have begun to look at providing case management in a relatively conflict free environment. In one part of Colorado, for example, the community center board contracts out all of its services with the exception of case management. In Pennsylvania, the state only funds new case management activities that are free of the conflicts noted above.

The issue of independent case management has become a topic for debate throughout the country. One argument is that if case management is totally independent, then there is no accountability. Advocates on the other side argue that case managers can only be effective in representing the interests of the people they serve if they are independent from the system of service delivery.

It is believed, given the aforementioned discussion, that case management can contribute to increased quality for individuals with developmental disabilities if, and only if, caseloads are manageable and independence is maximized. In a study performed by Temple University (Sokol-Kessler, Conroy, Feinstein, Lemanowicz & McGurrin, 1983), it was demonstrated that Pennhurst class members living in Philadelphia experienced better outcomes than individuals living in group homes who were not class members. The major difference between the two groups was in the court protections offered to class members, which included: an individual habilitation planning process, systematic monitoring, and case managers whose caseload did not exceed 30 individuals. Those court protections were demonstrated to have made a difference in the outcomes that are valued for individuals with developmental disabilities, including increased adaptive behavior and a decrease in the expression of challenging behavior.

Individual Written Plans

Another dimension of the service delivery system is the written plan. The individual habilitation plan sets out, in writing, the individual's strengths and needs, as well as the services required to produce positive outcomes. A careful dissection of the words "individual written plan" is revealing. "Individual" dictates that each plan should be written with the individual consumer as the primary focus of the plan. "Written" is an assumption made about how the plan will be documented. By the 1980s, most service systems required written plans.

Writing things down has several virtues. First, it assures that each individual who comes in contact with a consumer is operating from the same knowledge base with regard to what is to be delivered. Second, a written plan is a document that is available to everyone providing service to an individual so that if a new staff person becomes involved with the individual, the plan is there as part of an orientation to the needs of the individuals. Third, the existence of a written plan creates a means for holding people accountable for specific aims. A plan entails making, doing, or arranging something. The team of individuals who sit down to create the individual plan are doing just that—making, doing, and arranging.

The way in which individual plans are developed is variable. The field has changed over the years in terms of how planning is developed for individuals. The first step for planning development is the multidisciplinary team process. In this process, individuals from many disciplines come together and, each from his or her own perspective, describe an individual and write goals that are rigidly defined as "discipline specific." The second step is the interdisciplinary team process. (This was the buzz word of the 1970s and early 1980s.) In the interdisciplinary process, individuals from different disciplines come together with the individual and his or her family to develop a plan with implications for several disciplines. Eating skills training, for example, might involve both an occupational and speech therapist simultaneously. In the 1980s, the transdisciplinary team process came into vogue. In the transdisciplinary process, individuals from the various disciplines teach one another some aspects of how to perform their roles. This should create a more holistic approach to working with an individual in which the psychologist assists in eating techniques, the speech therapist assists in mobility training, and so on.

Whatever process is used, the key element is that there is a process for developing a written plan. In most cases, while one person may be the scribe, all individuals have an equal voice in the development of the plan. With one exception, one individual's voice should not be heard over another's. The consumer, to whom the process is ultimately accountable, should be given the opportunity to participate in the development of a written plan to the greatest extent possible. It is the consumer's voice that should be heard above the others'.

As mentioned before, it has been demonstrated empirically that the existence of a written plan is valuable. With regards to Pennhurst class members, a written plan was part of a constellation of factors that definitely made a difference in terms of positive outcomes to consumers.

Quality Monitoring

The next dimension that has been demonstrated to make a difference in the lives of consumers and the outcomes they experience is monitoring. When the deinstitutionalization movement first began in the early 1970s, one of the strongest arguments against small, community-based programs was that they would be more difficult to monitor than congregate care settings, because they were so spread out. Experience has shown, however, that this is not necessarily the case. Ten years of experience in the Pennhurst situation, along with similar studies in many other states, has shown that monitoring can be done in the community. It can be done effectively, and it can be done with minimal costs. An annual visit to the residential and day program setting of an individual costs no more than $200 per year. The subsequent benefits from such monitoring are major, making such outcome-oriented monitoring a highly cost-effective endeavor.

As noted earlier, there is a distinction to be made between process-oriented monitoring and outcome-oriented monitoring. In the former, efforts are devoted to looking at the "process" by which service is delivered. The process orientation focuses more on documentation, records, and procedures and less on the individuals being served. Types of process monitoring include that which is mandated as part of the ICF/MR regulations. This monitoring is aimed primarily to written documentation that is complete and appropriate.

ICF/MR reviews also look at the extent to which active treatment is provided. The major shortcoming of this approach is that the concept is ill-defined. In one of the training sessions for state surveyors in the new ICF/MR regulations, when asked, "How do we know when there is active treatment going on?" the surveyors were told, "You'll know it when you see it, you'll feel it in your gut" (M. Spaar, personal communication, November, 1988).

There are several other problems with this type of approach. Standards that are ill-defined and subjective may lead to ill-advised certification decisions. ICF/MR certification is an important issue, because a great deal of federal money depends on certification. (The federal share of payment for ICF/MR services is as high as 73%, and across the states the federal government is now spending more than $3 billion per year.) The fact that certification decisions may rest on hazy or ill-defined grounds would seem to be a serious problem from the point of view of the states.

In addition to being subjective, the ICF/MR standards have not been demonstrated to be reliable. In other words, certification judgments may vary between surveyors, and decisions may be dependent on the luck of the draw. When this possibility was raised with HCFA, the response was that the state surveyors were not under the control of the federal government; therefore, the federal government had no power to insist upon reliability testing (Smith, 1988). This does not mean, however, that individual states are precluded from testing the standards for both interrater and test-retest reliability.

There are other standards that suffer from some of the same problems as the ICF/MR regulations. Traditionally, the standards developed by CARF and the ACDD have used documentation as the principal indicator of quality. To the credit of both bodies, however, there has been a shift toward more outcome-oriented assessments. Nevertheless, neither of these sets of standards have been shown to be reliable. No serious attempts have been made to look at the extent to which two surveyors would rate a program similarly, nor has the issue been studied of how a surveyor would score the same program on a visit two weeks after the previous one (interrater and test-retest reliability, respectively).

Most states have process-oriented standard setting practices as well. In many states this takes the form of statewide licensing regulations. While licensing is a legitimate and necessary function performed by states, it should not be done in the absence of other types of monitoring activities, not the least of which is outcome monitoring.

Another area in which process-oriented standards become difficult in the community is in regard to the types of settings to be licensed or certified. Since community settings are by definition smaller than congregate care settings, the licensing or accrediting process may be perceived as unnecessarily intrusive. Examples include semi-independent living, supported employment, and family supports. Should traditional, process-oriented standards to such community integrated settings be applied? The authors think not. Any setting supported by public funds should be held accountable, but there comes a point where accountability contradicts the philosophies of normalization and independence, about which there is general consensus in the field. It is possible to hold service providers accountable without walking through people's homes with a clipboard and a red pen. Perhaps it is time for both state and national licensing and accrediting agencies to look at less intrusive ways of measuring the delivery of services. One way is to look at a more outcome-oriented way of monitoring.

Institution Versus Community

Investigations in many states have consistently revealed that outcomes are better in community settings than in any of the old institutional models, no matter how new or improved the institutions are (Bradley, Conroy, Covert, & Feinstein, 1986; Conroy, 1988; Conroy & Bradley, 1985; Conroy, Feinstein, & Lemanowicz, 1988; Lemanowicz, Conroy, & Feinstein, 1985).

The scientific literature on community placement of people with developmental disabilities has thus far produced no report that the average person is "worse off" after placement out of a "total institution" (Goffman, 1961) into some variety of smaller residential setting located in a regular residential community. In contrast, the number of studies showing positive outcomes has grown rapidly (Aanes & Moen, 1976; Craig & McCarver, 1984; Schroeder & Henes, 1978).

Therefore, the issue is believed to be settled. Other things being equal, community living in all its varieties is associated with better outcomes than institutional living. Although it is theoretically possible to construct a community service system that produces worse results than the institutional model, it must be very hard to do so; otherwise, it would have been done by now, and someone would have documented it. There is no shortage of scientists and others who have been skeptical of the community placement movement.

Daily Activities

There is good reason to believe that, as normalization presumes, the daily routine of life has a strong influence on individual development. In the early 20th century model of the total institution, people rarely traveled far from the place where they slept. Facilities had a dormitory-like sleeping area, closely joined to a "day room." In early studies on the quality of life at the Pennhurst Center in Pennsylvania, evidence indicated that people who were accorded a day program away from their sleeping area showed significantly greater developmental progress over time (Conroy & Lemanowicz, 1981).

The reasons for this finding include such assumptions as: changes may sharpen awareness, a daily routine may clarify social expectations, variation in social milieus may intensify individual needs to achieve approval, or the deadening "sameness" for years on end may hamper any kind of self-improvement. Regardless of these speculations, it seems that people benefit from a daily schedule that mirrors the norm of modern life. People do not generally spend their entire day and night in one place. People usually awaken and prepare themselves for activities "out there," in public and business locations. Whether it is school, a workshop, adult day activities, or a job, putting aside for the moment which of these is highest in "quality," the mere fact of having something to do during most of the days of the week appears to be an important contributor to good outcomes.

Valued Outcomes

In discussing outcomes and quality, it is important to emphasize that professionals, families, and primary consumers may place sharply different values on outcomes. Professionals tend to value the development model, achievement of maximal independence and self-care skills, and reduction of challenging behaviors. Families tend to place a higher value on basic life issues such as permanence, safety, health, and comfort. Primary consumers, although they have only rarely been asked (Conroy, Walsh, & Feinstein, 1987), tend to emphasize even more concrete issues such as choice-making, food, furniture, and recreational events.

These differences in values need not pose a problem for the outcome orientation. The implication is simply that each of the outcomes needs to be measured so that those who interpret the findings can assign their own priorities to each outcome. Beyond this elementary conclusion, it can only be said that it would be valuable to continue investigating these differences in what various stakeholders expect as results from the service delivery process.

Size

The best size of residential settings is a topic of considerable controversy. The issue was debated in federal court as part of the Willowbrook case (*New York State Association for Retarded Citizens and Patricia Parisi et al., v. Carey,* 1982). The plaintiffs in the case wanted to limit the size of community residential facilities to 10 consumers, but the New York state defendants wanted to construct new facilities for 50 residents and wanted to call these new facilities community group homes.

Most of the discussion regarding the size issue is in the section on "What Is Not Known About Quality Variables." However, a few points do seem clear to us. First, *very* big is definitely associated with inferior outcomes. As noted previously, the "total institution" model, whether it is for 100 or 3000 people, is associated with less integration, less productivity, less developmental progress, less consumer satisfaction, and less family satisfaction than the modern community living models. Even in the work of proponents for institutional settings, evidence clearly shows that smaller and more integrated settings are associated with greater individualization as opposed to regimentation (Balla, 1976).

Furthermore, the available evidence indicates that social integration is higher in small community settings than in the large congregate care facilities

(Bradley et al., 1986). This is in accord with common sense. Most of the nation's state institutions are located in relatively isolated rural areas. For residents of such facilities, opportunities to be in the presence of citizens without handicaps, other than staff, are rare as compared to residents living in a regular residential community.

WHAT IS NOT KNOWN ABOUT QUALITY VARIABLES

Discussed in this section are some of the issues about quality that continue to be a puzzle. Although evidence bearing on some of these issues may exist, the authors have not found it to be convincing.

First is the issue of the "right" size of a community residential setting. This issue was touched on in the previous section. Ideological trends point toward family size and style setting as the wave of the future, but economic trends appear to be pointing to the established group home models at sizes of roughly five to eight consumers. Could it be that different size settings are better for different kinds of consumers? Will consumers be able to have a choice in size of setting?

Second, what is the future of the relationship between the labor market and the quality of residential community staff? When food service industry and other minimum wage jobs are plentiful, what happens to the group home industry? Is it possible that, unless salaries in community facilities rise considerably above those offered in fast-food chains, community service systems might eventually deteriorate beyond redemption? Will there be a return to large scale settings in the next century if this happens?

A third issue is the question: What is the best way to move into a neighborhood? Is it with announcements and public education, or simply by doing it without fanfare? There is evidence on both sides of this issue. Pennsylvania has had good results since the 1970s with the covert approach. No zoning hearings were required because state judicial decisions had established that three or fewer unrelated persons could be considered to be equivalent to a family, and no zoning variance for the residential property was needed. Most group home providers, therefore, simply moved in, and anecdotal reports indicate that neighbor acceptance was generally achieved in about 6 months. In other areas, good results have been reported with intensive efforts to educate the community either before or after the fact. However, these good results seem to be the exception rather than the rule (Sigelman, 1976).

It is possible that there is also a relationship between the size of the community facility and the attitudes of the neighbors. In the extreme case, it is believed that neighbors would be far less accepting toward the people in a 20 bed newly constructed facility than toward three people in a regular house down the street. In any case, the ultimate question in this regard is how to teach, assist, and support community staff to be "good neighbors" so that they will be appreciated and welcomed rather than just tolerated and ignored (Bradley, Ellison, Knoll, Freud, & Bedford, 1989).

Another issue is the question of how people in the community can get high quality medical and dental care through a low quality "poverty-oriented" Medicaid system. One of the highest rated concerns of families of people in institutions and in residential community settings is health. As an indicator of quality, access to good medical care would seem to be basic. However, in most states, physicians receive only a token reimbursement for a regular office visit; yet an office visit from a person who cannot communicate certainly takes more time and effort on the part of the physician. For this and other reasons, even Medicaid doctors are often reluctant to take patients with a severe developmental disability. It is not clear how the nation is going to solve this quality related dilemma.

Also an issue is rate-setting for reimbursement to service providers. Many states have some form of rate-setting mechanism for community residential and day programs, but most do not. Even where they do exist, there is lacking a firm foundation of values. Should a group home serving people with profound deficits in adaptive behavior cost more than a home serving highly capable people who exhibit major challenging behaviors? If a set of price rules for community living is formulated, isn't there a danger of duplicating the disastrous misunderstandings and abuses of the "diagnosis-related groupings" concept in the hospital industry? The question of money is inextricably intertwined with issues of quality, so these are indeed important questions. Unfortunately, the nation seems to have no consensus about them.

As previously discussed in this chapter, consumers should be the primary judge of quality in services they receive. The question that now rises is if consumers and their families can be better involved in the quality assurance process. The consumers should be asked to help decide what to assess. This is being done to some extent with a series of focus groups about outcomes in California, but the process-oriented standards and licensing mechanisms should also have significant consumer input. Consumer involvement in long, working meetings with a great deal of jargon to develop standards is difficult to picture as a positive experience. There must be other ways to support the concept of consumer empowerment to define and measure quality.

Finally, is it possible to measure the things that are really difficult to measure? Love is the best example. Having loving relationships in one's life seems to be one of the most important aspects of a quality life. How can one reliably measure the amount of love a person feels, both from others and toward others? Similar measurement problems also exist for other important concepts such as dignity, self-esteem, choice-making, and happiness. These measurement problems are difficult for the general population, but for people who cannot communicate well, the problems may be insurmountable. Certainly the first step toward learning more about these dimensions of life is to ask consumers. As part of every data collection visit, the consumers should be asked about their views of the quality of life. However, in Philadelphia, for example, only 350 of the 900 individuals in residential settings can respond to a verbal or signed interview.

CONCLUSION

This chapter emphasizes the importance of thinking about, measuring, and continually monitoring outcomes. However, it is important to balance the picture presented here. If one is building a service system from scratch, it would be desirable to design a quality assurance system that included both process and outcome components.

In part, the reason that the process orientation is needed is that the ends do not justify the means. Results or positive outcomes are the sought after goal, but not at the cost of individual dignity or freedom. Therefore, attention must be given to both the processes and the outcomes in order to enhance quality.

REFERENCES

Aanes, D., & Moen, M. (1976). Adaptive behavior changes of group home residents. *Mental Retardation, 14,* 36–40.

Balla, D. (1976). Relationship of institution to quality of care: A review of the literature. *American Journal of Mental Deficiency, 81,* 117–124.

Bock, W., & Weatherman, R. (1979). *Minnesota development programming system.* Minneapolis, MN: University of Minnesota, College of Education.

Bradley, V., Conroy, J., Covert, S., & Feinstein, C. (1986). *Community options: The New Hampshire choice.* Concord, NH: New Hampshire Developmental Disabilities Council.

Bradley, V., Ellison, M., Knoll, J., Freud, E., & Bedford, S. (1989). *Becoming a neighbor: An examination of the placement of people with mental retardation in Connecticut communities.* Report prepared for Connecticut Office of Policy and Management. Cambridge, MA: Human Services Research Institute.

Bruininks, R.H., Hill, B.K., Weatherman, R.F., & Woodcock, R.W. (1986). *Instrument for client and agency planning.* Allen, TX: DLM Teaching Resources.

California Department of Developmental Services. (1979). *Client development evaluation report.* Sacramento, CA: Health and Welfare Agency.

Conroy, J. (1988). *Indicators of quality in Philadelphia's community service system* (Tech. Rep. No. 88-7-1). Philadelphia: Temple University, Developmental Disabilities Center/UAP.

Conroy, J.W., & Bradley, V.J. (1985). *The Pennhurst longitudinal study: A report of 5 years of research and analysis* (Pennhurst Study Rep. No. PC-85-1). Philadelphia: Temple University, Developmental Disabilities Center/UAP. Boston: Human Services Research Institute.

Conroy, J., Feinstein, C., & Lemanowicz, J. (1988). *Results of the longitudinal study of CARC v. Thorne class members.* (The Connecticut Applied Research Project Rep. No. 7). Philadelphia: Conroy & Feinstein Associates.

Conroy, J., & Lemanowicz, J. (1981). *Developmental growth among the residents of Pennhurst: What factors are related to growth?* (Brief Rep. No. 8). Philadelphia: Temple University, Developmental Disabilities Center/UAP.

Conroy, J., Walsh, R., & Feinstein, C. (1987). Consumer satisfaction: People with mental retardation moving from institutions to the community. In S. Breuning & R. Gable (Eds.), *Advances in mental retardation and developmental disabilities: Vol. 3* (pp. 135–150). Greenwich, CT: JAI Press.

Craig, E.M., & McCarver, R.B. (1984). Community placement and adjustment of deinstitutionalized clients: Issues and findings. In N. Ellis & N. Bray (Eds.), *International review of research in mental retardation* (Vol. 12, pp. 95–122). Orlando, FL: Academic Press.

Evaluation and Research Group. (1982, December). *Behavior development survey.* Philadelphia: Temple University, Developmental Disabilities Center/UAP.

Goffman, E. (1961). *Asylums.* New York: Doubleday-Anchor.

Lemanowicz, J., Conroy, J., & Feinstein, C. (1985). *Medical needs of clients: Perceptions of relatives and of staff* (Pennhurst Study Brief Rep. No. 6). Philadelphia: Temple University, Developmental Disabilities Center.

New York State Association for Retarded Citizens and Patricia Parisi et al., v. Carey. (1982). 72-Civ.-356, 357, E.D.N.Y.

Nihira, K., Foster, R., Shellhaas, M., & Leland, H. (1975). *Adaptive behavior scale.* Washington, DC: American Association on Mental Retardation.

Schroeder, S.R., & Henes, C. (1978). Assessment of progress of institutionalized and deinstitutionalized retarded adults: A matched-control comparison. *Mental Retardation, 16,* 147–148.

Sigelman, C.K. (1976). A Machiavelli for planners: Community attitudes and selection of a group home site. *Mental Retardation, 14,* 26–29.

Smith, W. (1988). Presentation at United Cerebral Palsy Association Governmental Affairs Seminar, Washington, D.C.

Sokel-Kessler, L., Conroy, J., Feinstein, C., Lemanowicz, J., & McGurrin, M. (1983). Developmental progress in institutional and community settings. *Journal of The Association for Persons with Severe Handicaps, 8,* 43–48.

Sudman, S. (1976). *Applied sampling.* New York: Academic Press.

U.S. Department of Health and Human Services (HHS). (1988). *State Operations Manual, Provider Certification, Advance Copy of Final Issuance* (Transmittal No. 212). Baltimore: U.S. Government.

QUALITY
ASSURANCE SYSTEMS

chapter 19 ⎯⎯⎯⎯

The South Carolina Model

⎯⎯⎯⎯ *Madeleine H. Kimmich* ⎯⎯⎯⎯

South Carolina is one of few states in the nation to undertake a major quality assurance effort in human services programs. In 1985, with the active support of the governor and the Joint Legislative Committee on children, South Carolina began addressing the issue of service quality on a broad scale, looking at all services funded under the federal Social Services Block Grant program. This effort represents the first major test of the new conceptual framework for quality assurance devised by the Human Services Research Institute in 1984. South Carolina is continuing to take significant steps in the direction of a comprehensive quality assurance system covering all seven of the major state human services agencies. It is useful to understand how South Carolina has achieved what it has, and to learn from its experience in developing a broad-based quality assurance system.

BACKGROUND

The South Carolina State Health and Human Services Finance Commission (referred to as the Commission), established by the South Carolina Legislature in 1984, has primary responsibility for administering Medicaid (Title XIX) as well as many of the federal block grants, including the Social Services Block Grant (SSBG, formerly Title XX), the Community Services Block Grant, and the Alcohol and Drug Abuse and Mental Health Block grant. The new agency was given a firm mandate to assure quality of services in contracts and was held accountable for client outcomes.

The Commission is a state-level agency with no direct service responsibility. Indeed, the major state-level service providers are SSBG contractors to the Commission, including the Department of Social Services, the South Carolina Commission on Alcohol and Drug Abuse (SCCADA), the Department of Mental Retardation, and the Department of Youth Services. With its unique position in the delivery system for human services, and its explicit mandate to assure service quality and accountability, the Commission was perfectly situated to embark upon a major enterprise in quality assurance.

Faced with major cutbacks in SSBG funds and a serious lack of information about how program monies were being used to assist consumers, South Carolina became the first state to pursue the development and implementation of a statewide comprehensive human services quality assurance system. The Commission funds 25 different services and 900 different providers with SSBG monies. In federal fiscal year 1985, the state faced a substantial reduction in federal SSBG support. By April 1985, the Commission had solicited bids and had awarded a 3-year contract to the URSA Institute and the Human Services Research Institute (HSRI) to assist in the development of a comprehensive quality assurance system for SSBG services. The request for proposal (RFP) and the winning proposal were based on the conceptualization presented in *Assessing and Enhancing the Quality of Services: A Guide for the Human Services Field* (Bradley, Ashbaugh, & Harder, 1984).

This chapter focuses on the experiences of the Commission, HSRI, and other involved parties in the development and implementation of a quality assurance system in South Carolina (Kimmich, 1986, 1987a, 1987b). By the third year of operation, 20 of the 25 services overseen by the Commission had been implemented. The remaining services were scheduled to be implemented in the fourth year.

THE IMPORTANCE OF A
COMPREHENSIVE QUALITY ASSURANCE SYSTEM

How can quality assurance be useful to a state agency responsible for the provision of human services? Quality assurance is a comprehensive approach for measuring all aspects of service delivery using the information to improve policy-making, service planning, program development, service delivery, and accountability. Quality assurance touches on all aspects of human services management and, indeed, offers an opportunity for coordination among the often numerous agencies sharing responsibility for particular functions related to consumer welfare—information and referral, eligibility determination, service assessment, case management, service delivery, follow-up, and evaluation. Once a comprehensive quality assurance system is in place, one vividly realizes how the operations of all human services organizations—at the state level as well as at the local, direct service level—are intertwined.

Quality assurance enables human services agencies to pursue five fundamental goals:

1. To assure that providers of human services have the capability to provide an acceptable level of service
2. To assure that client services are provided consistent with accepted beliefs about what constitutes good practice
3. To assure that a given commitment of resources produces a reasonable level of service
4. To assure that the services that are provided have the intended effect
5. To assure that the limited supply of services is provided to the clients most in need

As it developed its RFP, the Commission was clearly searching for something broader than program monitoring, deeper than client tracking, and more likely to be used in policy-making than is often the case with evaluation systems. Quality assurance promised a method that would involve all relevant players in the development process, that would produce a system to assess performance against a comprehensive vision of service quality, and that would foster utilization of the information gathered to facilitate improvement of services. By and large, the Commission has achieved its objective. The discussion that follows highlights the successes, and the remaining problems, of the intricate quality assurance system that governs the delivery of social services in South Carolina.

IMPORTANT FEATURES OF THE SOUTH CAROLINA EFFORT

Major Steps in System Implementation

The Commission followed five essential steps in establishing its quality assurance system, three of which correspond closely to the three principal components of a quality assurance system—standard setting, measurement, and control and enhancement mechanisms. The steps include: 1) understanding the current system, 2) developing service standards that enhance performance, 3) developing collaborative measurement approaches, 4) developing control and enhancement mechanisms, and 5) establishing a communication structure to facilitate development and implementation of the system.

Step 1: Understanding the System The first step was understanding the system of quality assurance as it existed in South Carolina (Kimmich, 1985). This involved systematic interviews with service providers, program administrators and managers, advocates, legislators, and others concerned in some way about the provision of human services. The investigation focused on identifying existing quality assurance elements and their usefulness; determining the aspects of service quality that were being adequately dealt with and those that were not; and determining how the service process actually occurred, from identification of a client to service authorization, service provision, and assessment of how the client fared after services were completed. The end product of this first step was a thorough analysis of the strengths and weaknesses of existing quality assurance components and recommendations for dealing with high priority problems. Among the major issues that came to light were:

1. The importance of having solid working relationships among the various agencies involved with the provision of human services
2. The critical role of training and technical assistance, especially at an early stage, to demonstrate the proactive nature of the system
3. The need to link monitoring to the provision of technical assistance, demonstrating how measurement results are fed into the system to improve service quality
4. The urgency of addressing the problem of routine reporting, a labor intensive activity that can be particularly burdensome to small agencies that tend to lack staff and automated information capabilities
5. The importance of having a clear connection between human needs, service priorities, and funding allocations that can be achieved through coordination among the various parts of the Commission responsible for needs assessment, quality assurance, and budget

Step 2: Developing Standards   Working within the context of the current system of quality assurance, the second step taken by the Commission was development of service standards. The standards form the basis for the rest of the system. Standards development must be a collaborative activity, involving representatives of all parties concerned about service quality, from client to provider, administrator, planner, and legislator. In South Carolina, the standards development process began with defining the service and developing a philosophy of service, including the who, what, where, when, why, and how of service provision. This task was performed by service subcommittees composed of representatives of agencies that provided the particular service, state agencies with oversight and/or policy responsibility, and others with particular interest in the service area.

Next came writing the standards, utilizing a matrix to ensure that all elements of the service enterprise were covered. Standards were based on the philosophies developed by the service subcommittees, and the state-of-the-art service standards in the particular areas of concern. HSRI examined standards developed by numerous national groups in order to design a conceptual framework for standards development. There are two dimensions to the framework: first, the types of standards needed that correlate directly with the five fundamental goals of quality assurance (see Table 1); second, the six aspects of

Table 1. Types of standards correlated to the goals of quality assurance

Goals of quality assurance	Types of standards
1. To assure *capability*	INPUT
2. To assure *good practice*	PROCESS
3. To assure *productivity*	OUTPUT
4. To assure *effectiveness*	OUTCOME
5. To assure serving those *most in need*	NEED

service provision and good program management. Putting these together, a formal matrix for standards development was created (see Figure 1).

Using the matrix in Figure 1, standards were created for each type of service funded through SSBG. However, it soon became clear that standards were not and could not be written specifically enough to be directly measurable, so a second order standard, called an indicator, was developed. The standard became the statement of policy while the indicator was a measurable definition of that policy. Table 2 includes several standards and indicators from the Commission's Standards for Developmental Services for Persons with Handicaps and Disabilities with notation of where they fit into the standards development matrix (Kimmich, 1987b).

The standards and their accompanying indicators were carefully reviewed and discussed by the relevant service subcommittees, and revisions were made accordingly. These revisions were suggested for numerous reasons: standards not relevant to South Carolina practice, standards too difficult to achieve at this stage, or standards already part of normal practice. The final standards were thus a necessary mix of state of the art and local wisdom. Since such a negotiation process is the key to local "ownership" of the

STANDARDS DEVELOPMENT MATRIX					
	Input	Process	Output	Outcome	Need
Human resources					
Facility					
Client					
Services					
Administrative and fiscal concerns					
Community relations					

Figure 1. Standards development matrix.

Table 2. Standards and indicators applied to the standards development matrix

Standards	Indicators
Standard 1.1: The personnel of the agency shall be appropriately qualified to carry out the agency's program of services.	1.1.3: 100% of persons providing professional or supervisory services have a bachelor's degree and 1 year of experience working with handicapped and developmentally disabled persons, or a master's degree in either child development, developmental disabilities, vocational rehabilitation, social work, or other area relevant to their job responsibilities. (Human Resources/Input)
Standard 3.6: Adults shall form friendships and engage in social relationships.	3.6.1: Opportunities are provided for clients to form and carry on friendships. (Client/Output) 3.6.2: At least 70% of clients and/or their families express satisfaction with the quality of their social contacts when responding to agency queries. (Client/Outcome)
Standard 3.7: The agency shall maximize opportunities for adult clients to achieve independence.	3.7.1: Adult clients are taught skills to lessen dependence, among which may be: community living skills, self-care skills, socialization skills, communication skills, vocational skills, educational skills, behavioral needs, and motor development. (Client/Output) 3.7.3: Within the past year, 80% of clients have achieved the objectives targeted in the areas identified in 3.7.1. (Client/Outcome)
Standard 4.5: Service coordination shall be maintained to ensure continuity and comprehensiveness of service to all clients.	4.5.5: The assigned service manager maintains regular contact with all service providers active with the client, including participating in case planning meetings at least annually and other meetings as needed to facilitate coordination of services to carry out the plan. (Services/Process)
Standard 4.8: The agency shall provide the full range of services and service activities in its service contract in response to the needs of its target population.	4.8.2: Those clients most difficult to serve are not systematically excluded from services. (Services/Need)

(continued)

Table 2. (continued)

Standards	Indicators
Standard 5.1: The agency shall formulate and maintain appropriate policies and procedures to govern agency activities.	5.1.3: The agency has policy and procedure manuals for case recording, case management, personnel, and for each of the basic services that it provides to adults and children with handicapping and disabling conditions. (Administrative/Input)
Standard 6.1: The agency shall develop community awareness of the needs of persons with handicapping and other disabling conditions.	6.1.1: The agency plans and conducts an ongoing program of community education, using a variety of techniques, to provide the general public with an understanding of its purposes, service offerings, and ways to access the service. (Community Relations/Process)

Adapted from Kimmich, M. H. (1987b). *Final report of phase II of the South Carolina human services quality assurance project.* Washington, DC: URSA Institute; reprinted by permission.

standards, any state developing its own standards for developmental services should use the South Carolina standards as a starting point, rather than adopting them wholesale.

Part of the standards review process included discussion of the way standards should be used; that is, should they be required in order for an agency to obtain a contract in the first place (a control function), or should assistance be offered to funded agencies to help them meet the standards over time (an enhancement function). It quickly became clear that a balance was needed between the minimal and the model standards. The service subcommittees had the authority to make the judgment of whether or not a particular standard would be required for initial funding. They made these decisions based on their sense of what was reasonable to expect from providers in the short term (a sense of the current state of the art in South Carolina), and on what was indeed necessary to protect the client's health and safety.

Step 3: Developing Measurement Approaches The third step in establishing the quality assurance system in South Carolina was developing measurement approaches. Measurement is the necessary link between standards and performance; it is the way to assess whether services meet the standards of quality. Measurement instruments must be designed to avoid duplication with existing reporting efforts to minimize any additional reporting burden on providers. In South Carolina, numerous measurement approaches were utilized, including what is called self-assessment, or the collection of data about the provider by the provider. Data are also collected from other state-level sources, and through on-site monitoring. The measurement instruments were questions directly reflecting the wording in the indicators.

Several important issues surfaced during instrument development, including the importance of having automated information systems to access needed data, the frequency with which information needed to be collected, and the changing role of monitors. Measurement methodology is important in that not all information has to be gathered frequently and by the same method (e.g., monitoring). Two significant discoveries were made. First, much of the information desired was already being collected by another agency. In these instances, direct access to the data was provided through automated systems; where adequate automated systems were lacking, other means were devised in order to obtain the information. Second, much of the information was more appropriately generated by provider staff themselves through what is called self-assessment. Self-assessment is an important technique because it reinforces the idea that quality assurance is a shared responsibility, built on mutual trust, and it also gives providers an active role in the measurement function.

Perhaps the biggest challenge occurred in the monitoring area. Monitoring became just one of several measurement activities, rather than being the only one, to find out how providers were performing. This meant that the monitors themselves suddenly had much less control over the process, a potentially threatening change. In addition, the monitors had a new role to perform—in the interest of providing quick turnaround to providers in a positive, enhancing way, monitors were expected to play a dual role of monitor and liaison to technical assistance sources. The attitude of monitors had to change dramatically; indeed, this has caused and continues to cause difficulties in some areas of implementation.

Step 4: Developing Controls and Enhancements The fourth step, developing control and enhancement mechanisms, was the link that guaranteed quick feedback to providers, assuring that the information gleaned in the measurement process was used to improve service delivery. Here lies a critical difference between quality assurance as conceived in South Carolina and how it is more typically regarded elsewhere: the system should be enhancement oriented, rather than sanction oriented; it should be assistive rather than punitive, to enhance the performance of low-level as well as high-level providers.

Development of the control and enhancement mechanisms proceeded with similar timing and in a similar manner to the development of standards. The Commission created a network of subsystem committees, each corresponding to a particular aspect of the emerging quality assurance system. There were subsystem committees for training and technical assistance, for licensing, for information management, and for contracting. These committees analyzed existing mechanisms for control and enhancement and designed a way to coordinate them to ensure best use of the resources. Committee members learned that many more resources were in place than they expected.

Two examples underscore the significance of this discovery. A primary enhancement mechanism is training and technical assistance to be provided either to remedy a problem faced by a provider (as reflected in the failure to meet certain standards and indicators) or to reward a provider for superior performance, such as special creative training for staff who have mastered all the routine case management tasks. The Commission discovered numerous training and technical assistance resources, relatively untapped by social services providers. They created an automated bulletin board as a central repository of information about training and technical assistance opportunities and as a way for agencies to announce that they needed help of a particular sort. Another example is performance contracting, used now in a limited fashion by the Commission. Contracts can be enhancement tools if the award level is based on the provider's level of performance (a sharp contrast to contracting based solely on whether the basic health and safety of clients is assured) and on lowest unit cost. Thus, one is rewarding higher performance as a positive incentive, rather than only punishing poor performance and virtually ignoring performance above the minimum.

One critical control and enhancement mechanism, which may go largely unnoticed when it operates well, is the analysis and reporting function (i.e., what to do with the masses of data generated by the quality assurance system). The effective and timely use of the information gathered is the key to the success of the entire system. The difficulties are numerous: how to physically handle the data, how to analyze it, how to use it to provide direct feedback to providers, how to use it to develop recommendations for policy change and for changes in the quality assurance system itself. The Commission established a subsystem committee specifically to look at these issues and developed some innovative ways to keep the volume of data from inundating the quality assurance division. The problems are by no means completely resolved, especially as the Commission proceeds to implement the third phase of the quality assurance system, but they are addressing the issues.

Step 5: Establishing a Communication Structure Interwoven throughout the steps described is the glue that holds all the pieces together—an extensive structure for communication. Communication involves both horizontal relationships (among agencies) and vertical relationships (within agencies). It may require an extensive committee structure to ensure full participation of needed parties. In South Carolina, the Commission established an advisory committee for the entire development effort, subcommittees to review the standards and measurement instruments for groups of services, plus subsystem committees to primarily address the issues of collaboration and building on what exists. These committees functioned throughout the development phases. An oversight committee, composed of selected members from all the development committees, continues to function during implementation and ongoing operation of the system, in an advisory capacity to the Commission.

Critical Characteristics of the Development and Implementation Process

There are several characteristics of a successful quality assurance development process that are worthy of mention, even as reminders to those experienced in designing and implementing systems such as the one in South Carolina. First and foremost is a shared vision of quality at the heart of the entire effort. The central tenet of quality assurance as conceived in South Carolina is the necessity to build the system on trust among the parties and on the commitment of all parties to the jointly created vision of service quality. This speaks to the vital importance of active involvement of many people at all levels of the service delivery system, including providers and consumers. This broad participation was achieved in the Commission's effort through the extensive network of committees, each with a unique role to play in the development process. In particular, the service subcommittees worked hard to define the services and to write appropriate philosophies, which in effect were the shared vision of good service, the ideal which was being defined through the standards.

The second critical element in successful quality assurance development is ownership. The system must be owned by all the participants in the system at all levels and across all agencies. Ownership stems from active participation in the early system decisions; more than that, it results from careful building of political support, obtaining high-level endorsements, and continually educating people. In South Carolina, this was a primary concern of the system planners. The intricate system of committees created by the Commission served to provide both needed manpower for development and the opportunity for a range of people to be actively engaged in the creation of the quality assurance system.

A third element in the creation of a successful quality assurance system is the essential modus operandi: being proactive rather than reactive, rewarding and assisting performance rather than policing and sanctioning. The task here is to convey this critical philosophy, different from traditional evaluation approaches, to all parties and to act on it consistently and promptly so that participants continue to believe what they have been told. In South Carolina, there was considerable resistance to this approach because of the dominant belief that fear of punishment is a stronger motivator than promise of reward. No matter how much training is done beforehand, this basic philosophical approach must be reinforced *repeatedly* during system implementation if the system is to have a real chance of working. This was successful in part, thoroughly changing the view of some small agencies, but not reaching deeply into other, larger agencies.

A fourth element in developing a system is taking advantage of what already exists, building on the strengths of current quality assurance mechanisms. In South Carolina, the entire project was geared to this approach. Work began with a detailed assessment of the strengths and weaknesses of the existing quality assurance activities. In addition, much of the work of the sub-system committees focused on just this issue, identifying in detail ways that the existing components could be used and modified. For example, the SCCADA used a model of monitoring and technical assistance that is compatible with what the Commission was developing. The Commission borrowed many elements from the SCCADA system, and even hired the SCCADA coordinator to manage the Commission quality assurance effort.

A final critical characteristic of the South Carolina system was attention to minimizing overlap and duplication, especially in the measurement arena. Direct service workers often bear the brunt of the reporting burden, so any effort to reduce repetition of data gathering is immediately beneficial to them. Monitoring is another labor-intensive area where duplication is frequently a problem. In South Carolina, the possibility of combining monitoring visits with other agencies, and even combining data collection forms for the monitoring visits, was explored. Many kinks have not worked themselves out, but monitoring has already become less burdensome for providers than it was previously.

REALITIES AND CONSIDERATIONS FOR INSTALLING A QUALITY ASSURANCE SYSTEM

The South Carolina project to establish a quality assurance system for all services funded through the Social Services Block Grant was the *first* statewide attempt to create a comprehensive system following the principles laid out by Bradley et al. (1984), in *Assessing and Enhancing the Quality of Services*. As such, it provided the opportunity for testing many of the theoretical precepts. The remainder of this chapter discusses what has been learned in the South Carolina experience. The discussion that immediately follows identifies some practical considerations for a state to address when it first begins to look at quality assurance. These concerns can and should be attended to before the design process gets too far along. They include both technical and organizational issues—the importance of building a solid philosophical base for system development, organizational structures to assist development, the critical distinction between minimum and model standards, the necessity for resource sharing, and the role of temporary solutions to long-term problems.

Building a Solid Philosophical Base

An important step in developing an environment conducive to quality assurance is comprehensive and repeated attention to the dramatic change in orientation that is required. Teaching participants about the philosophy of quality assurance, which is the conceptual framework, is essential groundwork. Since all change comes about slowly, such philosophical realignment needs regular, periodic assessment and renewal as part of training and technical assistance sessions, workshops, and any other routine meetings of people involved in the quality assurance effort. In South Carolina, a core group of people were successfully trained, and they, in turn, passed their new understanding to others in their organizations. However, the translation was not always consistent or thorough, and many direct service workers were left adrift, faced with major changes in their roles and responsibilities but with little understanding to help them change their attitude about the importance of evaluation and monitoring activities. As roles were redefined and job descriptions rewritten, many people were denied the opportunity to feel part of the decisions, and consequently, they developed an understandable resentment toward those who imposed the changes upon them. Particular efforts need to be made to reach people at all levels of the service delivery enterprise from the very beginning of the process, in order to spread the philosophy of quality assurance more widely at an earlier stage.

Organizing for Development

A second critical issue in development of a quality assurance system is designing a formal structure for developing the quality assurance components. Quality assurance quickly becomes large and all-encompassing, and there is an immediate need for an organizational structure to be imposed on the process. HSRI and the Commission worked collaboratively on this effort, with HSRI focusing on how to best formulate comprehensive standards and indicators and the Commission focusing on how to best integrate the new quality assurance elements within the existing system components. HSRI formulated standards using the standards development matrix described in Table 2. In theory, when each cell of the matrix is filled, one has covered all the necessary elements of the service activity and is assured a comprehensive and complete view of service quality. It should be noted that each cell need not be filled with a unique standard and indicator. Many indicators serve several purposes simultaneously, so one does not necessarily end up with hundreds of different indicators of quality.

This discussion points out one of the major implementation difficulties encountered in the South Carolina system—the sheer volume of information gathered in response to the number of standards and indicators. Initially at least, this was perhaps inevitable because of the primitive state of data collection and management when the quality assurance project began. Only by examining the data from the first round of implementation could the Commission begin to evaluate those pieces of information that would be needed repeatedly and those (the bulk of it, in all probability) that did not need to be gathered for many years. The burden of data collection, therefore, results in large part from the lack of baseline and background information on which to erect a comprehensive quality assurance system.

The Commission's organizational effort was implementing a multi-faceted subsystem network. The subsystems represent integral parts of the quality assurance system and are points of substantial interaction among different agencies and/or parties involved in the quality assurance effort. For example, training and technical assistance is a central enhancement mechanism. Training and technical assistance resources exist in many different places in the state. Many different service agencies have staff dedicated to such work, and it would be beneficial to coordinate such disparate resources for use by providers needing particular kinds of assistance. By the same token, there exist numerous ways to access these training and technical assistance resources, and it would be helpful if there was a central point of contact for these many activities. Therefore, the Commission created a training and technical assistance subsystem committee charged to identify training and technical assistance needs, identify training and technical assistance resources, design a method to best utilize what already exists to meet existing needs, design ways to meet remaining needs, and enumerate steps to reach the goal of a coordinated and responsive training and technical assistance subsystem (i.e., prepare an implementation plan).

Each of the subsystem committees follow comparable steps. Some of the implementation plans were fully in place less than two years after implementation of the quality assurance system began; others await development of major missing components such as a human services management information system.

Distinguishing Between Minimal and Model Standards

Once standards have been written, it is problematic how best to use them. Traditionally, in a quality controlled environment, standards represent the minimum acceptable level of performance. In an enhancement-oriented environment, standards describe the ideal or the model of good performance. Some compromise between these two extremes is necessary. In South Carolina, the standards review committees came up with a two-tier approach:

1) base requirements relating to health and safety considerations and other "musts" with sanctions applied for falling below the specified levels, and 2) standards describing the ideal vision of service performance with rewards for meeting or exceeding such levels. An interesting dynamic emerged during the process of deciding in which group a particular standard and indicator belonged. The committees discussed each item and, as part of the base requirements, included activities that went beyond minimal health and safety considerations but that represented average or somewhat above-average performance. The result has been that many providers (especially smaller, more rural ones) fall below the required base of performance. This is clearly a pitfall to the process since being labeled as "below minimum acceptable performance" is a negative, especially if it is not immediately followed by assistance to improve performance.

There are two possible explanations for this tendency to require standards beyond minimal health and safety considerations, both of which speak to a basic mistrust of the new quality assurance philosophy. In some of the larger statewide agencies, representatives wanted to set minimal standards at the level where they were already operating; no lower because they wanted practice to at least remain where it was, but also no higher because they did not want to be forced to suddenly improve practice. Such improvement would have both staff and funding implications. Difficulty arose in those instances where the representatives thought that current practice was at a higher qualitative level than in fact was the case, leading them to urge mandating standards that actually went beyond the current capabilities of their local service offices.

The second explanation for the relatively high minimal standards is that the high-performing providers pushed for a higher minimum for service quality to ensure that some other providers did not just quit trying when they reached the bare minimum level of performance. In both of these cases, the problem stems from a lack of faith in quality assurance philosophy, which says that there *will* be incentives to better performance so providers will not simply comply with the minimum and do nothing more. The whole episode seems to signal a reluctance on the part of providers to fully embrace a shared vision of quality and to trust that each and every provider is working (and will work) to improve performance.

Resource Sharing

Related to the issue of building on existing components is the issue of resource sharing. The extent of resource needs for development (and more so for implementation) means it is essential to tap resources of other agencies. If other agencies are to willingly share their own limited resources (i.e., their information gathering capacity and monitoring staff), there must be direct ways that the emerging quality assurance system will benefit them; for example, incorporating some of their data needs into the new measurement process.

The Commission approached this challenge in several ways. It constructed a formal administrative structure of committees, including quality assurance staff from many agencies, to support the system. It developed cooperative arrangements with other agencies to use monitors, data collection sources, technical assistance, and other efforts to sustain development and implementation. It also made important inroads to high-level human services coordinating bodies in the state to cement the commitment to collaborative quality assurance. The arrangements must go beyond the developmental needs of the system since quality assurance in the long term requires a permanent collaborative effort.

Need for Temporary Solutions

System designers and developers often are overly ambitious and stubborn about having everything done right the first time. It is important to recognize that all elements of the quality assurance system are not going to be implemented in the short term; indeed, there may be some major pieces missing. A management information system is an obvious example. The central importance of computer hardware and software to lessen the data collection (and analysis) burden cannot be overstated. There may be a need for temporary solutions while permanent ones are being developed. In South Carolina, the Commission developed a Personal Computer Information System (PCIS), a piece of software designed to gather some essential pieces of information on individual service cases until such time as a comprehensive computerized Human Services Information System is in place. It is designed to be user-friendly for those agencies with personal computers. It also may be completed manually with data entered into the computer system by the monitoring agency. It does represent an extra burden on direct service workers because the PCIS serves only one purpose, that of the quality assurance system, while not simultaneously meeting other data requirements. However, its value is two-fold—setting an example of how to simplify data collection efforts for workers by entering directly to a PC and highlighting the pressing need for an integrated computerized services information system.

LESSONS FROM SOUTH CAROLINA

This final section presents some lessons from the South Carolina experience, highlighting problems that are perhaps inevitable but that are helpful to anticipate and prepare for to ease the way for establishing a quality assurance system. Included are reminders to be attentive to the involvement of direct service workers, to the difficulty of reducing duplication, to the appeal of sanctions rather than rewards, to the importance of following through on enhancements, not just controls, to the potential threat in all that happens under the guise of quality assurance, and, especially, to the pitfall of promising too much too fast.

Lesson 1: Importance of Front Line Involvement

In the development phase in South Carolina, people were involved from all levels of the service delivery process, from direct service workers to managers to administrators. As committee members became more and more engaged in the process, and the demands on their time increased, there was a decrease in the participation of front line workers for both political and practical reasons. Agency administrators wanted to be sure that their views were fully represented, sometimes at the expense of the direct service perspective. From a practical standpoint, workers also withdrew from the process because of their client responsibilities and because many of them lacked the breadth of knowledge about the service area, such as knowing the administrative concerns. The result was that, by and large, the standards and indicators and the suggestions for control and enhancement mechanisms came largely from managerial staff. This presents several problems. First, involvement in the committees meant repeated doses of the philosophy and the conceptual framework underlying quality assurance. For various reasons such information was not always adequately passed down to lower levels by the managers. Second, those bearing most of the burden of data collection were *not* the ones involved in development, so they were being asked to do extra work without a strong sense of the shared vision of quality and without having some ownership in the system. Thus, they had little reason for expecting a different, better system or for changing their own attitudes about the worth of the activity. Perhaps a partial solution would be to involve direct service workers in reviewing just those sections of the standards that relate to their activities (i.e., facility, client, and service standards, perhaps not administrative, community relations, and personnel). Perhaps the process would take longer, but it would be time well spent.

Lesson 2: Difficulty of Reducing Duplication

One central rule in developing a quality assurance system is to reduce duplication, to build on what already exists, and to minimize the reporting efforts of the provider agencies and their staff. This is particularly true for front line, direct service workers, where just seeing the positive effects of reducing some duplication could make believers out of even the most resistant worker. However, duplication problems are not as easy to resolve as may first appear, because what is required is intensive negotiations over how to collaborate and share information, in what form to originally collect information, who gets the information and passes it on to others, and how to simultaneously meet varying, sometimes conflicting, goals. One example is accreditation. The Commission on Accreditation of Rehabilitation Facilities (CARF) has extensive standards that facilities must meet in order to receive the "good service" label from CARF. Many of these standards (but not all) are essential parts of the Commission's Standards for Services to Persons with Disabilities. How should the Commission deal with agencies accredited by CARF? If the agency is currently accredited, then it seems reasonable that the Commission could automatically waive certain standards, knowing that accreditation means those standards have been met. However, it is not that simple. CARF, like all accreditation bodies, has a complicated way of evaluating agency performance and may grant accreditation for some but not all services provided by the agency, or may allow the agency to fail to meet a certain number of standards and still be accredited. Those missed standards might include ones considered crucial by the Commission. It requires considerable effort to define precisely what the Commission cares about in the full collection of CARF standards and requirements, to understand how CARF evaluates and what "satisfactory" means, and to work out an efficient way to obtain from CARF what the Commission needs. Similar situations arise with multiple monitoring visits to a service provider agency. To truly reduce and eventually eliminate duplication may mean commitment of substantial resources early in the quality assurance development process.

Lesson 3: Appeal of Sanctions

Control and enhancement mechanisms are somewhat contrary elements to put together in one phrase. Control suggests punishment, restraints, lack of trust; enhancement suggests helping, improving, encouraging, rewarding. To embrace the concept of enhancement as having an equal if not greater role than control in a quality assurance system means a real change in viewpoint. There will often be pressure for sanctions rather than assistance and enhancements out of concern that not all providers share a common view of quality and, therefore, are not truly capable of improving themselves. Why waste enhancement resources trying to help someone who has little hope of doing better? The result of this is pressure for tougher minimums and more limited assistance until the agency proves "worthy." This is understandable in view of limited resources and clients' need for prompt, high quality service. But, it nonetheless points to a more fundamental problem in which the faith in the efficacy of enhancements and in the shared commitment to service improvements has not yet been established. In an ideal quality assurance system, agencies that do not meet minimum standards will get weeded out, enhancement support will be given promptly, and provider responses will be quickly judged. However, the ideal takes time to evolve; it must be given a fair chance to work, and should not be diverted to a more traditional "prove it and then

I'll help you" mentality. It is essential to break out of this punitive pattern that does not help clients, but only assures they are not too badly hurt.

Lesson 4: Importance of Following Through on Enhancements

Designers of human services policies can get so enthusiastic about what they are trying to create that it becomes more real for them than for the front line workers. Beware of trying to implement a partial system, especially of putting in place standards and measurement instrumentation without having the enhancement mechanisms ready to respond to the performance assessments. Such a step may undermine the carefully constructed system by going back on promises made that *this* system would be different and helpful. For direct line workers, and for administrators too, it may be hard to distinguish the new system with standards and measurement tools from the ordinary, punitive and burdensome system. This is especially true when not all providers received the philosophy training and participated in early development phases whereby their faith in the new approach to quality assurance might have been solidified. In short, the philosophy statement faces its first real test in early implementation.

If supportive, enhancement-oriented action follows closely on the results of measurement, the system is given a direct boost; if not, lack of supportive action may cause havoc, distrust, anger, and loss of much valuable ground so carefully gained in the development phase. The promise of better feedback and of a collegial relationship is only good for so long. Those responsible for system operation need to ensure rapid payback to the direct workers since they bear much of the initial burden of data collection. This is potentially a problem in South Carolina because the initial implementation involved so many providers and such extensive system design and redesign that it was virtually impossible to have everything ready at once. A possible solution might be to begin in only one service area initially, making sure that all the enhancement and control elements are in place. This approach, however, is politically less viable given the pressures to produce comprehensive results fast.

Lesson 5: Potential Threat of Efforts

Since quality assurance concerns reach into almost every department in an agency, any quality assurance development effort may be seen as threatening, internally in the agency initiating the effort and within other agencies affected by the system design. Quality assurance is not respectful of the established boundaries between evaluation, program development, contracting, and support services. The agency executive may be fully supportive of the quality assurance effort, but individual units in the agency and, indeed, individual staff persons may not share that view. Part of the problem is turf, concern that one branch may lose power as the branch responsible for quality assurance extends its reach. Also, part of the problem is individual fear of change; new roles can be challenging and unsettling. A prime example is the changing role of monitors since the monitor loses control over the process when other measurement approaches are used in addition to monitoring. The monitor is also asked to be ready to help in the field, where before he or she could simply make notes and go away, promising a full report soon. In ways such as this, quality assurance may lead to many internal organizational changes accompanied by turmoil, lost productivity, and lowered morale. Each agency will decide how best to address these problems within its own political and social environment. Designers should be aware of the potential and should take a proactive stance, acting before serious problems arise.

Lesson 6: Pitfall of Promising Too Much Too Fast

Quality assurance is not suited to development in a state of crisis, although it is frequently a crisis that provokes an agency to take a closer look at quality assurance concerns. As has been repeatedly noted, it takes time to get all the pieces in place, and all the pieces need to be there if the system is to get a fair test. If answers are offered too quickly, then they may be misleading and may violate whatever trust has developed at the local level. In South Carolina, implementation of the quality assurance system proceeded in phases, despite a constant demand for results, especially from political entities. Thus far, the powers-that-be have not forced publication of incomplete findings, and, in fact, the findings have led to improvements in relationships with many of the contracting agencies and changes in their ability and willingness to collect the needed information.

CONCLUSION

After 3 years of quality assurance development in South Carolina, it is still hard to identify a single path as the one to follow. However, many important lessons have been learned, and several phenomena that seem to be prerequisites to successful implementation can be pinpointed, including:

1. The philosophy of quality assurance must be explained again and again. There must be repeated opportunities for individuals involved in the service system to renew their commitment to the vision of quality and to renew their sense of a shared commitment, a shared effort to improve services.
2. Although political leadership is necessary to initiate the quality assurance effort, alone it is not sufficient to ensure continuity for the long haul. Quality assurance does not fall into place overnight; rather, it requires a sustained effort by an institutionalized group using formal avenues for interagency collaboration. For the Commission, this role was taken by the quality assurance division, which established a committee structure to

maximize cooperation and collaboration among all the involved state agencies.

3. The continuing involvement of local service providers is essential. A meaningful role must be provided not only during the development phase but also throughout the implementation and maintenance stages. Since the providers are the participants closest to the data collection and enhancement elements, they can serve as advisors in evaluating and modifying the system. Such an arrangement enables the providers to retain a sense of ownership in the system and the process, thus owning the outcomes as well; it also validates the entire collaborative development process since the collaboration is seen to continue throughout the life of the system.

The development of a quality assurance system can be a very exciting time for anyone involved in the human services field. It is an opportunity to visualize what can be, rather than being overwhelmed by the limitations of what is. It is a chance to work collaboratively rather than competitively with fellow human services professionals. It is an occasion to step back and look at the whole service enterprise, to recognize the strengths as well as the weaknesses, and to develop a more balanced sense of what is going on. Quality assurance can bring the heart back into the human services enterprise.

REFERENCES

Bradley, V.J., Ashbaugh, J.W., & Harder, P. (1984). *Assessing and enhancing the quality of services: A guide for the human services field*. Boston: Human Services Research Institute.

Kimmich, M.H. (1985). *Analysis of South Carolina's quality assurance system*. Washington, DC: URSA Institute.

Kimmich, M.H. (1986). *Final report of phase I of the South Carolina human services quality assurance project*. Washington, DC: URSA Institute.

Kimmich, M.H. (1987a). *Comprehensive final report of the South Carolina human services quality assurance project*. Washington, DC: URSA Institute.

Kimmich, M.H. (1987b). *Final report of phase II of the South Carolina human services quality assurance project*. Washington, DC: URSA Institute.

chapter 20 ————

The Connecticut Model

———— *Sue A. Gant* ————

Institutionalizing a quality assurance system begins with the mission statement, operating principles, and policies advanced by the organization's leadership. The process of designing and implementing a comprehensive state quality assurance system can be constrained if policies and purposes are vague. However, the process can be facilitated if policy, purpose, and ideology are clearly explicated. Quality assurance begins with a common shared ideology. This chapter highlights the experience of the Connecticut Department of Mental Retardation and the extent to which the department's mission statement, operating principles, and comprehensive policies provide the ideological and practical framework for the design of a quality assurance system. This chapter also addresses larger lessons for state quality assurance planners based on the author's experiences as a service provider, a federal court monitor, and director of the Division of Quality Assurance for the Connecticut Department of Mental Retardation.

INTRODUCTION

This country has struggled to recognize that people with developmental disabilities and mental retardation are in fact people with needs similar to those of their peers who are not disabled or mentally retarded, and they are not so different that they must be congregated in settings with those of their own kind. In order to meet the needs of those with disabilities, there has been rapid expansion and diversification of services designed for them, including personalized living options in their home communities, a variety of employment alternatives with personal supports, and the introduction of circles of support via natural community resources such as social clubs, churches, and neighborhood events. This effort to integrate people with developmental disabilities into the communities has challenged the designers and administrators of human services to question the traditional methodologies employed to evaluate the quality of services delivered in congregate settings. More specifically, state officials find themselves confronted with the challenge of maintaining the quality of services in outdated service delivery models while at the same time addressing the need to expand and modify the strategies to assess the new way of delivering services.

The impetus for many states to redesign their service delivery systems has been the result of both internal and external pressures. Changes in funding streams and public policy, intense advocacy, and legal obligations have influenced the design of state service systems.

These influences have also demanded greater accountability. Agency administrators have begun to recognize that the design and coordination of large systems requires the systematic application of management principles including supervising the improvement of the quality of the services delivered. Thus, there is a need to institutionalize certain practices that will assist administrators in evaluating whether the quality of the service is at desired levels. A look at the structure of the Connecticut quality assurance system provides a backdrop for the discussion in this chapter.

THE CONNECTICUT EXPERIENCE

The Connecticut Department of Mental Retardation (DMR) has made extraordinary progress since 1986 in establishing a system of community services for persons with developmental disabilities and mental retardation. The leadership of the department recognizes that a good system of services must have a strong quality assurance component that has high levels of regulatory compliance, while also encouraging service providers to work toward superior levels of performance. DMR expects that services for persons with developmental disabilities and mental retardation in Connecticut will be designed and managed in a manner that strives for optimal quality. The role of the division of quality assurance is to oversee and support the department's service mission and to assist in achieving its goal of excellence (Connecticut Department of Mental Retardation, 1989c).

DEFINITION OF QUALITY

Three assumptions underlie the quality assurance system in the Connecticut service system: quality cannot be assured or guaranteed (Human Services Research Institute, 1980); quality of services and the methods used to assess and enhance the quality of services is a fluid, evolutionary, and ever-changing process; and the process of enhancement of services requires a partnership among all participants in the system.

The definition of quality is dynamic and changes as the state of the art in service delivery advances. Quality is also a philosophical attitude that requires constant probing and examination.

Improving the quality of services is a learning process that requires constant monitoring (Taylor, 1980). New methods to assess and enhance services are continuously added as the system and its capacity to deliver services expands. A variety of measures should be applied at multiple levels, internally and externally, to determine if services are developed and offered consistently with the department's mission and to determine if the state of the art is maintained (Human Services Research Institute, 1984).

The policies and procedures affecting the department's quality assurance system rely upon a working partnership among multiple stakeholders. Partnerships must be forged among the various levels of government (federal, state, and local) and with the private sector. Other stakeholders included in the partnership are advocacy, consumer, and parent groups; court monitors; and community citizens.

Implementation of DMR policies on quality assurance has required the members of this vital partnership to accept the challenge of designing a quality assurance system that emphasizes optimal rather than minimal performance, proactive rather than reactive responses, and quality enhancement methods rather than enforcement activities. The challenge is to get all stakeholders to act in concert if optimal service quality is to be realized.

This partnership has served to expand public awareness of the services offered by DMR, allowing the department to be recognized for its responsive actions. The partners, while not always acting in concert, have communicated to one another that quality services are desired. Achieving optimal quality has become the central issue in planning and managing programs for Connecticut citizens with developmental disabilities and mental retardation.

The department's policies, mission, and operating principles have formed the basis for the definition of quality in service programs (Connecticut Department of Mental Retardation, 1985). Such documents serve as a guide to managing services and articulating an expected level of performance that is used as a standard in evaluating services. Connecticut has defined optimal quality services for people with mental retardation in its February 13, 1986 mission statement and operating principles (see Figure 1).

MONITORING APPROACH

A comprehensive quality assurance system recognizes the need to have a variety of assessment and enhancement strategies occurring at multiple levels throughout the system. Continuous monitoring is required at various levels if

MISSION STATEMENT

The mission of the Department of Mental Retardation is to join with others to create the conditions under which all persons with mental retardation experience:

. Presence and participation in Connecticut town life

. Opportunities to develop and exercise competence

. Opportunities to make choices in the pursuit of a personal future

. Good relationships with family members and friends

. Respect and dignity

OPERATING PRINCIPLES

1. DMR accepts responsibility to assure individuals with mental retardation uninterrupted essential services until the time a person no longer needs to depend on these services.

2. DMR believes that all individuals with mental retardation can grow, develop, make choices and participate in community life.

3. DMR will share responsibility for decision making with the people we serve, their families, friends and advocates.

4. DMR will promote or provide necessary adaptations and accommodations to ensure people's effective use of natural community resources and places, such as schools, workplaces, health services and homes.

5. DMR will promote or arrange services for individuals in groups that are appropriate with regard to age, size, and the compatibility of the group members.

6. DMR will invest its resources to the greatest extent possible in activities and programs that are most likely to advance our mission.

7. DMR will monitor department policies and operations to prevent practices that may undermine constructive relationships between program staff and the people they serve, and to effect changes in organizational design and management practices to improve these relationships where needed.

8. DMR will develop and adopt a variety of program evaluation methods that focus on the accomplishment of our mission and give the people we serve and their families an active role and a clear voice in the assessment of the services they receive.

9. DMR will support methods of regional planning and administration that ensure continual learning and innovation throughout the service network.

10. DMR acknowledges the essential contribution of advocates who call us to remain consistent with our mission.

Brian R. Lensink

Brian R. Lensink, Commissioner
February 13, 1986

Figure 1. Connecticut Department of Mental Retardation mission statement and operating principles. (From Connecticut Department of Mental Retardation. [1985]. *Mission statement,* East Hartford, CT: Author; reprinted by permission.)

optimal quality service is to be realized. A variety of alternatives and differing methods and techniques used in assessing and promoting quality support the principle that increased opportunities will maximize learning. The focal point of a responsive system is the quality of life of the individual being served. Therefore, a comprehensive quality assurance system involves reviews that focus on the impact of policies on an individual's life.

The Connecticut Department of Mental Retardation has chosen an approach to individual monitoring that occurs at multiple levels. The reviews, occurring over a period of time, are conducted by a variety of people both internal and external to the delivery system. Three mechanisms are involved. First, the individual review ensures that basic individual rights are safeguarded. Second, a longitudinal study is conducted to assess and monitor individual progress. Third, the program is reviewed based on efforts directed at enhancing the quality of life for individuals with disabilities. The purpose of each review follows.

Individual Review

The purpose of the individual review is to ensure that rights are safeguarded and protected (Connecticut Department of Mental Retardation, 1989a). This review is designed to identify potential crisis situations that an individual with disabilities might encounter. This review is administered by case managers on a quarterly basis.

Sometimes an individual with disabilities finds it difficult to cope with the stress of daily life. If the individual is not provided the necessary supports, his or her situation can escalate to the point of crisis. Such a situation can arise from many factors, including lack of trained staff, insufficient teaching strategies, no functional analysis of the situation, no opportunity to practice alternative means to gain attention or respect, and a lack of recognition where the individual is often the victim of a poorly managed situation.

Too many times, the only methods used to manage the situation have been chemical or mechanical restraint or confinement to an isolated and segregated environment as a punitive or a protective measure. Alternatively, routine analysis of the situation and positive teaching strategies applied with dignity and respect have proven successful in providing the person with a secure environment while living in the community. Active case management prevents a challenging situation from escalating to a crisis. With routine assessment of specific aspects of an individual's quality of life, immediate interventions can take place ensuring that all persons have the opportunity to live successfully in their home communities. This approach allows the individual to learn how to adjust to the stress and demands of everyday life while living in the community. The natural environment provides the individual with opportunities to gain positive personal recognition by building relationships with his or her neighbors, coworkers, and friends.

When a "red flag" or potential crisis situation is identified, the regional or training school director is informed and an assistant director is assigned to monitor and/or assist until the situation is under control. Through the team process, the case manager addresses the red flag situation and reports resolution to the regional director. The regional director reports resolution to the division of quality assurance. The director of the division of quality assurance publishes monthly reports identifying those areas in need of resolution and meets with the commissioner to review trends that identify systemic issues such as violation of department policy.

Longitudinal Study

The purpose of the longitudinal study conducted by Conroy & Feinstein Associates is to review individual progress on a yearly basis of a select number of people (*CARC v. Thorne* class members) receiving services from the Connecticut Department of Mental Retardation (Conroy & Feinstein Associates, Inc., 1987). This 3-year study of individual circumstances is conducted through a contract with the Connecticut Department of Mental Retardation. The data collectors complete individual surveys of a class of 1,300 people through visits to their homes and day programs along with interviews of the individuals and their staff.

Like the individual review conducted by case managers, any red flag situation identified through the survey is referred to the regional or training school director. The director assigns the responsibility for resolution to an area director and reports to the division of quality assurance when resolution has occurred. The director of quality assurance incorporates the resolution of the situation in the commissioner's monthly report. Trend analyses are conducted on a monthly basis that identify individuals whose rights are not safeguarded and who are experiencing barriers that impede individual progress. These individual data are used to identify systemic issues, and further support the need for department policy revision. The annual report published by Conroy & Feinstein Associates uses individual data to describe individual progress, program quality, and systems issues from a public social policy perspective.

Program Quality Review

This review process is facilitated by the department on a biannual basis for all community supervised residential settings and day programs (Connecticut Department of Mental Retardation, 1989b, Rammler, 1986). The purpose of this review is to evaluate the progress of individuals with regard to compliance with the DMR mission statement. Reviews are conducted by a team of individuals who are trained in program quality review practices.

The team members are professional and nonprofessional peers, interested community members, parents, and people with developmental disabilities who receive or have received services. This review assesses whether the quality of the program influences the quality of the individual's life. This review process examines whether DMR's mission is operationalized at an individual, program, and systems level.

The information is presented in such a manner that all stakeholders see this process as a learning experience. An exchange of views is encouraged since the goal of this review process is to introduce persuasive methods that will influence provider practice. Providers prefer this approach over the regulatory review process that involves coercive approaches to influence improvement of services.

Annual follow-up reviews are conducted by regional staff to monitor the implementation of the quality improvement plans. This information, among other sources, is used by regional department managers during service contract negotiations to evaluate the quality of performance during the past contract period. This information is also useful to case managers and is incorporated into the information used in the overall planning process for each individual.

The program quality review is also employed to design a quality improvement plan that targets those individual programs and activities that will further advance the mission statement. Information generated by the program and individual reviews is shared with program personnel, families, and residents of these sites.

OTHER QUALITY ASSURANCE FUNCTIONS

Regulating Measures

The regulatory and compliance unit of the division of quality assurance provides the following services.

Licenses Private Facilities   All private residential services are licensed upon initial application and annually thereafter. The licensing process consists of a review of policies, procedures, site visits, and observations of services delivered. This process is applied to all types of settings (i.e., residential schools, habilitative nursing facilities, and community-based services including group homes and community living alternatives where supports are required).

Certifies State Run Community Non–ICF/MR Residential Services All state run community non-intermediate care facilities for the mentally retarded (ICF/MR) residential services are certified upon initial application and annually thereafter. The certification process consists of a review of documentation, site visits, and observations of services delivered. This process is applied to all types of settings (i.e., group homes, supervised apartments, and other community living alternatives where supports are required).

Conducts Independent Reviews on all ICF/MR Programs Program reviews consist of observations and interviews with persons receiving services, observations and interviews with staff, and examinations of records on all Intermediate Care Facilities for the Mentally Retarded (ICF/MR) programs. Professional and utilization reviews are conducted to determine the adequacy of care and services provided to the individual, the feasibility of meeting the individual's needs through alternative placement, and whether or not the individual is receiving active intervention.

Requires Plans of Correction on Deficiencies Found Exit conferences are held with facility personnel to discuss findings from the reviews conducted. Positive aspects of the program are noted and common themes of facility service delivery performance are reviewed with personnel. Along with observations of facility practices that support the department's mission statement, deficiencies in the program are discussed. In all instances, the facility is required to submit a plan of correction within 10 working days of the receipt of the findings.

Reviews Plans of Correction If the plan of correction prepared by the provider is found not to be acceptable, the provider is required to address the area in question and resubmit the new plan within 10 days. Regional personnel and regulatory and compliance personnel provide technical assistance to ensure that the provider has the resources to address the problem area.

Follows Up on Implementation of Plans of Correction Additional site visits may be needed to ensure corrective action does address the findings. Reviews continue until the facility is free of any deficiencies. Facilities with outstanding deficiencies receive 30-day provisional licenses requiring the facility to respond to the status of the noted findings on an ongoing basis. Continuation of provisional licensure status places the program's license in jeopardy.

Reviews Problems with Plans of Correction Any program whose license is in jeopardy is included in a report published monthly. The commissioner distributes the report to the regional or training school director and requests that actions be taken to remedy any problems within those programs where licenses or certification are in jeopardy. The regional or training school director, or the designee, then meets with the provider to address the problems noted. If all deficiencies are then corrected, the provider's license is no longer at risk. If all deficiencies are not corrected, the region plans for alternative placement, recommends sanctions against the provider to the commissioner, or pursues revocation of licensure. If state-run programs continue to have deficiencies, the commissioner recommends personnel actions to the regional or training school director or takes actions against the director of the system.

In addition to these responsibilities, the regulatory and compliance unit also does the following:

Maintains an individual review and follow-up system

Ensures that corrective action is taken by the regional or training school director when a problem is identified in the individual review process

Maintains an automated system that receives, tracks, and follows-up on reports of abuse and neglect, use of restraint, client deaths, and other unusual incidents

Ensures that regions and training schools conduct abuse investigations in publicly run programs, monitor those conducted by private providers, file reports within required time frames, and develop and implement protective service plans when required

Conducts trend analyses and issues reports on abuse, neglect, use of restraint, and client deaths

Monitors the use of psychotropic medication through the department's medication tracking system, highlights problem areas, and makes recommendations to regions and training schools

The director of the division of quality assurance contacts line level staff and regional managers requesting resolution of issues and problems identified through the processes described above. If resolution fails, then the director reports to the commissioner the need for top level management assistance.

The director keeps the commissioner informed of ongoing concerns through management reports that are issued on a monthly basis. In addition, the commissioner and deputy commissioner meet on a biweekly basis to discuss issues relating to quality of services.

Enhancing Services

The program enhancement unit of the quality assurance division is responsible for:

Reviewing all day programs

Reviewing all residential programs

Reviewing individuals in all residential programs on a biennial basis

Monitoring quality improvement plans addressing the issues raised in the day program, residential, and individual program quality review

Monitoring required accreditation of community work service programs and notifying regions of accreditation status

Maintaining an automated data system that receives, tracks, and follows-up on issues identified during the various reviews

Ensuring family satisfaction with services

Facilitating empowerment of consumers

Ensuring consumer satisfaction with services

Maintaining an individual review and follow-up system

Regional Managers

Regional staff assist private providers to develop plans of correction in licensed and ICF/MR certified programs and are responsible for:

Providing ongoing technical assistance to the private sector to monitor and enhance quality improvement efforts

Developing plans of correction for publicly run, non-ICF/MR programs when deficiencies are identified by both inspection processes

Cooperating with quality assurance staff in follow-up certification inspections in both the public and private sectors

Providing technical assistance to community work services programs to assist them in maintaining national accreditation.

Submitting all reports of abuse, neglect, client deaths, and other unusual incidents to the division of quality assurance within the established time frames and guidelines

Report to the Court

Systematic collection of data, data analysis, and reporting of data serves as a means to report progress in the development of services for *CARC v. Thorne* class members. In Connecticut this class involves approximately 1,300 people; 250 of these individuals remain institutionalized. The remaining 1,050 people live in the community in approximately 500 different sites. These reports communicate the status of common concerns and, through trend analysis, identify the need for corrective action. Concerns identified for this class of individuals are often symptomatic of the larger system. Therefore, corrective actions can have an organized effect on the whole. This effective change then benefits the entire system, not just the protected class of individuals.

Report to the Public

The commissioner has publicly endorsed quality assurance as a high level priority and recognizes the need to not only develop and maintain a high visibility quality system, but also to take pride in finding and correcting problems in order to continually improve the level of quality in the future (Connecticut Department of Mental Retardation, 1989c). Periodic reports released to the public, based on quality assurance trends, can serve to emphasize this commitment.

OVERVIEW OF STATE QUALITY ASSURANCE ISSUES

The role of a state quality assurance system should be defined by the mission statement, the goals of the agency, and clearly defined objectives that support these goals. Many experienced policymakers recognize that one of the hallmarks of an effective quality assurance system is its value to the organization as manifested by its official and unofficial status in the organizational hierarchy (Ray, 1988). The choice of placement of the quality assurance organization within the agency hierarchy is significant. The organization's place sends a message to everyone regarding how important quality assurance is to agency management. Placement in the agency hierarchy reflects the role that oversight and support play in the agency's activities. If the quality assurance function is placed within the system at a level inferior to those entities that are being monitored, there is a likelihood that requests for actions will not be respected. The position of the organization must demonstrate that the administration considers quality assurance to be a top priority. This visibility within the organization communicates a commitment to improving services (Ray, 1988).

The manager of the quality assurance activity must have access to information about the system and must be seen as trustworthy in the use of this information. The manager should be included in top level management discussions of issues that influence the quality of the system. The quality assurance manager not only needs access to information but also needs access to the key decisionmakers. Easy access facilitates timely sharing of important information that could prevent a volatile situation from escalating into a crisis. It allows the key decisionmakers to shape the outcome of a particular problem by guiding the resolution with the support and problem-solving expertise of the quality assurance manager. Free access, including periodic planned meetings with prearranged agendas, provides the decisionmaker and the manager with opportunities to share information, to plan corrective or enhancement strategies, and to review the status of the overall system.

It also needs to be clearly communicated to the manager of the quality assurance organization and to the members of the agency that the manager of quality assurance is empowered to make independent decisions. This freedom allows immediate resolution of problems and facilitates corrective actions without involvement of the agency administrator. The manager needs to feel confident and free to make decisions without fear of retaliation. Likewise, managers of quality assurance need to feel assured that the information generated by the fact finding activities of the quality assurance organization will be used in meaningful ways and not shelved or swept under the rug.

Organizational Resistance

While the manager needs access to key decisionmakers, he or she also needs assurances that a "kill the messenger attitude" will not ensue when bad news is delivered. Placement in the organizational structure should be such that the quality assurance organization is insulated from the political pressures that could develop as a result of the bad news reported. The manager will not always bring good news and may be seen as the bearer of nothing but bad news while the system undergoes change toward improvement of services.

Another role of a quality assurance system is to bring about change. This requires the organization to have the necessary resources to produce meaningful reports demonstrating the rate of change. A commitment by a state agency to install a comprehensive quality assurance system requires key personnel to recognize that change is about to occur and certain behaviors will be manifested as a result. With change comes resistance, a sense of impatience, a need for a high degree of interest and support, and a commitment to maintain an objective outlook toward the future.

Even when a state agency publicly proclaims a desire for change, privately, resistance may be evident even for the most committed administrator. Resistance to change, particularly when self-analysis must occur, can be seen to follow a set of behaviors similarly exhibited during the grieving period when loss occurs. Criticism of the service delivery system can elicit responses by the agency's administrator that simulate the stages of grieving, including denial, anger, blame, and acceptance. The following are sets of circumstances that show how these behaviors may be manifested.

The Stage of Denial Information reaches the administrator of the state agency that the regulatory body of the quality assurance system identified a number of deficiencies in a state operated community program. The administrator who exhibits denial sends a message to the facility manager not to accept the deficiencies but, instead, question the survey methodologies, request a change in surveyors, and refuse to submit a plan of correction claiming the facts are unfounded and, thus, do not warrant a response. This administrator refuses to admit the truth or see reality and solicits his or her subordinates to behave in the same manner. The response is "kill the messenger."

The Stage of Anger In this stage the administrator's behavior toward receipt of information about the inferior quality of services may range from raging exasperation to sullenness. The administrator of a public agency, particularly an agency under court order, receives a great deal of scrutiny. Court officials and attorneys from opposing sides, by the nature of their monitoring roles, are often very critical of the quality of the service system. These parties often use individual examples as a means to convince the court and the state agency officials that the system is unresponsive and dysfunctional. Instead of using this information in a constructive manner to assess the larger system of services, the administrator who is resisting change first denies there is a problem and expresses this denial angrily. Administrators feel there is a "lack of appreciation" for what has been accomplished and have the feeling of being "slapped in the face." An atmosphere exists where there is resentment toward change and/or there is a lack of acceptance that change is about to occur.

The Stage of Blame Administrators of state agencies are extremely visible to the public. Performance appraisals are generated by private interest groups, legislative subcommittees, consumer groups, and the media. Information about the inferior quality of the service system is valuable information to these interest groups if the agency administrator does not have the same agenda. It is easy for these groups to blame the administrator for inferior services due to poor management. Likewise, the administrator who is unable to accept information as a tool to improve the quality of the system looks for ways to blame others for inferior services. This administrator puts the blame on anyone associated with the inferior service. It can be the fault of the union, staff turnover, the time of day, lack of notice, poor timing, and so forth. In any event, the action taken by an administrator in this stage is seldom constructive. Invariably, the response to any critical information will be in the form of a reprimand or condemnation against others who end up taking the rap.

The Stage of Acceptance   By this time, the administrator has a growing awareness of quality assurance information and usually has negative feelings about the information. He or she feels a sense of resignation and defenses are worn. He or she has had to succumb to self-analysis in front of his or her subordinates and superiors as well as the public. At this stage the administrator becomes acquiescent. The change in the system that has occurred since the introduction of a quality assurance system is beginning to become evident. Information about the quality of services is no longer seen as critical of the administrator's management style. The administrator no longer has to use the defenses of denial, anger, or blame in order to accept the information about the quality of the service system. The administrator now sees the valuable use of information and takes pride in correcting problems. With each corrective action, the administrator's management expertise is enhanced. The information is useful in targeting those areas in need of corrective action and is useful in identifying those services that are striving for optimal quality. A mature, responsible administrator sees change as good, and tolerates a quality assurance system that continuously challenges the delivery system to strive to a higher level of quality.

Guiding Principles

With a review of the literature, several years of study, and a number of professional experiences around the country, this author believes there is no one preferred method to the design of a quality assurance system. While there is no one method, there are basic principles that need to be recognized and adhered to in order to maintain the integrity of purpose.

The basic principles followed in the design of the Connecticut Quality Assurance System were the principles of regulating and enhancing its service system. The following discussion compares and contrasts the traditional method of regulating services with the more contemporary approach of enhancing services to improve quality. Figure 2 provides the reader with a graphic presentation of the discussion.

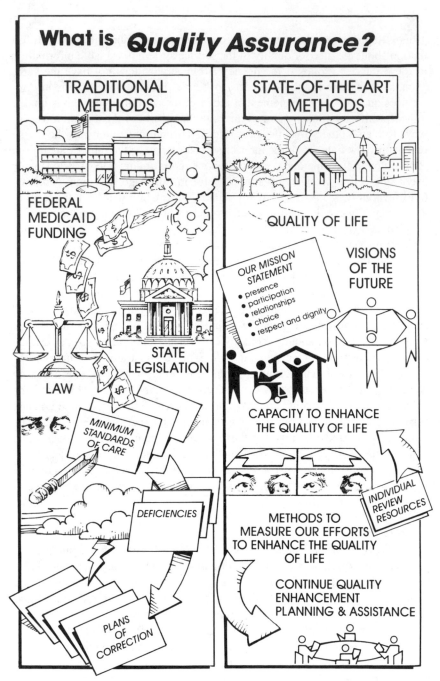

Figure 2. Graphic presentation comparing and contrasting traditional methods of regulating services with state-of-the-art methods.

Traditional Methods

The traditional method of quality assurance is to regulate a certain acceptable level or standard of service. Regulation typically includes minimum standards, detection of basic programming irregularities, and heavy reliance on documentation to verify that certain processes take place (Human Services Research Institute, 1980). The emphasis is on compliance with the letter of the law. Standards are usually generated as a result of an exception to appropriate codes of practice and often are used as a means to respond to an infraction by only a small number of service providers. An example is when certain policies or practices are required as a result of one incident of wrong doing, therefore causing extraneous safeguards that overwhelm the regulatory process. Regulatory standards generally communicate an interest in the building or facility with special emphasis on structural aspects, fire protection, and health and safety issues. Such regulations also tend to insist on definite types of trained personnel, prescribed staffing patterns, and particular groupings of individuals who are receiving services (Accreditation Council on Services for People with Developmental Disabilities [ACDD], 1987). The standards usually are stated in an objective criterion-referenced way for easy measurement and interpretation.

The regulatory review process involves rating compliance using a yes/no scoring method. This review is usually conducted by a single professional or a team of professionals who divide the review by their particular disciplinary expertise. The review process relies heavily on documentation as evidence to support compliance with the regulations. The reviewer spends a considerable amount of time looking at paper first and then verifying the paper by observations and interviews with staff and the individuals receiving services.

The findings of the review are presented to facility personnel during an exit from the program. This presentation is usually a pass/fail report, presented in a monologue manner with little if any expectation of discussion. Following this exit interview, a report listing the deficiencies is generated with a request to submit a plan of correction addressing the deficient areas within a few days. This plan of correction is the only opportunity for the provider of service to react. The plan of correction can become a document that is a written regurgitation of the problem, a denial that a violation exists, or a recitation of mea culpas and promises that the problems have been corrected and will not happen again.

The regulatory review is heavily process-oriented with emphasis on the quality of the program structure. The purpose of such a review is to satisfy taxpayers and provide administrators with a sense that at least the quality of services meets these minimum standards.

State-of-the-Art Methods

Contemporary administrators of large decentralized human services organizations recognize the need to balance the aims of regulating and enhancing services. The dynamic nature of the human services system has prompted administrators to seek new methods of enhancing the quality of service. This new method uses the regulatory process as a foundation of minimal quality and builds upward toward optimal levels of service delivery.

The first element of contrast between state-of-the-art and traditional methods is the recognition that any review process is based on the interests of the people being served by the program. The regulatory process assesses the program first and then assesses the quality of life of the individuals concerned. Enhancement methods are designed to teach service providers to learn to listen to people about their lives. The methods are person-oriented instead of facility or program focused. Enhancement methods are governed by the organization's mission statement and policies instead of by government mandates. Providers engage in enhancement methods voluntarily with the understanding that participation in the review process will be an educational experience. The standards or measures of quality are stated as subjective, probing, value laden questions. The yes/no scoring method is replaced with less quantifiable measures that use a combination of rating scales and narrative descriptions.

Interpretive guidelines use descriptions of state-of-the-art practices to set the criteria to measure against during the review process. Methods of enhancing services use multiple sources of data that contribute to the overall judgment about the quality of the program and how it influences the individual's quality of life. Observations of interactions and interviews with co-workers, neighbors, family members, staff, and the individual receiving services provide valuable information in assessing the quality of the program (Allen, 1988; Association for Retarded Citizens—Ohio, 1984; Blunden, 1988; Bradley, Allard, & Mullken, 1984; Danvers/Salem Area Mental Health/Mental Retardation Board, 1985; Evangelista & Hiltonsmith, 1985; Families and Friends for Community Living, 1988; Friedman & Conroy, 1985; Provencal & Taylor, 1983). The information is collected by a team of individuals who represent the partnership among consumers, providers, public officials, and interested community members. The findings are presented in a round table discussion where dialogue is encouraged and constructive criticism is embraced by the provider.

The findings are reported in a theme statement format instead of in the form of negative deficiency statements. The results of the review are then used as a basis for the design of a quality improvement plan that targets those general areas to be purposefully addressed by the provider. The methods to improve the quality are varied, can be implemented over extended periods of time, and generally tend to have a systemic effect. This method encourages creative approaches to improving services. The proactive nature of this effort to enhance quality is generally preferred over the more traditional reactive approach to improving quality. The overall state-of-the-art methods used to enhance service quality are outcome-oriented. It is not enough to simply document that policies exist as required in the regulatory process, but also what the outcome (the quality of life) is for the individual as a result of the policy application.

Enhancing methods are concerned with both the quality of the program and the quality of life of the person. The traditional methods of improving services were originally designed to satisfy the taxpayer and policymaker. These methods are dedicated to ensuring that first and foremost the consumer's needs, wants, and desires are recognized; second, that systems exist to address these basic human concerns in a responsive manner (Allen, 1988).

It is a challenge to balance regulating and enhancing methods to improve quality of a large state agency. Since most state agencies rely only on the regulatory process, marketing strategies to introduce the notion of enhancement to colleagues, service providers, and the community are needed. The best strategy is one where assistance is solicited from all parties who have a stake in wanting services improved (Commonwealth of Pennsylvania, 1986). A balanced system of quality assurance uses the regulating process as a method to safeguard basic rights by measuring compliance with applicable regulations and policies. The enhancement methods advance the agency's mission or ideological premise.

The real challenge is in balancing the design of the system so that the system protects individuals who are seen as vulnerable and in need of support, while at the same time designing strategies that empower individuals to speak out and participate in the review of their system of service delivery. This tension, though healthy, grows even stronger when consumer satisfaction surveys and home and residence review procedures are designed as strategies to enhance services.

In part, providers advocate that people with developmental disabilities should be fully accepted into community life to the extent that they are seen as typical citizens, leading typical lives. Yet, they continue to want to intrude into these typical lives to apply standards that protect, using measures of quality of life based on preconceived middle-class values. Thus, a conflict exists with the notion of quality. It is much easier to measure the characteristics of a homelike environment by counting the number of pictures on walls, rugs on floors, and presence of recreation. However, when one attempts to quantify the measures of a home, community presence, or relationships, increasing tension develops. Designers of a quality assurance system must remain sensitive to normal lives and must not allow the zeal and ardent interest in pursuing measures of quality to destroy the quality of a normal life (Bersani, 1986).

Characteristics of the Leadership

When searching for a director of a quality assurance system a number of factors need to be taken into consideration. The individual needs to have extensive experience in designing and managing services for individuals with developmental disabilities and mental retardation. Applied program knowledge and experiences in implementing programs for individuals with a variety of handicaps in institutions and community settings is necessary.

The personal characteristics to look for are as follows:

1. *Leadership Skills* The direction the quality assurance system takes depends on the ability of this person to direct, manage, and motivate staff.
2. *Human Relations Skills* Since partnerships that work in concert are a must, interpersonal skills including a positive temperament are required.
3. *Self-Confidence* Due to the stresses of this position, faith in oneself and one's ability should be evident by self-conviction.
4. *Good Communicator* All stakeholders must be fully informed orally and in writing of the policy, purpose, mission goals, and outcomes if cross fertilization activities and positive working partnerships are to exist.
5. *Strong Ideology* A vision of what can be and a passion for improvement must exist that will ignite the want to stretch services to a superior level of performance.
6. *Programmatic Knowledge* This person must have the ability to recognize state-of-the-art practices and any deviation from the norm.
7. *Systems Perspective* This person must have the ability to recognize that change occurs the fastest and lasts the longest when the systematic whole operates in an organized manner.
8. *Trustworthy* Conflicts and differing agendas and motives among stakeholders are inherent due to the nature of the work, requiring the individual to be reliable, unchanging, scrupulous, and truthful.
9. *Research Knowledge* Experience and knowledge in applied research methods, statistical analysis, and reporting of data in nontechnical, user friendly ways are required.
10. *Management Skills* The success of the system depends, in part, on the ability of this person to apply management principles and techniques.

Use of Information

The effectiveness of a quality assurance system is measured by the change in the system that occurs as a result of the information generated. Information is a powerful tool when it is used to support the need for change.

A comprehensive quality assurance system includes management of information that moves through a three-step planning cycle. The three steps include: planning, by describing the intended outcomes that will improve the quality of services such as advancing the mission, safeguarding rights, assessing individual progress, or building staff competence; doing, by developing systems that respond to the intended outcomes including tools that gather, track, analyze, and present data in meaningful ways; evaluating, by conducting quality improvement through agents within the organization such as employees, consumers, and family members and through agents external to the organization with the use of public forums and private research firms (Patterson & Wetzel, 1988).

The administrator of an effective quality assurance system recognizes the need for a certain number of tools if information generated by the system is going to be useful in bringing about change. These tools are as follows:

1. *Interpersonal Skills* The responsibility of a good manager is to create at every level among all employees and providers the motivation and training required to make the necessary improvements in the system.
2. *Statistical Surveys* The data about consumers and agents, such as number of injuries, turnover of staff, instances of use of restraint, number of deaths, or amount of wages, are used as measures of current status against future progress and identifies targeted areas that need further improvement.
3. *Statistical Techniques* Tracking, using clear charts and diagrams, helps identify trends or patterns, trace work patterns, and gauge progress, as well as indicates resolution.
4. *Statistical Process Control* The statistical charting of a process, whether program design or service delivery, helps identify and reduce variation through standardization.
5. *Observational Reporting Techniques* Educating the observer to recognize deviations from the norm clearly defines the acceptable standard of practice and trains the observer to recognize and report any deviation.
6. *Facilitation of Alternative Techniques* Identification of pockets of excellence and sharing of information, as exemplars, serve as a means to encourage alternative methods of delivering services.

These tools, when used in an integrated way, can serve the administrator of a human services agency in several ways—to assist the administrator during decision-making, as a means to persuade policymakers, and as a means to report progress toward specific goals or to evaluate system made efforts.

Decision-Making

The most important use of information generated by a quality assurance system is to provide management with information that will allow decisions to be based on objective data. Oftentimes management decisions are influenced by political pressures that force decisions that may not be consistent with the agency's overall plan, mission, or policies. Information generated by a quality assurance system provides decisionmakers with the tools to persuade those parties that may have individual interests that conflict with the overall interests of the agency's. Decisions can be supported with the use of objective information instead of influenced by antidotal scenarios and emotional pleas.

Furthermore, this information provides managers with the tools necessary for operationalizing program values into program standards and provides mechanisms for constant review of systems designed to protect and safeguard individual rights and well-being. This information can also assist the manager in assessing whether the strategies used to stretch the agency's services to superior levels of performance are having the desired effects.

CONCLUSION

Institutionalizing a quality assurance system begins with a clearly explicated policy, purpose, and ideology. The diversification of services and efforts to integrate people with developmental disabilities into life in their home communities has created a need to modify strategies to assess the new way of delivering services.

State systems can no longer rely only on regulatory processes to guarantee or assure quality, but must include enhancement strategies that focus on the quality of life of the person being served. Administrators of large decentralized human services systems need to balance the aims of consumers, family members, providers, and interested citizens as parties in the making of a comprehensive and responsive quality assurance system.

These methods assist the state system in ensuring that, first and foremost, the consumer's needs and desires are recognized, and systems exist to listen to basic human concerns in a responsive manner. A comprehensive quality assurance system generates information that reports the quality of life of those receiving services. A responsive manager uses this information to improve the quality of services. There is no one preferred method to improving services but a combination of strategies that safeguard rights while stretching the quality of services to optimal levels.

REFERENCES

Accreditation Council on Services for People with Developmental Disabilities (ACDD). (1987). *Standards for services for people with developmental disabilities: 1988 draft edition.* Boston, MA: Author.

Allen, W. (1988). *The right to be heard: Ways to increase consumer participation in the service system.* Sacramento, CA: Association of Regional Center Agencies.

Association for Retarded Citizens-Ohio. (1984). *Monitoring community residences handbook.* Columbus, OH: Author.

Bersani, H. (1986). *Making sure a house is still a home: Transition summary.* Washington, DC: National Information Center for Handicapped Children and Youth.

Blunden, R. (1988). Programmatic features of quality services. In M. Janicki, M. Krauss, & M. Seltzer (Eds.), *Community residences for persons with developmental disabilities* (pp. 117–121). Baltimore: Paul H. Brookes Publishing Co.

Bradley, V. Allard, M., & Mullken, V. (1984). *Citizen evaluation in practice.* Washington DC: U.S. Department of Health and Human Services.

Commonwealth of Pennsylvania. (1986). Quality assurance in community mental retardation programs. *Mental Retardation Bulletin, #99-86-08.* Harrisburg, PA: Office of Mental Retardation.

Connecticut Department of Mental Retardation. (1985). *Mission statement.* East Hartford, CT: Authors.

Connecticut Department of Mental Retardation, Division of Quality Assurance. (1989a). *Individual review.* Hartford, CT: Author.

Connecticut Department of Mental Retardation, Division of Quality Assurance. (1989b). *Program quality review of homes and residences.* Hartford, CT: Author.

Connecticut Department of Mental Retardation, Division of Quality Assurance. (1989c). *Statewide quality assurance methods.* Hartford, CT: Author.

Conroy & Feinstein Associates, Inc. (1987). *1989 site review package.* Philadelphia: Author.

Danvers/Salem Area Mental Health/Mental Retardation Board. (1985). *Danvers/Salem area quality assurance tool.* Salem, MA: Author.

Evangelista, N.J., & Hiltonsmith, R.W. (1985, August.). *From institution to community residence; Assessing environments for retarded people.* Paper presented at the annual meeting of the American Psychiatric Association, Toronto.

Families and Friends for Community Living. (1988). *Guidelines.* Milwaukee, WI.

Friedman, M., & Conroy, J.W. (1985). *Hiring consumers to interview consumers about day program satisfaction and hopes: A pilot test.* Philadelphia: Philadelphia Office of Mental Health and Mental Retardation.

Human Services Research Institute. (1980). *Assuring the quality of human services: A conceptual analysis.* Cambridge, MA: Author.

Human Services Research Institute. (1984). *Assessing & enhancing the quality of human services: A guide for human services.* Cambridge, MA: Author.

Patterson, J., & Wetzel, R. (1988). *Quality improvement planning.* Hartford, CT: Department of Mental Retardation.

Provencal, G., & Taylor, R. (1983, December). Security for parents: Monitoring of group homes by consumers. *The Exceptional Parent, 4*(12), 39–44.

Rammler, L. (1986). *A guide to program quality review of day programs.* Hartford, CT: Department of Mental Retardation.

Ray, Nancy K. (1988). *Defining a quality assurance capacity in human services: An introductory discussion.*

Taylor, S. (1980). *A guide for monitoring quality.* Syracuse: Syracuse University, Center on Human Policy.

chapter 21

Community Integration with Freedom and Choice

Gerald Provencal

There has been a major and heated debate in motion since the early 1980s in the field of developmental disabilities. The issue is whether or not a service system can adequately oversee community living arrangements for its consumers without suffocating them in the process. The debate occurs in virtually every state and province. The heart of the doubt and defense lies in the difficulty of monitoring people who are deliberately scattered throughout a community and living in situations that intentionally do not invite easy oversight.

The argument over what is possible, what is best and for whom, goes back and forth and is periodically brought into the center ring by an exposé of abuse or neglect in a community setting. When this happens there is invariably a reaction that puts proponents of integration on the defensive because the whole notion of community-based services comes under indictment. Hurst (1989b) wrote a three part series for the *Los Angeles Times* revealing the terrible conditions and practices in some California community-based housing programs. The most radical critics of community placement hold up such occasions, where poor community living arrangements are brought to the front page, as proof that placements cannot be monitored properly, that some people are just not right for integrated community life, and that a new improved institution has a vital role to play. Less severe critics call, instead, for the strictest of regulations and tightest of standards to be imposed on programs in the community.

The opinion of this author is that unscrupulous and incompetent providers of community-based services (whether they operate privately or publicly) have no place in the field of developmental disabilities. Furthermore, abuse and neglect in the community are not tolerable simply because it happens in the institution as well. When horrific conditions are found to exist in homes and programs that are intended to help people in need, everyone is disgraced. Thus, in order to prevent substandard conditions from prevailing in community-based programs, there is an absolute need for regulation, careful monitoring, and frequent evaluation of those programs. However, in the zeal to protect the consumer, one must also be careful not to let reactions to renegade providers and porous systems rush one to control the wrong things.

In order to make a dramatic difference in community programs so that they live up to their potential and never spawn shameful exposés, these programs must be regulated and monitored by certain agreed upon basics (e.g., high qualifications for providers, comprehensive staff training, budget accountability, positive appearance and appeal of homes, client satisfaction, and habilitation goals that are moored to meaningful achievements). At the same time, the monitors must be conscious of the potential for regulation and control to destroy the positive free spirit of a home. Nothing is accomplished if, for the sake of order, the positive textures and desirable expressions of the provider's unique style and the consumer's personal preferences are eliminated.

Furthermore, to ensure that community-based services achieve the quality desired, the outcomes of programs and the consumer's opinion can no longer be ignored. Without full-fledged respect for the outcomes of investments, and the voice of consumers, any expectation that rigorous standards will help save the day is a shot in the dark.

At the present time the United States is witness to a struggle over the "reforming" of Medicaid and as a result the old debate over monitoring community services is more alive than ever. Practitioners largely feel that the tight, process-orientation of Medicaid's Intermediate Care Facility (ICF) standards, which are now used so prevalently, in fact often strain the richness from the lives of the very people they are intended to protect. Many feel that this is so because the ICF standards tend to send staff in the wrong directions, working on matters of secondary importance while the real excitements in life are put on hold. In this regard, some would argue that ICF standards and the accompanying requirements for "active treatment" are reminiscent of the scene in Charles Dickens, *A Christmas Carol,* where the ghost of Christmas past told Ebenezer Scrooge: ". . . You have told me what you have gained. I will show you what you have lost."

Yet another reason to be mistrustful of standards (as they have come to be known) being the answer to poor community-based programs was brought home to this author upon receiving a copy of a memorandum written by the director of a large state department of developmental disabilities. In it, the director succinctly called for everyone in his organization to understand that "our primary goal for the client is active treatment." The memorandum did not say that "active treatment is the department's primary source of funding," rather the "client's primary goal." This was curious since a few years before, the primary goal of that same department was to have each institution gain accreditation.

What has happened, of course, is that this, like other departments, tends to chase the dollars that keep it alive or chase the symbols that have come to be associated with organizations of quality and security. It is not surprising that the state department cited above never had primary goals for helping each consumer achieve self-actualization and citizenship. It should be noted that there is no capital gain and there are no nationally recognized plaques declaring achievement of such goals. Therefore, what has tended to happen during the 1980s in this field is that the service community of developmental disabilities has drifted, one piece of paper at a time, one regulation at a time, away from self-actualization and citizenship ambitions.

The drift is not because of any disdain for the consumer, the drift is first because there has been a willingness to accept the terms that come with the money and the plaques; second, because when attacked, systems in developmental disabilities tend to over-react with over-regulations; third, and most significantly, the drift is because there is a long standing tradition in this field of never asking consumers what is important to them.

OBSERVATIONS ON THE "IS IT POSSIBLE TO MONITOR" DEBATE

After reading and talking about community placement failings in a variety of places and listening to countless skeptics of life's advantages outside of the institution, this author offers several observations.

Community-Based Program Reform

Virtually every region of North America has witnessed improvements in institutions for people with developmental disabilities; because of either conscience or litigation, public institutions have changed for the better, at least in that they are not as bad as they once were. They are not as crowded, not as bereft of activity, not as purposeless, nor indifferent to the people that live there. While they still only allow a slight approximation of the lives most other citizens enjoy, institutions by and large are not the same brutish warehouses of the late 1960s.

It is safe to say, however, that while there are many examples of good community-based programs, there has not been a parallel movement to improve the range of community-based programs on the same scale as there has been to improve the institutional model. While most every region has some exemplary community living initiatives underway, the attention given to enhancing and updating them has usually not been comprehensive. Community-based program reform has been more state-specific than its counterpart, institutional reform. There has also been a noticeable inclination to assume that reform work was over once the resident left the institution. As evidence of this, parents and professionals still clamor for the "money to follow the client," an argument that has been heard forever. In fact, some consumers leave institutional programs where staff have received 100 hours of training and move to homes where staff do not even know first aid.

Often discovered about community-based arrangements that have failed is that the public institutional system in that state, however poor, made steady and tangible improvements in environment and atmosphere over many years, while during the same time the community system idled. It is as if the system was relying on the magic of freedom to do the job or that the senses of security and belonging and adjustment to a whole new life experience outside the institution were enough to be self-executing. The result is often that a new high-tech version of the institution is compared against the frontier model of community integration.

Of course this is not the case everywhere nor need it be the case anywhere. In Michigan, for instance, while the state institutions responded to the call for attention to be given to humanization, normalization, and habilitation, community programs have progressed even more conscientiously. In Michigan, the movement from institution to community was accompanied by support services, follow along, monitoring, and accountability. It was also accompanied by consumer voice and active consumer participation. Michigan did not stand still with the interagency structure that was in place in 1969. Even though the state's institutions of the 1980s are quite good (by institutional standards) they are not on the same level when compared to community-based state-run or contracted programs for people with developmental disabilities.

While there is no suggestion that Michigan has not had its share of difficulties, they are not of the same magnitude as the problems that were reported in California. Hurst (1989b) reported in the *Los Angeles Times* his findings of the state's community-based services: "There is a growing concern that private facilities can be a lot more dangerous for patients than state hospitals, where living conditions for the retarded have greatly improved" (p. 1).

Agency Responsibility

States that have poor community-based operations are often characterized by a maddening lack of clarity in their interagency division of responsibilities, beginning with, "Who has ultimate statutory responsibility for the consumer's welfare?" to understanding which agency has the duty to ensure that the plumbing works, the staff are trained, and the provider is not an absentee. There is question to doubt responsibility, authority, and initiative. This level of wonder was common in the far western region where the state programs varied so greatly in quality that the father of a young woman who was leaving the institution said that his daughter's chances of going to a good home was like a game of "Russian roulette."

In areas where community-based programs have been caught in a kind of time warp, while public institutions have made recognizable progress, there invariably is an obvious lack not only of uniform standards or expectations that govern care, training, security, and monitoring, but the objectives of the program are covered with dust if they exist at all. Likewise, there is almost always an evidently weak foundation of policy, procedure, interagency agreements, and aggressive sharing of responsibility across the entire super structure of relevant human services agencies. Instead the roles played by each of the key agencies seem reactive at best and more likely they will appear passively frozen in nonownership. In regions where community-based services are the scenes of horror stories and exposés, agencies seem to be pointing their fingers at everyone else.

By contrast, in Minnesota, not only is there pride in the clarity and acceptance of assertive agency roles, the director of the Department of Developmental Disability Services and the director of the Developmental Disabilities Council have formed a group of parents whose children have disabilities but who are not yet consumers of state resources. The purpose is to tutor the group in whom they should hold accountable now and in the years to come.

Consumer Input

While strategies to make consumers true partners in the service delivery system will be discussed later in this chapter, it should be said now that experience has shown that when consumers are given responsible and active parts to play in the delivery system, the health of the community network improves noticeably. In fact, it is hard to imagine a single issue that has been raised as a weakness or a mistake in attempts at integration that would not have benefited from the insight of a person who was on the receiving end of the system's activity. More often than not their contribution will not only help with advice about reparation but will also identify potential trouble spots.

Substandard Community Services

Perhaps the one encouraging note about criticisms of most substandard community services is that the problems they have are invariably old, rather uncomplicated, correctable problems. The fact is that placement programs seldom fail for computer-age reasons, and exposés seldom reveal that an oblique detail in a top secret document had been misread. Programs fail and exposés are born because principles of basic decency are ignored. They fail because no one was conscientious enough to check the smoke detector (see Bersani, Chapter 6, this volume).

Placement failings and exposés are most common in regions where government agencies, and consumers alike, have been inclined to accept the status quo, to throw up their collective hands in a sign of resignation, or surrender to complexity. The encouragement comes from the fact that many more regions in this country (and other countries as well) have shaken the pessimism, the disbelief in remedy, and the indifference and have set about the job of assessing the old while erecting a new complementary framework to support a system of community living for all people with developmental disabilities.

With no intention of trivializing the serious problems and sad stories still heard in connection with community-based systems that fail, there is confidence that _none_ of them had to be nor do any have to be repeated. An interagency effort can be organized in any state to prevent consumer abuse and neglect, in all but the most extraordinarily exceptional cases. There is no acceptable reason to believe that in the United States people with developmental disabilities cannot be protected while they are cultivating their freedom. A proper mix can be created of provider expectations, relevant standards for care and treatment, consumer satisfaction, and the timely monitoring of services by responsible agencies. To do this, society neither has to control every action and reaction in the consumer's environment nor does it have to leave everything to faith.

THEMES OF CONCERN

The critics and cynics of the notion that integrated community life should be seen as an entitlement, as one of the ineludible basics of citizenship (regardless of whether the citizen has disabilities that were present in the developmental years or acquired sometime after) pound away at familiar themes:

1. The conditions within the homes are unacceptably substandard.
2. The staff in the homes are poorly paid and even more poorly trained. Some staff even have criminal records.
3. Private providers are making a fortune off community placement.

4. State and private agencies are slow to pick up on abuse and neglect in community homes and even slower to act once they discover its presence.
5. The homes are not appropriate for the most severely handicapped.
6. The residents of the homes are unable to speak for themselves and are exploited.

All across North America, in many parts of the United Kingdom, Australia, and New Zealand, professionals, parents, consumers, advocates, and government officials are working hard to remove these themes of concern from being elements that elicit anxiety.

The social climate in Michigan is one with a growing awareness of citizens with developmental disabilities. Checks and safeguards have been built against the previously mentioned themes of fear that can immobilize self-actualization and citizenship drives.

Conditions Within the Homes Are Unacceptably Substandard

Unfortunately, it is probably true that almost everyone has read about a group home that was discovered to be in a deplorable condition, where the furnace had made it a fire trap, where the landlady kept 28 cats in the basement, or where the building was an eyesore from the street and an eyesore from the living room. Such conditions are neither defensible nor inevitable in community-based programs, and they should never come as a surprise. The "condition" of each small group home (housing three to six residents) in Michigan's Macomb-Oakland Regional Center, for example, is a matter for which there is a clear understanding.

A legal contract exists that links the Macomb-Oakland Regional Center with the provider of the service given to the consumers who live in any group home. The contract requires that the group home be maintained so that it is not just clean and safe but warm, inviting, appealing, and presenting an atmosphere that any of the agency members or volunteer monitors would be pleased to live in. There is a case management system with a good ratio of staff to consumers (1-24) that permits the case manager to visit homes frequently (approximately two to four times each month) and stay in close touch with living condition issues. Additionally, the support staff of Macomb-Oakland that make up the remaining disciplines on the interdisciplinary team also visit the group homes frequently. Throughout the year, nurses, psychologists, speech therapists, occupational therapists, and other specialists each visit consumers in their homes several times.

The home licensing authority rests with a state agency separate from the Department of Mental Health. The agency must not only decide whether or not to relicense the group home each year, after a thorough inspection, but also act quickly on any complaint.

The Macomb-Oakland interdisciplinary team makes certain that each home resident has an active daily schedule that takes place in integrated situations outside of the home. Since every consumer leaves the home (to go to school, work, and engage in leisure activities in the community) at least once every day, there are a great many people whom they come in contact with on a frequent basis who can make complaints to the licensing agency. The high profile and public presence of the consumer alone has proven to be an important deterrent to abuse, neglect, or even indifferent treatment.

The state Public Health Department also must make a thorough inspection at least yearly. This is complemented by periodic dress rehearsals by the Department of Mental Health for the Health Department inspection. Each of these events offers another serious intrusion to any chronic condition of substandard living or interaction that might otherwise set in.

The Michigan Protection and Advocacy agency reacts primarily to complaints that are made on behalf of individual clients; however, the relationship between Protection and Advocacy, the responsible state agencies, and the provider network has become one built on candor, correction, and a great deal of pride rather than self-righteousness and disclaimers. The result is that no provider would be able to hold his or her head up if the kind of stories about classical exploitation or disgraceful neglect were published about him or her in the Macomb-Oakland region. While this "pride factor" is an intangible element in the makeup of a solid program, neither it's existence nor it's importance can be denied. Providers are taught that while they can make a good living in this line of work, more excitingly they are in the forefront of a great wave in social reform, where they have the rare opportunity to liberate people, make history, and be regarded as explorers and models. (Ego can be more important than money.)

The Michigan state Department of Mental Health has a free standing Office of Recipient Rights that both investigates every allegation of abuse and neglect and 10% of all reports of unusual incidents of any nature that are filed. Inadequate, improper, or questionable living conditions come to the attention of two full-time agents from the office of Recipient Rights who are assigned to the Macomb-Oakland Regional Center. The sources of the information they investigate come from the ranks of home staff, work program staff, parents, neighbors, volunteer monitors, professional staff at Macomb-Oakland, bus drivers, treating physicians, and others.

In many respects the very best safeguard against living conditions becoming insensitive to consumers (to say nothing of substandard) is the parent/consumer monitoring committee. This committee evaluates each group home, for example, six times each year, and they judge it through the eyes of a resident, a parent, and an interested party, who is outside of the paid professional circuit. The observations here are most often quite simple and have an unpretentious elegance in their fairness and legitimacy. All their observations are put into writing and then shared with the Macomb-Oakland director each month. By agreement the agency has 10 days to correct each situation, file a plan for correction, or stand and fight.

The parent/consumer monitors make it virtually impossible to develop chronic substandard living conditions in the group homes because of their frequent evaluations, their regular notation of trends in home atmosphere, management, and consumer demeanor, and their access to the Macomb-Oakland director. There is also an important closed loop of activity as the parent/consumer observations are made, presented, and reacted to each month.

Problems do not drag beyond 30 days. Even if a situation cannot be corrected in a month the agency action being taken must be communicated to the monitoring committee while remedy is in process.

Staff in Homes are Poorly Paid and Poorly Trained

The matter of wages paid to staff workers in community programs is troubling in virtually every state. It is no less so in Michigan. The starting salary for a direct care staff in a state institution in 1989 was $9.04 per hour. The average starting salary for a direct care staff doing virtually the same work in a community group home that Macomb-Oakland contracts averaged $4.50 per hour. The disparity is rooted in many things such as the community program being a new industry, and there being a strong union for state employees with a long history of successful bargaining and only the poorest beginning of one for community workers. Additionally, the rising cost of institutional care has left little resource or interest in spending new money to close the salary gap between the two work forces.

It is important to point out, however, that paying staff well does not necessarily assure anything to the consumer. The most flagrant abuses, for example, have come within state-run institutions where the staff was well paid and where the turnover rate was low. Staff wages, however, are not nearly as important to the consumer's development or happiness as staff training, staff supports, sensitive personnel practices, and helpful feedback by monitoring and regulatory agencies.

At Macomb-Oakland, as throughout Michigan's community-based program, there is a mandatory curriculum used to train every group home staff member in the system. Classroom and on the job training, with performance-based criteria required for completion, total 156 hours in the initial year of group home employment. By contractual agreement Macomb-Oakland provides the training and the provider assures that no staff member will work alone until they have completed the curriculum. The curriculum and its various methodologies are updated periodically to include new thinking, technology, and more practical ways of preparing staff for their jobs.

On occasion one hears placement critics point to a case where it is revealed that someone had been discovered to be working in a group home even though they had a criminal record. The note of apprehension, if not condemnation, is understandable and deserves a fair answer.

At Macomb-Oakland the criminal record matter is neutralized by the contractual requirement that calls for the provider to have all applicants state in writing whether or not they have ever been convicted of a felony. (While some might assume that no one would disclose that history it should be pointed out that conviction of a felony does not necessarily prevent an applicant from gaining employment. This is true in the public as well as private human services sector.) If the applicant has a criminal record, then the state licensing department is advised and a determination is made as to the applicant's suitability for the job. The determination is based upon the nature of the offense that resulted in the criminal record, how long ago it occurred, rehabilitation record, interviews with court or probation officials, and more. If it is found that an application has been falsified there is immediate dismissal of the employee or a refusal to hire.

The "horror stories" from the community about hardened criminals working in homes (and in some cases continuing their avocations) underscore the need for some central coordination of applicant information within given geographic areas, clear procedures on hiring, and required inservice for providers on staff qualities expected and those characteristics that will not be tolerated.

The procedure briefly described above is essentially no different than the one used in the institutional structure within the state of Michigan, and while probably not every employee who has lied about a lawless background has been detected, there is no reason whatsoever to believe that their presence would have been less likely found in the community system than in the institutional one. It is also important to recall that most of the sad tales regarding criminals working in community homes usually reveal that no one inquired about background to begin with, or they went ahead and hired before waiting to hear the results of the licensing official appraisal, or they never monitored the employee after the date of hire.

Rather than these cases being accepted as illustrative of the personnel problems in community programs, generally they should be seen as a situation-specific mix of provider incompetence and system passivity, both of which are responsive to better selection criteria for providers, assertive case management by professionals, and consultation with consumers and more.

Private Providers are Making a Fortune Off Community Placement

This perfectly legitimate accusation was never more vividly expressed than in an article titled, "Pair Prosper by Providing Homes, Care for Retarded," written by John Hurst (1989a) for the *Los Angeles Times*.

The article described the case of a married couple who, as the result of operating 13 large group homes and contracting for the out-of-home training programs for 800 individuals with developmental disabilities, were earning

$170,000 a year and had amassed personal property worth $1.6 million in just 10 years of operation. As difficult as it might be for the average citizen to justify that level of personal gain in a human services area more typically known for charity, it becomes all the more objectionable when it is revealed that the couple's corporation has received numerous, serious citations for neglect and mistreatment, including physical and sexual abuse. This example and similar ones that stimulate general criticism of providers who are seen as entrepreneurs making fortunes off the backs of citizens with handicaps, cries out for some order to govern the finances and provider performance in community-based systems. As policies and procedures relate to this particular case, it is evident that few limits and fewer high expectations for provider conduct were in place. It is evident that the limits and expectations were both wanting because in spite of the reported fact that the couple's operation was short on quality, and in spite of the fact that they had profited handsomely from community placement, the absence of comprehensive rules governing the program that reflect the values of both the consumer, community, and the public at large made it all possible. One may be angered by the couple's gains at the expense of the taxpayer and at a cost to people with disabilities, but the absence of restriction to prohibit the couple's level of return and meaningful sanction for abuse of consumers left the possibility open. There are, however, several things that can be done to reduce the likelihood that situations like this will occur.

The following initiatives have been taken at the Macomb-Oakland Regional Center in an effort to cultivate a relationship between the public and private sector that is fair to the providers of community-based services as it intends to be mindful of obligations to recipients of services and taxpayers as well.

Created a separation in the relationship between the owner of the home and the provider of the service. With only the rarest of exceptions, the provider of the home program does not own the home.

Constructed a detailed contract with very specific interagency responsibilities between the provider and all other relevant state agencies.

Established a percentage of the budget that is acceptable for the provider to earn for administration and management.

Determined how an acceptable not-for-profit corporation must be constructed; the composition of the board, presence of relatives on the payroll, existence of policies and procedures.

Placed limits on the resident capacity of homes to no more than six individuals. All capacities and residential movement in the home must be approved by Macomb-Oakland.

Avoided mixing disability groups within homes and in out-of-home day training and work settings.

Established incentives and mechanisms to help consumers form co-op housing, purchase their own homes, and have a voice in staff selection.
Developed healthy competition between providers so that there are desirable
alternatives to choose from if one provider is irresponsible or the system
fails.
Established consumer monitoring groups that regularly evaluate homes, report
findings, and receive appropriate satisfaction of actions taken from the
responsible agencies.
Established ambitious staff training programs for all direct care personnel in
group homes and require completion before they work independently.
Developed a mandatory provider training program.

These initiatives are not flawless by any means nor have they been
developed as fully as they might be, but they have filled enough of the void in
the public-private relationship to leave little room for doubt as to what is
expected from, and what is not tolerated by, any of the parties. They have
been good steps to take for removing public suspicion and periodic condemnation of community-based programs that are ripe for exploitation.

State and Private Agencies Are Slow to Act

In some ways the failure of government to respond with a sense of urgency is
the most disconcerting of all the characteristics of community-based programs
that stimulate apprehension. As a state employee that understands the difficulty in getting components of the bureaucracy to move quickly, the lack of
excitement and response to horrific conditions that have been described in
various community systems is bewildering. (The one thing that government is
usually rather good at is reacting after the fact.)

The government agency that is most accountable for the workings of any
community-based service owes the consumer participants of that program
(more fundamentally than anything else) every assurance that action will be
taken to eliminate a condition of abuse or neglect immediately after it has
been discovered. If the agency cannot do that it has no ethical right being
referred to as a service, and it is irresponsible to receive clients without
informing them of the agency's inability to make that commitment.

In addition to what has already been described as safeguards, the Macomb-Oakland community group home program has the following structure
and process in place that helps the agency act quickly on behalf of its
consumers:

Any "unusual incident report" must be reported in descriptive detail, in
writing, within 24 hours of occurrence. An unusual incident is an event
involving the consumer that could be potentially harmful, and it includes
everything from a consumer missing bedtime medication to a physical
injury.

Every "unusual incident report" is filed concurrently with the Office of Recipient Rights (the independent rights protection body of the Department of Mental Health) and the office of the director of the Macomb-Oakland Regional Center.

Investigations are begun immediately in matters that appear to be abusive or neglectful. The investigation ordinarily involves the Office of Recipient Rights and the administrative assistant to the Macomb-Oakland director; sometimes it also involves the protection and advocacy agency and the state police department.

Whenever it appears that there is suspicion that someone in the home might have been guilty of abuse or neglect they are suspended immediately pending the outcome of the investigation.

In situations where more than one staff is likely involved, or the provider is possibly a party, the residents might be removed, if the perpetrators in question are not.

There are many steps that can be taken beyond the point of investigation. If the harm done to consumers in the home was not serious and was unintentional, having come from lack of understanding, for example, the agency might increase the complement of staff in the home and tutor them in appropriate techniques. The agency might step up the monitoring schedule in the home or Macomb-Oakland staff might be sent into the home to work closely with the group home personnel.

If the infractions are more serious and the provider shows less concern than desired, Macomb-Oakland could demand that personnel be dismissed. Criminal charges may even be filed against staff and/or the provider. It is not unusual for Macomb-Oakland to place a home and provider on probationary status and require that a plan of correction be satisfied over the period of probation, nor is it out of the question for the agency to go to the board of directors that governs the provider and require that certain reparational action be taken. Macomb-Oakland has also required the dismissal of administrative providers from their boards. The agency may withhold payments in some situations and move to dissolve the operating contract and have the license to operate the group home revoked.

Obviously, none of these corrective or disciplinary actions is taken lightly, nor does the agency go from mild disappointment to license removal in a single motion. The fact is that the relationship between Macomb-Oakland and its providers is a very positive one. There is no hesitation to move immediately to take the consumer out of jeopardy. When it is time to act, the agency acts fast.

There are many parts of the noble objective to help people with disabilities be accepted as citizens, and have lives that are richly textured, that are hard to put into effect. Acting quickly to protect an individual with a disability from abuse or neglect, however, is rather basic. There is no doubt that systems can be taught to act with a sense of urgency.

Homes Are Not Appropriate for Individuals with Severe Handicaps

Over the years the judgment about who is too handicapped to be appropriate for living in the community has gradually worked its way down the tiers erected to hold back citizens with designated levels of disability. In the late 1950s, people below what was then called the "borderline" level of intelligence were often considered rather poor risks for successful community life, therefore, they were considered not "appropriate" to live there. Experience proved that assumption wrong, and the feeling was more likely than not that the individual was really brighter than the test score indicated. Opinion then descended down through the strata of handicapping conditions pronouncing that the members were too needy and therefore not appropriate for community life.

Among the many lessons taught by history is that no one has ever once been correct when using a person's disability to predict whether or not he or she can live a satisfying life down the street or next door to the mayor. Thus, it is a bit bewildering to find pockets of people who continue to designate a new tier, or their composite, as the next genuine article. Groups of people still remain, however, who believe that some should not be given the chance to live in a nice home nestled in an inviting neighborhood with a private yard, bedroom, and the eccentric paraphernalia others take pleasure in because two new tiers have been discovered that presumably now contain those who are "inappropriate once and for all." These new tiers are:

1. Those who have the most severe behavior problems
2. Those who are medically fragile

With the rarest of exceptions, this position of certain groups being inappropriate for integrated living settings ignores the facts and it inarguably ignores the possibilities.

This author has encountered only two individuals with mental retardation in all of Southeastern Michigan's mental health institutional system whose history of particular behavior clinically baffles and frightens one enough to create distrust in the system's capacity to help these individuals lead satisfying lives in a community setting and not place others in great jeopardy. When looking at individuals whose health is delicate enough for some people to refer to them as "medically fragile," the fact is that there are virtually no children or adults with any developmental disability, who are well enough to be discharged from a hospital, that cannot be provided better medical care in a Macomb-Oakland community home than in an institution or nursing home.

It has not always been this way. Macomb-Oakland, like so many other agencies, learned what its real capacities were as it increasingly embraced the consumer with special needs, and this question with the same honesty: "What is the best we can do?"

The experience with those individuals considered inappropriate for the community has been a rather uncomplicated one. Each person with a medical condition or behavioral condition who moved to a group home, foster home, or apartment, led the organization through another semester in the course on commitment and ingenuity.

Considering those with the most serious health care needs, the findings show that by cultivating relationships with locally practicing physicians, for both specialty medical care as well as primary care, consumers can be treated to medical services that are the best the metropolitan area has to offer, as well as live down the street. Health care equipment and hands-on nursing can be provided to people who live in any of the homes the Macomb-Oakland Regional Center monitors without difficulty. Foster parents and home staff can be taught simple treatment procedures with relative ease while health care professionals perform those treatments calling for special skill. Staffing ratios are increased differentially, and monitoring schedules adjusted to meet whatever level of care is required for a particular individual. A 24 hour on-call system, in addition to well rehearsed emergency procedures, not only keep home and consumer from being in jeopardy, more individual attention is actually given and homes are better prepared to handle emergencies than institutions and nursing homes that are often held up as the only places equipped to deal with the high level of need.

The experience with people who have the most complex behavior challenges is nearly identical to that which is found in working with their peers whose problems of health are extreme. The better ratio of caregivers to consumers that community homes offer increases the direct contact and attention given to the consumer; it reduces competition for staff time, reduces the contagion factors, and places the person with the behavioral challenge in a position to model socially acceptable behavior as well as take advantage of the rich mix of sights and sounds that largely stop at the front doors of segregated settings. Any of the specialty services from psychiatry or psychology or recreation can be provided to people in group homes, in foster homes, and in their own apartments.

The experience at the Macomb-Oakland Regional Center has taught that, with only the rarest of exceptions, people with any level or variety of developmental disability can live beautifully on most any street. The greatest challenge is not the disability, it is, as it always has been, the capacity to overcome mind-sets that are moored to tradition.

Residents Are Unable to Speak

After an important survey conducted by a professional team from an organization that evaluates human services agencies, the president of the Macomb-Oakland parent association asked, "Well, are we good or bad?"

This was the most active person in the association, the man who had been there since the agency was established, a man with a middle-aged son in the program, the energetic participant of hundreds of meetings, asking this question. This parent had experienced the "good" and the "bad" as bluntly as anyone could experience anything in life, yet, other than being invited to a large public forum where he could speak or listen as he chose, his opinion was of no real interest to the surveyors.

Fewer things have been clearer than the lesson from that day. Of the seven groups that came through the agency on a regular basis to judge the service and subsequently either award or withhold a license, certificate, an accreditation, or some other symbol of being "good enough to pass" their judgment, none had been interested in this parent's opinion. In fact, other than the large open meeting required by the one organization, no feedback from a recipient or his or her relatives was ever given audience much less solicitation. No consumer was ever asked:

Do you like it here?
Do you hate it here?
Does anyone hurt or threaten you?
Is the food good? Is there enough to eat?
Is there something you wish could be done for you here?

No family member or advocate was ever asked:

Has he or she learned anything here?
Is the care good here?
Do the staff seem to respect him or her?
Is there something you would like changed here?

The fact is that the field of human services totally ignored the consumers' opinion. It is also odd because great pains have been taken to alter behavior, and the behavior of others, to show consideration for people with disabilities. The language has been changed, and laws have been passed at all levels, and policies have been rewritten to assure every entry to normative experience in society. Yet, the field has continued to rely on elaborate apparatus to determine whether or not agencies serve the consumers well. Service providers have turned to the processes and the indicators that are thought to be reflective of good service organization without even asking the consumers themselves what they think.

In spite of all the rhetoric and good intentions, the consumers have largely been treated as if they are not part of the equation. Their individual thoughts for the most part have been irrelevant.

Lew Young (1980), Editor in Chief of *Business Week,* was quoted as saying:

> Probably the most important management fundamental that is being ignored today is staying close to the customer to satisfy his needs and anticipate his wants. In too many companies, the customer has become a bloody nuisance

whose unpredictable behavior damages carefully made strategic plans, whose activities mess up computer operations, and who stubbornly insists that purchased products should work.

It seems rather evident that the method used to determine whether a home or an agency is good enough to be given the document that signifies "quality" violates Young's fundamental management principle. By relying exclusively on process to gain the best picture of the product, the obvious has been overlooked. It is a bit like a restaurant critic making up his or her mind about a restaurant after reading the menu, checking the pantry, and watching the chef, without ever having eaten a bite there or talking to anyone else who has.

There are many ways to not only involve the consumer in the shaping of service systems but to make their presence the focal point of attention. The following suggestions are made as ways to better embrace the customers:

Require that all surveyors hold lengthy interviews with consumers, their family, and advocates if their records are selected for review and study.

Establish a consumer/parent monitoring committee that conducts unannounced on-site evaluation of homes on a frequent and periodic basis. The Macomb-Oakland Regional Center's monitoring committee has performed over 8,000 evaluations of group homes since 1978 for an average of six visits to every home per year.

Establish a contract between the service system and a consumer organization for the purpose of the latter performing a yearly survey of the system's quality from the consumer's perspective.

Establish a peer/consumer monitoring project where the residents of homes on one side of a region perform evaluations of homes on another side. This approach would tend to both gain the customer's frame of reference and reduce their anxiety over retaliation.

Experiment with a given number of situations where the consumers, their family, or advocates control the interdisciplinary team process and oversee the pursuit of the team's objectives.

Help residents of community-based housing establish their own tenant's unions so that they can gain legitimate platforms from which they may help resolve individual concerns and collect enough broad experience to make recommendations for systemwide change.

Organize service system advisory boards made up exclusively of community-based home residents, requiring that each home be represented by a single delegate at meetings held monthly. A single collective summit of all delegates could be held yearly. It would be expected that these boards would both give advice and take it seriously as is the case with other professional or community advisory bodies.

To those who might feel a little reluctant to have the recipients of service in positions of considerable influence it is interesting to remember the observation made by Peters and Waterman (1982), "The best companies are pushed around by their customers, and they love it" (p. 194).

CONCLUSION

When engaging in the great debate over whether or not the larger community should be traded for the larger institution, there are a few concluding thoughts to keep in mind. First, moving individuals from public institutions to privately operated homes should not have to mean a loss of government presence or responsibility. It need only mean that the medium of government participation change from direct provider to that of policy setting and aggressive monitor of standards.

The consumer already takes on enough risks when entering any part of society without having to contend with being abandoned by the only body that is obliged to protect them. At the heart of each community-based program scandal is a void left by government agencies that either deserted the consumer after they left the institution or never recognized their duty to give them protection as they struggled to avoid one.

Second, those who feel that it is the consumer's right to live in a flop house, to sit and stare at walls, pace their front porches, and go to bed at 7:00 P.M., along with most of the other 30 residents in their home, it is suggested that this version of a consumer's right is a mockery of the real thing. This is not an expression of preference, it is resignation and acquiescence. It is submission to the way things are. People do not accept degrading conditions by choice but by default.

The players in every segment of the field of developmental disabilities have to become activists in recognizing this fact that countless consumers need a champion, and they need to be rescued. People with disabilities are entitled to the access of honest and desirable choices between fine places to live and vigorous and fulfilling life experiences. The consumer should be helped to attain citizenship and strive for self-actualization.

This does not mean putting carpet in the flop houses. It means moving out of them. It means teaching, culturing, and persuading consumers and their families to be harder on the system than they have been and more ambitious on the consumer's behalf than they have been.

Finally, standards, as they have come to be used, do not get at the heart of the quality issue because they dance around the agony of truly disgraceful masquerades for community programs and supress the spirit of good ones with lethal threat and excruciating detail.

This author is convinced that the customer is far and away the best barometer for determining whether or not services are quality ones. The practice that has come to be accepted as sound, however, is one where professionals define the indices of quality in the life of a person with a developmental disability. They totally ignore the barometer.

The fact is that there would be few exposés if the consumer's participation, as a helpful critic, was sought. There would likely be no surprises. There probably would be little left to debate.

REFERENCES

Hurst, J. (1989a, January 10). Pair prosper by providing homes, care for retarded. *Los Angeles Times*, p. 1.

Hurst, J. (1989b, January 10). Private care for retarded: A gamble. *Los Angeles Times*, p. 1.

Peters, T.J., & Waterman, R.H., Jr. (1982). *In search of excellence.* New York: Warner Books.

Young, L.H. (1980, December). *Probably the most important: Views on management.* Paper presented at a meeting of Ward Howell International, New York.

section X

FUTURE CONCERNS

chapter 22

The Future
of Quality Assurance

It's Everybody's Business

Valerie J. Bradley
———— *and Hank A. Bersani, Jr.* ————

The authors of the preceding chapters paint a rich picture of the complex issues surrounding quality assurance for persons with developmental disabilities and mental retardation. This elaborate collage is a reflection of the multiple expectations associated with definitions of quality, the many levels at which monitoring and oversight take place, and the numerous participants and constituencies that of necessity should play a role in carrying out quality assurance activities.

The manifold vision of quality assurance outlined in this book is also a reflection of an increasing sophistication about the nature of the service delivery enterprise and a continuing redefinition of which goals and prerogatives should dictate how services are provided. Providing supports to people with disabilities is a much more subtle process than it was even 5 and certainly 10 years ago. It requires establishing a balance between the individual's particular needs and strengths and the mobilization of an array of services that maximizes change and minimizes dependency. Implementing services also requires a balance between indigenous supports and specialized services. The determination of scope, duration, and location of services, while still primarily a professional decision, is increasingly seen as a choice in which the client as well as his or her family should have a significant say.

Furthermore, the emerging picture of what will be required to ensure quality services is deeply influenced by the pluralism that characterizes the service system. Whereas, in the 1960s the major providers of services to people with developmental disabilities were states in large, remote institutions, the system now involves the federal government (through Medicaid), states, local government, voluntary advocacy organizations, and private for-profit and not-for-profit agencies. Virtually every community has been touched in some way by the development of day and residential programs. Such a range of agencies, sites, and auspices dictates multiple responsibilities for oversight.

It should be noted that the emerging outline of a responsive quality assurance system in this book is just that—emerging. Most quality assurance systems are still unidimensional and rely on basic regulatory approaches. Only a few federal, state, and local officials have begun to think more systematically about the construction of quality monitoring mechanisms.

As the design of quality assurance systems takes on an increased sense of immediacy, there are several major issues that are raised by the authors of this book that must be confronted and dealt with before viable mechanisms can be implemented. The remainder of this chapter discusses these issues and points out the possible ways in which these important concerns can be addressed.

PROBLEMS OF DECENTRALIZATION

As all of the authors in this book can testify, the expectations for where people with disabilities will live and work have changed drastically since the late 1960s. Individuals with disabilities and their families now expect to have options that include supports in their own homes, supported living, and real jobs with real employers. While large residential and sheltered workshops will continue to be a significant part of the service landscape in the foreseeable future, individuals with disabilities will increasingly live and work in regular neighborhoods and communities.

Protecting the interests of consumers through quality assurance is a profound challenge given the dispersal of sites. There will never be enough state employees to fulfill the range of quality assurance responsibilities discussed in this volume, nor should all of these responsibilities be carried out by public sector staff alone. In order to augment the traditional state quality assurance functions, it will be necessary to empower a variety of individuals to provide monitoring support, including parents, case managers, local citizens and neighbors, as well as people with disabilities themselves.

It will also be important to develop a more precise notion of what the service system should look like. State and federal government officials cannot continue to be the sole authorities for ensuring quality. They have to share the responsibility of establishing a unifying vision to guide the delivery of services and designing funding arrangements that support rather than constrain the realization of integrated community services. Without this vision, the current health pluralism that characterizes the system will begin to deteriorate into disorganization and incoherence.

Integration Versus Quality Assurance

There is a built-in tension that will continue to plague designers of quality assurance systems: How do you protect the privacy of people living in what should be their homes while making sure that their well-being is likewise protected? As the field strives to finally realize the promise of normalization, there will be pressure to remove real homes from the full range of bureaucratic scrutiny that characterizes quality assurance of programs.

As more people are served in homes and less in facilities, the standards that apply to physical structures and residential operations will become irrelevant. Requirements like keeping brooms and mops off the floor, posting menus, minimum bedroom square footage, exit signs, and so forth will be regarded as inappropriate and overly intrusive. As seen in the discussions about the federal regulatory role (see Smith and Gettings, Chapter 8, this volume), there is a growing fear that the regulatory approach of the past will stifle potential gains toward integration in the future.

Clearly, those who are concerned about individuals with disabilities cannot advocate for the abandonment of oversight but instead must support those approaches that minimize intrusion and enhance capacity and integration. One way to meet this goal is to assess the outcomes of people with disabilities, not just in terms of their acquisition of skills but the extent to which those skills have contributed to increased interdependence, relationship building, and community participation.

In addition to assessing the outcomes of services, utilizing people in the individual's natural environment to collaborate in monitoring and oversight minimizes the number of strangers "observing" and passing through a home or jobsite. Also, using other people with disabilities to serve as independent monitors can assist in maintaining the integrity of consumers and their living and working arrangements.

Finally, as people become more invisible—as they should be—in communities, the importance of grievance and complaint mechanisms is a sharp relief. People with disabilities, their friends and families, neighbors and coworkers must have easy access to forms of redress, and they must be aware of the ways in which problems and abuses can be brought to light and acted upon.

People Caught in the Transition

As noted earlier, the move to smaller, more integrated living arrangements continues, but many people still live and work in settings that were designed in the 1960s and that still reflect an earlier set of values and expectations. The challenge for designers of quality assurance systems is to create standards and monitoring systems that embody more contemporary assumptions about service delivery while protecting the interests of people who live in large congregate facilities and who work in large sheltered settings.

A related question is the extent to which the enhancement component of quality assurance should result in the allocation of scarce resources to programs and settings, such as institutions, that represent a diminishing part of the service system. The dilemma for planners and policymakers is how to protect and enrich the lives of people in these settings while building up community resources. Quality assurance provisions, especially those mandated by the courts and federal regulations, are squarely at the center of this debate.

There are no easy answers to this conundrum. Quality assurance mechanisms must be equally attentive to the well-being of people regardless of where they live and work. These mechanisms can also point out the dissonance between the older program conceptions and approaches designed around integration and independence. Furthermore, they can hold these programs to higher levels of accomplishment and enrich people's lives as a consequence. However, the needs of such programs for continued capital outlay and renovation could absorb enormous sums and jeopardize the continued growth of community programs.

The answer, therefore, is (as noted above) a coherent vision of the service system and an unequivocal statement about the future of such facilities and the schedule for the ultimate transition of people living there. It is only against the background of such a plan that clear choices can be made about the allocation of resources and the well-being of people caught between competing conceptions of service quality.

Protecting the Rights of People in the Community

The most poignant problem facing those who would design community quality assurance systems is how to ensure that people are not abused and exploited in neighborhoods as they were in institutional settings. Exploitation includes both physical harm and psychological intimidation, as well as inadequate and unhealthy living and/or working circumstances. The latter form of abuse can be managed by the multiple forms of monitoring described in this volume. The interpersonal abuse, however, may be more difficult to uncover, just as it is in larger institutional settings.

The chapter in this book (Chapter 4) by members of Speaking for Ourselves in the Philadelphia area illustrates the concerns that such individuals have and their reluctance to bring these concerns to the attention of those in charge for fear of retribution. The articulation of their concerns came only after they had come to know one another and to trust those volunteering as advisers. Monitors who visit residences irregularly and who do not form personal relationships with individuals with disabilities will find it hard to elicit information on abuse. This strongly suggests the importance of relationships in the lives of these individuals since it is through such relationships that people with disabilities will develop sufficient trust to confide any problems in their living or work settings. Again, it is critical that those who develop such relationships are knowledgeable about grievance mechanisms and the ways in which problems can be brought to the attention of the authorities.

MANY TASKS, MANY TOOLS

Each approach to quality assurance has its own attributes. Each state builds its own schema, and no two look exactly alike. The authors in this volume have articulated the diverse needs to be filled by quality assurance—from the enforcement of standards to the enhancement of quality. Along the way there are many tasks to be accomplished. Planners who wish to streamline their state bureaucracy may seek to develop a single quality assurance approach that will meet all the needs of the system. Certainly, this type of parsimony has an innate appeal. Imagine the efficiency of the perfect approach, a single tool that can carry out all applications and is cheap too. Some quality assurance methods seem to promise just that. The problem is that if it seems too good to be true, then it probably is. In fact, in an effort to be an all in one tool, these seemingly magical devices do none of the jobs successfully. But, they *are* cheap! (In the true sense of the word, inexpensive in the short run, and more expensive in the long run.)

The fact is that several inter-related approaches to quality assurance are needed. Some approaches, like parent monitoring, serve as enhancements to and not replacements for other approaches. For true quality assurance, experienced and competent players are needed in every position.

FACTORS IN THE QUALITY
ASSURANCE EQUATION: QUESTION OF BALANCE

There are many aspects to a quality assurance schema, and there are benefits derived from employing multiple approaches. To assist system planners and critics in identifying gaps in present schemas, the following list of factors should be balanced in any complete system.

Internal Versus External

There are definite merits to approaches across the spectrum from a totally external review process to one that is conducted totally from within. Clearly, internal reviewers know the program the best, and their recommendations may be direct and specific. However, bear in mind the potential conflict of interest of an agency evaluating its own performance. Outsiders (including funding bodies, taxpayers, consumers, and parents) may be less than confident in a positive evaluation that was conducted totally by agency staff. They will prefer to know that an external evaluation was conducted by an impartial group. The solution to these two extremes is not to choose between them because there is value in each. But, neither is the solution to strike a compromise between the two, again, because there is value in each. Rather, the recommendation must be to implement a variety of monitoring approaches, some external, such as accreditation, and some internal, such as performance contracts.

Formal Versus Informal

Likewise, there is no one "right" model to be selected from formal evaluation methods as compared to more informal methods. Rather, the strength of a schema is derived from an appropriate balance between one or more very formal reviews (HCFA assessments) and some more informal approaches (casual sessions where residents offer their opinions).

Professional Versus Volunteer

The benefits of quality assurance approaches directed by professionals are clear. However, with the growing pressure for consumer and parent involvement, and the new standards of "home" rather than "program," constructive criticism from volunteers (friends, family members, and consumers) cannot be underestimated.

Person-Focused Versus Program-Focused Evaluations

Most of quality assurance has focused on program level scrutiny and recommendations. However, in the age of decentralized, individualized, integrated living, there is a need to focus more on the person. Quality assurance schema must look at individuals as well as agencies and programs. Again, it is not recommended to totally replace program level evaluations with more individual-focused approaches, rather, the concern is to strike a balance where both approaches are utilized as appropriate.

Formative Versus Summative

Quality assurance schemas should be planned with an eye to each of two different functions. Most of the time, the need is for formative evaluations; that is, to offer constructive criticism on how to conform to standards or how to enhance quality. However, quality assurance systems must also have the capacity to take summative action. That is, the system needs to be able to determine that program deficiencies have been severe enough for a long enough period of time to warrant closure, decertification, or removal of accreditation. This capacity is not linked so much to a particular type of monitoring, but rather is a part of the sanction mechanism. The question to ask is, "What happens to programs that do not comply?" The response must be of the same magnitude as the breadth of the noncomplying activity.

Qualitative Versus Quantitative Data

In an effort to learn all there is about the nature of a service, data must not be restricted to only one kind. Many researchers and policymakers are most comfortable with traditional, quantitative forms of data. Clearly this form of information is useful and essential (see Conroy and Feinstein, Chapter 18, this volume). However, there is also a major role to be played by more qualitative types of data. Interviews with consumers, the subjective impressions of family members, and so forth are equally valid and essential. Each type of data is necessary; alone, neither is sufficient for assuring quality.

Multiple Levels of Accountability

Thus far, a suggestion for a single level of accountability for quality has not been made. If there is a decision rule, it might be to "render unto Caesar that which is Caesar's." As programs across the country receive matching federal funds ranging from 50–78% of their total budget through the Medicaid program, it is reasonable to expect that the Health Care Financing Administration (HCFA) will demand some accountability. Likewise, state and local governments will require some accountability as well as friends, family members, and direct consumers themselves. The authors' position is not that any one of these types of accountability should predominate. Rather, they suggest that a delicate balance be forged between all the major parties, each addressing a specific facet of the multidimensional nature of quality.

QUESTIONS FOR THE FUTURE

Even in the many chapters of this volume, these authors have not addressed all of the issues and problems in the area of quality assurance. As the face of the service system changes, new issues will emerge and (hopefully) others will resolve. Several areas can be anticipated that are as yet unresolved, which are likely to require direct action in the future.

Benefit/Harm Ratio

In human services the cost/benefit ratio is often of concern. People want to know if they are getting the most for their money. This concern holds in quality assurance as well. However, there is another ratio that in the future will take on more importance. By its very nature, quality assurance is intrusive, and at this point there seems to be no way of avoiding that fact. Intrusion must be seen as a potential "harm." Sometimes, as Michael Kennedy pointed out (see Chapter 3, this volume), the harm is perceived immediately by the consumers. Other times, the harm is less obvious but equally as pernicious. In the future the issue that will need to be wrestled with will be the appropriate ratio of the good derived from various quality assurance approaches relative to the harm associated with them. There will be an inverse relationship between the ability to offer people real homes and the ability to depend on old methods of minimal standards to protect people from harm and to assure quality.

Furthermore, greater creativity and flexibility will be needed in the future than ever before. In her discussion of ethical issues in the lives of people with severe handicaps, Boggs (1986) pointed out that in human services there is a range of ethical dilemmas in which two equally desirable ends are in conflict, such as the drive to ensure individual's autonomy and the pressure to protect them from harm. Surely the conflict between having one's own home and being assured quality and protection from harm represents one such dilemma.

Conflict of Interest

An old saying states that one would not leave a fox in charge of the chicken house because the potential for a conflict of interest is just too great. However, in services to people with developmental disabilities, one is faced with persistent conflicts of interest. In most states, the major provider of services is the state itself. The state also has the main responsibility for assuring quality (compliance and enhancement) in its own programs. How can reviewers paid by the state, using instruments approved by the state to evaluate services operated by the state, not experience a conflict of interest? When the provider (the state) receives a poor evaluation from the quality assurance team (the state) an appeal is then made to the licensing body (the state) to bring sanctions against the provider (the state). In the long run, the quality of services for some of society's most vulnerable citizens cannot be subjected to such strong conflicts of interest.

This dilemma is not restricted to the state. In many states, the so-called advocacy organizations, such as the United Cerebral Palsy Associations

(UCPA) and the Association for Retarded Citizens (ARC), are also major service providers. If the ARC (as in Ohio) is to serve as the vehicle for parent monitoring, then what happens in those states or counties where the ARC also operates services? Again, the potential conflict is unacceptable. One solution is to have the ARC monitors evaluate state programs, but not their own, but this does not provide for freedom from conflict of interest. In New York state for example, the ARC is a major sub-contractor of the Office of Mental Retardation and Developmental Disabilities. This means that even if ARC monitors services run directly by the state rather than their own, they are still in the dangerous position of evaluating the programs run by the same hand that feeds them. It isn't necessary to be particularly paranoid to appreciate the potential chilling of monitoring efforts that could come about if monitors feared that their organization would be subject to retribution from a state agency if their reviews were unfavorable.

What Is the Good Life?

What is the relationship of quality assurance to the ultimate quality of life for people who depend on human services programs? In the early days of quality assurance, there was little doubt about what kinds of changes would improve the quality of services to people with various disabilities. Services were so poor and conditions so impossible that there was literally room for improvement without ever questioning the ultimate goal of reform. Now, as more people are served in settings that are at least adequate and attention shifts to the enhancement of quality, there is a need to re-examine the definitions of quality and "the good life." For many people without disabilities, the good life is more than the absence of adverse conditions, and it is more than the presence of minimal amenities. The good life is even more than independence, productivity, and integration. It may include strong values for interdependence with loved ones, the choice to be more satisfied than productive, and the desire to elect privacy over integration.

CONCLUSION

In the final analysis, it may need to be admitted that quality assurance systems will always be flawed. There is no doubt that current systems can be made better: more responsive to need, tolerant of greater levels of individualization, and reflective of all of the state-of-the art innovations. However, in the long run, quality assurance, like human services, is a human endeavor. Inherently, society is made of fallible beings, and that is not likely to change in the near future. Evaluators will err, authorities will fail to follow-through, and in the end, quality will remain elusive. Success cannot be defined as achieving the ultimate in quality for everyone. The key is to keep aspirations somewhere just out of reach so that people can continue to grow and the systems that make this growth possible can continue to be renewed.

REFERENCE

Boggs, E. (1986). Ethics in the middle of life: An introductory overview. In P. Dokecki & R. Zaner (Eds.), *Ethics of dealing with persons with severe handicaps* (pp. 1–15). Baltimore: Paul H. Brookes Publishing Co.

index ―――――――――――――